Related Books of Interest

Rapid Portlet Development with WebSphere Portlet Factory
Step-by-Step Guide for Building Your Own Portlets

by David Bowley

ISBN: 0-13-713446-0

Expert developer David Bowley walks you through several of today's most common portlet development scenarios, demonstrating how to create powerful, robust portlets quickly and cost-effectively. Each walkthrough contains all the step-by-step instructions, detailed guidance, fast answers, and working sample code you need to get tangible results immediately.

As the best resource available on WebSphere Portlet Factory, this book reflects Bowley's unsurpassed experience constructing large enterprise portals. Bowley covers everything from back-end integration to user interface and AJAX techniques, helping you choose the right builder tool for each task and define high-level instructions that generate superior code artifacts. His example projects are simple enough to understand easily, but sophisticated enough to be valuable in real-world development.

WebSphere Business Integration Primer
Process Server, BPEL, SCA, and SOA

by Ashok Iyengar, Vinod Jessani, and Michele Chilanti

ISBN: 0-13-224831-X

Using WebSphere® Business Integration (WBI) technology, you can build an enterprise-wide Business Integration (BI) infrastructure that makes it easier to connect any business resources and functions, so you can adapt more quickly to the demands of customers and partners. Now there's an introductory guide to creating standards-based process and data integration solutions with WBI.

WebSphere Business Integration Primer thoroughly explains Service Component Architecture (SCA), basic business processes, and complex long-running business flows, and guides you to choose the right process integration architecture for your requirements. Next, it introduces the key components of a WBI solution and shows how to make them work together rapidly and efficiently. This book will help developers, technical professionals, or managers understand today's key BI issues and technologies, and streamline business processes by combining BI with Service Oriented Architecture (SOA).

Sign up for the monthly IBM Press newsletter at
ibmpressbooks/newsletters

Related Books of Interest

IBM WebSphere DataPower SOA Appliance Handbook

by Bill Hines, John Rasmussen, Jaime Ryan,
Simon Kapadia, Jim Brennan
ISBN: 0-13-714819-4

IBM WebSphere DataPower SOA Appliance Handbook begins by introducing the rationale for SOA appliances and explaining how DataPower appliances work from network, security, and Enterprise Service Bus perspectives. Next, the authors walk through DataPower installation and configuration; then they present deep detail on DataPower's role and use as a network device.

Using many real-world examples, the authors systematically introduce the services available on DataPower devices, especially the "big three": XML Firewall, Web Service Proxy, and Multi-Protocol Gateway. They also present thorough and practical guidance on day-to-day DataPower management, including monitoring, configuration, build, and deploy techniques.

WebSphere Engineering
A Practical Guide for WebSphere Support Managers and Senior Consultants

by Ying Ding
ISBN: 0-13-714225-0

In *WebSphere Engineering*, author Ying Ding shows how to maximize the WebSphere platform's reliability, stability, scalability, and performance for large enterprise systems. You'll find insightful discussions of each option and strategy for managing WebSphere, including practical guidance on making the right tradeoffs for your environment.

Coverage includes

- Planning, hiring, training, funding, and building a world-class WebSphere engineering support organization
- Implementing tight standards and consistent, comprehensive processes for managing the entire WebSphere engineering life cycle
- Creating optimal testing environments, administering parallel testing pipelines, and managing testing workloads
- Empowering production support teams with knowledge, system privileges, and the right tools

Related Books of Interest

Executing SOA
A Practical Guide for the
Service-Oriented Architect

by Norbert Bieberstein, Robert G. Laird,
Dr. Keith Jones, and Tilak Mitra

ISBN: 0-13-235374-1

In *Executing SOA*, four experienced SOA
implementers share realistic, proven, "from-the-
trenches" guidance for successfully delivering the
largest and most complex SOA initiative.

This book follows up where the authors' bestsell-
ing *Service-Oriented Architecture Compass* left
off, showing how to overcome key obstacles to
successful SOA implementation and identifying
best practices for all facets of execution—
technical, organizational, and human. Among
the issues it addresses include introducing a
services discipline that supports collaboration and
information process sharing; integrating services
with preexisting technology assets and strategies;
choosing the right roles for new tools; shift-
ing culture, governance, and architecture; and
bringing greater agility to the entire organizational
lifecycle, not just isolated projects.

Listen to the author's podcast at:
ibmpressbooks.com/podcasts

The New Language of
Business

Carter

ISBN: 0-13-195654-X

SOA Governance

Brown, Laird, Gee, Mitra

ISBN: 0-13-714746-5

Dynamic SOA and BPM

Fiammante

ISBN: 0-13-701891-6

The Greening of IT

Lamb

ISBN: 0-13-7155083-0

Enterprise Master
Data Management

Dreibelbis, Hechler, Milman,
Oberhofer, van Run, Wolfson

ISBN: 0-13-236625-8

Enterprise Java Programming
with IBM WebSphere,
Second Edition

Brown, Craig, Hester, Pitt, Stinehour,
Weitzel, Amsden, Jakab, Berg

ISBN: 0-321-18579-X

WebSphere Application Server Administration Using Jython

WebSphere Application Server Administration Using Jython

Robert A. Gibson, Arthur Kevin McGrath, Noel J. Bergman

IBM Press
Pearson plc
Upper Saddle River, NJ • Boston • Indianapolis • San Francisco
New York • Toronto • Montreal • London • Munich • Paris • Madrid
Cape Town • Sydney • Tokyo • Singapore • Mexico City

Ibmpressbooks.com

The authors and publisher have taken care in the preparation of this book, but make no expressed or implied warranty of any kind and assume no responsibility for errors or omissions. No liability is assumed for incidental or consequential damages in connection with or arising out of the use of the information or programs contained herein.

IBM Press Program Managers: Steven M. Stansel, Ellice Uffer

Cover design: IBM Corporation

Associate Publisher: Greg Wiegand
Marketing Manager: Kourtnaye Sturgeon
Acquisitions Editor: Katherine Bull
Publicist: Heather Fox
Development Editor: Kendell Lumsden
Managing Editor: Kristy Hart
Designer: Alan Clements
Project Editor: Anne Goebel
Copy Editor: Language Logistics, LLC
Indexer: WordWise Publishing Services, LLC
Compositor: Jake McFarland
Proofreader: Water Crest Publishing
Manufacturing Buyer: Dan Uhrig

Published by Pearson plc

Publishing as IBM Press

IBM Press offers excellent discounts on this book when ordered in quantity for bulk purchases or special sales, which may include electronic versions and/or custom covers and content particular to your business, training goals, marketing focus, and branding interests. For more information, please contact:

U.S. Corporate and Government Sales
1-800-382-3419
corpsales@pearsontechgroup.com.

For sales outside the U.S., please contact:

International Sales
international@pearson.com.

The following terms are trademarks or registered trademarks of International Business Machines Corporation in the United States, other countries, or both: IBM, the IBM logo, IBM Press, AIX, Cloudscape, DB2, developerWorks, Rational, Redbooks, WebSphere, and z/OS. Microsoft, Windows, and C# are trademarks of Microsoft Corporation in the United States, other countries, or both. Java, J2EE, EJB, JDBC, and all Java-based trademarks are trademarks of Sun Microsystems, Inc. in the United States, other countries, or both. UNIX is a registered trademark of The Open Group in the United States and other countries. Linux is a registered trademark of Linus Torvalds in the United States, other countries, or both. Other company, product, or service names may be trademarks or service marks of others.

Library of Congress Cataloging-in-Publication Data

Gibson, Robert A., 1954–
  WebSphere application server administration using Jython / Robert A. Gibson, Arthur Kevin McGrath, Noel J. Bergman.
      p. cm.

  ISBN 978-0-13-700952-7

  1. WebSphere. 2. Web servers. 3. Application software—Development. 4. Jython (Computer program language) I. McGrath, Arthur Kevin. II. Bergman, Noel. III. Title.

  TK5105.8885.W43.G53 2009

  005.1'17—dc22

                                         2009030406

ISBN-13: 978-0-13-700952-7
ISBN-10: 0137009526

Text printed in the United States on recycled paper at R.R. Donnelley in Crawfordsville, Indiana.
First printing October 2009

From the authors
Speaking with one voice, we wish to dedicate this book to the Gibson family.

From Bob Gibson
I thank God for his countless gifts and blessings and dedicate this work to my bride of 30 years, Linda, and our children. I'm sorry for all the time that this has required, but I have thought of you all throughout its development. I also thank everyone who helped make this book a reality. I could not have done this without your assistance, nor would it have been anywhere as good as you have helped make it.

From Arthur Kevin McGrath
I dedicate this book to Bob Gibson's children and to my niece, Katie Scalzo. Katie and the Gibson kids have a love for life and a dedication to their families that commands the respect and admiration of all of us.

From Noel J. Bergman
I thank my friends and family for putting up with my lack of social time while working on two books, a day job, and involvement with The Apache Software Foundation.

Contents at a Glance

Contents

Acknowledgments

Although it has been stated before, it bears repeating: Books do not come together without a great deal of time and effort. It is probably a good thing that we don't realize just how much time and effort we are committing to when we first sign up for a task of this size. Nor does a book make it through the process without help and support from an entire community. It is an enormous undertaking, and we could not have done it without a great deal of assistance.

First, we would like to thank IBM for providing its amazing WebSphere Application Server product. It is function-rich and contains so many features that it is difficult for any one person to know all of its capabilities. If it were not an important and valuable product, there would be little need for a book like this.

We would also like to thank our colleagues for their continued support during the time required to pull all of this information together. We would especially like to thank our reviewers who made time in their busy schedules to help make this a better book: Ty Shrake, Bill Holtzhauser, Mike Shenhouse, Rich Montjoy, Peter Neergaard, Peter Jakab, Preston Law, and Gale Botwick.

Bob would also like to thank the management at IBM, especially Wayne Sholtes, for providing the kind of environment that allows and encourages excellence and outstanding teamwork. Thank you also for making this such a wonderful place to work.

And last, but not least, we want to be sure to thank the IBM Press team that helped us through the challenge of driving this book to completion. Thank you to Katherine Bull, Pearson's acquisition editor, Steven Stansel, IBM's program manager for IBM Press, and most of all, Kendell Lumsden, our development editor. Your perseverance, dedication, professionalism, encouragement, and gentle guidance helped us immensely.

About the Authors

Bob Gibson is an Advisory Software Engineer who has more than 30 years of experience in numerous software-related roles at IBM, including Architect, Developer, Tester, Instructor, and Technical Support. For the last 10+ years, he has been working with IBM's WebSphere Application Server and is currently a team leader for the technical support group responsible for this amazing product. He holds both a Bachelor of Science degree in Engineering Science and a Master of Science degree in Computer Science from the University of Virginia.

Arthur Kevin McGrath has worked for Contract Engineers in a variety of positions since 1983. Kevin has lectured internationally on programming languages, management, and quality assurance subjects. He has authored and co-authored courses on programming, management, and quality topics and trained new instructors. Kevin received a BA in History in 1970 from Dowling College.

Noel J. Bergman is a Consultant and Contact Instructor. He has over 25 years of experience, 20 of which are with enterprise class distributed computing systems. Noel's areas of expertise include Java, JavaEE, SOA, WebSphere Application Server, Enterprise Service Bus, Process Server, and Portal, including both development and administration. Noel is a member of The Apache Software Foundation and vice president of the Apache Incubator. In his spare time, Noel enjoys hanging out on coral reefs with old friends.

## CHAPTER 1

Introduction

Why Is This Book Necessary?

For years we have been enthusiastically pounding the table, so to speak, saying that scripting is "where it's at!" for WebSphere® administrators. All the while, we (along with our students) have wished for a book that would enable more people to use Jython[1] for their scripting needs. We finally got together and set out to write one, and we hope this book addresses not only our own desires and demands but yours as well.

Websphere's robust and versatile scripting facility differentiates the IBM® WebSphere Application Server product from competitors in the Java™ EE server marketplace. As convenient and friendly as the Integrated Console can be, the true power for administrators is in scripting. This is probably evident to anyone who has had to configure something on multiple machines or perform the same configuration numerous times.

IBM's support for scripting that is built into the WebSphere platform is staggering. As you delve into it, you discover all sorts of hidden capabilities and ease-of-use features and quickly develop a greater understanding of how WebSphere fits together. Were we to deliver a book containing but a single page on each aspect of the available script objects, you'd need a forklift to take it home. Instead, we've hopefully provided you with a book that helps prepare you for a journey of discovery. We have documented and explained the scripting concepts, the core objects, and many of our favorite techniques, while demonstrating some new ones of our own.

---

[1] Jython is an implementation of the Python programming language that executes on a Java Virtual Machine.

If you will, think of WebSphere as a healthy, bio-diverse, coral reef, rich in wildlife. In this book, we teach you to master the core concepts necessary to explore the reef and introduce you to many of our favorite reef denizens. Afterward you will be prepared to explore more of the reef on your own, discovering for yourself more of the richness that IBM has built into WebSphere. Once you've mastered the core concepts, self-discovery becomes important; each new product layered on WebSphere (for example, WebSphere Enterprise Service Bus and WebSphere Process Server) and each new version adds more and more scripting capabilities. So in the way of the ancient parable, we will not only give you some fish, but also teach you to fish.

We hope that you enjoy the book...and the journey.

—*Bob, Kevin, and Noel*

About the WebSphere Application Server Product

The WebSphere Application Server is a large and complex product. As such, it is function-rich and can be configured and used in numerous ways. But you probably know that already. The kind of person likely to pick up this book and consider buying it is someone who has an understanding of what the WebSphere Application Server is and just how challenging its administration can be. It is also likely that you have either tried administering the product or might be wondering how to administer it using scripting. If you've gone down this road on your own, you have probably had some challenging moments (alright, hours) attempting to get your scripts to "behave." That is what this book is all about.

This book is not for the novice WebSphere Application Server administrator. It doesn't define or explain J2EE™ or an application server. Definitions and explanations of foundational topics are available elsewhere (see the online documentation[2]). This book is focused on the topic of scripting for the WebSphere Application Server environment.

In writing this book, we spent a great deal of time trying to understand this beast and what is required to administer a WebSphere Application Server using the examples that exist in the available documentation. As a WebSphere Application Server technical support analyst and team lead, and as instructors, we have also spent a great deal of time sharing our knowledge of this topic with others. That, too, is what this book is about—sharing some of what we have learned with those who are interested in learning.

This Book and Its Organization

We tried to organize this book in an easy-to-understand manner. To begin, we discuss Jython.[3] Chapters 2 through 5 describe Jython with enough detail that those unfamiliar with it should be able to readily "pick up" the language and use it effectively.

---

[2] http://www.IBM.com/software/webservers/appserv/was/library/.

[3] Python is a programming language, and Jython is an implementation of that language. We won't worry about this distinction and will continue to refer to it as the Jython programming language for simplicity's sake.

It should be noted that this book is not meant to be an introduction to programming or even an introduction to the Jython programming language. We could easily fill hundreds more pages on just the topic of "Programming with Jython." There are lots of books, papers, and websites that discuss the syntax and semantics of Python and therefore the Jython programming language.[4] This book is not intended to replace nor duplicate the information available elsewhere. If you already feel comfortable with Jython (or more precisely Python) as a programming language, you might be able to skip the chapters that describe Jython and begin with Chapter 6.

For those readers who might be less familiar with Jython as a programming language, this book attempts to present the rules, characteristics, and properties of Jython in a logical order, so as to build a solid foundation of information. A little is presented at time and then revisited and expanded upon, providing reinforcement through repetition. Additionally, each chapter is filled with working examples to help you better understand not only the Jython code, but the wsadmin scripting objects as well. Almost all of the examples described are available from the IBM Press website for this book[5] and are provided to minimize the need to search other sources for useful examples.

Chapter 6, "wsadmin," explores the **wsadmin** command in detail and explains the command and its parameters thoroughly. A number of the parameters don't seem to get a lot of use. That may be because when you first start using **wsadmin**, you can quickly get to a subset of the parameters that you use "all the time." For many tasks, this is a reasonable approach to getting the job done. However, in so doing, you might have forgotten or not even realize that some **wsadmin** parameter exists that might make your life easier. This chapter will help broaden your understanding of this command. You never know, you may even find something that you can use right away.

Chapter 7, "Introduction to Admin Objects," is a must-read because it explains how to configure **wsadmin** in order to use many of the examples shown later in the book. The **wsadmin** properties that are shown in this chapter (specifically the changing of the profiles directive) provide an environment upon which many of the later examples depend.

Chapter 8, "The AdminConfig Object," is the beginning of the explanation of the **wsadmin** scripting objects. Specifically, it explains the **AdminConfig** scripting object in great detail. Many administrative scripts deal primarily with the AppServer configuration use and depend upon this scripting object for the vast majority of these manipulations. A number of useful examples are provided to demonstrate just how helpful this scripting object can be.

Chapter 9, "The AdminControl Object," describes the **AdminConfig** scripting object in similar detail. This object is used by scripts that need to manipulate active AppServer objects (MBeans). So this chapter is full of useful information for those types of scripts.

---

[4] Please note, however, that the version of Jython that is provided and supported by the wsadmin utility does not include all of the features and facilities available in the "latest and greatest" version of Python. So, keep this in mind as you are writing your wsadmin scripts.

[5] http://www.IBMPressBooks.com/title/9780137009527.

Chapter 10, "The AdminApp Object," covers the **AdminApp** scripting object in detail. This object is used to list, view, install, uninstall, and modify AppServer applications. As such, this chapter explains how to perform these operations using the **AdminApp** object methods.

Chapter 11, "The AdminTask Object—Server Management," is where we begin the description of some of the **AdminTask** scripting object methods. The **AdminTask** object is enormous. Additionally, as is explained in this chapter, the methods included vary based upon a number of factors. The scope (as in breadth and depth) of this object is huge. It includes hundreds and hundreds of methods. As such, there is no way for it to be adequately covered in a single chapter. In fact, Chapters 12 through 15 largely deal with **AdminTask** object methods. That's not all they cover, but it is at the core of each of these chapters.

Chapter 12, "Scripting and Security," deals with scripting and security. As such, it addresses a number of security-related items. Anyone who needs to administer an enterprise application server should be familiar with the topics described in this chapter.

Chapter 13, "Databases and Authorization," covers databases and authorization. Even though the configuration and administration of database-related resources can seem overwhelming, this chapter presents these topics in a simple fashion. You discover the easy way to configure the database-related resources ("the plumbing," if you will) required for interactions with a database. These explanations include descriptions about the properties you can control and those that are automatically configured for you. The chapter then moves into exploring and manipulating the more complicated aspects and properties of database-related resources and then finishes with a detailed explanation of commonly used database and authorization **AdminTask** methods.

Chapter 14, "Messaging," is all about messaging. This complicated topic is explored in detail but explained simply. The chapter starts by discussing messaging basics and then adds a discussion of security. It ends by explaining the more commonly used messaging **AdminTask** methods in great detail.

Chapter 15, "Administering Web Services," is all about Web services. So what exactly are Web services? The IBM online documentation has this to say about Web services:

> Web services are self-contained, modular applications that can be described, published, located, and invoked over a network. They implement a services-oriented architecture (SOA), which supports the connecting or sharing of resources and data in a very flexible and standardized manner. Services are described and organized to support their dynamic, automated discovery and reuse.

This chapter describes Web services and explains how they should be managed. It also discusses policies, policy sets, bindings and even the use of keystores for the security-related aspects of Web services.

Lastly, Chapter 16, "Version 7.0 Scripting Libraries," is about the scripting object libraries that are included in version 7 of the AppServer product. These Jython libraries demonstrate some techniques for the management and manipulation of AppServer entities. Some people find the programming interface provided by some of the **wsadmin** scripting objects difficult to understand and even harder to work with. These libraries present another approach and provide methods that use simpler parameter lists to some of these scripting object methods.

## CHAPTER 2

Jython
Fundamentals

"Jython is an implementation of the high-level, dynamic, object-oriented language Python and is written in 100% Pure Java, and seamlessly integrated with the Java platform."

—Taken from http://jython.org

Even though this book isn't going to be a complete introduction to "Programming with Jython," we provide enough detail about the language that someone familiar with programming can learn its syntax and semantics. What does this opening quote mean for WebSphere Application Server administrators? It has a few implications. The fact that Jython is an implementation of Python means that Jython is based on a solid and well-designed language. The fact that it is implemented in Java means that it fits in seamlessly with the WebSphere product, which is also implemented in Java.

What does this mean for us? Simply put, it means that we can quickly and easily write scripts that allow us to access and manipulate our WebSphere Application Server environment. One of the biggest implications of this fact is that while a script is being written, the developer can interact with a WebSphere configuration or environment to validate their understanding of the situation. This allows scripts and commands to be tested as they are developed and demonstrates an important strength of interpreted scripting languages, sometimes called rapid software prototyping.

This book includes numerous examples of interactive **wsadmin** sessions that demonstrate a particular subject. We encourage you to have an interactive **wsadmin** session available as you are reading this book. Our hope is that you will try things out and reinforce your understanding of the topics being covered, as well as the various aspects of the scripting objects and the interface being explained.

One thing to remember, though, is that there are lots of places where you can find Jython and Python code examples (such as in books or on the Internet). It is important to note that the "latest and greatest" version of Python has language features that are not part of Jython. Additionally the "latest and greatest" version of Jython might, in fact, have features that are not part of the version of Jython provided with the WebSphere product you are using. That said, should you find code in a book or on the Internet, be sure to test it, perhaps even using an interactive **wsadmin** session, to ensure that it does what you expect.

Introduction

A scripting interface for the WebSphere Application Server environment has been available for numerous versions of the product. For example, versions 3.5 and 4.0 of the application server product included the WebSphere Control Program (WSCP), a command-line scripting interface that could be used to administer the application server using the Jacl scripting language.

Version 5.0 introduced significant changes in the way product configuration was performed. For this and other reasons, WSCP was replaced by **wsadmin** as the scripting tool for the application server product. At this point, Jacl was the only supported scripting language.

Version 5.1 introduced Jython as an alternative scripting language. Support for both Jacl and Jython continued and improved through version 6.0 of the product. Jython is now the preferred scripting language and as such is the topic of discussion for this book.

With the implementation of numerous alternative languages for the WebSphere Application Server Java Virtual Machine (JVM), you may wonder what sets Jython apart. A scripting language that is written in Java and that therefore can be executed on the JVM boasts many advantages. For one, Jython allows for close interaction between the administrative scripts and the application server environment. Additionally, Jython scripts can easily access Java (and therefore WebSphere Application Server) libraries, objects, properties, and resources. In the following sections, we look at some of the elements that comprise Jython's productivity advantage—namely data types and statement types.

NOTE   The examples in this book were written for and tested with the latest version of the WebSphere Application Server product generally available at the time of this book's writing (versions 6.1.0.23, and 7.0.0.3). Some issues might be encountered using an earlier version of **wsadmin** or the application server product. Should this occur, please check your version and consider upgrading to the latest available version. Details about the recommended versions of the product are available at http://IBM.com/support/docview.wss?rs=180&uid=swg27004980.

Data Types

Computer programs are tools. Like any other tool, every program is designed for a specific job. To build useful programs, we must be able to describe, in precise detail, what the computer needs to do and how it is to be done. Jython is no exception. It was designed to have a simple syntax that is easy to read, understand, and develop. After you've had a chance to work with some scripts, you will certainly agree.

One of the first "programs" to be demonstrated in many introductory programming classes displays a simple message (such as "Hello world") and terminates. Unfortunately, this kind of program isn't very exciting given that it only does one thing. Programs don't get interesting until they are able to manipulate information. Let's take a look at the kind of information, or data, Jython programs or scripts are able to manipulate.

Numbers

Jython programs can work with integers, floating point values, and even complex numbers.[1] Plain integers have values that range from -2147483648 to 2147483647. Long integers are indicated with an "L" suffix,[2] and are able to represent integer values in an almost unlimited range (subject to the memory limitations of the computer being used). Floating point values are represented using the IEEE Standard for Binary Floating-Point Arithmetic (ANSI/IEEE Std 754-1985), which allows at least eight significant digits and an exponent from approximately -300 through 300.

Jython represents complex numbers using two floating point numbers for the real and imaginary portions of the value. Complex numbers can be written using either a "j" or "J" suffix (note that 1J is the same as 1j). Complex numbers with a non-zero real component are written as (1.25+3.14j), where the first floating point value represents the real portion of the complex number and the second represents the imaginary portion. Using the complex (real, imaginary) function[3] is another option for creating complex numbers. Listing 2.1 shows an example of how complex numbers are written.

Listing 2.1   Sample Complex Numbers

```
1|wsadmin>1j
2|1j
3|wsadmin>complex(0,1)
4|1j
5|wsadmin>complex(0,1) * 1J
6|(-1+0j)
```

---

[1] Why one might want to use complex numbers in the administration of a WebSphere Application Server is beyond us.

[2] Because it is all too easy for human readers to misinterpret a lowercase L suffix as a digit (1), you are strongly encouraged to avoid the use of the lowercase L suffix for long integer values.

[3] Functions are described and discussed in Chapter 3, "Jython Statements."

Strings

One of the most frequently used data types in administrative scripts is the string, which is an immutable[4] sequence of zero or more characters. String literals are designated by enclosing the characters in matching single or double quote characters. Short string literals generally have the beginning and ending quote characters on the same line of text and are allowed to contain the quote character that wasn't used to start and end the string. Let's take a look at some sample string literals in Table 2.1.

Table 2.1   Sample String Literals

String Literal	Valid?	Comment
`' '`	Yes	Empty strings are valid, and either single or double quote characters may be used.
`'0'`	Yes	Strings containing a single character are also valid. Note, however, that a string containing digits is still a string and not a number.
`'WebSphere'`	Yes	The starting and ending quote characters match.
`'Oops!"`	No	The starting and ending quote characters must be the same.
`"Don't"`	Yes	Matching starting and ending (double) quote characters, with the string containing an embedded single quote character.
`'"Jython"'`	Yes	Matching starting and ending (single) quote characters, with the string containing embedded double quote characters.
`'He ' "won't"` `' go'`	Yes	A nice feature of string literals in Jython is the fact that adjacent string literals separated only by whitespace (space and/or tab characters) are automatically concatenated. The delimiting whitespaces are not included in the created string.

In addition to short strings, Jython has something called *long strings*. Long strings are enclosed in matching pairs of three identical (single or double) quote characters and are generally referred to as *triple-quoted strings*. These are called long strings because unlike short strings, the starting and ending triple-quote sequences don't have to be on the same line (at least in an input file). This allows long strings to contain newline characters that will become part of the string. For example, the long string shown in Listing 2.2 is possible in a Jython source file.

---

[4] Immutable simply means that the values in question are not allowed to be changed; they must be replaced.

Listing 2.2 Example Long (triple-quoted) String

```
'''Now is the time
for all good men
to come to the
aid of their
country.'''
```

The usefulness of this type of string will become abundantly clear the first time you create a multi-line message and want the message text to be aligned in a particular way. Triple-quoted (long) strings are ideal for this. You will find them used throughout the scripts provided with this book.

Regardless of the type, sometimes strings must contain special characters. The syntax used to identify these special characters is called an *escape sequence*. Escape sequences begin with the backslash (\) character, and are followed by one or more characters (depending on the special character to be represented). Table 2.2 identifies the character (or types of characters) that could be represented using each escape sequence.

Table 2.2 String Escape Sequences[5]

Escape Sequence	Character Being Represented
\\	Backslash
\'	Single quote
\"	Double quote
\a	ASCII Bell (BEL)
\b	ASCII Backspace (BS)
\f	ASCII Formfeed (FF)
\n	ASCII Linefeed (LF) character (also known as a newline)
\r	ASCII Carriage Return (CR)
\t	ASCII Horizontal Tab (TAB)
\uxxxx	16-bit Unicode character with the specified hexadecimal value

[5] Remember that even though these escape sequences require two or more characters, each represents an individual character in the actual string. For example, \\ actually represents a single character.

Table 2.2   String Escape Sequences[5]

Escape Sequence	Character Being Represented
\Uxxxxxxxx	32-bit Unicode character with the specified hexadecimal value
\v	ASCII Vertical Tab (VT)
\ddd	Character with the specified octal value, where ddd are three octal digits (that is, digits in the range 0–7 inclusive)
\xhh	Character with the specified hexadecimal value, where hh are two hexadecimal digits (that is, digits in the range 0–9 or the letters 'A'..'F' or 'a'..'f' where the letters are used to represent values from 10–15).

Additionally, if a string in an input file[6] has a backslash newline sequence (that is, if the last non-blank character on the line is a backslash \), the string is allowed to span multiple lines. The newline character is ignored, and the string is created as though the backslash and the newline were not present. Listing 2.3 demonstrates this more clearly.

Listing 2.3   Backslash Newline Sequence

```
1|C:...\bin>type string.py
2|print 'Now is the time for all \
3|     good men to come to the \
4|...'
5|
6|C:...\bin>wsadmin -conntype none -lang jython -f string.py
7|WASX7357I: ...
8|Now is the time for all          good men to come to the ...
```

The input file (string.py, as seen on lines 2–4) shows that the string spans multiple lines and contains the backslash newline sequence. The generated output (on line 8) shows that the string contains neither the backslashes nor the newline characters found in the input file. However, the leading spaces are present in the output.

---

[6] The distinction is made that these strings may occur in an input file because this construct is not supported in an interactive **wsadmin** session.

Additional details about strings, specifically the use of string methods, are discussed in Chapter 4, "Jython Classes," after we've had a chance to discover objects and methods.

Raw Strings

Is there an easy way to tell Jython not to interpret the backslash character as an escape sequence indicator? Yes—you would simply add an 'r' prefix to the string literal. For example, r'\n' is a two-character literal string, with the first character being a backslash and the second being the letter 'n'. Without the raw string prefix (that is, where 'r' immediately precedes the string literal), '\n' is recognized as a single character representing a "newline" (the ASCII character with the ordinal value of 10).

Be careful, though—the presence of the 'r' prefix is not simply an indication to Jython to leave the backslash alone. It just tells Jython to interpret the backslash and the character that follows differently. This means that r'\' is NOT a valid sequence. If you really want a single character backslash string, use '\\' instead. Raw strings are particularly useful for regular expressions and fully qualified file names where the backslash is used as a directory delimiter (for example, on the Windows® operating system).

Tuples

In addition to strings, Jython provides for an immutable sequence of heterogeneous values called a *tuple* (see Table 2.3). A tuple is an ordered sequence of values enclosed in parentheses and separated by commas.

Table 2.3 Sample Tuples

Tuple	Comment
()	An empty tuple.
(1)	This is not a tuple; it is an expression.
1,	This is a tuple, interestingly enough. The presence of the comma is sufficient to indicate to Jython that this is a single-element tuple.
(1,)	This is the proper syntax for a tuple containing a single element (note the presence of the comma).
(,1)	This is not a valid tuple and will cause a syntax error.
(1,2,3)	A three-element tuple contains only integer values.
("Testing",1,2,3 'testing')	A tuple containing elements of type string and integer.

The only differences between strings and tuples are the following:

1. The syntax (string values start and end with matching quotation marks, and tuples start and end with parentheses).

2. The values that may be present in the sequence (a string may only contain individual characters, whereas a tuple can contain other values such as strings, tuples, and lists).

Lists

Lists, in Jython, are modifiable sequences of heterogeneous items. A list is identified by enclosing items, or elements, in square brackets (' [' and '] '). One of the biggest differences between lists and other sequence types is the fact that a list may be dynamically modified. Table 2.4 shows some valid and invalid lists.

Table 2.4   Sample Lists

List	Comment
[]	An empty list.
[1,2,3]	A list containing only integer values.
['Testing', 1, 2, 3, 'testing']	A list containing strings and integers.
[1]	This list contains only 1 value. Note that unlike a tuple containing a single value, a trailing comma is not required.[7]
[,1]	This is not a valid list and will cause a syntax error exception.

We see more details and examples of lists and how they can be created, used, and modified in Chapter 4.

Accessing Sequence Elements

Each of the preceding data types is a *sequence*. One important property of a sequence is the order in which information occurs. There are times when it is appropriate to retrieve, or access, individual elements of a sequence[8] based upon their position. The property of a sequence element that is used to identify its position is called the index. The index value of the first element of a sequence is zero, and that of the last element in the sequence is 1 less than the number of elements in the

---

[7] Pease note, though, that how the value in brackets is interpreted is based on where it occurs.

[8] It is also quite common to process all of the elements of a sequence in order. We see how this is done a bit later.

sequence. The syntax used to reference an element of a sequence using an index is to surround the index value in square brackets.[9] The examples in Table 2.5 show how indexing can be used to access an element of a sequence.

Table 2.5 Indexing Sequence Elements

Indexed Sequence	Data Type	Value	Comment
`'Testing'[ 0 ]`	String	'T'	The first element of the string is accessed using an index value of 0.
`("Testing",1,2,3 ,'testing')[4]`	Tuple	'testing'	The tuple has five elements (the index values for which are 0 through 4 inclusive). So the index for the last element is one less than the number of elements in the sequence.
`[1,2,'buckle my shoe'][3]`	List	Index out of range error	An attempt to access an element past the end of the sequence will cause an error. Because there are only three elements in the sequence, they should be referenced using index values from 0 through 2.

Sometimes it is more convenient to access the elements at, near, or relative to the end of a sequence. In Table 2.5, we saw how the last element of a sequence can be accessed using the length of the sequence minus 1. Jython conveniently allows negative indices to be used to access elements relative to the end of the sequence. So, the last element of a sequence can be accessed using an index of -1, and the penultimate element can be accessed using an index of -2, and so on.

Table 2.6 shows some valid and invalid negative index values. Make special note of line 4 (`"['Bob'][0][1]"`), where a list containing a single string has two indexes provided to directly access an individual character of the string.

---

[9] Unfortunately some people, especially those for whom this syntax is a bit new, find it a little confusing. This is especially true when an index (in square brackets) is used to identify a particular element of a list, which also uses square brackets to identify elements of a list. Try to remember that a single numeric value in square brackets might be an index.

Table 2.6   Negative Indexes

Indexed Sequence	Data Type	Value	Comment
`'Testing'[-1]`	String	'g'	The last element of the string can be accessed using an index value of -1.
`'Testing'[-2]`	String	'n'	Accessing the next to last element of a sequence can be done using an index value of -2.
`['Bob'][-1]`	List	'Bob'	A sequence containing a single element can have that element indexed using either [0] or [-1].
`['Bob'][0][1]`	List	'o'	A nested sequence can have its elements indexed by adding additional indexes.
`('Testing',1,2, 3,'testing')[-5]`	Tuple	'Testing'	The last element of the sequence can be accessed using either the length of the sequence minus one, or more simply, using -1. Smaller index values (more negative) than -1 can be used to access elements closer to the beginning of the sequence.
`[1, 2,'buckle my shoe'][-4]`	List	Index out of range exception	An attempt to access a non-existing element will cause an exception.

Dictionaries

Another powerful data type that exists within Jython is the dictionary, which is especially useful when data is not best represented as a sequence. For situations where some unique key can be used to identify a particular value, dictionaries are likely to be the data structure of choice. Each item within a dictionary is defined as a key/value pair. A key may be of any immutable type (which excludes lists as a key) and is used as an index to access or retrieve the associated value, which can be of any data type supported by Jython.

Dictionary literals are enclosed in curly braces and have the key separated from the value by a colon ':'. Multiple dictionary elements (that is, key/value pairs) are separated by commas. Listing 2.4 shows how to define a multi-valued dictionary literal, as well as how to access an individual entry using the key 'spam' to retrieve the associated value.

Listing 2.4   Accessing a Dictionary Value Using a Key

```
wsadmin>print { 'bacon': 0, 'eggs': 1, 'spam': 2 }[ 'spam' ]
2
```

NOTE   Just in case you've been wondering about the topics used in some of the examples, the Python tutorial available at http://docs.python.org includes the following admonition: *"By the way, the language is named after the BBC show "Monty Python's Flying Circus" and has nothing to do with nasty reptiles. Making references to Monty Python skits in documentation is not only allowed, it is encouraged!"*

Additional Information Types

Now that we have had a quick exposure to the primitive data types, we take a look at how they can, and should, be used in scripts.

Literals (Constants)

Whenever a fixed value is used, be it an integer, a floating point value, or a string, it is simply a representation of the value of a particular data type. We have already seen examples of literals (`0`, `3.14159`, `'testing'`, and `[]`), and our scripts are likely to contain others. Up to this point, almost all of the example Jython code we have seen could only make use of these literal or constant values.

Variables Names (Identifiers)

In addition to constants, useful programs need to be able to work with values that are allowed to change over time. To do so, scripts must be able to identify or name these changeable and changing values. The identities for these changing values are called *variable names*. Jython variable names, also called identifiers, share these properties:

- Begin with an upper- or lowercase letter or an underscore
- Contain letters, digits, or underscore characters
- May be arbitrarily long
- Are case-sensitive (for example, Bob, bOb, and boB are all different)

Table 2.7 shows some examples of valid and invalid identifiers.

Table 2.7   Identifiers

Example	Valid?	Comment
Bob	Yes	Begins with a letter and is composed of letters.
a1a	Yes	Begins with a letter and is composed of letters and digits.
2do	No	Starts with a digit (isn't a valid number)—causes a syntax error.

Table 2.7   Identifiers

Example	Valid?	Comment
1L	No	This is a long integer literal constant and is therefore not a valid identifier.
_	Yes	Valid, but not very descriptive. It is far too easily overlooked and therefore is not recommended as a variable name.[10]

One of the ongoing challenges with programming is the choice of selecting reasonable, and hopefully intuitive, names for variables. Though a particular variable name makes sense to you while the program, or script, is being written, it might not resonate with someone else or even with you in the months to come. It is also important to remember that a long variable name is not always best.

Keywords

There are some identifiers, however, that should not be used as variable names. These identifiers have a specific meaning and are either reserved for use by Jython or have a special meaning to wsadmin. Jython reserved words, or keywords, cause syntax errors if you try to use them inappropriately. Table 2.8 lists these special identifiers in alphabetical order.

In addition to these special identifiers, another exists that is used to indicate that a variable has "no value." This special identifier is None. Interestingly enough, only one None object exists. Every reference to None within a script will be to the same object that has this special value. If the result of an expression is None, this value is evaluated as false.

Variables

Up to this point, we've used literals in the examples. This is because we had yet to describe variables. Now that we know what a variable is and how it can be named, let's learn how to define a variable and give it a value.

Variables are declared, or defined, using an assignment statement. The syntax of an assignment statement is that a variable name is followed by an equal sign ' = ', which is then followed by the value to be given to the variable. Table 2.9 shows some example assignment statements.[11]

---

[10] In fact, when wsadmin is being used in interpretive, or interactive, mode, this variable holds the value of the last printed expression. It is unlikely that ' _ ' as a variable name would be a good choice.
[11] Even though the whitespace around the equal sign and operators is not required, examples herein use whitespace for readability.

Table 2.8 Jython Special Identifiers[12]

and	break	def	else	exit**	from	import	lambda	pass	raise	while
as*	class	del	except	finally	global	in	not	print	return	with*
assert	continue	elif	exec	for	if	is	or	quit**	try	yield*

Table 2.9 Variable Assignment Statements

Statement	Identifier	Initial Value
rhyme = (1, 2, 'buckle my shoe')	rhyme	A three element tuple containing two integers and a string.
dict = { 'true' : 1, 'false' : 0 }	dict	A dictionary with two key/value pairs.
result = None	result	The "special" value, noted earlier, which is used to assign a "nothing", or non-value to a variable.

[12] Keywords flagged with an asterisk are (or will eventually become) keywords in Python. However, because changes to Python eventually find their way into Jython, it would be best to not use these identifiers in your Jython scripts. Those flagged with a double asterisk aren't really keywords but are "special" commands that are recognized by **wsadmin** when it is being used in interactive mode. Therefore, they are also poor choices for variable names in your scripts.

Some programming languages require that when a variable is declared, its data type is also identified. This means that for these programming languages, the data type of a variable is fixed, and the variable can only be assigned values matching this data type. This is not the case with Jython. Jython variables do not have a fixed type and may be assigned any value. In fact, you can assign a variable an integer value and then later assign that same variable a string or even a dictionary value. It just doesn't matter (at least not to Jython).

Expressions

Everyone should be familiar with arithmetic expressions, the most common of which have a value, followed by an operator followed by an expression. Table 2.10 shows some expressions, most of which should be familiar to you.

Table 2.10   Simple Arithmetic Operators

Operation	Operator	Expression	Result
Addition	+	1 + 2	3
Subtraction	–	2 – 3	–1
Multiplication	*	3 * 4	12
Division	/	20 / 4	5
Exponential	**	2 ** 3	8
Modulo (Remainder)	%	142 % 100	42

Some of these operations may warrant additional explanation. First, it is important to note that if operands do not share a common numeric data type, the values are converted to a common type before the operation is performed. Table 2.11 shows some conversion examples.

Table 2.11   Operand Conversion During Expression Evaluation

Expression	Result	Explanation
1 + 2L	3L	The plain integer (1) is converted to a long integer before the addition is performed.
1 – 2J	(1-2j)	The plain integer is converted to a complex number (with an imaginary portion of 0J) before the subtraction is performed.
8 / 9	0	Integer division is performed, and the fractional portion is discarded.
8 % 9	8	Integer division is performed, and the result is the integer remainder.
8.0 / 9	0.888. . .	The denominator is converted to a float (that is, a floating point value), and the result is also a float.

String Operators

In Table 2.1, we saw that adjacent string literals are automatically concatenated. (The usefulness of this string operation alone justifies its own operator.) An operator is provided to allow any two strings, not just literals, to be concatenated. The conventional operator used by many programming languages, Jython included, is the plus sign (+). So, when two string values and/or variables are separated by a plus sign, the result of this expression will be the concatenation of the strings. Please note, however, that the items to be concatenated both need to be strings. If you try to concatenate a string and a number, an exception is raised.

What a pain. Isn't there something that we can do to minimize these exceptions and allow us to concatenate a string with some other value? Yes, if you surround a value, or expression, or variable name in backticks, the result will be represented as a string. Listing 2.5 includes a demonstration of the backtick operator.

Another useful string operation is provided by the string repeat operator. It is sometimes much easier to have Jython duplicate, or repeat, a string a specified number of times than it would be for the programmer to specify a hard coded, literal string with a specified number of duplicated characters. The syntax for this operation is `string * number`.

Listing 2.5 shows some sample uses of string operators. Line 1 demonstrates how to make use of the string repeat operator using the asterisk ` * ` character, which is related to the multiplication operator that uses the same symbol. As you can see, using the repeat operator in this fashion makes it very obvious how many characters will exist in the generated string. Line 3 shows that the string being repeated can contain more than one character. Line 5 contains an expression composed of both the string repeat operations as well as string concatenation. It should also be noted how parentheses can be used to group a portion of the expression. Lines 7–14 show what happens when the wrong data type is provided for a string operator. And lines 15–16 show how the backtick operator can convert the value of a variable to a string so that the string concatenation operator may be used.

Listing 2.5 Sample String Operations

```
 1|wsadmin>'-' * 50
 2|'--------------------------------------------------'
 3|wsadmin>'---+' * 10
 4|'---+---+---+---+---+---+---+---+---+---+'
 5|wsadmin>( '-' * 4 + '+' ) * 10
 6|'---+---+---+---+---+---+---+---+---+---+'
 7|wsadmin>one = 1
 8|wsadmin>'---+---' + one
 9|WASX7015E: Exception running command: "'---+---' + one";
10| exception information: com.ibm.bsf.BSFException: exception
```

```
11| from Jython:
12|Traceback (innermost last):
13|  File "<input>", line 1, in ?
14|TypeError: __add__ nor __radd__ defined for these operands
15|wsadmin>'---+---' + `one`
16|'---+---1'
```

Operator Precedence

One aspect of expression evaluation that sometimes causes confusion is the order in which operations occur. Let's take a look at a simple expression containing multiple operators, specifically `1 + 2 * 3`. We have two possible ways to evaluate this expression:

1. **Addition first:** This would result in being evaluated as 3 * 3 resulting in 9.

2. **Multiplication first:** This would result in being evaluated as 1 + 6 resulting in 7.

Jython, like most programming languages, defines an order of precedence for expression evaluation. For the operators we've already seen, this precedence order is shown in Table 2.12, where the operators at the top of the table have the highest precedence, and the ones toward the bottom of the table have a lower precedence.

Table 2.12 Simple Operator Precedence

Operator(s)	Description
( )	Grouping using parentheses
**	Exponentiation
*, /, %	Multiplication/String repeat, Division, Modulo (Remainder)
+, -	Addition/String Concatenation, Subtraction

This means that if an expression has operators of different precedence, the operations with the highest precedence level will be evaluated first. If an expression has multiple operators of the same precedence level, then those sub-expressions will be evaluated from left to right. This is demonstrated in Table 2.13, where the steps used to evaluate an expression are shown.

Table 2.13 Expression Evaluation Using Precedence

Step	Current Expression	Action / Result
1	1 * 2 + 3 * 4 + 5	Given that multiple multiplication operators exist, the leftmost one is evaluated first.
2	2 + 3 * 4 + 5	The next multiplication operation is evaluated.
3	2 + 12 + 5	Multiple operators of the same precedence exist. The leftmost one is evaluated first.
4	14 + 5	The last operation is evaluated.
5	19	This is the result.

This is just the beginning as far as operators are concerned. The next ones described are called the *unary operators*. Unlike the simple arithmetic operators shown so far, unary operators deal with a single value. The four unary operators are shown in Table 2.14.

Table 2.14 Unary Operators

Operator	Example	Result	Description
+	+5	5	The unary plus yields the unchanged value.
-	-1	-1	The unary minus operator negates the given value.
~	~127	-128	The unary inversion operator is mathematically equivalent to computing -(value + 1).[13]
not	not 1	0	Boolean negation of specified value.

The next group of operators is used to manipulate integers and long integers as binary values. If necessary, values are converted to a common type as part of the expression evaluation.

Unfortunately, it would require too many pages to describe and explain binary arithmetic for the little that it is likely to prove useful in the administration of a WebSphere Application Server. Because of that, the operators are identified with a minimum of description. Should you find this material interesting, you are encouraged to investigate bitwise manipulation further. The bitwise operators Jython supports are shown in Table 2.15.

---

[13] The value generated by this inversion process is also called the *two's complement*.

Table 2.15   Bitwise and Boolean Operators

Operator	Example	Result	Description
<<	1 << 2	4	The left operand is left-shifted the number of bit positions specified by the right operand.
>>	256>>4	16	The left operand is right-shifted the number of bit positions specified by the right operand.
&	15 & 1	1	A bitwise "and" is performed using the given values.
|	10 | 5	15	A bitwise "or" is performed using the given values.
^	10 ^ 7	13	A bitwise "xor" (exclusive or) is performed using the given values.
and	1 and 0	0	A Boolean "and" of the two operands. *Note:* If the left operand is "false", the right is not evaluated. This is sometimes referred to as a *short-circuit evaluation*.
or	1 or 0	1	A Boolean "or" of the two operands. *Note:* If the left operand is "true", the right is not evaluated.

The last two operators in Table 2.15 are identified as Boolean. For these operators, the following values are considered `"false"`:

- Any numeric zero value (for example, 0, 0L, 0.0)
- Any empty sequence or dictionary (for example, [], (), ", {})
- None

All other values are considered `"true"`.

The last kind of (numeric) operators to be described are used much more frequently than the preceding bitwise operators. The following operators are used to determine the relationship between two values. The result of using one of these operators on two values yields either a value of 0 (also referred to as false), which is used to indicate that the specified relationship is not correct (does not hold), or 1, which is used to indicate that the specified relationship holds (or is correct). Table 2.16 shows these relationship, or comparison, operators and how they can be used.

Table 2.16   Relationship/Comparison Operators

Example	Result	Relationship Tested
1 < 3	1	1 is "less than" 3
1 > 3	0	1 is "greater than" 3
1 <= 5	1	1 is "less than or equal to" 5
1 >= 2	0	1 is "greater than or equal to" 2
1 == 2	0	1 is "equal to" 2
1 != 2	1	1 is "not equal to" 2
1 <> 2	1	1 is "not equal to" 2
		Note: This is the obsolescent form of the "not equal to" test. The != operator is preferred.

An interesting property of Jython relationship operators is that they may be "chained," which means that a relationship comparison expression like `"a relop b relop c"` (that is, a < b <= c) is evaluated as though it were written like so: (a relop b) and (b relop c) without actually evaluating any operand more than once. Listing 2.6 shows some examples of chained relationship operators. One thing that you should notice about these expressions is that the result is either a 0 or a 1, which, as mentioned earlier, are used to represent either the boolean false or true values (which are represented as 0 and 1, respectively).

Listing 2.6   Chained Relationship Operators

```
1|wsadmin>1 < 2 <= 3
2|1
3|wsadmin>'a' < 'b' <= 'x'
4|1
```

Next, we cover the remaining relationship or comparison operators. These are a little specific but are valuable nonetheless. Given a sequence, it is very useful to quickly and easily determine whether or not a specific value exists therein. It is also useful to be able to determine whether or not two objects are the same, or different. Listing 2.7 and Table 2.17 further explain these operators and demonstrate their use.

Listing 2.7   Sequence Membership and Identity Operators

```
 1|wsadmin>List = [ 1, 2, 3, 4, 5, 6, 7, 8 ]
 2|wsadmin>Tuple = ( 1, 2, 3, 4, 5, 6, 7, 8 )
 3|wsadmin>String = '12345678'
 4|wsadmin>
 5|wsadmin>0 in List
 6|0
 7|wsadmin>-1 not in List
 8|1
 9|wsadmin>5 in Tuple
10|1
11|wsadmin>'0' in String
12|0
13|wsadmin>a = b = []
14|wsadmin>a is b
15|1
16|wsadmin>b = []
17|wsadmin>a is not b
18|1
```

Table 2.17   Membership and Identity Operators Example Explained

Lines(s)	Description
1–4	Assign values to specified user variables.
5–12	Demonstrate the use of the in and not in operators that can be used to determine the presence or absence of a specific value in a sequence.
13–18	Show how the operators can be used to determine whether or not two items refer to the same object. *Note:* These operators do not compare the values of the operands, just their identities.

Table 2.18 is the revised operator precedence table and includes all of the operators that we have seen. Again, the operators closer to the top of the table have a higher precedence than those lower in the table. All operators on the same row have the same precedence and if they exist together in an expression, are evaluated from left to right.

Table 2.18 Operator Precedence—Revised

Operator(s)	Description
( )	Grouping using parentheses
**	Exponentiation
~	Bitwise inversion
+x, -x	Unary positive and negative
*, /, %	Multiplication/String Repeat, Division, Modulo (Remainder)
+, -	Addition/String Concatenation, Subtraction
<<, >>	Left and Right shift
&	Bitwise "and"
^	Bitwise "xor" (exclusive or)
|	Bitwise "or"
in, not in,	Membership
is, is not,	Identity
<, <=, >, >=, ==, !=, <>	Relationship/comparison
not	Boolean "not"
and	Boolean "and"
or	Boolean "or"

Statement Separator

Generally, it is considered a best practice to have one statement on a line. There are exceptional circumstances, however, where it is convenient to be able to violate this practice and have multiple simple statements on one line. This means that compound, or loop, statements (to be covered shortly) are not allowed. To do so, use a semicolon to indicate where the first simple statement ends and the next should begin. Listing 2.8 shows an example:[14]

---

[14] All statements separated by a semi-colon are considered to be at the same indentation level.

Listing 2.8   Statement Separator Example

```
1|wsadmin>a = -1; print 'Negative'; a = -a; print 'a =',a
2|Negative
3|a = 1
```

Comments

Jython is meant to be a very readable language. However, there are times when the program state-ments should be annotated with comments for the reader. This is especially true for scripts that are to be used more than once or if they are meant to be used by more than one person. Comments are provided in some of the examples and with all of the scripts made available with this book.

Comments can use the whole line, or they might be at the end of a line after another Jython statement. Comments begin with an octothorpe ('#') and continue to the end of line. An octothorpe in a string is not considered a comment, but rather it is simply a character.

Coding Conventions

Even though it isn't technically part of the Jython syntax, it is worth mentioning that adhering to rules, guidelines, and conventions for how scripts are to be written greatly enhances script read-ability. Therefore, you are encouraged to define and document the coding conventions you and your team use. For example, you might want to review the coding conventions used for the Python standard library, which are available from http://www.python.org/dev/peps/pep-0008/.

Summary

In this chapter, we started exploring the Jython programming language. We looked at the basic data types and the structures that are available to all Jython scripts. We also covered expressions, coding conventions, and the topic of operator precedence. In the next chapter, we see where these are used in Jython statements.

## CHAPTER 3

Jython Statements

In the previous chapter, we looked at the basic building blocks of Jython scripts—that is, the data types and structures used to represent information. In this chapter, we expand on these concepts and explore the next programming construct: *statements*.

Expression Statements

Expression statements are used to compute values and to invoke functions. They are frequently used in an interactive **wsadmin** session, where the result (if it is not None) is displayed. This can be seen in Listing 3.1 (lines 12–13). When **wsadmin** is not used in an interactive mode, the results of expression statements are discarded, as also shown in Listing 3.1 (line 8).

The `print` Statement

As has already been seen in the examples, the purpose of the `print` statement is to evaluate specified expressions and display the results. The `print` statement acts similarly to expression statements when **wsadmin** is in the interactive mode; however, the presence of `print` specifically indicates that the output be displayed, especially when the script is being executed. Listing 3.1 shows examples of print and expression statements.

Listing 3.1   `print` and Expression Statement Examples

```
1|C:...\bin>type print.py
2|1 + 2 * 3
3|print 'The result is:',
4|print 1 + 2 * 3
5|
6|C:...\bin>wsadmin -conntype none -lang jython -f print.py
```

```
 7|WASX7357I: ...
 8|The result is: 7
 9|
10|C:...\bin>wsadmin -conntype none -lang jython
11|WASX7357I: ...
12|wsadmin>1 + 2 * 3
13|7
14|wsadmin>print 'The result is:',
15|The result is:wsadmin>print 1 + 2 * 3
16| 7
17|wsadmin>quit
```

Lines 2–4 of Listing 3.1 show the contents of the example script file, print.py. Line 8 shows the output generated by the print statements within the script file, and lines 12–16 show the result of manually entering the same commands in an interactive **wsadmin** session.

While executing the script, the result of the expression statement in line 1 of the input file (that is, 1 + 2 * 3) is discarded or, rather, not displayed. Interestingly enough, what you see are the results of two different print statements displayed on a single line (line 8). This is because the first print statement (line 2) ends with a comma. The comma tells the print statement not to add a new line to the end of the information displayed. Note that the comma at the end of the interactive print statement (line 15) causes the **wsadmin** prompt to be displayed on the same line as the text generated by the print statement.

Assignment Statements

In simple terms, assignment statements are used to associate, or bind, a name to a value. A more complete and accurate definition would include that assignment statements can bind or rebind names to values and modify mutable items. Throughout this chapter, there are many examples of assignment statements that should make this point clearer. Now that you have some background, let's take a look at some of the forms assignment statements can take in Table 3.1.

Table 3.1   Assignment Statement Examples

Statement	Description
i = 0	This is the simplest form of the assignment statement. If the specified identifier, that is, i, already exists, then this statement replaces its current value with numeric integer value of 0. If the identifier does not exist, then this statement creates it and binds it to the specified value.

Table 3.1 Assignment Statement Examples

Statement	Description
`name = 'Bob'`	This is another simple assignment statement showing how the value to be assigned can be of any Jython data type. It could just as easily be an instance of any of the sequence types (string, list, tuple) or even a dictionary.
`i = i + 1`	The value to the right of the equal sign can be an expression. Just in case you are unfamiliar with it, this statement takes the current value of `i` and attempts[1] to add one to (increment) this value and assign the result of this expression to the variable on the left of the equal sign.
`a = b = c = 0`	This assignment statement binds the value of the expression (in this case 0) to each of the specified variable names.
`a = 1, 2`	Should the expression include commas and therefore provide multiple values, the expression is considered a tuple. In this case, if you were to follow this assignment statement with print a, then the generated output would be: `(1, 2)`.[2]
`a, b = 1, 2`	In this case, the number of identifiers on the left of the equal sign, also called targets, equals the number of comma separated values to the right of the equal sign. So, the values are assigned to the targets based upon the order in which they occur. Thus, this assignment statement is equivalent to "`a = 1; b = 2`."
`a, b = b, a`	This is a common Jython idiom used to exchange (swap) the values of the specified variables and is approximately equivalent to: `temp = a; a = b; b = temp`.
`a, b = 1, 2, 3`	The number of target variables must equal the number of values on the right side of the equal sign, so this is a syntax error.
`a, b = [ 1, 2 ]`	This shows that the contents of a list can be used to assign and bind values to variables as long as the number of elements in the list equals the number of target variables.
`a = b = [ 1, 2 ]`	This assignment statement binds the value of the expression (in this a two-element list), to each of the specified variable names. Notice how easy it is to misread this statement if you aren't careful. The only difference between this and the preceding one is this uses an equal sign between the a and the b and the other uses a comma. There is a subtle yet important difference between the values bound using the two techniques.

[1] Remember that `i` could be an immutable value, so an attempt to "add one to it" could cause an exception.

[2] See the "Packing and Unpacking" section.

Table 3.1 Assignment Statement Examples

Statement	Description
`a, b = '12'`	Strings are sequences too. As long as the number of target variables is the same as the length of the string, then each variable will be assigned the corresponding character from the source string, thus making this assignment statement equivalent to: `a = '1'; b = '2'`.
`a, b = [(1,2),'Buckle my shoe']`	This example is a little more complicated. The list (literal) has two elements, the first being a tuple `(1,2)` and the second a string. This statement will bind the tuple to a and the string to b.

Let's take a deeper look at the term "bind" as it applies to the action performed by an assignment statement. The term warrants further explanation, especially when we examine what actually occurs in Listing 3.2. It should be fairly clear that each of the target variables is associated with a two-element list. What might not be clear is the fact that after this statement is executed, a single list is created, and each variable refers to the same object.

Listing 3.2 Assignment Bindings

```
 1|wsadmin>a = b = [1,2]
 2|wsadmin>print 'a =', a, 'b =', b
 3|a = [1, 2] b = [1, 2]
 4|wsadmin>a[ 0 ] = -5
 5|wsadmin>print 'a =', a, 'b =', b
 6|a = [-5, 2] b = [-5, 2]
 7|wsadmin>c = b
 8|wsadmin>c[ 1 ] = 'Spam'
 9|wsadmin>print 'a =', a, 'b =', b
10|a = [-5, 'Spam'] b = [-5, 'Spam']
```

Lines 1–3 show how the assignment statement in line 1 binds each of the target variables to a two element list. Because a list is mutable, you can modify its value in place. This happens in line 4, where the first element of the list bound to the variable is changed to `"-5"`. Lines 5 and 6 show that each variable refers to the same object. Lines 7–10 show how this same binding occurs with simple assignment statements.

WARNING Assignments cause existing objects to be bound to identifiers. New objects are not created.

Packing and Unpacking

Some of the examples in Table 3.1 warrant additional explanation. As stated earlier, when multiple values exist on the right-hand side of an assignment statement (that is, are after the equal sign ' = ' and are separated by commas), a tuple is created. This process of combining comma sep-arated values into a tuple is called *tuple packing*. When multiple target identifiers exist on the left side of the assignment statement (that is, precede the equal sign) and multiple source values exist to be assigned to these identifiers, the inverse operation occurs and is called *unpacking*. Because unpacking can occur from any sequence, this operation is actually called *sequence unpacking*. Listing 3.3 demonstrates this, and Table 3.2 explains these statements in more detail.

Listing 3.3 Tuple Packing and Sequence Unpacking Examples

```
 1|wsadmin>a = 1,
 2|wsadmin>a
 3|(1,)
 4|wsadmin>a, b = 1, 2
 5|wsadmin>print 'a =', a, 'b =', b
 6|a = 1 b = 2
 7|wsadmin>a, b = b, a
 8|wsadmin>print 'a =', a, 'b =', b
 9|a = 2 b = 1
10|wsadmin>a, b = 'Hi'
11|wsadmin>print 'a =', a, 'b =', b
12|a = H b = i
```

Table 3.2 Packing and Unpacking (Explanation of Examples)

Lines(s)	Description
1	Tuple packing occurs to create the value to be bound to variable a.
2–3	The current value of variable a is shown to be the generated tuple.
4	Tuple packing is used to create a tuple, and sequence unpacking is used to assign (bind) the sequence values to the specified variables.
5–6	This shows that the values of a and b are individual integer values, and not a tuple as was seen previously.
7	Again, tuple packing is used to create a tuple containing the current values of the speci-fied variables, and then sequence unpacking is used to assign (bind) the values to the alternate variables.
8–9	This shows that the values of a and b have been exchanged (swapped).
10	This is an example of sequence unpacking from a string to the specified variables.
11–12	This shows the current values of both variables.

Augmented Assignment

One of the most common uses of the assignment statement is to modify an existing value of a particular variable. For example: `i = i + 1` is an idiom used to increment the value of `i`. This kind of thing (that is, having a variable as one of the operands in a binary operation and then assigning the result of the operation to the variable) is common enough to warrant a shorthand notation, which is called an "augmented assignment" statement. Table 3.3 shows these symbols and defines the augmented operation for each operator.

Table 3.3   Augmented Assignment Operators

Operator	Operation
`+=`	Addition or string concatenation
`-=`	Subtraction
`*=`	Multiplication or string repeat
`/=`	Division
`%=`	Modulo (Remainder) or string formatting
`**=`	Exponentiation
`>>=`	Right shift
`<<=`	Left shift
`&=`	Bitwise and
`^=`	Bitwise xor (exclusive or)
`|=`	Bitwise or

NOTE   It is important to remember that each augmented assignment operator of the form `a <operator>= b` is logically equivalent to: `a = a operator b`.

Understand, however, that the evaluation of the left operand (that is, the assignment target) only occurs once.

Slices

Now that you are aware of how assignment statements can bind multiple variable names to the same object, you might be wondering how to bind a variable to a copy of a sequence. This technique is called making a slice, or *slicing*. Square brackets with 0 to 3 numeric expressions, separated by colons, are used to indicate a slice.

These delimited expressions represent the following optional values:

1. The starting index (default = 0).

2. The ending (exclusive) index (default = sequence length).

3. The step, or stride, between values (default = 1).

The examples in Table 3.4 presume that the following assignment statements have been executed:

```
six = [ 0, 1, 2, 3, 4, 5 ]
lang = '"Jython"'
food = 'bacon, eggs, and spam'
```

Table 3.4 Simple and Extended Slices

Operator	Result	Operation
food[0:5]	'bacon'	The slice creates a copy of the specified string, copying only the characters from index [0] up to but not including the character with an index [5] (that is, the comma ',').
food[:5]	'bacon'	If the starting index is unspecified, an index of [0] is used. So the slice here is identical to the previous example.
food[17:]	'spam'	If the ending index is unspecified, the sequence length is used as the ending index. So, this is equivalent to food[17:21].
food[-4:]	'spam'	As noted earlier, a negative index can also be used. Any negative index value is added to the sequence length to determine the actual index to be used. Therefore, this is identical to the previous example.
six[-1:-2]	[]	Should the starting index (that is, -1) be greater than the ending index (that is, -2), the result is an empty sequence of the same type.
lang[:]	'"Jython"'	If both the starting and ending indexes are missing, the result is a complete copy of the source sequence and is equivalent to having used lang[0:8]. *Note:* Because of its usefulness, this is a frequently used idiom.
lang[1:-1]	'Jython'	This idiom is used to create a copy of the specified sequence without the starting and ending elements. In this case, notice how it can be used to remove the leading and trailing double quotes from the specified string value. You will see this idiom later with code that extracts information from strings.
six[::2]	[0, 2, 4]	The use of two colons indicates an extended slice. The expressions default the starting and ending indices, while providing or specifying the step, or stride, value. Use of an extended slice iterates over the sequence by adding the step value to the current index on each iteration.

Table 3.4 Simple and Extended Slices

Operator	Result	Operation
six[1:4:2]	[1, 3]	This extended slice indicates that the result should be generated by first selecting the element [1], then [1+2]. Because [1+2+2] is beyond the specified ending index of [4], it is not included.
lang[::-1]	'"nohtyJ"'	If the stride value is negative, then the default starting element is the last item in the sequence, and default ending index is logically before the first element of the sequence. The resulting slice will be generated by iterating over the specified range in reverse order. This example is equivalent to lang[7::-1]. Note, however, that you have to default the ending index if you want to include the first element in the sequence (that is, [0]) because attempting to reference [-1] is interpreted as the last element in the sequence.[3]

Slices can also identify a target portion of a mutable sequence (that is, a list) to be modified. Listing 3.4 shows some examples of this use of slices. Line 3 identifies the target slice of the list to be replaced. The interesting thing to note about this is how the result (line 5) might not be what you expect. If what was intended was to replace elements 1 and 2 with a single string element, then the syntax shown in line 6 should be used.[4] Note how one slice is used for the target, and a different slice can be used to specify a subset of the source. In this case, the source slice (that is, the [1:-1]) is a commonly occurring slice that is used to copy everything from the source sequence except the leading and trailing elements. If a complete copy of the source sequence were to be used, then the slice syntax would have been [:]. Additionally, lines 9–14 show the difference between assigning using an index (where no colon occurs) versus using a slice (where 1 or 2 colons occur). Lines 12 and 15 show how sequence unpacking from a list and a tuple could have been used to perform this particular assignment.

---

[3] Unfortunately, version 2.1 of Jython, which is the version provided with WebSphere Application Server 6.1, has a defect that doesn't implement lang[7:-1:-1] correctly. It results in '"nohtyJ"' instead of the correct empty string.

[4] Technically, the right-hand side of the assignment statement could be any sequence. However, it was felt that using the sequence unpacking from a list (i.e., the syntax shown) would be more easily understood than either of the sequence unpacking from a tuple—that is, either this: six[1:-3] = lang[1:-1] or this: six[1:-3] = (lang[1:-1],).

Listing 3.4   Assignment Using Slices

```
 1|wsadmin>six = [ 0, 1, 2, 3, 4 ,5 ]
 2|wsadmin>lang = '"Jython"'
 3|wsadmin>six[ 1:3 ] = lang[ 1:-1 ]
 4|wsadmin>six
 5|[0, 'J', 'y', 't', 'h', 'o', 'n', 3, 4, 5]
 6|wsadmin>six[ 1:-3 ] = [ lang[ 1:-1 ] ]
 7|wsadmin>six
 8|[0, 'Jython', 3, 4, 5]
 9|wsadmin>six[ 1 ] = [ 1, 2 ]
10|wsadmin>six
11|[0, [1, 2], 3, 4, 5]
12|wsadmin>six[ 1:2 ] = [ 1, 2 ]
13|wsadmin>six
14|[0, 1, 2, 3, 4, 5]
15|wsadmin>six[ 1:3 ] = (9, 8)
16|wsadmin>six
17|[0, 9, 8, 3, 4, 5]
```

Simple Statements

Up to this point, we have seen expression and assignment statements. Now it's time to start exploring the next programming construct, simple statements.

The assert Statement

assert statements are used to validate that conditions or relationships hold before an important calculation is performed. If you expect a specific variable to be non-zero, for example, you can use an assert statement to enforce this condition. The two forms of the assert statement are shown in Listing 3.5.

Listing 3.5   assert Statement Examples

```
1|wsadmin>x = 1 + 2 * 3
2|wsadmin>assert x
3|wsadmin>assert x == 0, 'Assertion failed.'
4|WASX7015E: Exception running command: "assert x == 0, 'Assertion
failed'";
5| exception information: com.ibm.bsf.BSFException: exception from
Jython:
6|Traceback (innermost last):
7| File "<input>", line 1, in ?
8|AssertionError: Assertion failed
```

Line 2 shows the first form of the assert statement, that is the assert keyword followed by a single expression. Line 3 shows the second form, where the assert keyword is followed by two comma separated expressions. Frequently the second expression is an "error" message or text string to be displayed should the assertion fail. In either case, the first expression is evaluated. If the result is non-zero, the assertion is considered to have succeeded, and execution continues. Should the expression result be a value of 0, the assertion is considered to have failed, and an exception is raised. Lines 4–8 show the results of an assertion failure. This should encourage you to have clear, complete, and concise assertion messages.

The break Statement

A break statement is used to terminate the nearest enclosing loop. Loop constructs and the use of the break statement are demonstrated in the "Compound Statements" section later in the chapter.

The continue Statement

A continue statement is used to initiate the next cycle of the nearest enclosing loop. Loop constructs and the continue statement are discussed the section, "Compound Statements."

The del Statement

The del statement is used to remove or unbind a name from a value. Essentially, it is the reverse of the assignment statement. Multiple items may be removed using a single del statement by separating the items to be deleted by commas. Elements and slices of mutable sequences (that is, lists) may also be removed using this statement. Listing 3.6 demonstrates using the del statement, and Table 3.5 explains these examples.

Listing 3.6   del Statement Examples

```
 1|wsadmin>lang = '"Jython"'
 2|wsadmin>del lang
 3|wsadmin>lang
 4|WASX7015E: Exception running command: "lang"; exception information:
 5|  com.ibm.bsf.BSFException: exception from Jython:
 6|Traceback (innermost last):
 7|  File "<input>", line 1, in ?
 8|NameError: lang
 9|
10|wsadmin>six = [ 0, 1, 2, 3, 4, 5 ]
11|wsadmin>del six[ 1:3 ]; six
12|[0, 3, 4, 5]
13|wsadmin>six = [ 0, 1, 2, 3, 4, 5 ]
14|wsadmin>del six[ 5 ], six[ 3 ], six[ 1 ]; six
```

```
15|[0, 2, 4]
16|wsadmin>six = [ 0, 1, 2, 3, 4, 5 ]
17|wsadmin>del six[ 1 ], six[ 3 ], six[ 5 ]
18|WASX7015E: Exception running command: "del six[ 1 ], six[ 3 ], six[
5 ]"; exception information:
19| com.ibm.bsf.BSFException: exception from Jython:
20|Traceback (innermost last):
21| File "<input>", line 1, in ?
22|IndexError: index out of range: -1
23|
24|wsadmin>six
25|[0, 2, 3, 5]
26|wsadmin>six = [ 0, 1, 2, 3, 4, 5 ]
27|wsadmin>del six[ 1 ]
28|wsadmin>six
29|[0, 2, 3, 4, 5]
30|wsadmin>del six[ 3 ]
31|wsadmin>six
32|[0, 2, 3, 5]
```

Table 3.5 del Examples Explained

Lines(s)	Description
1–9	These show how to create, or bind, a value to a variable name and then to use the del statement to remove, or unbind, that variable name. The exception seen in lines 4–8 should not be a surprise. Attempts to use an unassigned identifier generate a NameError exception.
10–15	These show how to use a slice in a del statement to remove elements from a list. Remember that the second expression in the slice syntax identifies the element past the end of the slice. In this case, 1:3 identifies elements 1 and 2.
16–32	These lines might surprise you a bit, at least until you consider what happens to the list as each of the specified elements is removed. This is why lines 24–32 are provided—so that you can see, as each of the del statements (in lines 27 and 30) are executed, the length of the list is reduced so that by the time the del six[5] is attempted, only four elements exist in the list, which is why the items in the list were removed in reverse order in line 15. So be careful when you are using the del statement to remove items from a list.

The exec Statement

The exec statement is used to dynamically execute Jython code. Listing 3.7 shows how a statement contained within a string can be dynamically executed and even change other values. Table 3.6 explains this example in more detail.

Listing 3.7   exec Statement

```
 1|wsadmin>cmd = 'print "Hello world"'
 2|wsadmin>print cmd
 3|print "Hello world"
 4|wsadmin>exec cmd
 5|Hello world
 6|wsadmin>cmd = 'a = [ 1, 2, 3 ]'
 7|wsadmin>a = 'Testing'
 8|wsadmin>exec cmd
 9|wsadmin>a
10|[1, 2, 3]
```

Table 3.6   Explanation of exec Examples

Line	Description
1	Assigns a string to the cmd variable, the contents of which are a complete print statement.
2	Display the current value of the cmd variable.
3	Shows the current value of the string.
4	Actual use of the exec statement to execute the contents of the cmd variable.
5	This is the output generated by the preceding print statement.
6	Assign an assignment statement to the cmd variable.
7	Assign a string to variable a.
8	Actual use of the exec statement to execute the contents of the cmd variable.
9	Interactive/interpretive expression used to display the current value of variable a.
10	Current value of the variable showing how the command executed in line 8 modified the value of variable a.

The import Statement

Discussion about the import statement will be deferred until Chapter 5, "Jython Modules."

The pass Statement

The pass statement does nothing. There are times when a statement is required syntactically but nothing needs to be done. In these cases, the pass statement is used.

The raise Statement

The raise statement is used to generate an exception condition. The syntax for this statement allows 0 to 3 comma-separated expressions. If no expression is present, Jython attempts to reraise the last exception that was raised. This form of the statement would normally occur within exception handling code.

When expressions are present, the first two expressions are evaluated to get objects. These objects are then used to determine the type and value of the exception. Omitted expressions are evaluated as None. If the third expression is present, and not None, it must be a traceback object. Unfortunately, discussions about traceback objects are outside the scope of this book.

Control Flow

So far, we've looked at only individual commands or statements that can be executed sequentially. For more useful programs, you need some statements that allow decisions to be made about what statements should and should not be executed and more importantly, in what order. Let's start with some simple statements and build upon them explaining as we go along.

Before discussing control structure, however, you first need to understand how Jython identifies groups of statements. Some programming languages use special symbols (for example, curly braces ' { ' and ' } '), or special identifiers (keywords) to indicate the start and end of a group of statements.

Jython is different. It uses indentation to identify the grouping and association of statements. For those unfamiliar with this technique, it can take a little getting used to. However, once you make this adjustment, many you will likely find that structuring your programs in this way is very intuitive. Many programming instructors feel that indentation makes programs more readable and therefore easier to understand. Jython takes this suggestion and enforces it by making indentation significant, thus making Jython scripts significantly easier to read.

How does it work? As Jython looks at each line, leading tab characters are replaced by the appropriate number of blanks (space characters) in order to have the "tab stop" position aligned on a column number that is a multiple of 8.

Listings 3.8 and 3.9 show an absurd example of how this works. There are two, almost identical, script files, absurd0.py and absurd1.py, the first of which is shown in Listing 3.8.

Each script file has a sequence of print statements. The statements on lines 2–9 are all considered (at least by Jython) to have identical indentation, which means that they are considered a statement-suite and will be executed in the order that they occur. The only difference in each line is the number of spaces ' ' that precede the tab character ' \t ' before the print keyword. In order to better understand where the tab is located, in this example, we use the ' • ' character to represent a tab. The quoted string after each print identifies the characters that precede the print on the given line.

Listing 3.8   absurd0.py

```
 1|if 0 :
 2|•print 'tab'
 3| •print 'space tab'
 4|  •print 'space space tab'
 5|   •print 'space space space tab'
 6|    •print 'space space space space tab'
 7|     •print 'space space space space space tab'
 8|      •print 'space space space space space space tab'
 9|       •print 'space space space space space space space tab'
10|print 'no tab'
```

Listing 3.9 shows what happens when the contents of the script files are displayed by the operating system and then executed by **wsadmin**. First, the contents of absurd1.py are displayed, and you can see that Windows interprets the indentation as expected. This is evidenced by the fact that the print statements (lines 3–10) are all aligned. With this indentation, these statements are logically grouped together by the reader, the operating system, and by Jython.

What about the other statements in the file (that is, lines 2 and 11)? They both begin in column 1, meaning that Jython also understands them to be associated in a sequential manner. Line 2 shows the first of the compound, or control flow, statements. The first word on the line is if, a keyword seen earlier. In its simplest form, the if keyword is followed by an expression to be evaluated, and this expression is followed by a colon ' : '. Should the result of the expression be evaluated as non-zero (that is, true), the indented statements immediately following the if are executed. If the result is evaluated as zero, the indented statement group is skipped, and any subsequent statement with the same indentation as the if is executed.

Listing 3.9   Absurd Indentation Example

```
 1|C:...\bin>type absurd1.py
 2|if 1 :
 3|        print 'tab'
 4|        print 'space tab'
 5|        print 'space space tab'
 6|        print 'space space space tab'
 7|        print 'space space space space tab'
 8|        print 'space space space space space tab'
 9|        print 'space space space space space space tab'
```

```
10|          print 'space space space space space space space tab'
11|print 'no tab'
12|
13|C:...\bin>wsadmin -conntype none -lang jython -f absurd0.py
14|WASX7357I: ...
15|no tab
16|
17|C:...\bin>wsadmin -conntype none -lang jython -f absurd1.py
18|WASX7357I: ...
19|tab
20|space tab
21|space space tab
22|space space space tab
23|space space space space tab
24|space space space space space tab
25|space space space space space space tab
26|space space space space space space space tab
27|no tab
```

Looking closely, you can see that the only difference between the two script files occurs in the first line, where absurd0.py contains "if 0 :" and absurd1.py contains "if 1 :".

Using this information you have a better chance of understanding the output seen in Listing 3.9. When absurd0.py is executed (lines 13–15), the expression to be evaluated is 0, so the indented statements are skipped, and execution continues with the subsequent statement. The next statement that has the same indentation as the if statement is executed. This results in the no tab output (line 15).

When absurd1.py is specified as the script file to be run (line 17), the expression is evaluated as 1, so the indented statements are executed in the order seen (lines 19–26). After the last indented print statement is executed, execution continues with the next (and last) statement in the file, which is why we again see the no tab output on line 27.

This example clearly illustrates how difficult it can be to interpret the indentation when space and tab characters are mixed. This is especially true if the text editor you are using allows you to define your own tab stops and you are inconsistent with the characters used for indentation. Should this occur, you will see a SyntaxError when wsadmin tries to execute the script file.

Compound Statements

The next level of complexity involves compound statements that determine whether or not associated statements should be executed and how many times.

The if Statement

As seen in the previous section, one of the compound statements available to us is the `if` statement, the syntax of which is as follows:

```
if <expression> :
    statement-suite
else :
    statement-suite
```

This statement is used when a choice needs to be made between two different statement groups. Should the expression evaluate to `true` (non-zero), the first statement-suite is executed. At the end of the statement-suite, control skips over the second statement-suite and continues with the next logical statement of the same indentation level as the `if`. Should the expression evaluate as `false` (that is, zero), the first statement-suite is skipped, and the second statement-suite is executed. Occasionally a choice needs to be made among more than two groups of statements. For this kind of situation, one or more `elif` clauses can be added, as shown here:

```
if <expression> :
    statement-suite
elif <expression> :
    statement-suite
else :
    statement-suite
```

In this case, the expressions are evaluated in the order they occur until a non-zero result is encountered. The associated statement-suite is executed, and control continues after the last of the statement-suites in this construct. Should none of the expressions evaluate as `true`, the statement-suite following the `else` keyword is executed (that is, if the optional `else` clause is present).

loop Statements

The following compound statements can cause the statement-suite to be executed zero or more times. Because of this, they are know a as `loop`, or `looping` statements. However, be sure these loops include some way to exit the loop constructs. If there is no way for the loop to terminate, an unfavorable condition known as an *infinite loop* occurs.

The while Statement

It is important to note that the `else` and subsequent statement-suite are optional. The expression portion of the `while` is evaluated, and as long as the result of the evaluation is `true` (that is, non-zero), the statement-suite is executed. Once the expression evaluates as `false` (that is, zero), the statement-suite associated with the `else`, if one is present, is executed. The syntax of the `while` statement is shown here:

```
while <expression> :
    statement-suite
else :
    statement-suite
```

Listing 3.10 shows a sample `while` loop. Line 1 initializes the variable that will be used in the `while` expression. The first time the expression is evaluated, count has a value of 10, so the expression result is `true` (that is, 10 is greater than 0), and the indented statement-suite is executed. Line 3 prints the current value but does not include a newline character because of the presence of the comma at the end of the `print` statement. Line 4 decrements the value of the count variable (using an augmented assignment statement). Because the end of the statement-suite has been reached at this point, control is returned back to the `while` statement so that the expression can be re-evaluated. Lines 2–4 are executed in turn as long as count is greater than 0.

Eventually, the expression evaluates as `false` when the value of count equals 0, and control passes to the statement-suite associated with the `else` portion of the `while` statement. Because this example was used in an interactive **wsadmin** session, you can see the output that was generated by the `while` statement on line 8.

Listing 3.10 Sample while Statement

```
1|wsadmin>count = 10
2|wsadmin>while count > 0 :
3|wsadmin>   print count,
4|wsadmin>   count -= 1
5|wsadmin>else :
6|wsadmin>   print 'done'
7|wsadmin>
8|10 9 8 7 6 5 4 3 2 1 done
9|wsadmin>
```

Listing 3.11 shows two more examples of the `while` statement. This time, including the `break` statement mentioned earlier. For the first `while` loop, seen in lines 4–10, execution includes the evaluation of the expression in line 4, which is used to determine if the loop execution has checked every element in the values list for an occurrence of 5. Eventually, the expression evaluation results as `false`, and control is passed to the `else` statement on line 10. The result is the `"5 was not found"` message shown on line 12.

The `while` loop (lines 15–21) of Listing 3.11 is nearly identical; however, this time the value to be checked is present and is eventually located. When it is, the `print` statement (line 17) is executed, followed by the `break` statement (line 18). When a `break` statement is executed, as noted earlier, the nearest enclosing loop is terminated. When it is, any associated `else` clause is skipped. That is why we only see the `4 is present` message printed (line 17) and not the one from the `else` suite (line 21).

Listing 3.11   Example `while` and `break` Statements

```
 1|wsadmin>values = [ 0, 2, 4, 6, 8, 10 ]
 2|wsadmin>length = 6
 3|wsadmin>index = 0
 4|wsadmin>while index < length :
 5|wsadmin>  if values[ index ] == 5 :
 6|wsadmin>    print '5 is present'
 7|wsadmin>    break
 8|wsadmin>  index += 1
 9|wsadmin>else :
10|wsadmin> print '5 was not found'
11|wsadmin>
12|5 was not found
13|wsadmin>
14|wsadmin>index = 0
15|wsadmin>while index < length :
16|wsadmin>  if values[ index ] == 4 :
17|wsadmin>    print '4 is present'
18|wsadmin>    break
19|wsadmin>  index += 1
20|wsadmin>else :
21|wsadmin> print '4 was not found'
22|wsadmin>
23|4 is present
24|wsadmin>
```

The for Statement

The syntax of the `for` statement is shown next. The `<sequence-expression>` is evaluated once to generate the sequence over which the loop iterates. The statement-suite is then executed for each target value in the sequence (one at a time). If the sequence is empty or once the values have been exhausted, control transitions to the optional `else` suite, and the loop terminates:

```
for <target> in <sequence-expression> :
    statement-suite
else :
    statement-suite
```

Listing 3.12 has some `for` statement examples to study. The first for loop (lines 3–6) sum up the values in the specified sequence. When the loop has processed each element in the list, control transitions to the `else` statement-suite (lines 6–7). The output (line 8) should not be too much of a surprise.

The second `for` statement (lines 10–15) includes another of the previously mentioned `continue` statements. When a `continue` statement is executed, control is transferred to the end of the nearest enclosing loop, in this case the `for` loop, and the next iteration value is assigned, should one exist. If the sequence values are exhausted, control transitions to the `else` statement-suite. In this particular example, the `if` statement (line 11) is executed to look for any values of 10. If any are encountered, the continue statement is executed to skip over any remaining statements within the loop (that is, the augmented assignment statement to add the current value to the sum). Because only one instance of the value of 10 exists in the list of values, the result of this test and the `continue` statement should be straightforward and easily understood. Notice how the else statement-suite still gets executed, even though the `continue` was executed while processing the last value in the sequence.

Listing 3.12   for Statement Examples

```
 1|wsadmin>values = [ 0, 2, 4, 6, 8, 10 ]
 2|wsadmin>sum = 0
 3|wsadmin>for val in values :
 4|wsadmin>  sum += val
 5|wsadmin>else :
 6|wsadmin>  print 'sum =', sum
 7|wsadmin>
 8|sum = 30
 9|wsadmin>sum = 0
10|wsadmin>for val in values :
11|wsadmin>  if val == 10 :
12|wsadmin>    continue
13|wsadmin>  sum += val
14|wsadmin>else :
15|wsadmin> print 'sum =', sum
16|wsadmin>
17|sum = 20
18|wsadmin>sum = 0
19|wsadmin>for val in values :
20|wsadmin>  if val % 2 == 0 :
21|wsadmin>    print 'even number encountered'
22|wsadmin>    break
23|wsadmin>  sum += val
```

```
24|wsadmin>else :
25|wsadmin>   print 'sum =', sum
26|wsadmin>
27|even number encountered
28|wsadmin>
```

The last for statement example in this listing can be found in lines 19–25. In this case, the test is for even numbers. This check is made using the modulo operator '%', which divides the quotient (that is, the left operand) by the dividend (the right operand). The value returned by this operator is the remainder after performing integer division. The purpose of this example is to show that when a break statement is executed, the nearest enclosing loop is terminated, and any associated else statement is skipped.

WARNING   Don't directly modify the list over which the for statement is iterating. To demonstrate this, we need to reference something that the book has not yet discussed, and that is the list method named "remove()," the purpose of which is to delete the specified value from the list. An example of this is shown on lines 4 and 11 of Listing 3.13.

The problem is demonstrated by the first for loop seen in lines 2–4. The expectation is that the if statement within the loop would remove all of the even values in the list. Unfortunately, this does not happen when the for loop iterates over the list being modified. Remember to make a complete copy of the list using the slice construct (that is, [:]), as shown on line 9. By making this simple change, every element of the list is processed correctly.

Listing 3.13   for Statement Caveat

```
 1|wsadmin>values = [ 0, 0, 1, 2, 2, 3, 4, 4, 5, 6, 6 ]
 2|wsadmin>for val in values :
 3|wsadmin>   if val % 2 == 0 :
 4|wsadmin>     values.remove( val )
 5|wsadmin>
 6|wsadmin>print values
 7|[0, 1, 2, 3, 4, 5, 6]
 8|wsadmin>values = [ 0, 0, 1, 2, 2, 3, 4, 4, 5, 6, 6 ]
 9|wsadmin>for val in values[:] :
10|wsadmin>   if val % 2 == 0 :
11|wsadmin>     values.remove( val )
12|wsadmin>
13|wsadmin>print values
14|[1, 3, 5]
```

The try Statement

The `try` statement is used to set up an exception handler for a suite of statements, which means that should an error condition occur during the execution of the statement-suite, the specified error types are compared to look for a match. The complete form of the `try` statement is shown here:

```
try :
    statement-suite
except <expression>, <target> :
    statement-suite
else :
    statement-suite
finally :
    statement-suite
```

The `except` and associated statement-suite can occur zero or more times, but each time it occurs, a unique exception expression identifying an exception handler must be specified. When an exception occurs in the `try` statement-suite, the exception handlers are checked, in the order specified, until a match is found or the list of handlers is exhausted. It is also valid to specify an expressionless `except` clause. However, if so, it must occur last in the list, and it will be a match for any exception.

The optional `else` clause can only occur if at least one `except` clause exists and is invoked if none of the exception handlers has been executed. Additionally, the optional `finally` clause is supposed to be invoked as a cleanup handler. If an unhandled exception is encountered in any of the statement-suites, the exception information is saved, and the `finally` suite is supposed to be executed. At the end of the `finally` statement-suite, the exception is reraised unless the `finally` suite executes a `return` or `break` statement, in which case the saved exception is lost.

Listing 3.14 shows a little more complex example that has a `try` statement within a `for` loop construct. Essentially, the `for` statement has a statement-suite that consists of a single `try` statement (lines 2–16). The `for` loop iterates over the values in the list, assigning each value, in turn, to the loop control variable `"i"` (line 1).

Listing 3.14 "try" Statement Within a `for`

```
1 | wsadmin>for i in [ 0, 1, 2 ] :
2 | wsadmin>  try :
3 | wsadmin>    if i == 0 :
4 | wsadmin>      print 'Divide by zero test'
5 | wsadmin>      x = 1 / i
6 | wsadmin>    elif i == 1 :
7 | wsadmin>      print 'NameError exception test'
```

```
 8│wsadmin>        x = unassigned
 9│wsadmin>      else :
10│wsadmin>        print 'No error'
11│wsadmin>    except NameError :
12│wsadmin>      print 'NameError exception caught'
13│wsadmin>    except :
14│wsadmin>      print 'unknown exception caught'
15│wsadmin>    else :
16│wsadmin>      print 'success - no exception raised'
17│wsadmin>
18│Divide by zero test
19│unknown exception caught
20│NameError exception test
21│NameError exception caught
22│No error
23│success - no exception raised
24│wsadmin>
```

The first time through the loop, the value of `"i"` is 0. When control gets to line 3, the expression evaluation is successful, and the statement-suite on lines 4–5 are executed. The `print` statement on line 4 generates the first line of output seen on line 18. Then the division by 0 on line 5 causes the `try` statement to search for a matching exception handler. First, a test is made (line 11) for a NameError. Then the expression-less `except` is checked (line 13), and a match is found (given that this kind of except matches any exception).[5] This causes the suite in line 14 to be executed, and the output is generated, seen on line 19.

Control then completes the execution of the `try` statement, and the `for` loop iterates to the next value (that is, 1), and the `try` statement is again executed. The `if` expression in line 3 fails, so control transfers to line 6 where the `elif` expression succeeds, and the statement-suite in lines 7–8 are executed. The print statement in line 7 generates the output seen on line 20. The attempt to access the variable unassigned in line 8 causes the NameError exception to be raised. The `try` begins looking for a matching exception handler in line 11 and finds a match. Thus, control is transferred to line 12, and the generated output is seen on line 21.

Control then completes the execution of the `try` statement, and the `for` loop iterates to the next value (that is, 2), and the `try` statement is again executed. This time, the `if` and `elif` expressions fail, and control transfers to the `else` statement-suite found on line 10, which generates the output seen on line 22. Because no exception was raised in the try suite, control is transferred to the `else` found in line 16, which generates the output seen on line 23. Control attempts

---

[5] Just in case you are wondering, there is a way in an `except` statement-suite to find out about the exception that was raised. Unfortunately it will make a bit more sense if we wait until Chapter 5, where we discuss the sys module.

to iterate to the next for value and finds that the sequence values have been exhausted. Control transfers to the statement following the for, which does not exist, so you can see the **wsadmin** command prompt on line 24 that indicates that the for loop has completed successfully.

If you were reading the paragraphs ahead of Listing 3.14 carefully, you would have noticed references to the phrase "...is supposed to..." with regard to the optional finally clause. This is because of the fact that the finally clause has a problem and doesn't work properly. This defect should be fixed in a future version of Jython. In the meantime, you must use a different technique to make use of a finally cleanup handler.

To work around this problem, have an outer try/finally as a wrapper for an inner try statement without a finally clause. An example of this nesting is shown in the following code sample, with extra indentation used to emphasize the inner try statement.

```
try :
    try :
        statement-suite
    except <expression>, <target> :
        statement-suite
    else :
        statement-suite
finally :
    statement-suite
```

Functions

Most programming languages have a method of gathering statements together for easy reuse. In Jython, this is done by defining a function using the syntax shown here:

```
def <function_name>( <parameter-list> ) :
    statement-suite
```

A function definition, like an assignment statement, binds the function name to the specified statement-suite. Because the intent of a function is to allow it to be easily reused, Jython allows a way to easily document the role of the function and how it should be used. This technique allows using the definition of a documentation string as part of the function definition.

Function Definitions

Listing 3.15 shows how to define and use some simple functions. Three function definitions appear on lines 1–16. Once a function has been defined, it can be executed (invoked or called) using the function name followed by parentheses (on lines 19, 21, 22, 24, and 25).

When a function is executed (for example, test1(), on line 19), Jython "remembers" where the call originated[6] and begins the execution of the specified function statement-suite. The statements in this particular function try to reference a variable named x. The question though is to which identifier does this refer?

NOTE   If you don't include the parentheses, you are simply referencing the function, not calling it (see line 17). In interactive mode, this expression statement causes information about the function to be displayed.

Listing 3.15   Functions and Global/Local Variables

```
 1|wsadmin>def test1() :
 2|wsadmin>  try :
 3|wsadmin>    if x :
 4|wsadmin>      print 'non-zero x =', x
 5|wsadmin>    else :
 6|wsadmin>      print 'x is zero'
 7|wsadmin>  except :
 8|wsadmin>    print 'x is undefined'
 9|wsadmin>
10|wsadmin>def test2() :
11|wsadmin>  x = 1
12|wsadmin>
13|wsadmin>def test3() :
14|wsadmin>  global x
15|wsadmin>  x = 1
16|wsadmin>
17|wsadmin>test1
18|<function test1 at 1970435442>
19|wsadmin>test1()
20|x is undefined
21|wsadmin>test2()
22|wsadmin>test1()
23|x is undefined
24|wsadmin>test3()
25|wsadmin>test1()
26|non-zero x = 1
27|wsadmin>
```

---

[6] Jython needs to know where the call originated so that when the function is complete, control can go back to any statement that follows.

Namespaces

A namespace is a mapping used to determine to which object a name refers. For each context, Jython has both a global and a local mapping.[7] This allows a distinction to be made between local and global variables. It's not until we discuss functions that this makes sense though. When a function is defined, a local namespace is created and populated with name and object references based on what identifiers are assigned within the function. If no assignments are made to an identifier within the function, then this identifier is not added to the local namespace. References to it use the global namespace mapping.

Because no assignments to x occur in the test1() function, all references to this identifier are to the global namespace. The first time test1() is called, x does not exist in the global namespace, so the except statement-suite (line 8) is executed. This causes the x is undefined message to be displayed. The function then completes, and control returns to the place from where the function was called. In this case, control returns to the statement after the function call (line 19). Because no statement exists to be executed, a **wsadmin** prompt is displayed (line 21), indicating that user input is expected.

The next function call (line 21) is to the function named test2(). The only action performed by this function is to assign the value 1 to the variable named x. Because an assignment occurs to this identifier within the function, it is added to the local namespace, and references to it within this function will be to a local variable. This explains why the output on line 23 is seen. It shows that no global variable was created by the assignment statement.

The global Statement

Is there a way to assign a value in a function to a variable outside of, or global to, the function? Yes, by using the global statement. This statement should be used to define a list of identifiers that are identified as existing outside of the function, so assignments to these identifiers will bind the specified value to these global identifiers.

```
global <identifier-list>
```

Listing 3.15 shows that the identifier-list is simply a comma separated list. Line 14 shows that when a single identifier is used, no comma should be present.

By having this global statement, the assignment to x (line 15) binds the specified value to a global variable with this name. It is important to note that before this function was executed, the global variable x did not exist, so the result of the assignment causes the global variable to be created in the global namespace so that when test1() is again executed, it is able to access the global identifier x. This, in turn, causes the output generated (line 26).

---

[7] There is also a "built-in" namespace that contains the names and references to all of the objects known to Jython (for example, None).

Listing 3.16 shows how an assignment to an identifier within a function makes all references to that identifier local to the function. Without the assignment statement within the function, on line 6, all references to the identifier x would be to a global variable. However, because an assignment to this identifier occurs within the function (even though the assignment occurs at the end of the function), all other reference to this identifier within the same function are considered to be to local variables. This is shown by the output generated on lines 9 and 12.

Listing 3.16   "local" Precedence

```
 1|wsadmin>def fun() :
 2|wsadmin>  try :
 3|wsadmin>    print 'x =', x
 4|wsadmin>  except :
 5|wsadmin>    print 'oops'
 6|wsadmin>  x = 0
 7|wsadmin>
 8|wsadmin>fun()
 9|x = oops
10|wsadmin>x = 1
11|wsadmin>fun()
12|x = oops
```

The output on line 9 might be a little confusing at first, but it does make sense once you understand what is happening. As the function is executing, the print statement in line 3 begins to execute. The first part of this statement generates the literal string "x =" before any attempt is made to access the value of the local variable x. At this point, an exception occurs because the local variable has not yet been assigned a value. Control transfers to the exception statement-suite on line 5, and the remainder of the message is generated (that is, the oops).

Line 10 defines a global variable named x, which has no effect on the execution of the function because all references to this identifier within the function are considered to be to a local variable having this name. Hence, we see the same output generated on line 12 as we saw on line 9. If the reference to x in line 3 were to a global variable, then the output in line 12 would display the value of the global variable instead of the oops message.

Function Parameters

The syntax of a function definition, seen earlier, showed that parameters can be passed to functions. The simplest form of a function parameter list is a group of comma-separated identifiers within the parentheses. It is important to understand how function parameters work, so take a look at the following simple example.

Listing 3.17 shows how to define a function, f(), and specify one formal parameter, a. As far as the function is concerned, this formal parameter is an identifier that is local to the function.[8] When the function is called (line 7) an actual parameter is provided for each formal parameter listed. For this particular example, the current value of the actual parameter (that is, variable x) is used as the initial value for the "formal parameter" (that is, variable a). This can be verified by observing the output generated by the print statement (line 8).

Listing 3.17 Simple Function Parameters

```
 1|wsadmin>def f( a ) :
 2|wsadmin>  print 'f(), a =', a
 3|wsadmin>  a += 1
 4|wsadmin>  print 'a =', a
 5|wsadmin>
 6|wsadmin>x = 0
 7|wsadmin>f( x )
 8|f(), a = 0
 9|a = 1
10|wsadmin>x
11|0
```

You can also see that although the value of this formal parameter (local variable) is modified, when control returns to the place where the function was called, the value of the actual parameter is unchanged (as evidenced by the output shown on line 11). This kind of parameter passing is sometimes referred to as "pass by value."[9] Because only a value is needed as an actual parameter, you could have just as easily called the function using a literal (such as, f(0)).

Optional Function Parameters

There are times when it is convenient to define functions that allow a variable number of parameters. Jython supports the following types of optional parameters.

Default Function Parameters   Frequently, it is useful to define an initial value of a formal parameter. The syntax for this is to have an equal sign followed by an expression representing the initial value for the parameter. Listing 3.18 shows how to define a default value (on line 1) and how the default value is used should an actual parameter not be specified where the function call occurs (on line 7). You can also see (on lines 9–10) that when an actual parameter is specified, its value is used instead of the default.

---

[8] Should a global identifier exist with this name, it is inaccessible within the function.

[9] The way in which parameters are passed to functions is not, technically, "pass by value." A more accurate description would be "pass by object reference." However, because we have yet to describe or discuss objects, it is much easier at this point to simply say that parameters are "pass by value."

Listing 3.18   Default Function Parameters

```
 1|wsadmin>def countdown( start=10 ) :
 2|wsadmin>  while start > 0 :
 3|wsadmin>    print start,
 4|wsadmin>    start -= 1
 5|wsadmin>  print 'done'
 6|wsadmin>
 7|wsadmin>countdown()
 8|10 9 8 7 6 5 4 3 2 1 done
 9|wsadmin>countdown( 5 )
10|5 4 3 2 1 done
```

What happens if we have multiple parameters (sometimes called arguments)? Can default values be used? Yes, but all parameters without default values must precede any and all parameters with default values. This can be seen in Listing 3.19 (lines 1–2) where the proper way to define a function having parameters with and without default values is shown.

Next (lines 4–10) you can what happens if you try to define a formal parameter list having a parameter with a default value before one without a default value. Jython is nice enough to tell us how silly this would be (lines 7–10). The reason this is unacceptable is that because it would be ambiguous. If it were allowed, and the user specified a single actual parameter value, to which formal parameter should this single actual parameter value be applied?

Additionally (lines 11–16) you see what happens should a required parameter value not be specified. Again, Jython is nice enough to point out the problem with an easily understood error message. And lines 18–36 show some valid and invalid function calls, with the examples in lines 18–25 being valid, and those on lines 26 and 31 being invalid and causing (easily understood) error messages.

Named Parameters   An interesting feature of function parameters is that they may be specified using their keyword or formal parameter names. This is demonstrated on lines 20–25 of Listing 3.19. These lines demonstrate that when the formal parameter names are not specified, then the actual parameter values are associated with the corresponding formal parameter in the order in which they occur. This is sometimes called *positional parameter passing*.

However, should a formal parameter name exist in the actual parameter list, then all subsequent parameters in the actual parameter list must have the appropriate formal parameter name specified. Lines 27–30 show the error message generated should this requirement not be met.

Listing 3.19   Optional Versus Required Parameters

```
1|wsadmin>def ok( a, b=1 ) :
2|wsadmin>  print 'a =',a,'b =',b
3|wsadmin>
```

```
 4|wsadmin>def bad( a=0, b ) :
 5|wsadmin>  print 'a =',a,'b=',b
 6|wsadmin>
 7|Traceback (innermost last):
 8| (no code object) at line 0
 9| File "<input>", line 0
10|SyntaxError: non-default argument follows default argument
11|wsadmin>ok()
12|WASX7015E: Exception running command: "ok()"; exception information:
13| com.ibm.bsf.BSFException: exception from Jython:
14|Traceback (innermost last):
15| File "<input>", line 1, in ?
16|TypeError: ok() takes at least 1 argument (0 given)
17|
18|wsadmin>ok(42)
19|a = 42 b = 1
20|wsadmin>ok(a=123)
21|a = 123 b = 1
22|wsadmin>ok(3,b=0)
23|a = 3 b = 0
24|wsadmin>ok(a=123,b=456)
25|a = 123 b = 456
26|wsadmin>ok(b=2,0)
27|Traceback (innermost last):
28| (no code object) at line 0
29| File "<input>", line 1
30|SyntaxError: non-keyword argument following keyword
31|wsadmin>ok(1,a=0)
32|WASX7015E: Exception running command: "ok(1,a=0)"; exception
information:
33| com.ibm.bsf.BSFException: exception from Jython:
34|Traceback (innermost last):
35| File "<input>", line 1, in ?
36|TypeError: ok() got multiple values for keyword argument 'a'
```

Additionally, lines 31–36 show another type of error message that is displayed, also related to the use of formal parameter names. The message is pretty straightforward and should require no additional explanation.

Arbitrary Parameters Jython also allows for functions with a variable number of arguments. These are referred to as arbitrary parameters, and the syntax for this type of parameter is shown in

Listing 3.20 (line 1). Subsequent lines show how you can use this type of argument. Note that when arbitrary parameters are used, the "formal parameter" (that is, local variable) value will be a tuple containing the actual values specified.

Listing 3.20   Arbitrary Function Parameters

```
 1|wsadmin>def fun( *args ) :
 2|wsadmin>  print 'args =', args
 3|wsadmin>
 4|wsadmin>fun()
 5|args = ()
 6|wsadmin>fun( 1, 3, 5 )
 7|args = (1, 3, 5)
 8|wsadmin>fun( [ 2, 4, 6, 8 ], "Who do we appreciate?" )
 9|args = ([2, 4, 6, 8], 'Who do we appreciate?')
10|wsadmin>a = [1, 2, 3]
11|wsadmin>fun( a )
12|args = ([1, 2, 3],)
```

NOTE   An arbitrary parameter entry (there can only be one) must occur after positional and/or default formal parameters.

The last few examples in Listing 3.20 might leave you asking, "Given a list, or a tuple, is there a way to specify its contents as the actual parameter list?" The reason for this question can be explained by revisiting lines 11 and 12 in Listing 3.20, where you can see a list variable as the actual parameter, and the result of this call being a single element tuple with the list as `args[ 0 ]`. If the desired outcome were to have the contents of the list passed to the formal parameter, a way to unpack the sequence as part of the function call is needed. To do this, precede the actual parameter with an asterisk '*', as seen in Listing 3.21. Look closely and you will see how this unpacking can be used on any sequence (lines 12–17). Note, however, what happens when it is used on a string (lines 16–17), which might not be what you intended.

Listing 3.21   Unpacking Sequence Parameters

```
 1|wsadmin>def fun( *args ) :
 2|wsadmin>  print 'args =', args
 3|wsadmin>
 4|wsadmin>fun( 1, 3, 5 )
 5|args = (1, 3, 5)
 6|wsadmin>a = [ 1, 2, 3 ]
 7|wsadmin>b = ( 9, 8, 7 )
```

```
 8|wsadmin>fun( a )
 9|args = ([1, 2, 3],)
10|wsadmin>fun( b )
11|args = ((9, 8, 7),)
12|wsadmin>fun( *a )
13|args = (1, 2, 3)
14|wsadmin>fun( *b )
15|args = (9, 8, 7)
16|wsadmin>fun( *'spam' )
17|args = ('s', 'p', 'a', 'm')
18|wsadmin>
```

Keyword Arguments Using a Dictionary   As with arbitrary parameters, there are times when it is convenient to use the contents of a dictionary to satisfy or provide the actual function parameter values. To do this, the dictionary identifier is prefixed by '**' to indicate that it should be unpacked, much like the sequence unpacking prefix discussed previously. Listing 3.22 demonstrates this situation.

Listing 3.22   Unpacked Dictionary Parameters

```
 1|wsadmin>def fun( a=1, b=2 ) :
 2|wsadmin>  print 'a=', a, 'b=', b
 3|wsadmin>
 4|wsadmin>d = { 'a' : 'bacon', 'b' : 'eggs' }
 5|wsadmin>fun( **d )
 6|a= bacon b= eggs
 7|wsadmin>d = { 'a' : 'bacon', 'b' : 'eggs', 'c' : 'spam' }
 8|wsadmin>fun( **d )
 9|WASX7015E: Exception running command: "fun( **d )"; exception
information:
10| com.ibm.bsf.BSFException: exception from Jython:
11|Traceback (innermost last):
12| File "<input>", line 1, in ?
13|TypeError: fun() got an unexpected keyword argument 'c'
```

Unfortunately, lines 9–13 display one of the potential problems of using the dictionary unpack prefix. The question is, what can and should be done about possible "extra" name/value pairs within the unpacked dictionary? Is there a way to allow these extra, or arbitrary, name/value parameter pairs?

Yes, Jython includes a notation similar to arbitrary parameters for arbitrary keyword parameters. To identify a parameter for arbitrary keyword parameters, the last formal parameter may have a double asterisk (" ** ") prefix specified. Listing 3.23 demonstrates both kinds of arbitrary parameters, as well as how to use the unpack prefix on the actual parameters.

Listing 3.23 Arbitrary Keyword Parameters

```
 1|wsadmin>def fun( a, b=1, *args, **keywords ) :
 2|wsadmin>  print 'a=', a, 'b=', b
 3|wsadmin>  print 'args=', args
 4|wsadmin>  print 'keywords=', keywords
 5|wsadmin>
 6|wsadmin>fun( 0 )
 7|a= 0 b= 1
 8|args= ()
 9|keywords= {}
10|wsadmin>parms = { 'a':42, 'b':3.14159, 'spam':'yes, please' }
11|wsadmin>fun( **parms )
12|a= 42 b= 3.14159
13|args= ()
14|keywords= {'spam': 'yes, please'}
15|wsadmin>evens = [ 2, 4, 6, 8 ]
16|wsadmin>breakfast = { 'bacon' : 'no thanks', 'eggs' : 'fried',
'spam' : 'yes, please' }
17|wsadmin>fun( *evens, **breakfast )
18|a= 2 b= 4
19|args= (6, 8)
20|keywords= {'bacon': 'no thanks', 'eggs': 'fried', 'spam': 'yes,
please'}
```

The return Statement

Although the return statement is a simple statement, it is better addressed in the discussion of functions. The primary purpose of this statement is to indicate that the processing within a function is complete, and the execution of control should return to the place from which the function was called. The alternate purpose for this statement is to supply 0 or more values as part of the "return of control" process.

In many of the simple functions shown, a return statement has not been needed. This is because when the last statement of a function is reached, an implicit return is executed so that control transfers, or returns, to the calling location. However, there are instances when it is convenient and even necessary to indicate that the processing of the function is complete somewhere within the function statement-suite. At these times, the return statement can and should be used.

A `return` statement may include an optional expression list (that is, a collection of expressions separated by commas). When this is done, the function call, with any actual parameters, should occur where an expression is allowed by the Jython syntax.

Listing 3.24 shows how return statements can include various optional expressions and some ways in which these functions can be called. Notice that when an implicit return is used (line 1), the returned value is `None` (line 14). Because functions return values (remember, `None` is a value), they can be used anywhere that allows the data type returned by the function. This is why we see each of these function calls as the expression on `print` statements on lines 13–23. In each instance, the specified function is called, and the returned result is displayed on the subsequent line.

Listing 3.24   Return Values

```
 1|wsadmin>def nothing() : pass
 2|wsadmin>
 3|wsadmin>def Integer() : return 0
 4|wsadmin>
 5|wsadmin>def String() : return 'spam'
 6|wsadmin>
 7|wsadmin>def Tuple() : return nothing(), Integer(), String()
 8|wsadmin>
 9|wsadmin>def List() : return [ 1, 2, 3 ]
10|wsadmin>
11|wsadmin>def Dict() : return { 'food':'bacon, eggs, & spam' }
12|wsadmin>
13|wsadmin>print nothing()
14|None
15|wsadmin>print Integer()
16|0
17|wsadmin>print String()
18|spam
19|wsadmin>print Tuple()
20|(None, 0, 'spam')
21|wsadmin>print List()
22|[1, 2, 3]
23|wsadmin>print Dict()
24|{'food': 'bacon, eggs, & spam'}
25|wsadmin>
```

Default Parameter Evaluation

Some features of Jython can catch the unwary by surprise. One of the most common of these features relates to the evaluation of default function parameters. The function definition on line 1 of Listing 3.25 has a default parameter L that is assigned an empty list. You might think this means the initialization of the formal parameter L to the specified expression occurs every time the function is invoked. Unfortunately, this understanding is incorrect. The expression is actually evaluated only once, when the function definition (def statement) is first encountered, and every invocation of the function will initialize the formal parameter to this same object, each and every time the function is called.

Listing 3.25 Functions and Default Value Evaluation

```
 1|wsadmin>def f( a, L=[]) :
 2|wsadmin>  L.append( a )
 3|wsadmin>   return L
 4|wsadmin>
 5|wsadmin>print f(1)
 6|[1]
 7|wsadmin>print f(2)
 8|[1, 2]
 9|wsadmin>print f(3)
10|[1, 2, 3]
11|wsadmin>def f( a, L=None ) :
12|wsadmin>  if L == None :
13|wsadmin>    L = []
14|wsadmin>  L.append( a )
15|wsadmin>   return L
16|wsadmin>
17|wsadmin>print f(1)
18|[1]
19|wsadmin>print f(2)
20|[2]
21|wsadmin>print f(3)
22|[3]
```

What does this mean? It means that you may not get the intended result if you aren't careful. Notice how lines 5–10 display an ever lengthening list of values. You might have expected the formal parameter L to be assigned an empty list each time the function was called. In fact, when the def statement is executed, the default expression is evaluated, and a list object is created. Each time the function is called, the formal parameter, L, is assigned to the current value of this list object. Because lists are mutable objects, every change to the list that occurs within the function will persist across function invocations. This is shown on lines 5–10, where you see the number of elements increasing every time the function is invoked.

There are times when this is exactly how you want your function to work. If you want the default value for your parameter to be an empty list object, you need to use a technique similar to what is shown on lines 11–13. Here, the expression that is evaluated during the execution of the def statement is the value None. When the def statement is executed, the default value for the L parameter is None. When the function is called, the if statement (line 12) checks to see if the value for L is the special None (that is, the default) value. If this is the case, then L can be initialized as an empty list (on line 13).

Function Documentation String

If the first executable "statement" of a function statement-suite is a string literal, this string is the function documentation string (also called the function docstring). The docstring must be a string literal, not an expression. The value of a function docstring can be accessed using 'functionName.__doc__'. If no docstring is specified in the function definition, the value of the docstring attribute (that is, functionName.__doc__) is None. Listing 3.26 shows how we can define and access a function docstring.

Listing 3.26   Documentation String (docstring)

```
1│wsadmin>def nothing() :
2│wsadmin>   "It's nothing! ... merely a fleshwound."
3│wsadmin>   pass
4│wsadmin>
5│wsadmin>print nothing.__doc__
6│It's nothing! ... merely a fleshwound.
7│wsadmin>
```

> **NOTE**   Remember that the interactive mode of **wsadmin** does not support multi-line triple-quoted strings. So multi-line docstrings should to be defined, or specified, in an input (text) file containing the complete function definition. Another alternative is to include newline characters in the docstring using an escape sequence for each newline character (that is, '\n').

In his book *An Introduction to Python*, Guido van Rossum, the author of the Python programming language, recommends the following conventions for documentation strings:

- The first line should be a short and concise summary of the function purpose.

- Strings need not restate the function or object name unless the name happens to be a verb describing the function's operation.

- The first word of a string should be capitalized, and the line should end with a period.
- If additional lines are appropriate, include a blank line between the summary and the remainder of the text to separate the summary from the description.
- The remainder of the string text should describe how the function or object is to be used, any results and/or side effects, and so on.

When multiple lines of text exist, a triple-quoted string is generally used for the docstring.

Summary

In this chapter, we saw the various Jython statement types. We started with something simple, that is, expression statements, progressed into assignment statements, with a little side excursion to discuss slices, and then resumed our discussion by talking about simple statements. These then led to compound statements, and finally we saw how these different types of statements could be put together as function definitions.

Jython Classes

Object-oriented programming (OOP) is an enormous concept and unfortunately not the topic of this book. A wealth of information about OOP is available from a variety of other resources. Therefore, this chapter is limited to the syntax and semantics of Jython OOP constructs. However, consider the fact that in Jython we use scripting objects to interact with the WebSphere Application Server environment, and objects are created using classes.

Class Statement

To create an object, you must be able to define the data type for the object. To do so, use the class statement, the simplified syntax for which is shown here:

```
class ClassName :
   <statement>
   <statement>

   . . .
```

Like function definitions, class definitions are executable statements. When one is executed, information about the specified class is collected by Jython. Generally, the statements within a class definition are function definitions. In addition to function definitions, a class documentation string (docstring) is also allowed. As with function definitions, if the first non-blank expression statement in a class definition is a string literal, it is considered the class docstring and can be accessed using either ClassName.__doc__ or objectName.__doc__.

This use of a period (' . ') after a class or object name is significant. It identifies that the name/identifier that follows is an attribute, or method, of the specified class or object. The "Modules" section in this chapter notes that this "dot qualifier" is also used to indicate that the identifier after the dot (period) is qualified by the identifier preceding the dot. So ClassName.__doc__ identifies that the __doc__ (docstring) attribute for the specified class is being referenced.

Example class Definition

Listing 4.1 shows a simple class definition for class Thing. The Thing class has two attributes (data values) and two methods (functions). Remember that even though it is not explicitly identified as such, the class documentation string (docstring) is an attribute. It is also useful to remember that methods, like functions, can also have docstrings.

Listing 4.1   Simple Class Definition

```
 1 | # - - - - - - - - - - - - - - - - - - - - - - - - - - - - - - - - - - - -
 2 | # Name: Thing
 3 | # Role: Define a Thing object
 4 | # - - - - - - - - - - - - - - - - - - - - - - - - - - - - - - - - - - - -
 5 | class Thing :
 6 |
 7 |   'A simple Thing object'       # class docstring
 8 |
 9 |   myName = 'anonymous'          # default instance name
10 |
11 |   # - - - - - - - - - - - - - - - - - - - - - - - - - - - - - - - - - -
12 |   # Name: Thing.setName()
13 |   # Role: Used to set the name attribute
14 |   # - - - - - - - - - - - - - - - - - - - - - - - - - - - - - - - - - -
15 |   def setName( self, name ) :
16 |     'Assign the instance name' # method docstring
17 |     self.myName = name         # bind to instance attribute
18 |
19 |   # - - - - - - - - - - - - - - - - - - - - - - - - - - - - - - - - - -
20 |   # Name: Thing.getName()
21 |   # Role: Used to get the name attribute
22 |   # - - - - - - - - - - - - - - - - - - - - - - - - - - - - - - - - - -
23 |   def getName( self ) :
24 |     'Return the instance name' # method docstring
25 |     return self.myName         # return instance attribute
```

Also note that the name of the first parameter defined in class methods is not required to be self. This is merely a convention, not a requirement. However, using something other than self is probably a bad idea because of the potential confusion that it could cause to the human reader.

Jython (and Python) programmers are comfortable with the convention of using `self` to indicate when the first parameter of a function (method) is used to identify the object with which the function is associated.

Listing 4.2 demonstrates how to instantiate (create) two objects of this new data type using the same notation used to execute a function—that is, to use the class name followed by parentheses. Table 4.1 explains each line in Listing 4.2 in more detail.

Listing 4.2   Example Object Creation and Use

```
1|wsadmin>thing1 = Thing()
2|wsadmin>thing1.setName( "I'm thing1" )
3|wsadmin>thing2 = Thing()
4|wsadmin>print thing2.getName()
5|anonymous
6|wsadmin>print thing1.getName()
7|I'm thing1
8|wsadmin>print Thing.setName.__doc__
9|Assign the instance name
```

Table 4.1   Example Object Creation Explained

Line	Description
1	Create a `Thing` object by calling the `class` like a function.
2	Execute the `setName()` method for the object passing it a literal string.
3	Create another `Thing` object.
4	Call the `getName()` method for `thing2` to obtain, the object name value.
5	The displayed attribute value for this object instance has not been defined, so the default value is displayed.
6	Call the `getName()` method for `thing1` to obtain the object name value.
7	The displayed value for this object instance attribute is the value that was provided using the `setName()` method call (line 2 in Listing 4.2).
8	Statement used to display the method docstring for the class `setName()` method.
9	This line shows the value of the method docstring.

Unlike some object-oriented languages, Jython does not rigidly restrict or even limit access to attributes and methods within an object. It is the responsibility of the programmer to use good sense and not abuse the openness of the language. Use the object methods to access the instance data. If your code ignores this convention, it will be more difficult to maintain. Imagine what happens to your scripts if the underlying class definition changes in some way (that is, the attributes or their types are modified). Things that were previously working now either cause exceptions or (even worse) invalid results. Exceptions are easy to see, whereas a incorrect value somewhere in the middle of your script is much more difficult to understand and locate. Therefore, it is a best practice to use the interface provided by the object methods to access and update the underlying information.

What does this mean? Generally, it means that you should not write code that "looks into" an object to access or manipulate its attributes. Use the provided methods to "get" or "set" values within the object. If the class is almost but not quite what you need, consider creating and defining a descendent class that extends the existing class to do what you need it to do.

Object Instantiation

One of the things we have yet to discuss is object customization during the creation process. In some programming languages, the terminology for a method to be executed during the object creation process is a *constructor*. In Jython, if a method named __init__ exists within the class, it will be called as part of the instantiation process. The syntax for this method is shown here:

```
def __init__( self ) :
   <statement-suite>
```

> **NOTE** There are no special methods that are automatically executed when an object instance is no longer needed (that is, there are no destructor methods).

Built-in Constants

You should be aware that the only "constants" in Jython are the numeric (and string) literal values. Even the "special" identifier, None, is not a constant.[1] Hopefully it won't be too difficult for you to restrain from assigning a different value to it. Listing 4.3 shows an example of how dangerous this can be.

If you were to do something silly like this (that is, assigning a value to None), someone (either you or someone who tries to make use of your script) is likely to lose time trying to figure out why scripts are not working as expected or even worse, debugging scripts that apparently worked fine previously. So be careful not to do this kind of thing.

Listing 4.3 None Is Not (Yet) a Constant

```
1|wsadmin>print None
2|None
```

---

[1] None became a constant in version 2.4 of Python. It is not clear when the version of Jython that is used by **wsadmin** will do the same.

```
3|wsadmin>None = 'Hi there'
4|wsadmin>print None
5|Hi there
6|wsadmin>del None
7|wsadmin>print None
8|None
```

Built-in Data Types

Built-in data types (that is, numbers, strings, tuples, lists, and dictionaries) were one of the first things covered in this book. Of these, only lists and dictionaries are mutable. Each data type is, in essence, a class. These built-in data types have associated methods that are used to manipulate the object. This section identifies and describes these methods. In some cases, sample code snippets are provided as part of the explanation or to help clarify how the method should be used.

List Methods

The following methods are available for all list objects. It is very doubtful that you will be reading this in order from start to finish, so you can use the following as a reference when you need to check what methods exist for list objects.

append(item)

Lengthen the list by adding the specified item. Logically, equivalent to:

```
List[ len( List ) : len( List ) ] = [ item ]
```

count(item)

Return the number of times that item occurs in the list.

extend(item)

Lengthen the list by adding the specified item. This differs from the append() method when the item to be added is a sequence. When a sequence is added using append(), it is added to the end of the list as an individual item. The extend() method appends each sequence element individually, as can be seen in Listing 4.4.

Listing 4.4 List extend() Method Example

```
1|wsadmin>L = []
2|wsadmin>L.append( 'spam' )
3|wsadmin>L
4|['spam']
5|wsadmin>L.extend( 'spam' )
6|wsadmin>L
7|['spam', 's', 'p', 'a', 'm']
```

index(item)

Return the index of the first occurrence of item in the list, if it exists. If it doesn't exist in the list, a `ValueError` exception is raised.

insert(index, item)

Inserts the specified item at the indicated index position. Logically, equivalent to:

`List[ index : index ] = [ item ]`

pop([index])

If the optional index is specified, remove and return that item from the list; otherwise, remove and return the last item in the list. Should the list be empty or should the specified index element not exist, an `IndexError` exception is raised.

remove(item)

Remove the first occurence of the specified item from the list, should it exist. If the item does not exist in the list, a `ValueError` exception is raised.

reverse()

Reverse the list contents "in place." Listing 4.5 provides an example of how you would use the `reverse()` method.

NOTE   This method returns `None`, not another (reversed) list instance.[2]

Listing 4.5   List `reverse()` Method Example

```
1 | wsadmin>L = range( 8 )
2 | wsadmin>L
3 | [0, 1, 2, 3, 4, 5, 6, 7]
4 | wsadmin>print L.reverse()
5 | None
6 | wsadmin>L
7 | [7, 6, 5, 4, 3, 2, 1, 0]
```

sort([compareFunction])

Sort the list contents "in place." The `compareFunction`, if specified, is used to determine the ordering of the list elements. This is especially useful when the list elements are not simple types. If the `compareFunction` is provided, it is called and passed two items from the list. It should return the following:

---

[2] As shown in Listing 4.5 (lines 4–5).

- −1—To indicate that the first item is less than the second.
- 0—To indicate that the first item is equal to the second.
- 1—To indicate that the first item is greater than the second.

NOTE This method returns None, not another (sorted) list instance.

Dictionary Methods

Dictionaries are also objects. Each dictionary has the following methods available to it. Again, it is unreasonable to expect you to read and remember all the methods described in this section. It is more likely that it will be used as a reference while using dictionary objects.

clear()

Remove all items from the dictionary.

copy()

Return a "shallow" copy of the dictionary, which means that the copy will have the same keys, but each value will refer to the same value object, should one exist. Listing 4.6 provides a copy() method example, and Table 4.2 explains this listing in detail.

Listing 4.6 Dictionary copy() Method Example

```
1|wsadmin>D = { 1: [ 'bacon' ], 2: [ 'eggs' ], 3: [ 'spam' ] }
2|wsadmin>E = D.copy()
3|wsadmin>E
4|{3: ['spam'], 2: ['eggs'], 1: ['bacon']}
5|wsadmin>D[ 0 ] = [ 'spam', 'eggs' ]
6|wsadmin>D
7|{3: ['spam'], 2: ['eggs'], 1: ['bacon'], 0: ['spam', 'eggs']}
8|wsadmin>E
9|{3: ['spam'], 2: ['eggs'], 1: ['bacon']}
10|wsadmin>D[ 1 ].append( 'spam' )
11|wsadmin>D
12|{3: ['spam'], 2: ['eggs'], 1: ['bacon', 'spam'], 0: ['spam', 'eggs']}
13|wsadmin>E
14|{3: ['spam'], 2: ['eggs'], 1: ['bacon', 'spam']}
```

Table 4.2   Dictionary `copy()` Method Example Explained

Line(s)	Description
1	Create a dictionary D.
2	Use its copy() method to create a shallow copy.
3–4	Use an expression statement to display the contents of E.
5	Add a new element to D.
6–7	Display the contents of D.
8–9	Display the contents of E. Note the lack of key 0.
10	Modify the list of key 1.
11–12	Display the complete dictionary contents, including the modified element of key 1.
13–14	Display the contents of E, including the shared value of key 1.

get(key [, defaultValue])

Return the value associated with the specified key. If the key isn't in the dictionary, this method returns the optional `defaultValue`, should it exist, or `None` if `defaultValue` isn't specified. Conceptually, this is like the `get()` function shown in Listing 4.7.

Listing 4.7   Dictionary `get()` Method Concept

```
1|def get( dict, key, defaultValue = None ) :
2|  try :
3|    result = dict[ key ]
4|  except KeyError :
5|    result = defaultValue
6|  return result
```

has_key(key)

Return 1 if the specified key exists in the dictionary; otherwise, a 0 is returned.

items()

Return a list of the dictionary key/value (tuple) pairs.

keys()

Return a list of the dictionary keys.

setdefault(key [, defaultValue])

If the specified key exists in the dictionary, return the associated value. Otherwise, return the optional `defaultValue` while adding this `key`/`defaultValue` pair to the dictionary. If `defaultValue` is not specified, `None` is used.

update(dict)

Use the key/value pairs from the specified dictionary to add or replace key/value pairs in the current dictionary.

values()

Return a list of the dictionary values.

String Methods

Strings are also objects, and have their own set of methods. Since string use in scripts is so common, we expect that this will be a frequently referenced section of the book.

capitalize( )

Return a copy of the string with the first character capitalized.

center(width)

Return a space padded string of the specified width containing the given string centered in the middle.

count(substring[, start[, end]])

Return the number of occurrences of the given substring, where the optional `start` and `end` parameters are used like slice values to indicate the portion of the string to be checked.

endswith(suffix[, start[, end]])

Return 1 if the string ends with the specified suffix; otherwise, return 0. The optional `start` and `end` parameters are used like slice values to indicate the starting and ending indices.

expandtabs([tabsize])

Return a copy of the string with all tab characters are expanded using spaces. If the optional `tabsize` parameter is not specified, 8 is used.

find(substring[, start[, end]])

Return the lowest index in the string where the substring is located. The optional `start` and `end` parameters are used like slice notation values to indicate the portion of the string to be checked. Return -1 if the substring is not found.

index(substring[, start [, end]])

Like `find()`, but a `ValueError` exception is raised should substring not be present.

isalnum( )

Return 1 if at least one character exists and all characters in the string are alphanumeric (that is, `'0'` through `'9'`, `'a'` through `'z'`, or `'A'` through `'Z'`). Otherwise, a 0 is returned.

isalpha( )

Return 1 if at least one character exists and all characters in the string are alphabetic ('a' through 'z', or 'A' through 'z'). Otherwise, a 0 is returned.

isdigit( )

Return 1 if at least one character exists and all characters in the string are numeric ('0' through '9'). Otherwise, a 0 is returned.

islower( )

Return 1 if at least one letter character exists and all letters in the string are lowercase. Otherwise, a 0 is returned.

isspace( )

Return 1 if at least one character exists and all characters in the string are whitespace characters (space, tab, newline, carriage return, vertical tab). Otherwise, a 0 is returned.

istitle( )

Return 1 if at least one character exists and all characters in the title follow capitalization rules (uppercase letters may only follow non-letters, and lowercase letters may only follow letters). Otherwise, a 0 is returned.

isupper( )

Return 1 if at least one letter character exists and all letters in the string are uppercase. Otherwise, a 0 is returned.

join(sequence)

Return a string that is the concatenation of the strings in the sequence. The separator between elements is the string whose method is being used. Keep in mind that if an empty delimiter string is specified, the sequence strings are simply concatenated. Listing 4.8, on line 5, shows how the string for which the join() method is being called is a single space.

Listing 4.8   split() and join() String Methods

```
1|wsadmin>food = 'bacon, eggs, & spam'
2|wsadmin>asList = food.split( ' ' )
3|wsadmin>print asList
4|['bacon,', 'eggs,', '&', 'spam']
5|wsadmin>asString = ' '.join( asList )
6|wsadmin>asString
7|'bacon, eggs, & spam'
```

ljust(width)

Return a string of the specified width, padded on the right with spaces. If width is less than or equal to length of given string, return a copy of the given string.

lower( )

Return a copy of the string with all uppercase characters converted to lowercase.

lstrip( )

Return a copy of the string with all leading whitespace characters removed.

replace(old, new[, count])

Return a copy of the string after replacing a maximum of the count occurrences of old replaced by new. If count is not specified, all occurrences are replaced.

rfind(substring[,start [,end]])

Like find(), but the highest index is returned or -1 if the substring is not found in the string. The optional start and end parameters are used like slice notation values to indicate the portion of the string to be checked.

rindex(substring[, start[, end]])

Like rfind(), but a ValueError exception is raised if the substring is not present.

rjust(width)

Return a string of the specified width, padded on the left with spaces. If width is less than or equal to length of the original string, return a copy of the given string.

rstrip( )

Return a copy of the string with trailing whitespace characters removed.

split([separator [,maxsplit]])

Return a list of substrings delimited by the given separator. If the optional maxsplit parameter is specified, its value is used to limit the maximum number of split operations performed. If maxsplit parameter is not specified, all possible split operations are performed. If the optional separator parameter is not specified, whitespace characters are used (after removing any leading and trailing whitespace characters). Listing 4.8 has a simple example of using the split() method using a single blank as a parameter.

splitlines([keepends])

Return a list of the lines in the string, breaking at end-of-line boundaries. If the optional keepends parameter is specified and is non-zero, then each list element will include the end-of-line delimiter.

startswith(prefix[, start[, end]])

Return 1 if the string begins with the specified suffix; otherwise, return 0. The optional start and end parameters are used like slice values to indicate the portion of the string to be checked.

strip( )

Return a copy of the string with leading and trailing whitespace characters removed.

swapcase( )

Return a copy of the string with lowercase characters converted to uppercase and vice versa.

title( )

Return a copy of the string where words start with uppercase characters; all other characters are lowercase.

upper( )

Return a copy of the string where all lowercase characters are converted to uppercase.

zfill(width)

If width is greater than the given input string, return a copy of the string left padded with zeros to the specified width. Otherwise, return a copy of the input string.

String Formatting

It is difficult to precisely control the appearance of output generated using the `print` statement. For example, to perform an action on a group of names that have "user" as a prefix and a numeric suffix (from 0..5), you might be tempted to try something like what is shown in Listing 4.9.

Listing 4.9   "Formatted Output"—Attempt #1[3]

```
1|wsadmin>for i in range( 6 ) : print 'user', i,
2|wsadmin>
3|user 0 user 1 user 2 user 3 user 4 user 5wsadmin>
```

Unfortunately, by using the comma between the "prefix" string and the number, a space is inserted between the each value (as in line 3). What if you use a plus sign to concatenate the user `string` with the loop control value? Let's take a look at Listing 4.10.

Listing 4.10   "Formatted Output"—Attempt #2

```
1|wsadmin>for i in range( 6 ) : print 'user' + i
2|wsadmin>
3|WASX7015E: Exception running command: ""; exception information:
4| com.ibm.bsf.BSFException: exception from Jython:
```

---

[3] Remember that when the statement-suite of a compound statement is a single simple statement, it can occur on the same line as the statement keyword.

```
5|Traceback (innermost last):
6| File "<input>", line 1, in ?
7|TypeError: __add__ nor __radd__ defined for these operands
```

What does that mean? Oh, yeah, that's right. String concatenation is only defined for two strings, not a string and a number. Can you convert the number to a string and then concatenate? Certainly, you can use the backtick operator described in Chapter 2, "Jython Fundamentals." Listing 4.11 shows how this might be done.

Listing 4.11   "Formatted Output"—Attempt #3

```
1|wsadmin>for i in range( 6 ) : print 'user' + `i`,
2|wsadmin>
3|user0 user1 user2 user3 user4 user5wsadmin>print
```

Is there a better way to perform string formatting? Yes, but it is much more involved than the simple display output seen previously. A string format operator exists that allows you to completely control how data should be represented. The operator uses the percent sign ("%"), and has a "format string" as the left operand and the value(s) to be displayed as the right operand.

The way to do this is to use the Jython string format operator ("%") to identify the kind of data to be displayed and how it should be displayed. When a string is followed by the percent sign, Jython processes the string and the values that follow, the result of which is a formatted string.

```
formatString % values
```

The string format operation involves the processing of the formatString, looking for format specification sequences, and using these sequences to format the associated data from the right operand. For any other text in the format string, the data is copied "as is" to the result string.

Each format specification begins and ends with a required character. The character used to indicate the start of a format specification is the percent sign ("%"), and the ending character identifies the type of data to be processed. A complete and detailed description of all the available string format options is beyond the scope of this book; however, some of the scripts will make use of this feature, so it is appropriate to provide the following information, examples, and explanations.

Section "3.6.2" of the Python Library Reference, "String Formatting Operations," describes this topic more completely, and is available at http://docs.python.org/lib/typesseq-strings.html.

String format examples are provided in Listing 4.12 and explained in Table 4.3.

Listing 4.12   String Format Examples

```
1|wsadmin>values={'str':'spam','int':42,'float':3.14,'char':'*'}
2|wsadmin>format = 'String = "%(str)s"\nInteger = %(int)d\n'
```

```
 3|wsadmin>format += 'Float = %(float)7.2f\nChar = "%(char)c"'
 4|wsadmin>
 5|wsadmin>print format % values
 6|String = "spam"
 7|Integer = 42
 8|Float = 3.14
 9|Char = "*"
10|wsadmin>format='Small = %e\nMedium = %10.5e\nLarge = %20.10E'
11|wsadmin>print format % ( 1.23456e-127, 0, 9.87654e+128 )
12|Small = 1.234560e-127
13|Medium = 0.00000e+000
14|Large = 9.8765400000E+128
15|wsadmin>print 'James Bond is %03o' % 7
16|James Bond is 007
```

Table 4.3   String Format Examples Explained

Line(s)	Explanation
1	Defines a dictionary containing some values to be displayed.
2–3	This format string contains four format specifications, like this: • `%(str)s`—Format the value named `str` as a string. • `%(int)d`—Format the value named `int` as a signed integer. • `%(float)7.5f`—Format the value named `float` as a floating point value using seven places and five digits after the decimal point. • `%(char)c`—Format the value named `char` as a (single) character.
5–9	Shows how you can use the string format operator with a `print` statement to display the values indicated in the specified ways. Note how the presence of the newline (i.e., `'\n'`) in the format string causes each value to be display on a separate line.
10	Defines the format string to be used for three "unnamed" values.
11–14	Because the format specifiers do not include a "name" in parentheses, the right operand of the string format operator must be a tuple containing the exact number of

Table 4.3   String Format Examples Explained

Line(s)	Explanation
11–14	values for which format specifiers exist. The values in the tuple are displayed in the order they occur: • `%e`—Format the value as a floating point using the default exponential notation. • `%10.5e`—Try to format the value as a floating point using a total of ten places, with five digits after the decimal point. Looking closely at the result shows that a total of 12 places were required to display a value having five decimal digits. • `%20.10E`—Format the value as a floating point using 20 positions and five decimal places. The `'E'` specifier indicates that the exponent on the formatted value should use an uppercase `'E'`.
15–16	A trivial example where a three-digit octal value is displayed with leading zeroes (`%03o`). Because only one format specification exists in the format string, a single value can be used as the right operand for the string format operator.

Built-in Functions

A number of built-in functions exist in Jython. They can be used without having to do anything special to make them available. One unfortunate difference between Python and Jython is that in Python, there is a special module named __builtins__ that contains all of the built-in functions identified in the following list. This is not the case with the version of Jython provided with WebSphere Application Server version 6.1. This has been corrected in version 7.0, where you are able to list these functions simply by using dir(__builtin__).

abs(x)

Return the absolute value of the specified numeric expression. For integers, long integers, or floating point values, the absolute value represents the positive value. If a value is negative, the sign is dropped. For complex values, the result is the square root of the sum of the squares of the values, which is sometimes referred to as the *magnitude of the value*. A simplistic definition is provided in Listing 4.13.

Listing 4.13   Simplistic Definition of abs()

```
1|def abs( x ) :
2|  if x < 0 :
3|    x = -x
4|  return x
```

`callable( object )`

Return `1` if the specified object appears to be callable; `0` otherwise. If this returns `1`, it is still possible that an attempt to call the object could fail. But if the returned value is `0`, calling the object cannot succeed.

`chr( i )`

Return a single character string whose ASCII value is the specified integer, which must be in the range [0..255] inclusive. For example, uppercase letters have values from [65..90], and lowercase letters have values from [91..122]. This is the inverse of `ord()` (defined in this section).

`compile( string, filename, kind )`

Compile the string into a code object. Code objects can be executed by an `exec` statement or evaluated by a call to `eval()`. If the string was read from a file, the filename parameter should specify the name of the file. Otherwise, pass some recognizable value (for example, `'<string>'`). The kind parameter indicates how the code contained within the string is to be compiled. The value should be one of the following:

> **`'exec'`**
>
> If the string contains a sequence of statements.
>
> **`'eval'`**
>
> If the string contains of a single expression.
>
> **`'single'`**
>
> If the string contains of a single interactive statement.

`complex( real[, imag ] )`

Create a complex number with the specified real and imaginary components. If the imaginary parameter is omitted, it defaults to zero. The function serves as a numeric conversion function like `int()`, `long()`, and `float()`.

`delattr( object, name )`

The name parameter is a string and must be an attribute name of the specified object. The role of this function is to delete the specified object attribute. For example:

`delattr(obj,'spam')` is equivalent to `del obj.spam`

`dir( [object] )`

The `dir` function returns a sorted list of names. If no object parameter is specified, the returned list contains the names of the local objects. If an object parameter is specified, the returned list contains the attribute names of the specified object.

`divmod( a, b )`

The parameters must be non-complex numbers, and the result is a tuple of two numbers representing of the quotient and remainder of the expression `a / b`.

`eval( expression[, globals[, locals] ] )`

The parameters are a string and two optional dictionaries, which can be used to represent the global and local name spaces. The expression string parameter is parsed and evaluated as a Jython expression using either the specified or default globals and locals dictionaries. The return value is the result of the evaluated expression, as shown in Listing 4.14.

Listing 4.14   Sample `eval()` Example

```
1|wsadmin>pi = 3.141592653589793
2|wsadmin>r = 2
3|wsadmin>print eval( 'pi * r ** 2' )
4|12.566370614359172
```

`execfile( filename[, globals[, locals ] ] )`

Like the `exec` statement, the `execfile` function parses the specified input—in this case, the contents of the file named by the string. As with the `eval` function, the second and third parameters are optional dictionaries used to represent the global and local namespaces.[4]

`filter( function, sequence )`

Build a list from those sequence elements for which the specified function returns 1. If the specified function is None, then the result contains sequence elements that are not zero, or None. `filter( function, sequence )` is approximately equivalent to definition represented in Listing 4.15.

Listing 4.15   Simplistic `filter()` Definition

```
1|def filter( function, sequence ) :
2|   result = []
3|   for item in sequence :
4|     if function and function( item ) :
5|        result.append( item )
6|     else :
7|        if item : result.append( item )
8|   return result
```

`float( x )`

Convert a noncomplex number or a string to floating point. If the parameter is numeric, Jython returns the closest approximation of this value using the available floating point precision. Otherwise, the string must contain a "well-formed" numeric value with

---

[4] Unfortunately, versions of the Application Server earlier than 6.1.0.15 appear to have a defect requiring that the filename to be executed should be specified as a literal string that does not have blanks between the parentheses and the quotation marks.

optional leading and/or trailing whitespace characters, and Jython again returns the closest approximation of this value.

getattr(object, name [, default])

The name parameter must be a string and should contain the name of an attribute of the specified object. If the name is of an existing attribute of the specified object, the current value of that attribute is returned. If the specified attribute does not exist, and the default parameter is provided, its value is returned. Otherwise, an `AttributeError` exception is raised.

globals( )

Return a dictionary representing the current global namespace.

WARNING   Do not modify the contents of this dictionary.

---

hasattr(object, name)

Return 1 if the string contains the name of an existing attribute of the specified object, 0 otherwise.

hash(object)

Return an integer value representing the hash value of the specified object.

hex(x)

Return a string of hexadecimal characters equivalent to the specified integer value.

id(object)

Return the (possibly long) integer representing the "identity" of the specified object. The identify of an object is guaranteed to be unique and constant for the object during its lifetime.

input([prompt])

The string representation of the optional prompt parameter is displayed, the user response is evaluated (using the `"eval"` function), and the result is returned. Therefore, this function is equivalent to `eval(raw_input(prompt))`. An example of using `input()` is provided in Listing 4.16.

Listing 4.16   Sample Use of `input()`

```
1|wsadmin>pi = 3.141592653589793
2|wsadmin>r = 2
3|wsadmin>print input( 'expression: ' )
4|expression: pi * r ** 2
5|12.566370614359172
```

WARNING   This function is unsafe because no checks are used to validate the user input before it is evaluated.

Using the `raw_input()` function allows your script to verify and validate the user specified input.

int(x[, radix])

Return the specified value converted to integer form. If the value parameter is a string, it must be a well-formed number and is allowed to have leading and trailing whitespace characters. The optional radix parameter specifies the conversion base to be used (and defaults to 10). The radix value can be 0 or 2 to 36 inclusive and can only be specified when the first parameter is a string. A radix value of 0 indicates that Jython should interpret the value as it does integer literals. Conversion failures cause exceptions to be raised.

isinstance(object, classinfo)

Return 1 if the object parameter is an instance of or a subclass of the specified `classinfo` parameter; otherwise, return 0.

issubclass(class, classinfo)

Return 1 if the class parameter is a subclass of the specified `classinfo` parameter; otherwise, return 0.

len(s)

Return the number of items (for example, length) of the specified object. The object could be a string, a tuple, a list, or a dictionary.

list(sequence)

Return a list built from the items in the specified sequence. Note that if the specified sequence is a list, the list and not a copy is returned.

locals( )

Return a dictionary representing the current local namespace.

WARNING   Do not modify the contents of this dictionary.

long(x[, radix])

Return the specified value converted to long integer form. If the value parameter is a string, it must be a well-formed number and is allowed to have leading and trailing whitespace characters. The optional radix parameter specifies the conversion base to be used (and defaults to 10). The radix value can be 0 or 2 to 36 inclusive and can only be specified when the first parameter is a string. A radix value of 0 indicates that Jython should interpret the value as it does integer literals. Conversion failures cause exceptions to be raised.

map(function, sequence, ...)

Return a list containing the results of passing each sequence element to the specified function. Multiple sequences should be provided for functions requiring multiple parameters. The sequence elements are processed in parallel, passing the paired sequence items to the function for processing. Should the sequence lengths be different, the None value is supplied for the "missing" elements from the shorter sequence.

max(sequence)

Return the largest item of a non-empty sequence.

min(sequence)

Return the smallest item of a non-empty sequence.

open(filename[, mode[, bufsize]])

Return a file object identified by the filename (string) parameter. If the file can't be opened, an IOError exception is raised. The optional mode parameter is a string identifying how the file is to be opened:

'r'—Open for "read" (default)

'w'—Open for "writing"

'a'—Open for "append" (i.e., writing at the end)

NOTE   Append 'b' to one of the mode letters shown here to indicate that the file is to be opened in "binary" mode (end-of-line characters are not respected as such).The optional bufsize parameter identifies a requested buffer size. A detailed description of this function is beyond the scope of this book. Please review the Python documentation for this information.

ord(c)

Return the ordinal value of the specified single character (which may be a Unicode character).

pow(x, y[, z])

Return x ** y, or (x ** y) % z if the optional third parameter is specified.

range([start,] stop[, step])

Return a list containing a range of plain integer values generated using the specified (plain integer) parameters.[5]

---

[5] It is very easy to generate a very large list using range, consider how many values are generated should you use something silly like range(2147483647). Attempts to do so, however, require a large amount of memory and could cause heap exhaustion. You might want to consider using xrange() (described and explained later in this section).

NOTE If a single parameter is specified, start defaults to 0, step defaults to 1, and the value is used as stop. If two values are specified, step defaults to a value of 1. The value of step must not be zero, or a ValueError exception is raised.

---

raw_input([prompt])

Display the optional prompt string, if one exists, then read a single line of text from "standard" input, remove the tailing newline character, and return this string as the function result. An example is shown in Listing 4.17.

Listing 4.17 Sample Use of `raw_input()`

```
1|wsadmin>raw_input( 'What is your favorite color? ' )
2|What is your favorite color? Green
3|'Green'
```

reduce(function, sequence[, initialValue])

Return the result of calling the specified function on the values in the specified sequence in a cumulative fashion in order to "reduce" the sequence of values to a single result. The specified function must allow two parameters and is expected to return some operation using the specified input. If the optional initialValue parameter is specified, it is used as the initial, or default, value for the processing. If the specified sequence contains a single value, reduce() returns that value. An example is shown in Listing 4.18 and explained in detail in Table 4.4.

Listing 4.18 Examples of `reduce()`

```
 1|wsadmin>def add( a, b ) : return a + b
 2|wsadmin>
 3|wsadmin>def mul( x, y ) : return x * y
 4|wsadmin>
 5|wsadmin>def cat( s, t ) : return str( s ) + str( t )
 6|wsadmin>
 7|wsadmin>reduce( add, range( 101 ) )
 8|5050
 9|wsadmin>reduce( mul, range( 1, 5 ) )
10|24
11|wsadmin>reduce( cat, 'abc', '->' )
12|'->abc'
13|wsadmin>reduce( cat, '', '*' )
14|'*'
```

```
15|wsadmin>reduce( cat, ( 0, ) )
16|0
17|wsadmin>reduce( cat, ( 0, 1 ) )
18|'01'
```

Table 4.4   reduce() Examples Explained

Line(s)	Explanation
1–6	Define some binary functions to be used for this example.
7–8	Note how function calls can be nested. In the first case, the result of range(101) is a list containing the integers from 0 through 100 inclusive, and the result of the reduce() function is the sum of these values.
9–10	The result of the reduce() call on line 9 is equivalent to 1 * 2 * 3 * 4.
11–12	Don't be confused. The string 'abc' is the sequence to be reduced, and the '->' is the initialValue parameter. The reduce concatenates all of the elements of the string sequence to the initialValue. This also shows that reduce() can process other than integer values.
13–14	This shows how reduce() works given an empty sequence.
15–18	The last two examples show how reduce() can be used to process elements of a tuple. The interesting thing to note about the former is that the input sequence contains a single element tuple containing the integer 0 and that the result of using reduce() on this sequence is an integer and not the string that is returned by the specified cat() function. This is more evident when the input sequence has at least two elements, as seen on lines 17–18.

reload(module)

Reload a previously imported module. Unfortunately, the restrictions, limitations, and caveats related to this function are a bit beyond the scope of this book. For specific details about this function and how it should be used, look at some Python documentation, one example of which is available at http://docs.python.org/lib/built-in-funcs.html.

repr(object)

Return a string containing a displayable, or printable, representation of the specified object.

round(x[, digits])

Return the specified value as a floating point after rounding to the specified number of digits after the decimal point. If the digits parameter is unspecified, it defaults to 0, thus truncating any existing decimal points from the specified value. That rounding is "away from" the value 0, as seen here in Listing 4.19.

Listing 4.19 `round()` Example

```
1|wsadmin>print round( 0.5 ), round( -0.5 )
2|1.0 -1.0
```

`setattr( object, name, value )`

This is the opposite of `getattr()`, with the following parameters:

- The target object
- A string containing the attribute name
- The value to be bound (assigned)

`str( object )`

Return a string containing a displayable representation of the specified object.

`type( object )`

Return the type of the specified object.

`unichr( i )`

Return the Unicode string of characters having a Unicode code of the specified integer value.

`unicode( object[, encoding [, errors ] ] )`

Return the Unicode string representation of the specified object. The optional encoding parameter is a string identifying the name of the encoding code page to be used. The optional errors parameter is a string that can have one of the following values defined in Table 4.5.

Table 4.5 `unicode()` Error Values

Value	Meaning
`'strict'`	Raise a `ValueError` exception when an conversion error is encountered.
`'ignore'`	Silently ignore any conversion errors.
`'replace'`	Use the official Unicode replacement character (i.e., `U+FFFD`), as a replacement for any characters that can't be converted.

vars([object])

Return a dictionary containing details about the local variables, or those of the specified object, if one is provided.

WARNING   Do not modify the contents of this dictionary.

---

xrange([start,] stop[, step])

This function is very similar to `range()`, but instead of returning a list of all the specified values, it returns an `xrange` object. This special sequence type is used to obtain the same values as the corresponding list, without generating them at the time the function is called. For example, use the code shown in Listing 4.20 to see how long it takes to generate 1 billion (that is, `1E9`) values, with a `'.'` being displayed every 10 million (`1E7`) values. Don't be surprised by the time required to execute this loop. It does, however, run to completion. Trying to use `range()` on the same value is likely to cause an out of memory (OOM) error.

Listing 4.20   Sample Use of `xrange()`

```
1 wsadmin>for item in xrange( int( 1e9 ) ) :
2 wsadmin>   if item % int( 1e7 ) == 0 : print '\b.',
3 wsadmin>
```

Summary

This chapter continued our discussion of Jython, specifically related to object-oriented programming constructs (such as classes, attributes, and methods). In addition, references are provided for the built-in list, dictionary, and string methods, as well as functions that exist as part of the language. We also took a short side trip to explore the topic of string formatting.

## CHAPTER 5

Jython Modules

Classes, functions, and variable definitions can be collected into files for easy reuse and maintenance. A file containing these kinds of definitions is referred to as a *module* and has a suffix of .py. In this chapter, we take a closer look at Jython modules.

Jython Module Basics

As with functions and classes, when Jython processes a module file, new global and local namespaces are defined to identify the objects that are directly accessible within the file. For example, given a simple module, as shown in Listing 5.1, how are the objects in this file used by other scripts?

Listing 5.1   Simple Module File (countdown.py)

```
 1|# - - - - - - - - - - - - - - - - - - - - - - - - - - - - - - - - - - - - - - -
 2|# Name: countdown.py
 3|# Role: Simple demonstration of a Jython Module
 4|# - - - - - - - - - - - - - - - - - - - - - - - - - - - - - - - - - - - - - - -
 5|'A holding place for some potentially useful functions'
 6|
 7|# - - - - - - - - - - - - - - - - - - - - - - - - - - - - - - - - - - - - - - -
 8|# Name: countdown()
 9|# Role: Simple function
10|# - - - - - - - - - - - - - - - - - - - - - - - - - - - - - - - - - - - - - - -
11|def countdown( start=10 ):
12|   'Simple function used to display countdown data'
```

```
13|   while start > 0 :
14|     print start,
15|     start -= 1
16|   print 'done'
17|
18|#- - - - - - - - - - - - - - - - - - - - - - - - - - - - - - - - - - - - - - -
19|# Statements executed when the file is loaded
20|#- - - - - - - - - - - - - - - - - - - - - - - - - - - - - - - - - - - - - - -
21|if  __name__ == 'main' or __name__ == '__main__' :
22|   print 'countdown.py executed as a stand-alone script file'
23|else :
24|   print 'countdown.py loaded as a module'
25|
26|print 'dir():', dir()
```

The import Statement

The `import` statement is used to access the objects defined within a module file. A few different ways exist to do this. The first is to use an `import` statement of the form: `import FileName`, an example of which is shown in Listing 5.2.

Listing 5.2   Example Use of the `import` Statement

```
1|wsadmin>import countdown
2|countdown.py loaded as a module
3|dir(): ['__doc__', '__file__', '__name__', 'countdown']
4|wsadmin>countdown.countdown()
5|10 9 8 7 6 5 4 3 2 1 done
6|wsadmin>dir( countdown )
7|['__doc__', '__file__', '__name__', 'countdown']
8|wsadmin>countdown.__doc__
9|'A holding place for some potentially useful functions'
```

Line 1 shows, by specifying the name of the module file, Jython can execute the contents of that file. Notice that the generated output (lines 2–3) show that the statements contained within the file were, in fact, executed. It is also important to note that the output on line 3 lists the names of the identifiers that are defined and available within the module. If you remember, one of the actions performed by the execution of a function definition is to bind the function statement-suite to the function identifier. That is why the local function (`countdown`) is listed in the namespace.

Line 4 shows how to execute a function defined within a module. The general form for this is `moduleName.functionName()`. This also points out one of the challenges related to naming and using modules, which is when an `import` statement is executed, the module (file) name is bound to the module (file) contents. Another form of the `import` statement is available that helps with this issue, namely `import FileName as name`. This means that instead of simply using `import countdown`, as shown in Listing 5.2, you could identify the name (or alias) by which we want this module known. An example of this is shown in Listing 5.3.

Listing 5.3 Example of `import as`

```
1 | wsadmin>import countdown as spam
2 | countdown.py loaded as a module
3 | dir(): ['__doc__', '__file__', '__name__', 'countdown']
4 | wsadmin>spam.countdown()
5 | 10 9 8 7 6 5 4 3 2 1 done
6 | wsadmin>dir( spam )
7 | ['__doc__', '__file__', '__name__', 'countdown']
8 | wsadmin>spam.__file__
9 | 'C:\\IBM\\WebSphere\\AppServer\\bin\\.\\countdown.py'
```

Both of forms of the `import` statement bind all of the module contents to a name in the given namespace. However, doing so means that to access any of the objects within the module, the object must be qualified using either the module name or an alias (if the second form of the `import` statement was used). There are a few different ways around this, all of which are related to binding individual identifiers in the local namespace to module objects.

1. Assign a local identifier to a module object. Listing 5.4 shows how a module object (function) can be bound to a local identifier. Note that in order to bind a module function to a name does not involve the function being called, so the parentheses after the function name are not included in this assignment.

Listing 5.4 `import <moduleName>`

```
1 | wsadmin>import countdown
2 | countdown.py loaded as a module
3 | dir(): ['__doc__', '__file__', '__name__', 'countdown']
4 | wsadmin>count = countdown.countdown
5 | wsadmin>count()
6 | 10 9 8 7 6 5 4 3 2 1 done
```

2. Another alternative is to use the last form of the `import` statement, which is `from ModuleName import objectName`, which only adds the specified object to the namespace, as shown in Listing 5.5.

Listing 5.5   from <moduleName> import <objectName>

```
1|wsadmin>from countdown import countdown
2|countdown.py loaded as a module
3|dir(): ['__doc__', '__file__', '__name__', 'countdown']
4|wsadmin>countdown
5|<function countdown at 1409569796>
6|wsadmin>countdown()
7|10 9 8 7 6 5 4 3 2 1 done
```

   3. Another alternative is to use a variation of the `from` form of the `import` statement, which allows the identification of an alias for the given module object, as shown in Listing 5.6.

Listing 5.6   from <moduleName> import <objectName> as <name>

```
1|wsadmin>from countdown import countdown as lancelot
2|countdown.py loaded as a module
3|dir(): ['__doc__', '__file__', '__name__', 'countdown']
4|wsadmin>lancelot
5|<function countdown at 82838768>
6|wsadmin>lancelot()
7|10 9 8 7 6 5 4 3 2 1 done
```

   4. The last form of the "from" variant of the `import` statement is to use an asterisk `'*'` as the list of module objects to be bound to the current namespace—for example, `from FileName import *`. This form is not recommended because it not only clutters the namespace with module objects, but can also override existing object definitions with ones from the specified module.

nested_scopes

Previously mentioned was the fact that three namespaces exist for identifiers:

   1. **Local**—These names (identifiers) are defined and assigned within a function, class, or module.

   2. **Global**—These names are defined outside of a function, class, or module.

   3. **Built-in**—These names exist as part of the environment and are available without any special action on the part of the script writer.

As shown previously, when a reference is made to an identifier within a function, the order in which the namespaces are checked for this identifier becomes an issue. The `nested scope` issue was discovered and was fixed in Python 2.2. This problem is demonstrated by the code shown in Listing 5.7.

Listing 5.7 nested scope Issue

```
 1|wsadmin>def f() :
 2|wsadmin>  def g() :
 3|wsadmin>   print 'g(): x =', x
 4|wsadmin>  x = 'local to f()'
 5|wsadmin>  print 'f(): x =', x
 6|wsadmin>  g()
 7|wsadmin>
 8|<input>:1:[SyntaxWarning]: local name 'x' in 'f' shadows use as
global in nested scopes
 9|wsadmin>x = 'global'
10|wsadmin>f()
11|f(): x = local to f()
12|g(): x = global
13|wsadmin>
```

The issue arises when a function is defined local to another function. In this case, note how the reference to the variable x in function g() can only access a local or global value. The original definition of scoping rules meant that there was no way for the code in a nested function (for example, g()) could access items local to the enclosing, or outer, function (for example, f()) without them being passed as parameters. The desired effect is to allow intermediate scopes to be checked instead of being ignored.

This is why the SyntaxWarning is generated. This shortcoming was corrected in version 2.2 of Python. The Jython used by **wsadmin** is based on Python version 2.1 and therefore includes this shortcoming. Because this "correction" to the language involves a change to the way in which scripts function, the developers of the language provided a way that script writers would be warned about the potential impact to existing scripts. Additionally, it allows script writers to communicate to Jython that it should make use of this "future language feature." This involves using the from variant of the import statement, and shown in Listing 5.8.

Listing 5.8 nested scope Resolution

```
 1|wsadmin>from __future__ import nested_scopes
 2|wsadmin>
 3|wsadmin>def f() :
 4|wsadmin>  def g() :
 5|wsadmin>   print 'g(): x =', x
 6|wsadmin>  x = 'local to f()'
 7|wsadmin>  print 'f(): x =', x
 8|wsadmin>  g()
 9|wsadmin>
```

```
10|wsadmin>x = 'global'
11|wsadmin>f()
12|f(): x = local to f()
13|g(): x = local to f()
14|wsadmin>
```

By adding the statement shown (line 1), the script writer is telling Jython to change the way in which Jython processes the script. Without it, Jython will "generate a SyntaxWarning" message for each script that will be affected by this language change when the feature is fully implemented.

> **NOTE**   The profile script that we provide and recommend using (that is, WAuJ.py) includes this `import` in order for you to simplify your scripts.

Packages

A package is a collection of modules (files) collected into a directory or directory tree. Each directory in the tree is required to have a file named `__init__.py` (which may, in fact, be empty). Unfortunately, Jython packages are outside the scope of this book. To learn more about them, consider reviewing the Python documentation about packages that is available from http://docs.python.org/tut.

Errors and Exceptions

In general, there are two kinds of problems that can occur with Jython scripts: Syntax errors and exceptions. Syntax errors are identified by Jython as it checks that the program "follows the rules" before execution of the script begins. Syntax errors include (but are not limited to) the following:

1. Unterminated string literals
2. Invalid identifiers
3. Misuse of a reserved identifier
4. Inappropriate indentation

Exceptions occur while the script is executing. The preceding chapters have provided numerous examples of exceptions and the associated messages. Additionally, you have seen that the language includes the `try` statement that allows programs to recognize and deal with these exceptional conditions. What hasn't been previously discussed, however, is defining new exceptions specifically for the script to handle. To do this, first you must understand how to define a Jython object. Listing 5.9 shows how to define a simple exception class.

Listing 5.9 Defining a New Exception

```
 1|# - - - - - - - - - - - - - - - - - - - - - - - - - - - - - - - - - - - -
 2|# Name: Lumberjack
 3|# Role: Define an exception object type
 4|# - - - - - - - - - - - - - - - - - - - - - - - - - - - - - - - - - - - -
 5|class Lumberjack( Exception ) :
 6|
 7|  def __init__( self, value ) :
 8|    self.value = value         # Save parm as instance attrib
 9|
10|  def __str__( self ) :
11|    return repr( self.value )  # Return value as string
```

Listing 5.10 shows an example of how this user-defined exception can be used. This allows exception conditions to be specifically designed for the scripts being written. Line 2 shows the creation of an exception object, and line 3 shows how the exception object instance is associated with a particular identifier (that is, e). Line 4 shows how, by simply referencing the object identifier, that the class __str__() method is invoked to return the string representation of the instance attribute value.

Listing 5.10 Example Use of a User-Defined Exception

```
1|wsadmin>try :
2|wsadmin>  raise Lumberjack( "I'm ok" )
3|wsadmin>except Lumberjack, e :
4|wsadmin>  print "I'm a lumberjack, and", e
5|wsadmin>
6|I'm a lumberjack, and I'm ok
```

Built-in Exceptions

Jython uses the same kind of exception class hierarchy as Python. However, some differences do exist due to recent changes in Python. You may encounter exceptions in some Python code that do not exist in Jython.

Listing 5.11 shows the names of the exceptions that can be generated by Jython, as well as their relationship to the base Exception class. Should you decide to create an exception class for your application, this information may help you decide on how to do that.

Listing 5.11 Exception Class Hierarchy

```
- Exception
  - StandardError
    - ArithmeticError
      - OverflowError
```

```
          - ZeroDivisionError
          - FloatingPointError
      - AssertionError
      - AttributeError
      - EnvironmentError
          - IOError
          - OSError
      - EOFError
      - ImportError
      - KeyboardInterrupt
      - LookupError
          - IndexError
          - KeyError
      - MemoryError
      - NameError
          - UnboundLocalError
      - RuntimeError
          - NotImplementedError
      - SyntaxError
          - IndentationError
              - TabError
      - SystemError
      - TypeError
      - ValueError
          - UnicodeError
      - SystemExit
      - Warning
          - DeprecationWarning
          - SyntaxWarning
          - RuntimeWarning
          - UserWarning
```

Functional Programming

Jython also includes facilities that allow scripts to be written more concisely. These facilities are related to a subject called *functional programming* and include the following:

- Lambda expressions
- The `filter()`, `map()`, and `reduce()` built-in functions
- List comprehension

This topic is somewhat involved and requires quite a bit of explanation. Fortunately, this explanation is readily available elsewhere. Specifically, there are some very nice and readable articles related to this subject available on the developerWorks® website (http://www.IBM.com/developerworks/). Take a look at these developerWorks articles on Functional Programming:[1]

- *Charming Python: Functional Programming in Python*

  Part 1: http://www.IBM.com/developerworks/linux/library/l-prog.html

  Part 2: http://www.IBM.com/developerworks/linux/library/l-prog2.html

  Part 3: http://www.IBM.com/developerworks/linux/library/l-prog3.html

- *Using the full potential of Jython to build compact and maintainable **wsadmin** scripts*

  http://www.IBM.com/developerworks/websphere/library/techarticles/0801_simms/0801_simms.html

Using Java Objects and Libraries

As mentioned earlier, one advantage of Jython is the accessibility it has to Java libraries, objects, and properties. To demonstrate this, let's take a quick look at an example function that can be used to load the contents of a properties file into a Jython dictionary. Listing 5.12 shows a file, Properties.py and the function it contains, `propfileToDict()`, that can be used to perform this task. Table 5.1 dissects Listing 5.12, line by line. Listing 5.13 provides example uses of Properties.py.

Listing 5.12   Properties.py

```
 1|#- - - - - - - - - - - - - - - - - - - - - - - - - - - - - - - - - -#- - - - - - - - - -
 2|# Name: Properties.py
 3|#- - - - - - - - - - - - - - - - - - - - - - - - - - - - - - - - - -#- - - - - - - - - -
 4|'Create a dictionary from a properties file.'
 5|
 6|def propfileToDict( fileName ) :
 7|  'Create a dictionary from a properties file.'
 8|
 9|  import java.io.FileInputStream
10|  import java.util.Properties
11|
```

---

[1] It is necessary to mention, however, that the "listings" in Parts 1 and 2 of the *Charming Python* articles are a little hard to read because of the way they are represented. For some reason, the significance of the end-of-line markers for these listings was lost, so they require a little bit more study to understand. It helps if you remember that ' # ' is used to indicate the beginning of a comment, and the ' >>> ' is the Python interpreter command prompt.

```
12|  try :
13|     istream = java.io.FileInputStream( fileName )
14|     props   = java.util.Properties()
15|     props.load( istream )
16|     istream.close()
17|     result = {}
18|     e = props.keys()
19|     while e.hasMoreElements() :
20|        key = e.nextElement()
21|        result[ key ] = props.getProperty( key )
22|     return result
23|  except java.io.FileNotFoundException :
24|     raise IOError, 'FileNotFound: ' + fileName
```

Table 5.1   Properties.py Explained

Line(s)	Description
1–3	A simple block comment used to identify the source file.
4	A documentation string (docstring) used to identify the role of the file contents.
6	Function definition statement.
7	Function docstring definition.
9–10	Import statements used to load the Java resources needed to perform the desired action.
12	Try statement used to handle possible errors that might occur.
13	Creation of a Java FileInputStream object using the specified file name.
14	Creation of a Java Properties object for accessing the specified properties file.
15	Calling of the properties method for processing the specified file as a properties file.
16	Closing of the FileInputStream object.
17	Initialization of the result object as an empty dictionary.
18	Creation of a Java enumeration object using the properties keys() method.
19	while loop used to process all property key values in the enumeration.
20	Retrieval of the next property key from the enumeration.
21	Assignment to the dictionary using the given key and the associated value.

Table 5.1 Properties.py Explained

Line(s)	Description
22	After the loop completes successfully, the generated dictionary is returned to the caller.
23	Exception handler for a specific error (for example, the Java `FileNotFoundException` thrown by the `FileInputStream` constructor).
24	By raising an `IOError` exception, the caller of `propfileToDict()` has a greatly simplified call stack, as well as an easy to understand error message.

Listing 5.13 Example Use of Properties.py

```
 1|wsadmin>import Properties
 2|wsadmin>d = Properties.propfileToDict( 'jmx.properties' )
 3|wsadmin>keys = d.keys()
 4|wsadmin>keys.sort()
 5|wsadmin>for key in keys :
 6|wsadmin>  print '%s = %s' % ( key, d[ key ] )
 7|wsadmin>
 8|JmxConsoleLog = off
 9|JmxCoreLogLevel = 3
10|JmxLoadingLogLevel = 3
11|JmxLog = off
12|JmxLogFile = Tmx4j_.log
13|JmxMaxLogFileSize = 1024
14|JmxMaxLogFiles = 2
15|JmxModelMBeanLogLevel = 3
16|JmxMonitorLogLevel = 3
17|JmxRelationLogLevel = 3
18|JmxSyncLog = true
19|JmxTimerLogLevel = 3
20|JmxUserLogLevel = 3
21|JmxUtilsLogLevel = 3
```

Jython Standard Library

Interestingly, when reading about the Python (and therefore Jython) programming language, you'll notice it is described as having "batteries included." What this phrase intends to convey is that unlike some systems or programs, Jython has an enormous collection of resources readily available for the programmer to use and build upon. This collection is much too large to describe here and includes code for all sorts of things, such as the following:

- Date and time manipulation
- Calendar-related functions
- Containers (for example, heaps, trees, lists, vectors, and so on)

Provided with this book are a few very useful and powerful modules used often by the scripts, as discussed in the following sections.

sys Module

Rather than being a simple regurgitation of the Python documentation on this built-in and (almost) always available module, let's take a look at techniques for finding out what is in a module like this. These same techniques prove useful later as you start learning about the WebSphere Application Server scripting objects.

Listing 5.14 shows a trivial script that can be used to display information about the items in the sys module. Lines 5–6 gets and sorts the list of items names in the sys module. Line 8 uses list comprehension to determine the longest name for later use in the alignment of the output. The most likely areas of confusion are lines 11–14 and line 16. Lines 11–14 are used to obtain the type() of each named object as a string. Unfortunately, trying to use the type() on some items causes an exception to be raised, which is why the try/except statement is needed.

This leaves line 16 to explain. It uses formatted string output to display the pertinent information in a nicely aligned fashion. The '%2d:' formation string is used to format the item number, right-justified in a two-digit field, followed by a colon. The '%*s' format string uses two values: the width to define the width of the output field and specify the fact that the value should be left justified in this field and the 's' to indicate that the value of name should be output as a string. This is then followed by '%s' to have the value of kind output as a string. See Listings 5.14 and 5.15 for examples.

Listing 5.14   SysInfo.py

```
 1 | # - - - - - - - - - - - - - - - - - - - - - - - - - - - - - - - - - - - - - - -
 2 | # Name: SysInfo.py
 3 | # Role: Display details about the built in sys module items
 4 | # - - - - - - - - - - - - - - - - - - - - - - - - - - - - - - - - - - - - - - -
 5 | names = dir( sys )                        # List of item names
 6 | names.sort()                              # Sort the list
 7 |
 8 | widest = max( [ len( x ) for x in names ] ) # find longest
 9 | count  = 0                                #
10 | for name in names :                       # For every name ...
```

```
11|   try :                                    #    get the item type
12|     kind = str( eval( 'type( sys.%s )' % name ) )
13|   except :                                 #
14|     kind = '<unknown>'                      #    some don't type...
15|   count += 1                               # item number
16|   print '%2d: %*s = %s' % ( count, -widest, name, kind )
```

Listing 5.15 SysInfo.py Sample Output

```
. . .
14: argv                = org.python.core.PyList
. . .
22: exc_info            = org.python.core.PyMethod
. . .
26: exit                = org.python.core.PyMethod
. . .
34: maxint              = org.python.core.PyInteger
35: minint              = org.python.core.PyInteger
36: modules             = org.python.core.PyStringMap
. . .
38: path                = org.python.core.PyList
. . .
56: version             = org.python.core.PyString
57: version_info        = org.python.core.PyTuple
. . .
```

We will only look at a few of the results in order to demonstrate how to use this kind of information. Let's start with lines 34 and 35, which show that the `sys` module has two integer values to define the smallest and largest integer values. The value of `sys.version` for both version 6.1 and 7.0 of the AppServer is 2.1. Line 26 shows that a function called `sys.exit()` exists, and investigation shows that this routine can be called to terminate the script being executed. Other values of interest include `sys.argv`, which contains the list of parameters specified when the script was executed. You will see how it can be processed shortly.

Some of the most important items in the `sys` module have been left for last. Sys.path is a list of directories that is used by Jython to locate modules (for example, when an `import <moduleName>` (of any form) is executed, Jython looks in the directories specified in this list. Chapter 7, "Introduction to Admin Objects," describes how this can be used.

One of the most important entries in the `sys` module is the `sys.modules` directory object. It contains the names of the modules and reference information about modules that have been loaded. Chapter 7 discusses how it can be used to get around one of the challenges that exist for WebSphere Application Server Administration script authors.

And finally, `sys.exc_info()` is a method that is used within an `except` clause. The result of calling this function is a tuple containing the following information about the exception that is currently being handled:

- Type
- Value
- Traceback

Listing 5.16 shows one way in which this function might be used. You will see this function used elsewhere in some of the scripts provided with this book.

Listing 5.16   Example Use of `sys.exc_info()`

```
 1 | wsadmin>try :
 2 | wsadmin>  1 / 0
 3 | wsadmin>except :
 4 | wsadmin>  format = 'type = %s\nvalue = %s\ntrace = %s'
 5 | wsadmin>  print format % sys.exc_info()
 6 | wsadmin>
 7 | type  = exceptions.ZeroDivisionError
 8 | value = integer division or modulo
 9 | trace = <traceback object at 1580097070>
10 | wsadmin>
```

getopt() Module

One reason for using scripts is that they can be tailored to process user input specified when the script is invoked. Many of the scripts provided with this book are written to do just this. Command-line process has been around for quite some time. To make things easier for C programmers, the `getopt()` library routine was provided and has been used extensively. For this reason, the same kind of facility for processing Python command-line values has been developed and made available as a module. The documentation for the `getopt` module is available on the web at http://docs.python.org/lib/module-getopt.html.

The code shown in Listing 5.17 represents the main structure of many of the scripts provided with this book.

Listing 5.17   `parmTest.py` Outline

```
1 | # - - - - - - - - - - - - - - - - - - - - - - - - - - - - - - - - - - - - -
2 | # Name: parmTest()
3 | # Role: Show one technique for processing command line parms
4 | # - - - - - - - - - - - - - - - - - - - - - - - - - - - - - - - - - - - - -
```

```
 5|import getopt, sys
 6|
 7|#- - - - - - - - - - - - - - - - - - - - - - - - - - - - - - - - - - --
 8|# Global dictionary to hold the user specified options&values
 9|#- - - - - - - - - - - - - - - - - - - - - - - - - - - - - - - - - - --
10|Opts = {}
11|
12|#- - - - - - - - - - - - - - - - - - - - - - - - - - - - - - - - - - --
13|# Name: parseOpts()
14|# Role: Process the user specified (command line) options
15|#- - - - - - - - - - - - - - - - - - - - - - - - - - - - - - - - - - --
16|def parseOpts( cmdName ) :
17|   ...
18|
19|#- - - - - - - - - - - - - - - - - - - - - - - - - - - - - - - - - - --
20|# Name: Usage()
21|# Role: Display script usage information, and exit
22|#- - - - - - - - - - - - - - - - - - - - - - - - - - - - - - - - - - --
23|def Usage( cmdName ):
24|   ...
25|
26|#- - - - - - - - - - - - - - - - - - - - - - - - - - - - - - - - - - --
27|# Name: parmTest()
28|# Role: Process the user specified (command line) options
29|#- - - - - - - - - - - - - - - - - - - - - - - - - - - - - - - - - - --
30|def parmTest( cmdName = 'parmTest' ) :
31|   ...
32|
33|#- - - - - - - - - - - - - - - - - - - - - - - - - - - - - - - --
34|# Role: main entry point
35|# Note: Ensure script is executed, and not imported
36|#- - - - - - - - - - - - - - - - - - - - - - - - - - - - - - - - - - --
37|if ( __name__ == 'main' ) or ( __name__ == 'main' ) :
38|  parmTest()
39|else :
40|  Usage( __name__ )
```

Some things to note about this code are the following:

1. The import getopt makes the option processing facilities available.
2. The definition and initialization of 'Opts' as a global dictionary.

3. The definition of the `'parseOpts'` function for processing the command-line parameters/arguments.

4. The definition of the `'Usage'` function for providing details of how the script should be used.

5. The definition of the `'parmTest'` function (which uses the same name as the file in which the function is contained).

6. The `'main'` code at the bottom that determines whether or not the "named" function (that is, the function named the same as the script file) or the `Usage()` function should be invoked.

Let's look at these routines in the order in which they might naturally be invoked. Specifically:

1. `Usage()`
2. `parmTest()`
3. `parseOpts()`

Usage()

This routine, the skeleton for which is shown in Listing 5.18, is quite straightforward. Things to note include the following:

1. `cmdName` parameter used to simplify the use of the script name in the output.

2. Jython triple quotes (long) string used to format usage information in a readable manner.

3. Use of named format specification (for example, `%(cmdName)s`) and the formatted string operator (`... % locals()`) greatly simplifying the use of the script/routine name in the usage information.

4. Use of `sys.exit()` to terminate the script when usage information is displayed.

Listing 5.18   Usage() Outline

```
 1 | #- - - - - - - - - - - - - - - - - - - - - - - - - - - - - - - - - - - - - - -
 2 | # Name: Usage()
 3 | # Role: Display script usage information, and exit
 4 | #- - - - - - - - - - - - - - - - - - - - - - - - - - - - - - - - - - - - - - -
 5 | def Usage( cmdName='scriptName' ):
 6 |   print '''
 7 | Command: %(cmdName)s\n
 8 | Purpose: WebSphere (wsadmin) script used to demonstrate the
 9 |          parsing of command line parameters.
10 |   Usage: %(cmdName)s [options]\n
11 | Required switches:
12 | ...
```

```
13|\nOptional switches:
14|...
15|\nNotes:
16|...
17|Examples:
18|...
19|''' % locals()
20|  sys.exit( 1 )
```

parmTest()

This is the "named" routine, the one that is executed by the main test at the bottom of the script to initiate the action work to be performed. As shown in Listing 5.19, in this case, the routine is used to check how many user-specified parameters were provided and if enough are present, "parse" (process) them, looking for the required and optional parameters.

Listing 5.19 parmTest() Function

```
 1|#- - - - - - - - - - - - - - - - - - - - - - - - - - - - - - - - - - - - - - -
 2|# Name: parmTest()
 3|# Role: Process the user specified (command line) options
 4|#- - - - - - - - - - - - - - - - - - - - - - - - - - - - - - - - - - - - - - -
 5|def parmTest( cmdName = 'parmTest' ) :
 6|  fewParms = '%(cmdName)s: Insufficient parameters provided.'
 7|
 8|  argc = len( sys.argv );                  # Number of parms
 9|  if ( argc < 1 ) :                        # Too few?
10|    print fewParms % locals();             #    Error...
11|    Usage( cmdName );                      #
12|  else :                                   # otherwise
13|    parseOpts( cmdName );                  #    Parse the data
14|
15|  #- - - - - - - - - - - - - - - - - - - - - - - - - - - - - - - - - -
16|  # Assign values from the user Options dictionary, to make
17|  # data access simpler, and easier.  For example, instead of
18|  # using: Opts[ 'servName' ]
19|  # we will be able to simply use:
20|  #    servName
21|  # to access the value.  Additionally, this allows us to make
22|  # use of mapped error messages (e.g., see parms below)
23|  #- - - - - - - - - - - - - - - - - - - - - - - - - - - - - - - - - -
24|  for key in Opts.keys() :
```

```
25|     cmd = '%s=Opts["%s"]' % ( key, key )
26|     exec( cmd )
27|
28|   #- - - - - - - - - - - - - - - - - - - - - - - - - - - - - - - - - - - - - - -
29|   # Result of parsing command line parameters
30|   #- - - - - - - - - - - - - - - - - - - - - - - - - - - - - - - - - - - - - - -
31|   parms  = '%(cmdName)s:'
32|   parms += ' --serverName %(servName)s'
33|   parms += ' --nodeName %(nodeName)s'
34|   if ( boolName != None ) :
35|     parms += ' --boolName'
36|
37|   print parms % locals()
```

Table 5.2 explains the parmTest() function.

Table 5.2   parmTest() Function Explained

Line(s)	Comments
5	Defines the default cmdName parameter value.
6	Assignment of mapped error message containing named format specifier.
8–13	Test for number of user parameters specified. Remember, if Usage() is called, it never returns; sys.exit() is invoked to terminate the script.
24–26	The result of calling parseOpts() will be to populate the global Opts dictionary with the user-specified values. The purpose of this code is to use the information in this dictionary to assign variable names to make access to the values simpler.
31–35	Build a mapped message containing multiple named format specifications.
37	Use the mapped message string to display the user-specified values.

parseOpt() Function

This is the routine that is only called by parmTest() to parse (process) the user-specified parameters. Table 5.3 provides important items to note about the parseOpt() function shown in Listing 5.20.

Listing 5.20   parseOpts() function

```
1|#- - - - - - - - - - - - - - - - - - - - - - - - - - - - - - - - - - - - - - - -
2|# Name: parseOpts()
```

```
 3| # Role: Process the user specified (command line) options
 4| #--------------------------------------------------------------
 5| def parseOpts( cmdName ) :
 6|   sOpts  = 's:bn:'
 7|   lOpts  = 'serverName=,boolName,nodeName='.split( ',' )
 8|   badOpt = '%(cmdName)s: Unknown/unrecognized parameter%(plural)s:
%(argStr)s'
 9|   optErr = '%(cmdName)s: Error encountered processing: %(argStr)s'
10|
11|   try :
12|     opts, args = getopt.getopt( sys.argv, sOpts, lOpts )
13|   except getopt.GetoptError :
14|     argStr = ' '.join( sys.argv )
15|     print optErr % locals()
16|     Usage( cmdName )
17|
18|   #--------------------------------------------------------------
19|   # Initialize the global Opts dictionary using these keys (indexes)
20|   #--------------------------------------------------------------
21|   keys = 'servName,nodeName,boolName'.split( ',' )
22|   for key in keys : Opts[ key ] = None
23|
24|   #--------------------------------------------------------------
25|   # Process the list of options returned by getOpt()
26|   #--------------------------------------------------------------
27|   for opt, val in opts :
28|     if opt in   ( '-s', '--serverName' ) : Opts[ 'servName' ] = val
29|     elif opt in ( '-n', '--nodeName' )   : Opts[ 'nodeName' ] = val
30|     elif opt in ( '-b', '--boolName' )   : Opts[ 'boolName' ] = 1
31|
32|   #--------------------------------------------------------------
33|   # Check for unhandled/unrecognized options
34|   #--------------------------------------------------------------
35|   if ( args != [] ) :
36|     argStr = ' '.join( args )
37|     plural = ''
38|     if ( len( args ) > 1 ) : plural = 's'
39|     print badOpt % locals()
40|     Usage( cmdName )
41|
```

Table 5.3   `parseOpts()`—Things to Note

Line(s)	Comments
5	Use of default `cmdName` parameter, which is passed to `Usage()` should that routine be called (see lines 16 and 43).
6	String identifying "short form" options; that is, a single letter with an optional colon to indicate that this option switch requires an associated value.
7	List of long form options. Note the use of string `split()` method to create the list and the use of an equal sign at the end of an option to indicate a required value.
8 and 9	Mapped error messages containing named format specifications.
11–16	Use of `getopt()` routine to use the short and long option lists to parse/process the user-specified parameters and the use of an exception handler to deal with an error in the user-supplied information (for example, missing or unrecognized option or missing value).
21–22	Initialization of the global Opts dictionary.
27–30	Using `getopt()` results to populate the Opts dictionary.
35–40	Checking for unknown/unrecognized parameters and providing an appropriate error message should one occur.
41	Implicit return—should `Usage()` and therefore `sys.exit()` not be invoked.

One of the powerful things about using `getopt()` to process the command-line parameters is how it allows you to focus on making your script useful without having to spend all sorts of time testing the command-line processing code. That has all been done for you by the people who wrote and provide the `getopt` module. Take a look at the notes and examples provided with the `parmTest` usage statement to understand this further. Listing 5.21 demonstrates this. First we see the very end of the `Usage()` output (for example, the `Examples:` section) when the script is invoked and no parameters are specified. Then, the long forms of the parameters names are shown, and finally, the short forms of the same parameters are also shown. The use of `getopt()` to process the command-line parameters allows the remainder of the script to focus on the actual role of the script and minimize the amount of effort required to validate and make the user command-line input easily accessible to the script. The scripts provided with this book with make use of `getopt()` for just this purpose.

Listing 5.21   `parmTest`—Example Output

```
C:...\bin>wsadmin ... -f parmTest.py
WASX7357I: ...

...

Examples:
  wsadmin -lang jython -f parmTest.py  -serverName=s1  -nodeName N
```

```
wsadmin -lang jython -f parmTest.py -ss1 -b -n ragibsonNode01
```

```
C:...\bin>wsadmin ... -f parmTest.py  -serverName=s1  -nodeName N1  -
boolName
WASX7357I: ...
parmTest:  -serverName s1  -nodeName N1  -boolName
```

```
C:...\bin>wsadmin ... -f parmTest.py -b -ss1 -n N1 WASX7357I: ...
parmTest:  -serverName s1  -nodeName N1  -boolName
```

Regular Expressions (RegExp)

Regular expressions, sometimes called RegExp, are one of the most powerful mechanisms available for the string processing. Unfortunately, it is a very involved topic, about which numerous books, articles, and web pages have been written. Therefore, a complete discourse on this topic is well beyond the scope of this book. However, the power and versatility of regular expressions for processing strings is such that it is not something that can be ignored. They will be used in some of the scripts described in this book, so it is important that enough information be provided that allows you to have a chance of understanding how and why they are being used.

The purpose of regular expressions is to allow the programmer to specify patterns for searching for information in text strings. For example, say that the result of some configuration-related query of the Application Server is a string containing the following kind of information:

```
Name1(cells/Name2/nodes/Name3/servers/Name1|server.xml#Server_#)
```

A regular expression could be used to verify that the string "matched" this pattern and extract the various name values from this string. The way that regular expressions work is that "normal" characters, by definition, match identical characters in strings. Additionally, there are special, or meta-characters, that have special meanings. A subset of the total list of meta-characters and their roles are listed in Table 5.4.

Table 5.4   Regular Expressions—Some Meta-Characters

char	Matches
'.'	Generally, this matches any character except a newline.
'^'	Matches the start of the string (or after a newline in MULTILINE mode).
'$'	Matches the end of the string (or before a newline in MULTILINE mode).

Table 5.4   Regular Expressions—Some Meta-Characters

char	Matches
[ ]	Identifies a set of characters to be matched. Any character within the square brackets will match.
|	Separates two patterns and indicates that either is allowed to match.
( )	Identifies a group to be matched (and held).
\#	Where # is a numeric value (1..99). Matches the specified parenthetical group.
\d	Matches a digit (that is, equivalent to [0–9]).
\D	Matches a non-digit.
\s	Matches a whitespace character (for example, space, tab, newline, form-feed, vertical tab).
\S	Matches a non-whitespace character.
\w	Matches a "word" character (alphanumeric and underscore).
\W	Matches a non-word character.
\A	Matches only at the beginning of string.
\Z	Matches only at the end of string.
\	Escape prefix, which can be used to allow a meta-character (for example, ' . ') to occur in the string and be matched.

These represent some of the most frequently used "special" characters and allow scripts to be written that match a large variety of patterns. In addition, there are some modifiers that allow these characters to occur a specific number of times. These modifiers are listed in Table 5.5. The reason they are called "greedy" is that they indicate that "as many as possible" matches will be used.

Table 5.5   Regular Expression—'greedy' Modifiers

Modifier	Modification
*	Preceding char/meta-char is allowed to exist zero or more times.
+	Preceding char/meta-char is allowed to exist one or more times.
?	Preceding char/meta-char is allowed to exist zero or one time.
{n}	Preceding char/meta-char must exist exactly 'n' times.
{m,n}	Preceding char/meta-char must exist at least 'm' times and at most 'n' times.

For those instances where a "greedy" match is not desirable, the modifiers shown in Table 5.6 can be used instead. For these, the shortest matching sequence is preferred.

Table 5.6 Regular Expression—'minimal' Modifiers

Modifier	Modification
*?	Preceding char/meta-char is allowed to exist zero or more times.
+?	Preceding char/meta-char is allowed to exist one or more times.
??	Preceding char/meta-char is allowed to exist zero or one time.
{m,n}?	Preceding char/meta-char must exist at least 'm' times and at most 'n' times.

Searching for and matching of regular expressions are the most common operations that can be done with RegExp patterns. However, they are not the only things that can be done. The methods that exist for RegExp objects are listed here.

Regular Expression Functions

`compile( patternString [, flags ] )`

Create a regular expression pattern object using the specified pattern string and optional flags if any are included.

`escape( string )`

Return a copy of the input string with each non-alphanumeric character escaped with a backslash.

`findall( pattern, string )`

Return a list containing the non-overlapping matches of the pattern object in the specified string.

`match( pattern, string [, flags ] )`

Return a match object if the pattern object matches the beginning of the specified string; otherwise, return None.

`search( pattern, string [, flags ] )`

Return a match object if the pattern object matches text anywhere in the specified string; otherwise, return None.

`split( pattern, string [, maxsplit ] )`

Return a list of strings after using the specified pattern object to identify the separation positions in the input string. If maxsplit is provided, it identifies the maximum number of split operations that should occur.

```
sub( pattern, replacement, string [, count ] )
```

Return a string created by replacing occurrences of text matching the specified pattern object by the replacement string. If count is provided, it indicates the maximum number of substitutions that should occur.

```
subn( pattern, replacement, string [, count ] )
```

Perform the same operation as the sub() method, but return a tuple containing the updated string and the number of substitutions that were made.

Regular Expression Object Methods

A regular expression object, created by using the re.compile() function, has the following methods:

```
findall(string [, startPos [, endPos ] ] )
match( string [, startPos [, endPos ] ] )
search( string [, startPos [, endPos ] ] )
split( string [, maxsplit ] )
sub( replacement, string [, count ] )
subn( replacement, string [, count ] )
```

All just like the re functions of same names.

Regular Expression Match Object Methods and Attributes

A regular expression match object, created by using either the match or search methods, has the following methods and attributes:

```
group( [group] )
```

Return the specified captured group.

```
groups()
```

Return a tuple containing all of the captured group.

```
groupdict()
```

Return a dictionary containing all of the named groups.

```
start( [group] )
```

Return the starting index associated with the specified group. Group defaults to zero if it isn't specified.

```
end( [group] )
```

Return the ending index associated with the specified group. Group defaults to zero if it isn't specified.

span([group])

Return a tuple containing the starting and ending position for the specified group. If no group number is specified, group defaults to 0.

pos

The starting position specified on the match or search or 0 if none was specified.

endpos

The ending position passed to the match or search method used to create the match object. If no value was specified, it represents the length of the specified string.

lastindex

The integer value representing the number of captured groups.

lastgroup

The name of the last captured group, or None.

re

The regular expression object used to perform the match or search.

string

The string on which the match or search was performed.

Listing 5.22 shows an example interactive **wsadmin** session in which Regular Expressions are used.

Listing 5.22   Regular Expression Example

```
 1|wsadmin>server = AdminConfig.list( 'Server' )
 2|wsadmin>import re
 3|wsadmin>cidPat = r'(\w+)\(cells\/(\w+)\/nodes\/(\w+)\/servers'
 4|wsadmin>cidPat += r'\/\1\|(\w+\.xml)#([a-zA-Z_0-9]+)\)'
 5|wsadmin>reo = re.compile( cidPat )
 6|wsadmin>mo  = reo.match( server )
 7|wsadmin>for i in range( 1, mo.lastindex ) :
 8|wsadmin>  begin = mo.start( i )
 9|wsadmin>  fini  = mo.end( i )
10|wsadmin>  data  = mo.group( i )
11|wsadmin>  print '%d [%2d:%2d] = %s' % ( i, begin, fini, data )
12|wsadmin>
13|1 [ 0: 7] = server1
14|2 [14:33] = localhostNode01Cell
15|3 [40:55] = localhostNode01
16|4 [72:82] = server.xml
```

Table 5.7 explains the regular expression example shown previously.

Table 5.7   Regular Expression Example Explained

Line(s)	Description
1	This statement is better understood after reading Chapter 8, "The Admin Config Object," which describes the **AdminConfig** administration object. In the single application server environment on which it was executed, it returns a configuration id string for the application server.
2	This statement is used to load the regular expression (re) library code and creates a namespace for this module.
3–4	These statements build a regular expression pattern string to be used to identify and extract portions of a configuration id.
5	This statement invokes the compile function in the re namespace to create a regular expression object, a reference to which is saved in the variable named reo.

6	The match method of the previously created regular expression object is used to process the string variable named server that contains the configuration id. *Note:* Alternative techniques for performing this same action and that don't save the regular expression object are:
	
	`mo = re.match( re.compile(cidPat ), server )`
	
	`mo = re.compile( cidPat ).match( server )`

7	The lastindex attribute of the match object can be used to access the match object captured groups. *Note:* group(0) contains a copy of the entire string that matched specified pattern.
8–11	This demonstrates a string formatting technique to display the index value, the starting and ending positions for the group, and the value of the group.
12	This is the empty line that indicates the end of the for statement to wsadmin.
13–16	These are the four lines output by the print statement within the for loop.

Summary

In this chapter, we brought together a number of the concepts from the preceding chapters on Jython (Chapters 2–4, specifically). We made use of this information in order to present the enormously valuable concept of Jython modules. In subsequent chapters where we discuss WebSphere scripting objects, you will better understand these objects because of the information found herein.

wsadmin

"Make it so!"

—Jean-Luc Picard, USS Enterprise-E commanding

The **wsadmin** program can and should be considered a scripting engine for performing administrative tasks on an application server or its configuration. It can be used to execute individual commands or multiple commands in an interactive/interpretive fashion, or it can be used to execute script files. Just as Jean-Luc Picard commands the astronauts who control the starship Enterprise, **wsadmin** commands and controls how WebSphere Application Server behaves and configures the way WebSphere Application Server starts.

The operating system being used defines how the **wsadmin** program should be executed. The examples included in this chapter show how the command to start the **wsadmin** program looks in a Unix® and a Windows type of environment. The `. /` before the name of the file to be executed on a Unix environment is an indication that the specified file is located in the current directory. The `options` in square brackets is simply a notation used to indicate that user-specified options are, in fact, optional.

- AIX®—`wsadmin.sh [options]`
- Linux®—`wsadmin.sh [options]`
- z/OS®—`wsadmin.sh [options]`
- Windows—`wsadmin`[1] `[options]`

Let's begin by looking at the **wsadmin** "help" (usage) information. Specifying `-?`, `-h`, or `-help` after **wsadmin** on the command line will cause **wsadmin** to display its help details, and terminate.

---

[1] Windows executable files extensions (e.g., .bat) are optional.

Listing 6.1 shows a significant portion of the **wsadmin** help, and Table 6.1 describes values that are allowed for individual options. From the number and variety of these options, it should be clear that an assortment of things can be specified on the **wsadmin** command line to identify and indicate what **wsadmin** should do for a particular invocation. Unfortunately, what may not be as easily understood are the implications of the selections that can be made or the default settings that exist and how these defaults can be changed to suit your particular needs. The purpose of this chapter is to explain these aspects of the **wsadmin** program.

Listing 6.1   wsadmin Help Information

```
C:\IBM\WebSphere\AppServer\bin>wsadmin -?
WASX7001I: wsadmin is the executable for WebSphere scripting.
Syntax:

wsadmin
        [ -h(elp)   ]
        [ -?  ]
        [ -c <command> ]
        [ -p <properties_file_name>]
        [ -profile <profile_script_name>]
        [ -f <script_file_name>]
        [ -javaoption java_option]
        [ -lang  language]
        [ -wsadmin_classpath  classpath]
        [ -profileName profile]
        [ -conntype
                SOAP
                        [-host host_name]
                        [-port port_number]
                        [-user userid]
                        [-password password] |
                RMI
                        [-host host_name]
                        [-port port_number]
                        [-user userid]
                        [-password password] |
                NONE
        ]
        [ -jobid <jobid_string>]
        [ -tracefile <trace_file>]
```

```
[ -appendtrace <true/false>]
[ script parameters ]
```
. . .

Table 6.1 **wsadmin** Command Invocation Explained

Command	A command to be passed to the script processor.
properties_file_ name	A java properties file to be used.
profile_script_ name	A script file to be executed before the main command or file.
script_file_name	A command to be passed to the script processor.
classpath	A classpath to be appended to built-in one.
-conntype	Specifies the type of connection to be used; the default argument is "SOAP" a conntype of "NONE" means that no server connection is made and certain operations will be performed in local mode.
host_name	Is the host used for the SOAP or RMI connection; the default is the local host.
password	Is the password required when the server is running in secure mode.
script parameters	Anything else on the command line. These string values are passed to the script in the sys.argv variable.
jobid_string	A jobID string to be used to audit each invocation of **wsadmin**.
trace_file	Is the log file name and location where **wsadmin** trace output is directed.

To better understand these things, it is best to begin by describing what happens when **wsadmin** starts executing. Looking at the **wsadmin** help output, you find a number of available options. Unfortunately, the way that they are presented might make them a bit difficult to understand, but grouping the options into categories might make things a little clearer.

wsadmin Options

It's probably a good idea to familiarize yourself with the **wsadmin** command-line options. Even though you may eventually get into a habit of using only a subset of these options, it is good to realize which ones exist, just in case you need to do something different.

Usage Information

The first category of options might best be called *usage information* or documentation. The options that fit this category are used to display the **wsadmin** usage details and were shown earlier.

If no command or script is specified, an interpreter shell is created for interactive use. To leave an interactive scripting session, use either the quit or exit commands.

Several commands, properties files, and profiles may be specified on a single command line. They are processed and executed in the order they are specified.

The Java Virtual Machine Initialization Phase

The **wsadmin** program is written in Java. It requires a Java Virtual Machine (JVM) in order to execute. So the next category of options is related to the JVM and its initialization.

```
-javaoption <java_option>
```

This option allows values to be provided that define how the JVM should be initialized. Any valid JVM option may be included. For example, to define the maximum size to be used by the Java heap, one can use something like -javaoption -Xmx1024m.

```
-wsadmin_classpath <classpath>
```

This option should be used to add Java class files to the classpath. Multiple entries should be separated using a semicolon. Should a space exist in any of the directory names, surround the entire value in double quotes. The example option, shown next, demonstrates how to add the specified archive (.jar) file to the wsadmin classpath. If you have Java libraries that you would like to add to the **wsadmin** code base, this is how you would do that. If you have some Java code that uses the Java Management Extensions (JMX) to monitor and control the behavior of WebSphere, this is how you would load that code into **wsadmin**:

```
-wsadmin_classpath "C:/Program Files/classes/myClasses.jar"
```

The wsadmin Environment Initialization Phase

The next category of options is related to the tailoring of the **wsadmin** environment, which in many ways is an extension of the settings used to configure the JVM environment. To better understand this, it is best to begin by explaining that some **wsadmin** configuration information is specified on the command line, and other information is provided using Java property files. Property files are simple text files containing directives and optional comment statements.

Comment statements are exclusively for the use of any human reader and are ignored by **wsadmin**. The first non-blank character on these lines is an octothorpe # or an exclamation mark!. Fortunately, the default property files contain numerous comments explaining each directive statement, the possible values to which it can be assigned, and the default value should the directive not exist.

Directive statements are of the form `key=value` and frequently correspond to command-line options. The keys and values found in the default property files are created either during the installation of the WebSphere Application Server product or during the creation of a profile and have a prefix of `com.ibm.ws.scripting`. Table 6.2 shows the property key suffix, its default value, and the corresponding command-line option (should one exist).[2]

It should be easy to understand that **wsadmin** performs its job depending on the options that are provided on the command-line. What may not be clear is that the property files exist to define "default" values should command-line options not be provided. It should be no surprise that the primary property file that is processed during the initialization of **wsadmin** is named **wsadmin.properties**. So should you decide that particular properties are appropriate for your environment, you can either modify the existing property files or create your own to reflect your individual or group needs.

Table 6.2   **wsadmin** Property Keys and Command-Line Options

Property Key Suffix	Default Value (in Properties File)	Command-Line Option
connectionType	SOAP	-conntype
port	8880	-port
host	localhost	-host
defaultLang	jacl	-lang
echoparams	true	
traceFile	.../wsadmin.traceout	-tracefile
validationOutput	.../wsadmin.valout	
traceString	*=info	
appendTrace	false	-appendtrace
profiles	.../securityProcs.jacl; .../LTPA_LDAPSecurityProcs.jacl	-profile
emitWarningForCustom SecurityPolicy[3]	true	

---

[2] Remember that each property key begins with `com.ibm.ws.scripting`.

[3] This property suffix is all one camelcase word.

Table 6.2   `wsadmin` Property Keys and Command-Line Options

Property Key Suffix	Default Value (in Properties File)	Command-Line Option
tempdir	java.io.tmpdir	
validationLevel	HIGHEST	
crossDocumentValidation Enabled	true	
classpath		**-wsadmin**_classpath

Another thing that you should realize is that multiple instances of the property files exist (especially when multiple profiles exist), which brings up a major "pet peeve" with this and, unfortunately, many other products—the use of very similar terminology for different things. Specifically, the use of `profile` here actually refers to the `profileName` command-line option. If you take a moment to search the online documentation for the term "profile" or "profiles," the vast majority of references are related to the topic of `profileNames`. In fact, choosing one of the first pages[4] that is located, you find that it contains the following statement:

"A profile defines the runtime environment. The profile includes all of the files that the server processes in the runtime environment and that you can change."

It is not until you reach a topic entitled "Setting up profile scripts to make tracing easier using scripting" that you encounter the first reference to the command-line option identified by the -profile option. The topic of profile scripts is discussed shortly; however, first we need to finish the discussion about the `profileName` option, which has the misfortune of being referred to as `profile` in many places in the documentation. In this book, every effort is made to distinguish between the concept of `profile` as in `profileName` and `profile` as in `profile script file`.

Anyway, it may not be immediately obvious which of the property files will be used when **wsadmin** is executed and that values from multiple property files might be read and used during one execution of **wsadmin**. What determines which files are used? Determining factors can include the following:

1. Which **wsadmin** command script (for example, `.bat` or `.sh`) file was executed?

    The answer to this question identifies that the **wsadmin** program, as is the case with any of the command script files provided with the WebSphere Application Server product,

<hr/>
[4] http://publib.boulder.ibm.com/infocenter/wasinfo/v6r1/index.jsp?topic=/com.ibm.websphere.base.doc/info/aes/ae/cpro_overview.html.

can, by its location, imply a "default" `profileName` to be used should one not be specified on the command line. For example, should the "**wsadmin**" command script from a particular profile bin directory (that is, `"...\WebSphere\AppServer\profiles\ AppSrv01\bin"`) be executed, then this is exactly the same as having executed the "**wsadmin**" command script from the <WAS_HOME>\bin (for example, `"...\WebSphere\AppServer\bin"`) directory and having specified `"-profileName AppSrv01"` as a command-line option.

2. Which `profileName` has been identified as the "default?"

   This question is important should the "**wsadmin**" command script from the <WAS_HOME>\bin directory be executed without providing the `profileName` option, in which case this identifies the `profileName` to be used should one not be provided.

3. What **wsadmin** command-line options were specified?

The answer to this question is especially important because it can change the "default" behavior of **wsadmin** command. So regardless of the answers to the previous questions, if the `profileName` command-line option is specified, it takes precedence over the default `profileName` value. Furthermore, there is an option that allows you to specify additional property files (for example, the `"-p"` option, as described later).

   If you don't know or can't remember which `profileName` has been defined as the default, there is an easy way to find out which will be used by the **wsadmin** command script. From a command prompt, execute the `manageprofiles` command script and specify the `-getDefaultName` option, as shown in the example:

```
...\bin>manageprofiles -getDefaultName
AppSrv00
```

Should you decide that a different `profileName` be used as the default for your environment, the `manageprofiles` command may be used to change the default, as shown in this example:

```
...\bin>manageprofiles -setDefaultName -profileName AppSrv00
INSTCONFSUCCESS: Success: The default profile has been set.
```

Once you have determined the `profileName` being used when the **wsadmin** starts executing, the next question to be answered is, "Which properties file(s) will be used during the initialization of **wsadmin**?" During its initialization, **wsadmin** looks for a file named **wsadmin.properties** in each of the following locations:

1. Below the installation root directory—For example, <WAS_HOME>\profiles \<profileName>\properties\wsadmin.properties.

2. The user default, or home directory—For example, <USERPROFILE> \wsadmin. properties.

3. The file specified by the WSADMIN_PROPERTIES environment variable (should one exist)—For example, %WSADMIN_PROPERTIES%.

What does it mean that **wsadmin** "looks" for a file in each of these places? If the specified file exists, any properties (for example, `key=value` statements) contained therein are read and saved—meaning that a `key=value` statement occurring in the first file found may be overridden by another occurrence of the same key in a subsequent property file. So be careful. You might need to override a property file setting with a command-line option (for example, `-tracefile`) and review the messages contained therein to understand exactly which properties files are loaded and in which order to understand how the initialization of the **wsadmin** environment occurs.

In addition to the properties files listed here, the `-p` command-line option can be used to specify one or more additional properties files to be loaded and processed during the initialization of **wsadmin**. Again, any of these files may be used to override existing key values set by any of the previously identified property files.[5] The syntax of this command-line option is seen here:[6]

`-p <properties_file_name>`

The **wsadmin** tool uses information from the property files to determine things such as:

- The default communication protocol to be used, if any
- The hostname of the default application server
- The default port number to which the connection request should be sent
- The user and password to be used for authentication.

Fortunately, the information in the property files is very well documented and easily understood. However, not all option values are identified in the comments (for example, even though NONE is a valid communication protocol, its availability is not documented in the **wsadmin** `.properties` file).

The Connection Phase

After all of the **wsadmin** environment property values have been loaded, the next phase of the initialization can take place. This is when **wsadmin** uses the connection type value to determine whether a connection to an application server should be attempted. If not, that is, should `-conntype none`[7] be specified on the command line or in the property file(s), **wsadmin** initialization does not attempt to connect to an application server and could be used to view and manipulate the application server configuration details. When **wsadmin** is not connected to an application server, it is called being in *local mode*.

---

[5] Because of the potential confusion that can occur, a best practice would probably include a limitation of the number of properties files to be specified and processed as part of the initialization of **wsadmin**.

[6] Remember to enclose the `properties_file_name` in double quotes if a space exists anywhere in the value. For example: `-p "C:\Program Files\properties\my.properties"`.

[7] The IBM InfoCenter shows the word "NONE" in uppercase. In fact, you can use either upper- or lowercase.

WARNING   Changes made to the configuration in local mode should be made with extreme caution because they can make the configuration invalid.

If the connection type identifies that either a SOAP or RMI/IIOP connection should be established, then additional property settings are used to determine the host and port number to which the connection request should be sent. Additionally, when security is enabled on the target application server, the user and password information need to be communicated to the application server so that permission to communicate with the server can be authenticated.

The properties and/or command-line options that are used during this connection phase are as follows:

* `conntype`
* `host`
* `port`
* `user`
* `password`

You can choose to save the user and password authentication values in communication protocol-specific files (for example, `soap.client.props` or `sas.client.props`). However, you should be aware of the security implications of saving user and password information on your file system. Additionally, you should also be aware of the implications of providing the user and password information as **wsadmin** command-line options, given that it is possible to display the command-line options of any executing program on all of the operating systems on which the application server product is supported.

If security is enabled on your application server and the user and password information is not available in the property files, or as command-line options, **wsadmin** attempts to open a dialog box and prompt you for the user and password information.

One of the useful characteristics about the **wsadmin** program is the fact that it explains what it is doing, as well as what it is trying to do. For example, when **wsadmin** is started and is able to connect to an application server, the first line of output generated indicates the name of the server with which the connection was made (or attempted), the communication protocol that was used, and the kind of application server to which the connection was made (if the connection was successful). Listing 6.2 contains two examples of this connection message.

Listing 6.2   WASX7209I Connection Message

```
C:\IBM\WebSphere\AppServer\bin>wsadmin
WASX7209I: Connected to process "server1" on node ragibsonNode00 using
SOAP connector;  The type of process is: UnManagedProcess
...
C:\IBM\WebSphere\AppServer\bin>wsadmin -profileName Dmgr01
```

WASX7209I: Connected to process "dmgr" on node ragibsonCellManager01
using SOAP connector; The type of process is: DeploymentManager

---

Defining the Scripting Language

After the connection phase, the environment initialization phase determines the scripting language using the -lang option (from either a wsadmin.properties file or a command line option).

The only valid entries are the case sensitive values jacl and jython. Because this book is only concerned with the latter, it is recommended that you locate the directive in your property file named com.ibm.ws.scripting.defaultLang and change the value from jacl to jython. Remember to also change the profile script names if you do this.[8]

NOTE   For the remainder of this book, it is presumed that this change has been made to the wsadmin.properties file. Therefore the use of the "-lang jython" command-line parameters will no longer be included in any of the examples.

If you change language, you should also change the names of the security profile scripts in wsadmin.properties from something.jacl to something.py or remove them if no corresponding something.py file is available. Otherwise, **wsadmin** will attempt to find Jython versions of the Jacl scripts by looking for the .py file in the same directory and complain if none exists.

Trace-Related Options

Another of the things that can be controlled about the environment initialization is related to tracing. Three command-line options exist that relate to tracing of **wsadmin**:

- tracefile
- appendtrace
- jobid

The first two of these have corresponding settings in wsadmin.properties (for example, traceFile and appendTrace). The other (-jobid) is only available as a command-line option and is used to add a text string to the **wsadmin** trace file. This entry can be used to correlate the contents of the trace file with a specific invocation of **wsadmin**. If the jobid text string contains spaces, then the string should be enclosed in quotation marks:

```
wsadmin -jobid "Ports used" -f ListPorts.py
```

---

[8] If you change the language setting, it is very important to also change the names of the default profiles. See the section "wsadmin Profile Script Files" for very important details.

Another trace-related option is only available using `wsadmin.properties` file. Looking therein, you can see that, by default, this `key=value` is commented out, which means that a default level of tracing is selected:

```
AbstractShell A   JobID=Ports used
```

After executing this command, the trace file (`wsadmin.traceout`) will contain a line like that shown in the code example that follows. This can prove to be especially useful should the `appendtrace` option be specified, which could cause the trace messages from multiple invocations of the **wsadmin** tool to be contained in the trace file. This allows the section of the trace file associated with a specific **wsadmin** invocation to be quickly located by searching for the appropriate `jobid` text string:

```
#com.ibm.ws.scripting.traceString=com.ibm.*=all=enabled
ManagerAdmin  I   TRAS0017I: The startup trace state is *=info.
```

wsadmin Profile Script Files

Once the language property is set and the associated scripting portion of the **wsadmin** tool is initialized, the next option to come into play is associated with the processing of profile script files. These script files must be of the appropriate language, which in this case is Jython. The default property file directive for this option is shown in the code example provided here:

```
com.ibm.ws.scripting.profiles=.../securityProcs.jacl;
   .../LTPA_LDAPSecurityProcs.jacl
```

Remember to change the file extension for these profile files from `.jacl` to `.py`, and verify that the specified files exist in the indicated locations. During the initialization of **wsadmin**, any files specified here will be used to configure the **wsadmin** scripting environment before any command or script is executed.

After you've made that change and started an interactive **wsadmin** session, you can use the `dir()` command to find out what objects exist in the default namespace. Listing 6.3 shows an example of this. When we first encountered this information, our initial reaction was, "Wow, from where did all of these objects come?"

Listing 6.3   Default **wsadmin** Namespace

```
1|C:\IBM\WebSphere\AppServer\bin>wsadmin
2|WASX7209I: Connected to process "server1" on node ragibsonNode00
3| using SOAP connector;  The type of process is: UnManagedProcess
4|
5|WASX7031I: For help, enter: "print Help.help()"
6|wsadmin>dir()
7|['AdminApp', 'AdminConfig', 'AdminControl', 'AdminTask', 'Help',
8|'LTPA_LDAPSecurityOff', 'LTPA_LDAPSecurityOn', 'TypedProxy',
9|'__doc__', '__name__', 'bsf', 'cellName', 'checkuserpw',
```

```
10|'doAuthenticationMechanism', 'doGlobalSecurity',
11|'doGlobalSecurityDisable', 'doLDAPUserRegistry', 'domainHostname',
12|'exportLTPAKey', 'flag', 'forceSync', 'generateLTPAKeys',
13|'getLDAPUserRegistryId', 'getLTPAId', 'getSecId',
14|'getSecurityAdminMbean', 'java', 'ldapPassword', 'ldapPort',
15|'ldapServer', 'ldapServerId', 'ldapUserRegistryId', 'lineSeparator',
16|'ltpaId', 'nodeName', 'secMbean', 'securityId', 'securityoff',
17|'securityon', 'sleep', 'sys', 'whatEnv']
18|wsadmin>
```

You might not like to have the namespace cluttered with things that you're not planning on using. So let's remove the default profile script files that were used by commenting out the com.ibm.ws.scripting.profiles directive in the wsadmin.properties file. After doing this, you can see that the number of items made available in the default namespace is greatly reduced. Listing 6.4 demonstrates the contents of the default Jython namespace when no profile script files are specified.

Listing 6.4   Minimum **wsadmin** Namespace

```
1|C:\IBM\WebSphere\AppServer\bin>wsadmin
2|WASX7209I: ...
3|WASX7031I: For help, enter: "print Help.help()"
4|wsadmin>dir()
5|['AdminApp', 'AdminConfig', 'AdminControl', 'AdminTask', 'Help',
6|'TypedProxy', '__doc__', '__name__', 'bsf', 'sys']
7|wsadmin>
```

Because these specified files are Jython script files, you can use a text editor to find out what they are doing and how it is being done.

securityProcs.py contains definitions for these functions:

- **checkuserpw()**—Takes a user and password as arguments and checks with the MBean server to see if they are valid.

- **securityon()**—Takes a user and password as arguments and enables security.

- **securityoff()**—Disables security "enabled" flag.

And the other file, LTPA_LDAPSecurityProcs.py, contains all of the other items and objects that show up in the namespace in Listing 6.5. Is there an easy way to get a list of these items? Yes, first look at wsadmin.properties and the profiles directive to locate the fully qualified name of the directory containing the file. Then use the steps identified in Table 6.3 to generate this list of items, as seen in Listing 6.5. In fact, it is quite a list—32 objects in all. Granted, some of them are automatically provided by Jython ('__doc__', '__file__', and '__name__' for example), but you get the idea. If you take the time to open the script file in a text editor, you will see that half of the items are functions, and the remainder are variables.[9]

Table 6.3   Listing a Module Namespace Explained

Line	Action
1	Import the module in question (in this case, `LTPA_LDAPSecurityProcs.py`)
2	Use the `dir()` function to display the module namespace.
3–12	Review the module namespace contents.
13–14	Nest the `dir()` function within the `len()` function to determine the number of items added to the namespace.

Listing 6.5   Listing a Module Namespace

```
 1|wsadmin>import LTPA_LDAPSecurityProcs
 2|wsadmin>dir( LTPA_LDAPSecurityProcs )
 3|['LTPA_LDAPSecurityOff', 'LTPA_LDAPSecurityOn', '__doc__',
 4|'__file__', '__name__','cellName','doAuthenticationMechanism',
 5|'doGlobalSecurity', 'doGlobalSecurityDisable',
 6|'doLDAPUserRegistry', 'domainHostname', 'exportLTPAKey',
 7|'flag', 'forceSync', 'generateLTPAKeys',
 8|'getLDAPUserRegistryId', 'getLTPAId', 'getSecId',
 9|'getSecurityAdminMbean', 'java', 'ldapPassword', 'ldapPort',
10|'ldapServer', 'ldapServerId', 'ldapUserRegistryId',
11|'lineSeparator', 'ltpaId', 'nodeName','secMbean','securityId',
12|'sleep', 'whatEnv']
13|wsadmin>len( dir( LTPA_LDAPSecurityProcs ) )
14|32
```

Based on this information, you can decide whether to include the `securityProcs.py` or `LTPA_LDAPSecurityProcs.py` as profile script files or not. For simplicity sake, remove these default script files from the directive. If there are circumstances when you would like to occasionally use one of these files, then you might want to consider using the `-profile` command-line option to do so. It allows you to add one or more profile script files without modifying your properties files.

---

[9] Please be careful, though. When we viewed `LTPA_LDAPSecurityProcs.py` in a text editor, we were very surprised to find that indentation was done using a mixture of spaces and tab characters. This is an extremely bad practice and should be avoided.

Another use for the -profile command-line option is that it allows you to test profile script files and their contents before you decide that they are stable enough to be added to one of the wsadmin.properties files. It is easy to create a profile script file containing a function to be tested. Then this script file can be defined and loaded using the -profile command-line option and thoroughly tested using an interactive **wsadmin** session. When you're confident that the function works as you want it to, you can either move the function to an existing profile script file or simply add this file to the list of profile script files in the profiles directive in the appropriate wsadmin.properties file.

Commands and Script Files

The last group of **wsadmin** command-line options are related to script files, or commands. Let's first take a look at the -c **wsadmin** command-line option, which is used to execute one or more commands. To execute multiple commands, you can either specify each with a -c option, or you can use a semi-colon (line separator) between the statements. Because it is very likely that the command(s) to be executed will contain one or more spaces, it is very likely that you will need to surround the command(s) to be executed by double quotation marks, as shown in Listing 6.6.

Listing 6.6   Specifying Multiple Commands

```
...\bin>wsadmin -c "J='Jython'; print J"
WASX7209I: Connected to process "server1" ...
Jython

...\bin>wsadmin -c "J='Jython'" -c "print J"
WASX7209I: Connected to process "server1" ...
Jython
```

After all of the commands that have been specified using this option have been executed, the **wsadmin** program exits gracefully and automatically commits any configuration changes you have made. This is exactly the same effect as adding AdminConfig.save() immediately after your command.

Thinking quickly about this might make you wonder whether this has any value at all. The reason for this concern is the fact that there is a non-trivial amount of overhead related to starting up a **wsadmin** session, and if all you are going to do is have a single command executed, why bother? Well, the answer to that question is yes; there is some overhead associated with using the -c command-line option to execute a single, or even a few, **wsadmin** command(s). However, there are times when this technique can do exactly what you need it to do. Additionally, there are times when the output of a single command can be voluminous, in which case, using the -c command-line option to execute this command allows you to redirect the output of a command to a file for later review.

Because we have yet to discuss any of the administrative objects, it is a little difficult to provide a good example for this option. However, Listing 6.7 shows an example that should be easily understood. It shows how a method (`reportConfigInconsistencies()`, for example) of an administrative object (**AdminTask**) can be invoked, and the return value of this call (a string) can be display using a `print` statement. It should be fairly clear from both the name of the method and the generated output what this particular statement does.

Listing 6.7 Example Use of `-c <command>`

```
1|C:\IBM\WebSphere\AppServer\bin>wsadmin -conntype none -c "print
AdminTask.reportConfigInconsistencies()"
2|WASX7357I: By request, ...
3|Configuration consistency report for cell ragibsonNode01Cell
4|
5|No consistency problems were found.
6|C:\IBM\WebSphere\AppServer\bin>
```

The final command-line option to be discussed is `-f`, and is used to specify a Jython script file to be executed. If you execute the **wsadmin** command from the directory containing the script file, then you don't have to include any path or directory references as part of the `-f` option. For example, let's look at this code:

```
C:\temp>set WAS_HOME=C:\IBM\WebSphere\AppServer
C:\temp>%WAS_HOME%\bin\wsadmin -conntype none -f ListPorts.py
```

If the fully-qualified path to the script file contains spaces, then this parameter should be enclosed in double quotes, as shown:

```
wsadmin -f "C:\Program Files\scripts\ListPorts.py"
```

Another thing shown in the **wsadmin** usage information is something like [script parameters]. This simply means that anything specified on the **wsadmin** command line that is not recognized as a **wsadmin** command-line option is made available to the script. For Jython scripts, parameters are made available via the `sys.argv` list. Listing 6.8 shows how to specify script parameters and how they can be accessed using `sys.argv` data structure. It also shows how the parameters are identified as unrecognized **wsadmin** options and are therefore being passed on to the scripting environment. This topic was discussed in the section "getopt() Module" in Chapter 5, "Jython Modules."

Listing 6.8 Script Parameters and `sys.argv`

```
1|C:\IBM\WebSphere\AppServer\bin>wsadmin spam and eggs
2|WASX7209I: Connected to process ...
3|WASX7411W: Ignoring the following provided option: [spam, and, eggs]
4|WASX7031I: For help, enter: "print Help.help()"
5|wsadmin>print sys.argv
6|['spam', 'and', 'eggs']
7|wsadmin>
```

Interactive/Interpretive wsadmin Session

Each of the following options causes **wsadmin** to exit after performing requested function:

- `help (or -?)`
- `c <command>`
- `f <script_file>`

If one of these options is not specified, the **wsadmin** scripting environment is initialized, and a "command prompt" (for example, **wsadmin>**) is displayed to indicate that **wsadmin** is awaiting user input to determine what needs to be done. You have seen examples of this previously.

An interactive **wsadmin** session can be a very useful and educational experience. The immediate response to the user input allows for code fragments to be entered and tested for syntax errors, as well as logic error. It can also be used to interact with administrative objects to learn about the application server configuration and the commands used to manipulate it.

Should you later determine that the interactive session would be useful as a function, you can make use of the fact that the commands that were executed are automatically written to the **wsadmin** trace file (identified by the `traceFile` directive in a properties file or by the `-traceFile` command-line option). It requires some editing on your part to extract the useful commands into a function, but it is certainly worth knowing that the commands that were executed are written somewhere should you need them.

Summary

wsadmin is a command shell. This chapter showed some different ways in which the **wsadmin** environment can be configured, including the Java Virtual Machine used by **wsadmin**. We also saw some configuration information that may be used to control **wsadmin** and its access to an enterprise security service. Finally, we showed you the mechanics of using the **wsadmin** command shell. In the chapters that follow, we see how to use the scripting objects that exist within the **wsadmin** environment.

Introduction to Admin Objects

"Help! I need somebody."

—*The Beatles*

We all need help at one time or another, and trying to use or learn how to administer the Web-Sphere Application Server product is no exception. It should be no surprise that the administrative scripting objects and the scripting environment are complicated and complex. So complex, in fact, that a Help scripting object is included, and each of the other scripting objects have help methods to assist with the understanding of the object and how it can be used. This chapter discusses and describes the kind of help that is available from the `Help` object, the scripting object methods, and active MBeans.

The Administrative Scripting Objects

To administer the WebSphere Application Server environment, **wsadmin** includes some specialized administrative objects. It also includes a way to get help for using these objects and some of the things these objects manipulate. The administrative objects are listed and briefly described in Table 7.1.

Each of the administrative objects is described in more detail in this and subsequent chapters. However, a "frequently asked question" occurs when dealing with these objects, especially when trying to create and use modules. The issue can be easily demonstrated using a simple module, like that shown in Listing 7.1. The problem is seen when displaying the default namespace using the `dir()` command.[1] A very different result is seen when this module is imported and the same command is executed. This demonstration can be seen in Listing 7.2 (lines 4–8).

---

[1] See Chapter 6, "wsadmin," in the section "wsadmin Profile script files."

Table 7.1   WebSphere Administrative Objects

Object Name	Description
AdminConfig[2]	Object used to view and manipulate configuration elements (xml files).
AdminControl[3]	Object used to view and manipulate active application server objects (MBeans).
AdminApp[4]	Object used to install and manipulate applications.
AdminTask[5]	Object used to execute administrative and server management commands.
Help	Object used to provide usage information about the administrative objects.

Listing 7.1   simpleModule.py

```
#- - - - - - - - - - - - - - - - - - - - - - - - - - - - - - - - - - - - - - -
# Name: simpleModule
# Role: Show the difference between module & profile namespaces
#- - - - - - - - - - - - - - - - - - - - - - - - - - - - - - - - - - - - - - -
print 'simpleModule namespace: ' + str( dir() )
```

If you look at the namespace displayed for the imported module (line 8), you see that the WebSphere administrative objects (that is, **AdminApp**, **AdminConfig**, **AdminControl**, **AdminTask**, and **Help**) are not listed.

Although there are several ways for an imported module to gain access to the administrative objects, the best way appears to be to make use of the fact that the administrative objects *are* present and available for scripts processed as profile files, as shown in Listing 7.2 (lines 11–15).

Listing 7.2   simpleModule Example[6]

```
1|...\bin>wsadmin
2|WASX7209I: Connected to process ...
```

---

[2] See Chapter 8, "The AdminConfig Object," for detailed information about this object.

[3] See Chapter 9, "The AdminControl Object," for detailed information about this object.

[4] See Chapter 10, "The AdminApp Object," for detailed information about this object.

[5] See Chapters 11 through 15 for detailed information about this object.

[6] Exactly what you see when you type dir() within **wsadmin** will vary depending on your version of WAS and depending on what you have written in profile scripts for **wsadmin**. See Chapter 6, in the section "**wsadmin** Profile script files," for more details.

```
 3|WASX7031I: For help, enter: "print Help.help()"
 4|wsadmin>print dir()
 5|['AdminApp', 'AdminConfig', 'AdminControl', 'AdminTask',
 6|'Help', 'TypedProxy', '__doc__', '__name__', 'bsf', 'sys']
 7|wsadmin>import simpleModule
 8|simpleModule namespace: ['__doc__', '__file__', '__name__']
 9|wsadmin>quit
10|
11|...\bin>wsadmin -profile simpleModule.py
12|WASX7209I: Connected to process ...
13|simpleModule namespace: ['AdminApp', 'AdminConfig',
14|'AdminControl', 'AdminTask', 'Help', 'TypedProxy', '__doc__',
15|'__name__', 'bsf', 'sys']
16|WASX7031I: For help, enter: "print Help.help()"
17|wsadmin>
```

You can use a simple technique that works well, has a minimum chance of making a mistake, and is also very easy to add to your environment.

The technique involves using a property of the sys.modules dictionary. By adding entries for each of the administrative objects to sys.modules, imported modules can access these objects. The first attempt is a simple profile file (WSASobjects.py), shown in Listing 7.3.

Listing 7.3 WSASobjects.py

```
sys.modules[ 'AdminApp'     ] = AdminApp
sys.modules[ 'AdminConfig'  ] = AdminConfig
sys.modules[ 'AdminControl' ] = AdminControl
sys.modules[ 'AdminTask'    ] = AdminTask
sys.modules[ 'Help'         ] = Help
```

A simple module file (moduleTest.py) is shown in Listing 7.4.

Listing 7.4 moduleTest.py

```
#------------------------------------------------------------
# Name: moduleTest
# Role: Show the difference between module & profile namespaces
#------------------------------------------------------------
print 'moduleTest.py'
```

```
print 'namespace before import: ' + str( dir() )
import AdminApp, AdminConfig, AdminControl, AdminTask, Help
print 'namespace  after import: ' + str( dir() )
```

What happens when you add WSASobjects.py to the list of files processed as profiles? Take a look at Listing 7.5 to see if the issue has been resolved.

Listing 7.5 WSASobject Example

```
 1|C:\IBM\WebSphere\AppServer\bin>wsadmin -profile WSASobjects.py
 2|WASX7209I: Connected to process ...
 3|WASX7031I: For help, enter: "print Help.help()"
 4|wsadmin>import moduleTest
 5|moduleTest.py
 6|namespace before import: ['__doc__', '__file__', '__name__']
 7|namespace  after import: ['AdminApp', 'AdminConfig',
 8|'AdminControl', 'AdminTask', 'Help', '__doc__', '__file__',
 9|'__name__']
10|wsadmin>
```

This is really simple! Unfortunately, however, it is an incomplete solution. What's required is a slightly more complicated script to deal with two situations: The target server is stopped, or **wsadmin** was started with -conntype none.

If **wsadmin** is unable to connect to its target server (that is, the target application server is stopped), the **AdminTask** object is not available, as seen in Listing 7.6. If you start **wsadmin** in local mode, that is,

```
    wsadmin -conntype none
```

the **AdminControl** object will not be available. In either case, you will get a **NameError** exception any time you try to use an administrative object that is not available.

Listing 7.6 AdminTask Object Unavailable

```
 1|C:\IBM\WebSphere\AppServer\bin>wsadmin -profile WSASobjects.py
 2|WASX7023E: Error creating "SOAP" connection to host "localhost";
 3|exception information: ...ConnectorNotAvailableException:
 4|WASX7213I: This scripting client is not connected to a server ...
 5|WASX8011W: AdminTask object is not available.
 6|...
 7|NameError: AdminTask
```

```
 8 |
 9 | WASX7031I: For help, enter: "print Help.help()"
10 | wsadmin>
```

To eliminate this exception, you can create a useful profile, which here is called WAuJ.py,[7] that we will add to the wsadmin.properties file as the only profile file to be loaded. Once this is done, the start up of **wsadmin** looks a little different, as shown in Listing 7.7. This example also demonstrates that a module can access the available administrative objects.

Listing 7.7   Using **WAuJ.py** as a Profile

```
 1 | C:\IBM\WebSphere\AppServer\bin>wsadmin -conntype none
 2 | WASX7357I: By request, this scripting client is not connected...
 3 | - - - - - - - - - - - - - - - - - - - - - - - - - - - - - - - - - - - - - -
 4 | Actions performed by WAuJ.py:
 5 | > from __future__ import nested_scopes
 6 | > sys.modules.update( WSASobjects )  # All admin objects added
 7 | > sys.modules[ 'sys' ] = sys
 8 | > wasroot = r'C:\IBM\WebSphere\AppServer'
 9 | > sys.path.append( r'C:\IBM\WebSphere\AppServer\scripts' )
10 | - - - - - - - - - - - - - - - - - - - - - - - - - - - - - - - - - - - - - -
11 | WASX7031I: For help, enter: "print Help.help()"
12 | wsadmin>import modifiedModuleTest
13 | modifiedModuleTest.py
14 | namespace before import: ['__doc__', '__file__', '__name__']
15 | Unable to import AdminTask
16 | namespace  after import: ['AdminApp', 'AdminConfig',
17 |   'AdminControl', 'Help', '__doc__', '__file__', '__name__']
```

The modifications made to the example module that allow it to check for and import available modules are shown in Listing 7.8. A module can check for each of the administrative objects that is needed using a simple try/except statement and determine if execution should continue should an object be unavailable.

---

[7] WSAS Administration using Jython (WAuJ)—where WSAS is an acronym for WebSphere Application Server.

Listing 7.8   Checking for Administrative Object Availability

```
1|try :
2|  import AdminTask
3|except :
4|  print 'Unable to import AdminTask'
```

Based on the usefulness of this profile, the remainder of the book makes use of this module, and it's automatically loading by the following line in the `wsadmin.properties` file:

```
com.ibm.ws.scripting.profiles=C:/IBM/WebSphere/scripts/WAuJ.py
```

> **NOTE**   If you do use the `WAuJ.py` profile and dislike the banner, seen in Listing 7.7 (lines 3–10), that gets displayed when **wsadmin** starts, there is a way to tell the profile not to display the banner. Just add `'-WAuJ'` as a command-line parameter when you start **wsadmin.** If found, this command-line parameter is removed (so your scripts don't need to check for or deal with it), and the banner isn't displayed.

Help for the Help Object

Each execution of **wsadmin** that causes it to enter interactive mode makes note of the Help object, and its `help()` method. The line of text immediately preceding the **wsadmin** prompt looks like this:

```
WASX7031I: For help, enter: "print Help.help()"
```

If you simply execute this help method, the result is shown to be a text string. Listing 7.9 shows part of the result and how it looks using the recommended `print` statement.

Listing 7.9   `Help.help()`—Result

```
 1|wsadmin>Help.help()
 2|'WASX7028I: The Help object has two purposes: \n\n\tFirst,...
 3|wsadmin>print Help.help()
 4|WASX7028I: The Help object has two purposes:
 5|
 6|    First, provide general help information for the objects
 7|    supplied by wsadmin for scripting: Help, AdminApp,
 8|    AdminConfig, and AdminControl.
 9|...
10|attributes      given an MBean, returns help for attributes
```

```
11│operations        given an MBean, returns help for operations
12│...
13│all               given an MBean, returns help for all the above
14│help              returns this help text
15│AdminControl      returns general help text for ...
16│AdminConfig       returns general help text for ...
17│AdminApp          returns general help text for ...
18│AdminTask         returns general help text for ...
19│wsadmin           returns general help text for ...
20│message           given a message id, ...
```

Looking at this output shows two distinct types of methods:

1. Those that provide help for active MBeans[8] (for example, attributes, operations, and so on).

2. Those that provide help for other administrative objects (such as help, **AdminControl**, and so on).

At first glance, it might seem to be a lot of information to absorb. Fortunately, grouping it using these categories seems to help. Another thing that helps is the realization that the help text associated with this object has object method names starting on the left edge immediately after the newline character.

As was mentioned earlier, regular expressions (RegExp)[9] are particularly useful for extracting information from a text string. What you want to do is to find all of the method names from this help text using the knowledge that each method name begins after a newline and is composed only of letters. Because it is conceivable that a method name might also include digits and possibly underscore characters, you can make use of a special RegExp meta-character to easily locate exactly this kind of character. After the method name, some whitespace occurs, followed by some text, in which you need not be particularly interested at this point. Listing 7.10 shows how you can use a regular expression to extract the method names from this help text.

Listing 7.10   Extracting Method Names with RegExp

```
1│wsadmin>import re
2│wsadmin>mNames=re.compile(r'^(\w+)(?:\s+.*)$',re.MULTILINE)
3│wsadmin>mNames.findall( Help.help() )
```

---

[8] See Chapter 9, "The AdminControl Object," for information about MBeans and how to use them.

[9] See Chapter 5, "Jython Modules," in the "Regular Expressions (RegExps)" section for more information.

```
4|['attributes', 'operations', 'constructors', 'description',
5|'notifications', 'classname', 'all', 'help', 'AdminControl',
6|'AdminConfig', 'AdminApp', 'AdminTask', 'wsadmin', 'message']
7|wsadmin>
```

Table 7.2 explains the regular expression in this example in more detail. Unfortunately, as you can see, regular expressions can be both powerful and hard to understand all at the same time. You can write a very terse and somewhat cryptic pattern that allows you to extract exactly the information you want from a text string.

Table 7.2   Method Name RegExp Explained

RegExp	Meaning
r'...'	Raw strings simplify regular expression sequences containing back-slashes.
^	Match the "beginning of line" in multiline mode.
(...)	Capture group. The matching text is saved.
\w+	One or more "word" characters (letters, digits, or underscore).
(?:...)	Non-capturing group, the matching text is discarded.
\s+	One or more whitespace (blanks and/or tabs).
.*	Zero or more characters (matches everything except a newline).
$	Match the "end of line" in multiline mode.
re.MULTILINE	Multiline flag identifies that newline characters indicate the "end of line."

Help for MBeans[10]

Given these method names (Listing 7.10, lines 4–6), you can generate the help text for each method by executing the `Help.help()` method and passing in the name of each method. An example is shown in Listing 7.11.

---

[10] See Chapter 9, "The AdminControl Object," for information about MBeans and how to use them.

Listing 7.11 Method Help

```
 1|wsadmin>print Help.help( 'attributes' )
 2|WASX7268I: Method: attributes
 3|
 4|     Arguments: MBean
 5|
 6|     Description: Display information about the attributes of
 7|     the specified MBean.
 8|
 9|     Method: attributes
10|
11|     Arguments: MBean, attribute name
12|
13|     Description: Display information about the specified
14|     attribute on the specified MBean.
15|wsadmin>
```

You can make use of the list of method names, looping over each, and generate the help for the method using a really simple group of statements. A first attempt of this is shown in Listing 7.12. It's not perfect, but it's a reasonable start.

Listing 7.12 Help for Help Methods—Attempt #1 (Helphelp1.py)

```
 1|wsadmin>import re
 2|wsadmin>mNames=re.compile(r'^(\w+)(?:\s+.*)$',re.MULTILINE)
 3|wsadmin>methods = mNames.findall( Help.help() )
 4|wsadmin>for name in methods :
 5|wsadmin>   print 'Help.help( "%s" )\n%s' % ( name, '-' * 70 )
 6|wsadmin>   print Help.help( name )
 7|wsadmin>   print '-' * 70
 8|wsadmin>
```

With minor revisions, the output looks quite reasonable. The modified version of this script is called Helphelp2.py and is available from the book's website. A small portion of this modified output is shown in Listing 7.13.

Listing 7.13 Helphelp2.py Sample Output

```
# - - - - - - - - - - - - - - - - - - - - - - - - - - - - - - - - - - - - - -
# Help.help( "attributes" )
# - - - - - - - - - - - - - - - - - - - - - - - - - - - - - - - - - - - - - -
```

```
WASX7268I: Method: attributes

        Arguments: MBean

        Description: Display information about the attributes of
        the specified MBean.

        Method: attributes

        Arguments: MBean, attribute name

        Description: Display information about the specified
        attribute on the specified MBean.
...
```

Help for MBean Attributes

Now you can finally start to develop some useful utility routines for the administration of a Web-Sphere environment. Let's begin by using the method shown in Listing 7.13. This method can be used to retrieve attributes for a given MBean.[11] For example, if you have an MBean for an active application server (svr), then the attributes for this application server can be obtained using `Help.attributes( svr )`. Remember, though, that the result of this call will be a text string, as shown in Listing 7.14.

Listing 7.14   Subset of Active Application Server Attributes

```
wsadmin>svr
'WebSphere:name=server1,process=server1,platform=proxy,node=...
wsadmin>print Help.attributes( svr )
Attribute                    Type                      Access
name                         java.lang.String          RO
shortName                    java.lang.String          RO
threadMonitorInterval        int                       RW
threadMonitorThreshold       int                       RW
...
```

Notice how each attribute has an attribute name, a type, and an access indicator showing whether the attribute value is Read-Only (RO) or Read-Write (RW). Wouldn't it be nice to have a

---

[11] Techniques for obtaining MBeans are discussed in Chapter 9, where we discuss the **AdminControl** object.

routine that could be used to retrieve all of the attributes for a given MBean and store them in a nice Jython data structure? We've written such a routine, and called it `MBattrAsDict()`, which is available in a utility module called `WAuJ_utilities`.[12] Listing 7.15 demonstrates how this routine can be used.

Listing 7.15   Example Use of `MBattrAsDict` Utility Method

```
 1 wsadmin>import WAuJ_utilities as WAuJ
 2 wsadmin>svr = AdminControl.queryNames( 'type=Server,*' )
 3 wsadmin>svrDict = WAuJ.MBattrAsDict( svr )
 4 wsadmin>names = svrDict.keys()
 5 wsadmin>names.sort()
 6 wsadmin>print '\n'.join( names )
 7 Modifiable
 8 cellName
 9 cellShortName
10 deployedObjects
11 ...
12 wsadmin>fields='name,platformName,platformVersion,processType'
13 wsadmin>for name in fields.split( ',' ) :
14 wsadmin>  print '%-15s : %s' % ( name, svrDict[ name ] )
15 wsadmin>
16 name            : server1
17 platformName    : IBM WebSphere Application Server
18 platformVersion : 6.1
19 processType     : UnManagedProcess
20 wsadmin>
```

Table 7.3 explains this example in more detail. Next, you'll see how the technique used to understand the `Help.attributes()` method can be used with other methods of this and all of the WebSphere administrative objects. In fact, the next Help method used is `Help.operations()`. Passing this method the same MBean value (`svr`) results in the list of operations available for this same MBean.

It should be no surprise when the output contains a number of routines, most of which relate to the attributes listed earlier. In fact, you should find a correlation between the attribute values and operations that can be used to get the named attribute value. These types of operations are frequently called *getters*. For those attributes identified as having Read/Write (RW) access,

---

[12] For the import in line 1 to succeed, the `WAuJ_utilities` module must be available in one of the `sys.path` directories.

Table 7.3   Example Use of `MBattrAsDict` Explained

Line(s)	Description
1	Import the `WAuJ_utilities` module using an alias (`WAuJ`).

2	Obtain an MBean identified. *Note*: This could return multiple results, so you may have to use something like:
	
	`svr=AdminControl.queryNames( 'type=Server,*'`
	`).splitlines()[ 0 ]`

3	Use `MBattrAsDict` to build a dictionary of the server attribute names and values.
4–11	Get the attribute names and display some of them in alphabetical order.
12	Specify the attribute names to be displayed.
13–14	For each of the specified attribute names, display the name and associated value.
15	In interpretive mode, a blank line is used to identify the end of the `for` statement.
16–19	Formatted output of the specified fields.

you should also find an operation that allows you to modify (set) a new value for the attribute. These types of operations are also called *setters*.

Help for MBean Operations

How do you go about figuring out how to use these operations? Let's look at a complete example, as shown in Listing 7.16. The MBean used earlier (svr) happened to be for an unmanaged server. Just as you used the `Help.attributes()` method to obtain the names of the attributes for this object, you can now use the `Help.operations()` method for the same MBean to get information about the available operations (line 5). Then, you can use the information from these two methods to identify operations for which no attribute exists. In this example, the first such operation name is `getProductVersion()` (line 8). Because you aren't familiar with this operation, you can get some additional details from the `Help.operations()` method by passing it the same MBean and the name of a specific operation in question (line 12). The output of this provides a little more specific information about this operation, but it doesn't explain how to figure out what kind of productID should be provided. However, looking a little further in the previous output from the `Help.operations()` for this same MBean, you can see an apparently related operation named `getVersionsForAllProducts()` (line 10).

Line 15 shows how to use the `AdminControl.invoke()` method to call this operation.[13] This use of the `invoke` method shows how to call an operation associated with a specific MBean when no parameters need to be provided. The output of this call (specifically, line 19) includes an example `productID` value. Given this information, line 26 shows how to invoke an MBean operation and pass it a parameter. In this case, the output from this call happens to be identical to what is seen on lines 16–24, so are not displayed. So, you're all set.

Listing 7.16   Attributes, Operations, and Invoke (Oh My!)

```
 1|wsadmin>svr = AdminControl.queryNames( 'type=Server,*' )
 2|wsadmin>print Help.attributes( svr )
 3|Attribute                    Type                      Access
 4|...
 5|wsadmin>print Help.operations( svr )
 6|Operation
 7|...
 8|java.lang.String getProductVersion(java.lang.String)
 9|...
10|[Ljava.lang.String; getVersionsForAllProducts()
11|...
12|wsadmin>print Help.operations( svr, 'getProductVersion' )
13|java.lang.String getProductVersion(java.lang.String)
14|...
15|wsadmin>print AdminControl.invoke( svr, 'getVersionsForAllProducts' )
16|<?xml version="1.0" encoding="UTF-8"?>
17|<!DOCTYPE product SYSTEM "product.dtd">
18|<product name="IBM WebSphere Application Server - ND">
19|   <id>ND</id>
20|   <version>6.1.0.17</version>
21|   <build-info
22|     date="5/28/08"
23|     level="cf170821.07"/>
24|</product>
25|
26|wsadmin>print AdminControl.invoke(svr,'getProductVersion','ND')
27|...
```

---

[13] Additional details about the invoke method are covered in Chapter 9, where we discuss the **AdminControl** object.

Help for Additional MBean Information

The `Help.constructors()` method can be used to display the parameter information for MBean types that have constructor methods. Which MBean names have constructors? You can figure it out. How should you go about finding the answer to this question? To begin, you first need to figure out how to determine the valid MBean names. Then, for each name, you can call the `Help.constructors()` method to see if it has actual usable information. When an MBean name doesn't include a constructor, what is the result of calling the `Help.constructors()` method? After you determine this, you can then use the `Help.constructors()` method to see which MBean names have other than the default, or empty, response. Listing 7.17 shows one technique for doing just this, and Table 7.4 describes the statements in detail.

Listing 7.17   Finding Constructors

```
 1|wsadmin>names = AdminControl.queryNames( '*' ).splitlines()
 2|wsadmin>Help.constructors( names[ 0 ] )
 3|'Constructors\r\n'
 4|wsadmin>len( Help.constructors( names[ 0 ] ) )
 5|14
 6|wsadmin>sep = '-' * 70
 7|wsadmin>fString = '%(sep)s\n%(name)s\n%(sep)s\n%(text)s'
 8|wsadmin>for name in names :
 9|wsadmin>  text = Help.constructors( name )
10|wsadmin>  if len( text ) > 14 :
11|wsadmin>    print fString % locals()
12|wsadmin>
13|----------------------------------------------------------------------
14|WebSphere:type=ExtClassLoader
15|----------------------------------------------------------------------
16|Constructors
17|(p1 java.lang.String)
18|(p1 java.lang.ClassLoader)
19|(p1 java.lang.String, p2 java.lang.ClassLoader)
```

Making this interactive **wsadmin** session into a script file is quite easy. Some of the things that should be done as part of this process include the following:

- Add comments and usage information to clarify what is being done and why.
- Decide whether the file should be executable as a script or imported as a module.
- Add error handling code for commonly occurring and unexpected situations.

This has been done, and the script file that was created is named `beanConstructorys.py`.

Table 7.4   Finding Constructors Explained

Line(s)	Description
1	Get the list of active MBean names.[14]
2–3	Display the constructor details for the first MBean name.
4–5	Display the length of an "empty" constructor response.
6–7	Create a separator line containing 70 hyphen characters and a `formatString` to display the data.
8–9	For each MBean name, get the constructor text for the given MBean name.
10–11	If the constructor response is not empty, display it using string formatting.
12	While using **wsadmin** as an interpreter, an empty line is needed to end a `for` loop.
13–19	Formatted output of the only MBean name that has a non-empty constructor response.

In a similar fashion, you can write a script to display the `Help.description()` information for each available MBean. The script that does this is `beanDescriptions.py`. Example output from the execution of this script file is shown in Listing 7.18.

Listing 7.18   Example Output from `beanDescriptions.py`

```
AdminOperations
  Management interface for a miscellaneous set of admin functions
AdvisorNotificationMBean
  MBean for Performance and Diagnostic Advisor Notifications
AntAgent
  null
AppManagement
  Management interface for application management functions.
Application
  Management interface for a J2EE Application.
ApplicationManager
  Interface for managing the lifecycle of applications.
...
```

It should be noted at this point that this particular script does not process the `Help.descriptions()` text much at all. Some of the descriptions are quite long and as such may

---

[14] The **AdminControl** object and associated methods are discussed in Chapter 9.

benefit from some additional code to rearrange the text. This enhancement code is also left as an exercise to the reader.

Similarly, another script has been written, named `beanNotifications.py`, to display the notifications that are available for the active MBeans. Unfortunately, because of space limitations, additional information about notifications is beyond the scope of this book.

The output from the `Help.classname()` method is, for almost all of the active MBeans in an unmanaged application server, `javax.management.modelmbean.RequiredModelMBean`. So although a script named `beanClassnames.py` is provided, no additional discussion should be needed.

The last of the MBean-related help methods can be used to obtain all of the preceding help-related information in one place, meaning that the result of calling `Help.all()` for a particular active MBean is very similar to calling all of the following for the same MBean and merging the resulting text:

```
Help.attributes()
Help.operations()
Help.constructors()
Help.description()
Help.notifications()
Help.classname()
```

A script named `beanInformation.py` is provided that shows a simple way to display this information. Unfortunately, as was mentioned earlier, very little effort has been put into making this output "pretty."

Help for Other Administrative Objects

Can you write a simple script that captures some help for the other administration objects? For most of them, the answer is yes. For each of the following administrative objects, the main help text has methods that start at the beginning of a line and are followed by whitespace: **AdminApp**, **AdminControl**, **AdminConfig**, **Help**.

So the same kind of code used to display the help for all of the **Help** methods would work for them. In fact, with a little bit of work, you can combine all of these objects into a single data structure and use this to produce all of the help for all of these objects and their methods with one little script. The script that does this is called `ObjHelp.py` and is included with the other scripts for this chapter. As its usage information shows, it can be used as shown in Listing 7.19.

Listing 7.19   ObjHelp Usage

```
Unix:
    ./wsadmin.sh  -conntype none -WAuJ -f ObjHelp.py >ObjHelp.out


Windows:
    wsadmin[.bat] -conntype none -WAuJ -f ObjHelp.py >ObjHelp.out
```

Used like this, an output file approximately 1,800 lines long is generated that has the help text for four of the five administrative objects all in one place. This gathering of information can be much easier to use and search with a text editor.

The last administrative object, **AdminTask**, is a different beast, as can be seen by looking at its help. Instead of having a collection of methods, the **AdminTask** has commands and commandGroups. Looking at the output of print AdminTask.help('-commands'), you can see that the "command names" look very much like the "method names" that exist for the other Help objects. In fact, we can reuse the same RegExp to extract the command names from this text as you used for extracting the method names for the other **Help** object.

If you take a close look at the AdminTask.help() output, you will see that in addition to being able to execute AdminTask.help(commandName), you can also specify an optional stepName parameter for extra information.

Looking at the output of the script as it exists, you have to go a long way before finding a command that includes a step. So enhancing this script to add checks for stepName checks and displaying the associated help text is left as an exercise for you.

Help for WebSphere Messages

This is the last of the **Help** methods and can be used to (possibly) obtain addition additional information about a particular WebSphere Application Server message identifier. For example, should the default application server not be available when **wsadmin** is invoked, an error message with the identifier 'WASX7023E' is displayed as in Listing 7.20.

Listing 7.20   Example Use of Help.message() Method

```
C:\IBM\WebSphere\AppServer\bin>wsadmin
WASX7023E: Error creating "SOAP" connection to host "localhost"; ...
wsadmin>print Help.message('WASX7023E' )
Explanation: An error was reported from the connector when trying to
establish a connection to the host.
User action: Examine the accompanying exception information and the
information in the wsadmin.traceout file to determine the cause of the
error.
```

Useful Information

One of the things that we have done to it a little bit easier for ourselves is to bookmark some frequently used pages in the online documentation.

Following pages can be particularly useful:

- Commands for the **AdminApp** object

- Commands for the **AdminConfig** object
- Commands for the **AdminControl** object
- Commands for the **AdminTask** object
- Commands for the **Help** object

Occasionally, while providing technical support for the WebSphere Application Server distributed product, we have encountered some people who did not know how to get to either the WebSphere Application Server support or the Application Server documentation pages. The URL for the Application Server support page is http://IBM.com/software/webservers/appserv/was/support.

On the left side of this page, you can find a link labeled Library that can be used to get to the main documentation page. On this page, select the tab corresponding to the version of the Application Server product you are using (for example, V 7.0, V 6.1). Next, select the link for the product edition (such as, "Network Deployment—distributed platforms").

At this point, you should see a page showing general information entitled "WebSphere Application Server documentation" on the right and a section hierarchy for different editions of the selected product version on the left. If you selected the "Network Deployment" edition, then that portion of the documentation hierarchy will be selected, with the sub-headings for that document expanded below it.

When you first access the documentation, the "Search scope," just above the contents section on the left, shows as "All topics." We find this particular choice somewhat frustrating because it means that whenever we search for word or phrase, its existence in each edition of the documentation will be located. Therefore, we suggest that you take a moment and click the "Search scope" link to open the "Select Search Scope" dialog box.

If the topic section is blank, then no topic groups have been defined. Click the "New..." button to open the "New Search List" dialog box. To define a topic, you can select an entire "book" (Network Deployment, for example) or something more granular (such as expand the Network Deployment section by clicking on the plus ' + ' beside it and locating a section of special interest, such as, "Scripting the application serving environment"). Once one or more selections have been checked, provide a unique name that has some specific meaning to you and enter it into the "List name" input field at the top. Clicking the "OK" button causes the dialog box to close and the named entry to appear in the topic selection area. Selecting the "Search only the following topics" radio button, selecting one of the topics listed, and clicking the "OK" button causes the "Select Search Scope" dialog box to close and the "Search scope" value adjacent to the link to reflect the portion of the documentation to be searched.

For this example, we created a search scope labeled "6.1 ND" to search all of the Network Deployment document for the 6.1 version of the product. This allowed us to enter a search string, "**AdminApp**," in the Search input field, and press enter. The result showed the page in which we were interested at the top of the list.

At this point, we found it best to click the list to display the page of interest; then, in the right pane (on the page that shows "Commands for the **AdminApp** object"), we right-clicked and selected "This Frame, Show Only this Frame." This forced the address as well as the table of contents pane on the left to be updated. This is the point that we suggest you bookmark.

Scrolling to the bottom of this page we found a link for the "Options for the **AdminApp** object..." page referenced earlier. We suggest that you use this link to view the page and then "Show Only this Frame" and bookmark this page as well. Scrolling to the bottom of this page, you find the link for the "Usage table..." page mentioned earlier. Then, you can search for the other administrative objects and use this same technique to bookmark these pages as well. This will provide you with a useful set of bookmarks for the **wsadmin** administrative objects.

Summary

In this chapter, we discussed the **wsadmin** Help object, as well as the help method that exists in each of the other administrative scripting objects. Hopefully, the discussion and examples provided leave you with a more thorough understanding of what is available from the Help object.

The AdminConfig Object

"Architecture starts when you carefully put two bricks together."

—*Ludwig Mies van der Rohe*

One of the most valuable things that **wsadmin** allows us to do is manipulate the AppServer configuration. In fact, what is really important about this is the fact that **wsadmin** can perform this configuration manipulation when the AppServer is stopped. To perform this manipulation, you must know how to use the **AdminConfig** scripting object, which this chapter covers in great detail.

AdminConfig Overview

Looking at the **AdminConfig.help()** text,[1] you see that this object can be used to perform several operations on WebSphere Application Server configuration objects. These operations include the following:

- List
- Create
- Remove
- Display
- Modify

WARNING   Modifying a WebSphere Application Server configuration using scripting can render it invalid.

---

[1] This is explained further in Chapter 7, "Introduction to Admin Objects."

Hopefully this warning encourages you to be careful when modifying a configuration. Additionally, if changes are made to a managed node configuration while in "local mode,"[2] a subsequent node synchronization request can cause any such changes to be discarded. Before making changes to your configuration, you should familiarize yourself with the `backupConfig` command script and make sure to save your configuration. Visit the WebSphere Application Server Information Center for documentation on the `backupConfig` and `restoreConfig` utilities.

There are some challenges to learning how to use the WebSphere administration scripting objects within **wsadmin**, the greatest of which is the confusion about which administrative objects deal with which kinds of items. Some objects require a configuration identifier (config ID), while others require an MBean identifier. How, then, do you know which is to be used and when?

Configuration Identifier (config ID)

The simple answer is that administration objects that deal with configuration information require a config ID, whereas objects that deal with active application server resources require an MBean identifier. Let's take a quick look at an example config ID, as shown in Listing 8.1.[3]

Listing 8.1   Example config ID

```
server1(cells/ragibsonNode01Cell/nodes/ragibsonNode00/servers/
server1|server.xml#Server_1219933843508)
```

Figure 8.1 shows a slightly different perspective of the information specified in this config ID. This listing shows the directory structure under the WebSphere Application Server installation directory for which this config ID applies (that is, `.../profiles/AppSrv00/config`). Notice how we can use each portion of the config ID, in Listing 8.1, to traverse the directory structure shown in Figure 8.1 to the exact location of the applicable configuration file (`server.xml`). Each portion of the config ID from Listing 8.1 is underlined in Figure 8.1 to more easily locate and identify each element.

What about that "stuff" after the filename, specifically the `Server_1219933843508`? If you look at the contents of the specified file, you find that this information is contained within the file as an attribute of the `process:Server` tag (that is, `xmi:id="Server_1219933843508"`). So not only does the config ID point directly to a specific file, but it also identifies a unique element within that XML configuration file.

The fact that you can use a config ID to locate a specific file and XML tag within the file should not be taken as encouragement to do so. Please let **wsadmin** and the scripting objects do this for you. Manual manipulation of an XML configuration file could easily invalidate the configuration.

---

[2] Starting **wsadmin** with –conntype none as one of the command-line options forces it to be in local mode.

[3] Unfortunately, config IDs can be so long that they won't fit on a single line unless you use a very small font. The config ID shown should, in fact, be a contiguous string containing no end-of-line characters.

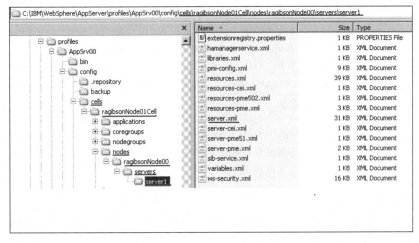

Figure 8.1   Directory structure view of config ID

Containment Path

Another frequently asked question is, "How do I get the config ID for a particular configuration object?" Well, there a few different ways to do it. Choose one technique over the other based on your personal preferences and the information you have available.

In the documentation, the most common technique uses the `AdminConfig.getid()` method to obtain a config ID. However, this call requires that a containment path be provided. A *containment path* is a collection of one or more name/value pairs in a specific order. The name portion is required and is a configuration object type and is followed by a colon and an optional value. The name/value pairs are delimited using the slash character `'/'`. Some example containment paths would be `'/Cell:/'`, or `'/Cell:myCellName/'`. Each containment path, when passed to the `AdminConfig.getid()` method, result in zero or more config IDs. Listing 8.2 shows some example calls to `AdminConfig.getid()` using a containment path (lines 3 and 5).

Listing 8.2   Example Use of `AdminConfig.getid()`

```
1|wsadmin>cell = AdminControl.getCell()
2|wsadmin>node = AdminControl.getNode()
3|wsadmin>print AdminConfig.getid( '/Cell:%s' % cell )
4|ragibsonNode02Cell(cells/ragibsonNode02Cell|cell.xml#Cell_1)
5|wsadmin>print AdminConfig.getid( '/Node:%s' % node )
6|ragibsonNode03(cells/ragibsonNode02Cell/nodes/ragibsonNode...
7|wsadmin>print AdminConfig.getid( '/Node:%s/Cell:%s' % ( node, cell ) )
8|
9|wsadmin>
```

Should multiple name/value pairs exist within the containment path, the sequence of the name/value pairs must match the hierarchy of the types in the WebSphere environment. This means that the first type specified should contain objects of the second type specified, and so on. For example, a containment path in which the first type specified was `Cell` and the second type specified was `Node` would be valid because a cell is composed of node objects. However, a containment path where the first type is `Node` and the second type is `Cell` would not be valid because the hierarchical relationship does not match that of the WebSphere objects. Listing 8.2 (lines 7–8) shows that using an invalid containment path results in no match being found in the configuration. Additional information about this configuration object relationship is covered in the "Create and Modify Methods" section later in the chapter.

Configuration Types

What configuration object types exist? A call to `AdminConfig.types()` can be used to get a list of all valid types. A small, stand-alone script (`AdminConfigTypes.py`) is provided that displays these types, identifies the number of types, and gives the length of the shortest and longest.

When you execute the script on a version 6.1 installation, almost 600 supported types exist. For a version 7.0 installation, it was closer to 800. This means you can't possibly cover these types in any amount of detail. What you can try to do is to present some techniques for investigating types and the object methods that use them. Hopefully these techniques will assist you in your investigations about those types in which you are interested that are not discussed within this book.

In addition to the `getid()` method, the `AdminConfig.list()` method can also be used to find one or more config IDs. For example, the config ID shown in Listing 8.1 happens to be for an unmanaged application server. The technique used to obtain this server config ID depends upon your environment. For an unmanaged application server, it can be as simple as using something like `print AdminConfig.list('Server')`.

What's the difference between using the `getid()` and `list()` methods to obtain a config ID, and why might you prefer one method over the other? The primary difference is that when the `AdminConfig.list()` method is used, a type is specified (for example, `'Server'`) instead of a containment path. The result of this call can therefore include multiple objects.[4] By using the `getid()` method and providing qualified name/value pairs, the result might already be "filtered."[5] In this case, additional processing to identify or select one of the results might not be necessary. For example, Listing 8.3 shows how an unqualified containment path (lines 5–8) is the same as using the call to `AdminConfig.list()` and specifying the same type (lines 1–4). However, by qualifying the containment path (lines 9–10), no additional code is needed to get to the specific config ID in question (that is, server1).

---

[4] For example, the result of calling `AdminConfig.list('Server').splitline()` in a clustered environment should result in a list containing all of the config IDs of all of the application server in the cell.

[5] The result of calling `AdminConfig.getid('/Cell:cellName/Node:nodeName/').splitlines()` contains only config IDs of items within the specified containment path, not the entire cell.

Listing 8.3 `AdminConfig.list()` and `getid()` Method Examples

```
 1│wsadmin>print AdminConfig.list( 'Server' )
 2│dmgr(cells/ragibsonCell01/nodes/...#Server_1)
 3│nodeagent(cells/ragibsonCell01/nodes/...#Server_1219937362939)
 4│server1(cells/ragibsonCell01/nodes/...#Server_1219934689484)
 5│wsadmin>print AdminConfig.getid( '/Server:/' )   .
 6│dmgr(cells/ragibsonCell01/nodes/...#Server_1)
 7│nodeagent(cells/ragibsonCell01/nodes/...#Server_1219937362939)
 8│server1(cells/ragibsonCell01/nodes/...#Server_1219934689484)
 9│wsadmin>print AdminConfig.getid( '/Server:server1/' )
10│server1(cells/ragibsonCell01/nodes/...#Server_1219934689484)
```

Because both the `list()` and the `getid()` method can result in multiple values, it is best to have your scripts takes this into account. To do so, use the string `splitlines()` method to convert the string into a list of strings, with each element being the config ID of an application server. The `splitlines()` routine uses end-of-line markers as line delimiters.[6] Should the result of the `AdminConfig.list()` call be a single entry (for example, a single application server), the result of the `splitlines()` call will be a single element list.

Using a config ID

What can be done once you have a config ID? One of the most useful **AdminConfig** methods is `AdminConfig.show()`, which can be use used to provide information about the specific attributes and values that exist for the resource identified by the specified config ID. As seen in Listing 8.4 (lines 3–14), you can see that the result is many lines of text, with each line containing something that looks like a name/value pair. Interestingly enough, each line starts and ends with square brackets (`'[]'`). One way to use this information would be to process, or parse, each line, searching for entries of interest. However, there is an easier and better way.

Listing 8.4 `AdminConfig.show()` Example

```
1│wsadmin>server = AdminConfig.list('Server').splitlines()[ 0 ]
2│wsadmin>print AdminConfig.show( server )
3│[components "[...]"]
4│[customServices []]
5│[developmentMode false]
6│[errorStreamRedirect (...)]
7│[name server1]
```

---

[6] Please note that the string `splitlines()` method that exists in the version of Jython in WebSphere Application Server 6.0 doesn't work as expected, so you should use `split('\n')` instead.

```
 8|[outputStreamRedirect (...)]
 9|[parallelStartEnabled true]
10|[processDefinitions [...]]
11|[serverType APPLICATION_SERVER]
12|[services "[...]"]
13|[stateManagement (...)]
14|[statisticsProvider (...)]
```

Using the understanding of how the text result of the show() method is formatted, it is a simple matter to create a routine to call the show() method for a given config ID and convert the result into a dictionary, which can then be returned. A routine to do just this was created and is part of a collection of utility routines provided in a module name WAuJ_utilities. Listing 8.5 shows an example use of this routine to demonstrate its usefulness, and Table 8.1 explains this example in detail.

Listing 8.5 Example Use of showAsDict Function

```
1|wsadmin>import WAuJ_utilities as WAuJ
2|wsadmin>server = AdminConfig.list( 'Server' ).splitlines()[ 0 ]
3|wsadmin>dict    = WAuJ.showAsDict( server )
4|wsadmin>for name in 'name,serverType'.split( ',' ) :
5|wsadmin>  print '%-10s : %s' % ( name, dict[ name ] )
6|wsadmin>
7|name       : server1
8|serverType : APPLICATION_SERVER
9|wsadmin>
```

Table 8.1 showAsDict Example Explained

Line(s)	Description
1	Import the utility module using an alias (WAuJ).
2	Assignment statement used to obtain the config ID of the first Application Server.
3	Use of the showAsDict() method to call AdminConfig.show() using the specified config ID and to convert the output into a dictionary.
4–9	The dictionary keys, or indexes, can be used to display individual dictionary entries that correspond to the names seen in Listing 8.4. For this example, only the name and serverType name/value pairs are displayed.

The usefulness of a routine like showAsDict() should be readily apparent, especially to anyone who has tried writing code to extract a particular piece of information out of the text returned by an **AdminConfig** or any of the other object methods. Being able to write something simple like dict['name'] to access the name attribute of a given object is very powerful (and intuitive).

Show and Tell Methods

Other **AdminConfig** methods exist that can also be used to learn more about specific types with which you are working. For example, the attributes() method can be used to "show the attributes for a given type," where the show() method will "Show the attributes of a given configuration object." We have already discussed and seen the results of using the AdminConfig.show() method. The parameter for the AdminConfig.attributes() method is a configuration type, so you use print AdminConfig.attributes('Server') to display the attributes that are available for application servers.

Listing 8.6 contains a more complicated interactive session that demonstrates one way to process the results of the AdminConfig.show(), and attributes() methods in order identify attributes that don't exist in the output of show() for a particular application server. Table 8.2 explains the interactive session in detail. Note how the showAttribute() method is used to display the attribute information for a given configuration object.

Listing 8.6   Missing Attributes with No Default Value

```
 1|wsadmin>from WAuJ_utilities import showAsDict
 2|wsadmin>import re
 3|wsadmin>server=AdminConfig.list('Server').splitlines()[0]
 4|wsadmin>sDict =showAsDict(server)
 5|wsadmin>aPat  = re.compile('^(\w+)(?:\s+.*)$', re.MULTILINE)
 6|wsadmin>aNames=aPat.findall(AdminConfig.attributes('Server'))
 7|wsadmin>missing=[x for x in aNames if not sDict.has_key( x )]
 8|wsadmin>for name in missing :
 9|wsadmin>  try :
10|wsadmin>    attr = AdminConfig.showAttribute( server, name )
11|wsadmin>  except :
12|wsadmin>    attr = '<unknown>'
13|wsadmin>  print '%-17s %s' % ( name, attr )
14|wsadmin>
15|adjustPort          <unknown>
16|clusterName         None
17|modelId             None
18|processDefinition None
19|serverInstance      None
20|shortName           None
21|uniqueId            None
```

Table 8.2   Explanation of Missing Attributes with No Default Value

Lines(s)	Detailed Explanation
1	Import the `showAsDict` utility method for converting `AdminConfig.show()` results to dictionary form.
2	Import the regular expression (`re`) module.
3	Use `AdminConfig.list()` to locate a valid application server config ID.
4	Use `showAsDict()` to get a dictionary of the available attributes for the specified server.
5	Create a RegExp pattern object to extract attribute names from multi-line text string.
6	Use the RegExp object to extract the attribute names from the `attributes()` text.
7	Use list comprehension to build a list of attribute names that don't exist in the `show()` result for the given application server configuration object.
8–13	Try to use `AdminConfig.showAttribute()` to obtain the value of the missing attribute in the given server and format the `showAttribute()` result.
14	Blank line used in interactive mode to designate the end of the preceding `for` loop.
15–21	Formatted output generated by the `for` loop, showing that `showAttributes()` returns `None` for almost all of the undefined attributes.

Note the use of a `try/except` clause to define an exception handler for special cases. |

Interestingly enough, some of the entries listed from the `attributes()` method call don't appear from the earlier call to the `show()` method. If you look again at the methods listed in the help text, you see that another method called `defaults()` exists. Printing the help for this method shows what appears to be an overlap of function between the two methods (`attributes` and `defaults`). However, if you print the output from each method in which you specify the type parameter as `'Server'`, the descriptions are significantly different. The output of the two routines might also raise some questions.

If an attribute doesn't have a configured value, then you would expect that attribute to have a default value. Why do we find attributes for which no default value is provided? And there is yet another **AdminConfig** method called `required()`. If you display the required attributes for type `'Server'`, using a statement like `print AdminConfig.required('Server')`, you see that only the name attribute is required. How is it that so few are required as well as so few default attributes? Does the `AdminConfig.showAttribute()` method return a value for the undefined attributes that don't have a default value? Unfortunately, these are questions only the developers could answer.

The last of the "show and tell" methods, as we like to think of them, is the `AdminConfig.showall()` method. The difference between the `show()` and `showall()` methods is that the `show()` method returns the attributes of the specified configuration object, and the `showall()` method does that as well as recursively including all of attributes of the referenced configuration objects. For example, given a configuration object for an unmanaged application server (e.g., as seen in Listing 8.4) using `AdminConfig.show()` results in 12 attributes. On the other hand, using `AdminConfig.showall()` results in almost than 650 attributes and nested attributes.

The unfortunate thing about the results of using the `showall()` method is that the result is difficult to analyze at least programmatically. Is there anything that we can do to traverse a configuration object hierarchy searching for a specific attribute? Well, nothing is provided, so you have to develop your own.

How might you go about doing this? Let's begin by taking a look at the information that exists in the output from calling the `AdminConfig.show()` method using some config ID. Because the `showAsDict()` routine does this and returns a dictionary, it should be easy to realize that each line of the result should contain a name/value pair. What kind values are returned? It depends on the kind of configuration object that was passed to the `show()` method.

Listing 8.4, shown earlier, details possible values such as the following:

- Empty lists (that is, open and closed square brackets [])
- Names, or identifiers (for example, `true`, `false`, `server1`, `APPLICATION_SERVER`)
- Numeric values (such as port numbers, threshold values, and timeouts)
- Single config ID (with or without the leading name)
- Config ID lists (contained within [...])

The ones of special interest at this time are the ones containing either a single config ID or a config ID list. What you need to be able to do in order to traverse the configuration object hierarchy is to be able to recognize, extract, and use these config IDs in order to process the referenced configuration object.

The best way to identify a single config ID is by using a regular expression (RegExp). How do you build a RegExp to identify a config ID? Very, very carefully. The important part is to realize that they begin and end with parentheses (with an optional identifier prefix). What would this kind of RegExp look like? Simply stated, the expression is `'^(\w*\([^)]+\))$'`. Table 8.3 explains this RegExp in detail.

Table 8.3 config ID RegExp Explained

Metachars	Meaning
^	Match beginning of string
(...)	Identify the "group" of text to be captured
\w*	Zero or more "word" characters (i.e., letters, digits, or underscore)
\(	Match an open parenthesis character

Table 8.3   config ID RegExp Explained

Metachars	Meaning
[^)]+	Match one or more characters that are not a closing parenthesis
\)	Match a closing parenthesis character
$	Match end of string

A similar RegExp for config ID lists is `'^"?\[([^\]]+)]"?$'`. It differs from the previous RegExp in the following aspects:

- Optional surrounding double quotation marks
- Surrounding square brackets ([])
- Space between each config ID

The good news is that these work great for the vast majority of config identifiers. The bad news is that in testing, we found something that we did not expect. It is valid to have a config ID that has a name (the portion before the opening parenthesis) containing blanks. If a blank exists in the name, the whole config ID is surrounded by double quotes. This means that the simple RegExp pattern (for example, the `'\w*'`) isn't valid for all config IDs. So the new and improved RegExp to match this more complete understanding of config IDs would be `'(\w*\([^)]+\))|"[ \w]+\([^)]+\)")'`. The first part of this RegExp pattern (the portion before the `'|'`) is the same. The second part allows double quotes as well as spaces within the name. The revised code is available in findAllAttributes.py, and includes code that demonstrates how the function can be used.

The "test" code that is included within findAllAttributes.py script (that is, the code executed when the file is executed instead of being imported) tries to find attributes having the name "port." Interestingly enough, this code doesn't provide information about all of the ports that are used by an application server. Unfortunately, this code is quite a bit harder to understand and follow. Additionally, it is not clear how useful or applicable that it might be without additional experimentation and testing.

A better and more useful example would be a script that could be used to find and display the port numbers configured for an application server. Interestingly enough, this script is very easy to create and, in fact, has been provided in the script named ListPorts.py.[7] The sample output of this script is shown in Listing 8.7. To perform this task, the script only needs to:

---

[7] It is not as easy as using an existing method like AdminTask.reportConfiguredPorts(), but we haven't gotten to the **AdminTask** scripting object yet. Additionally, the output of ListPorts.py looks better.

1. Obtain the list of ServerEntry config IDs using:

   ```
   SEs = AdminConfig.list( 'ServerEntry' ).splitlines()
   ```

2. For each ServerEntry config ID, get the NamedEndPoint config IDs using:

   ```
   NEPs = AdminConfig.list( 'NamedEndPoint', SE ).splitlines()
   ```

3. For each NamedEndPoint, use the `endPoint` attribute to get the port number:

   ```
   for NEP in NEPs :
     NEPdict = showAsDict( NEP )
     EPdict  = showAsDict( NEPdict[ 'endPoint' ] )
     print EPdict[ 'port' ], NEPdict[ 'endPointName' ]
   ```

This shows how challenging it can be to access a particular kind of information from the configuration. It requires quite a bit of knowledge (such as the configuration type names of the objects), as well as some perseverance to get the information you want displayed in a specific format. However, it also shows how easy and intuitive it can be to use a utility routine like `showAsDict()` to simplify your programs at the same time they are being made easier to read and understand.

Listing 8.7 Sample Output of `ListPorts.py`

```
Server name: server1

Port#|EndPoint Name
-----+-------------
 2809|BOOTSTRAP_ADDRESS
 8880|SOAP_CONNECTOR_ADDRESS
 9401|SAS_SSL_SERVERAUTH_LISTENER_ADDRESS
 9403|CSIV2_SSL_SERVERAUTH_LISTENER_ADDRESS
 9402|CSIV2_SSL_MUTUALAUTH_LISTENER_ADDRESS
 9060|WC_adminhost
 9080|WC_defaulthost
 9353|DCS_UNICAST_ADDRESS
 9043|WC_adminhost_secure
 9443|WC_defaulthost_secure
 5060|SIP_DEFAULTHOST
 5061|SIP_DEFAULTHOST_SECURE
 7276|SIB_ENDPOINT_ADDRESS
 7286|SIB_ENDPOINT_SECURE_ADDRESS
 5558|SIB_MQ_ENDPOINT_ADDRESS
 5578|SIB_MQ_ENDPOINT_SECURE_ADDRESS
 9100|ORB_LISTENER_ADDRESS
```

Create and Modify Methods

Another category of **AdminConfig** methods is associated with the creation and modification of objects. Let's begin by taking a look at what is required to create a configuration object like an application server. Looking at the help for the create() method,[8] you find that the Type, the Parent, and Attribute parameters are required.

The Type parameter is pretty straightforward because it is used to identify the kind of object to be created. But what does the Parent parameter represent? To understand that, it is important to realize that you can't create stand-alone configuration objects. Every object has a place in the configuration hierarchy. So the Parent parameter is the config ID of an existing object that is allowed to "contain" the kind of object being created. This means that each object type can only occur in specific places in the object hierarchy.

Is there a way to find out the kinds of objects that are allowed to be parents for a specific type? Yes, there is. To do this, you can use the AdminConfig.parents() method and pass it the configuration type you want to create. For example, executing print AdminConfig. parents('Server').splitlines() results in ['Node', 'ServerCluster'] being displayed. This means that to create a server object, you must provide the config ID of either a Node object, or a ServerCluster object.

Can you use the AdminConfig.parents() method and the AdminConfig.types() method to determine all of the allowed parent/child object relationships? Sure, to do so, you first need to find out what is returned by the AdminConfig.parents() method when a type is specified for which a parent type does not exist. Once that is done, you can build a simple script to generate the list of configuration type names. For each type name, you can also determine the valid parent types that can contain objects of the current type.

Our first attempt at writing a script to use this technique can be found in parents.00.py. It includes no "unnecessary" code and simply displays the configuration types for which the AdminConfig.parents() method returns a "valid" result. This is kind of alright, but the output is hard to read. With a little additional code (as found in parents.01.py), the information can be displayed in an easier to read format. The main thing wrong with this output though, is the fact that the information is displayed from the perspective of the different configuration types. For each type, you can see the valid parent types listed.

How can you turn this around? Instead of listing the valid parent types for each type, what would it take to list the valid child types for parent type? That's what happens with the parentTypes.py script. This provides an easier to understand representation of the hierarchical relationships. A portion of the output from this script is shown in Listing 8.8. The types on the left are allowed (by the WebSphere Application Server product) to be parent types. For each of these valid parent types, the right column shows the allowed "child" types.

---

[8] That is, print AdminConfig.help('create').

Listing 8.8 Example `ParentTypes.py` Output

```
- - - - - - - - - - - - - - - - - - - - - - - - - - - - - - - - - - - - - - - - -

Parent type                   : Allowed child type(s)

- - - - - - - - - - - - - - - - - - - - - - - - - - - - - - - - - - - - - - - - -

AuthorizationGroup            : AuthorizationTableExt
CacheProvider                 : CacheInstance
                                ObjectCacheInstance
                                ResourceEnvEntry
                                ServletCacheInstance
Cell                          : AuthorizationGroup
                                AuthorizationTableExt
                                CORBAObjectNameSpaceBinding
                                CacheProvider
                                CoreGroup
. . .
```

Now that you understand what the Parent parameter represents, you can use the following steps to create a new configuration object:

1. Decide the type of object to be created.
2. Locate the type name using the `AdminConfig.types()` method.
3. Verify that an object of this type can be created using `AdminConfig.parents()`.
4. Identify the required, default, and allowed attributes for this type using the `AdminConfig.required()`, `AdminConfig.defaults()`, and `AdminConfig.attributes()` methods.
5. Identify the appropriate Parent type of the new object.
6. Locate the config ID of the object under which the new object is to be created.
7. Determine the necessary attribute values that need to be provided to the create call.
8. Call the `AdminConfig.create()` method to create the desired object using the appropriate parameters.

For something like a `Server` (which only requires that the name attribute be specified), this could be as simple as the following:

```
node = AdminConfig.getid('/Node:/').splitlines()[-1]
attr = [['name','serverName']]
server = AdminConfig.create( 'Server', node, attr )
```

Wow, that's pretty simple. Is that all there is? Almost, but not quite. One of the things that **wsadmin** does is to provides a level of protection. When any configuration change is made, this change is not actually made to the existing configuration. These changes are kept in a workspace separate from the permanent configuration. All changes to the configuration are stored in this workspace until the changes are committed (using the `AdminConfig.save()` method) or discarded, either by terminating **wsadmin** (using either the quit, or exit command[9]) or by calling the `AdminConfig.reset()` method.

What if you change your mind about the object you created? If that was the only change made, you could simply discard all of the changes. However, if you are uncertain about all of the changes, you can first display the list of modified files (using the `print AdminConfig.queryChanges()` statement), or you can obtain the config ID of the created object and then use the `AdminConfig.remove()` method to remove this object from the configuration. Remember, though, that should you invoke the `remove()` method, the specified object is not actually removed from a saved configuration until the `AdminConfig.save()` method is called.

A call to the `AdminConfig.hasChanges()` method can be used to determine whether or not changes have been made to the configuration. The result of this call is either 0, which indicates that no changes have been made, or 1, which indicates that unsaved changes exist in the workspace.

The last method in this category is the `AdminConfig.modify()` method. As you might expect, it can be used to make changes to the attributes of a particular configuration object. To do so, a config ID is required, as well as the list of attributes to be modified. A trivial example to demonstrate this would be the following:

```
node = AdminConfig.list( 'Node' ).splitlines()[-1]
server = AdminConfig.create( 'Server', node, [['name','A']] )
AdminConfig.modify( server, [['name','B']] )
print AdminConfig.show( server )
AdminConfig.reset()
```

From this, you would see that the `name` attribute of the created server object was modified by the call to the `AdminConfig.modify()` method.

Configuration Verification/Validation

This chapter started with a warning about the possibility of corrupting a configuration using scripting. A number of questions come to mind related to what you can do to protect your WebSphere configuration from corruption. Is there a way to check for a corrupt or invalid configuration? What can be done to minimize the possibility of configuration corruption? What happens if conflicts exist in the configuration?

The **wsadmin** utility is configured, by default, to use the highest level of protection and verification available. As was discussed in Chapter 6, in the section "The **wsadmin** Environment Initialization Phase," many of these default settings are configurable in the `wsadmin.properties` file

---

[9] Should modification be made when either the quit or exit command are issued, a warning message will be displayed to remind you to save your changes should you desire to do so.

that is loaded when **wsadmin** starts. The settings provided in the properties file that are related to validation/verification are as follows:

- `validationOutput`
- `validationLevel`
- `crossDocumentValidationEnabled`

Each of these attributes has a prefix of `com.ibm.ws.scripting`, and each has a comment block in the properties file identifying the role provided by each attribute, as well as the default value, should one exist.

If your script needs to query or change either of the last two attribute values, the **AdminConfig** object has getter and setter methods to do so. Specifically, you would use `getValidationLevel()`, `setValidationLevel()`, `getCrossDocumentValidation Enabled()`, and the `setCrossDocumentValidationEnabled()` methods.

Interestingly enough, both the getter and setter for each of these values returns a string containing the requested setting. In each case, the last blank delimited word in the result is either the current value (in the case of the getter method) or the value after making the requested change (in the case of the setter method). So, in order to save, or access this value, you can use something like `val=AdminConfig.setValidationlevel('high').split(' ')[-1]`.

Another related setting exists for which only getter and setter methods are available (i.e., no corresponding attribute is available within the `wsadmin.properties` file). The possible `saveMode` values are `'rollbackOnConflict'` (the default) and `'overwriteOnConflict'`. This value defines the action to be performed should a configuration conflict occur during a request to save the configuration.

So some amount of checking is performed during a configuration save request. Additionally, a call to the `AdminConfig.validate()` method can be used to perform a configuration validation. The result of this call will be a string identifying the number of validation messages generated (and written to the specified file) based on the current workspace contents, the value of the cross-document validation-enabled flag, and the validation level setting.

Please note that with the highest level of validation enabled (which is the default setting), calling the `AdminConfig.validate()` method can result in messages being written to the validation output file even before any change to the configuration has been made.

The result of calling the `AdminConfig.validate()` method is a string that includes the name of the validation output file and the number of each severity message written to the output file.

Should you be interested in determining the number of messages of each severity that were written to the output file without parsing the `validate()` result string, another method exists. Calling `AdminConfig.getValidationSeverityResult()` and passing a numeric (severity) value returns a number representing the number of messages of the specified severity that were written to the validation output file.

Document Manipulation Methods

Another category of methods exists that should be used with caution. These methods are related to the direct manipulation of files, or documents in a specific portion of the application server configuration hierarchy. The methods are `checkin()`, `createDocument()`, `deleteDocument()`, `existsDocument()`, and `extract()`.

An example script has been provided (`documents.py`) that shows one way in which these methods might be used. Please note the restriction that exists that limits the location(s) of these "documents" within the application server hierarchy.

WARNING   Just because you can use these methods to copy WebSphere Application Server configuration (i.e., XML) files out of the directory structure and then edit and replace them, this should not be taken as encouragement to do so. It is extremely important that WebSphere configuration files be managed by the administrative objects.

Miscellaneous Methods

The remainder of the **AdminConfig** methods are grouped together simply as a matter of convenience. The first of these methods are related to clusters:

- `convertToCluster()`—Used to convert an existing server configuration object to ServerCluster configuration object.

- `createClusterMember()`—Used to create a new ServerCluster configuration object in an existing cluster and on an existing node.

The former is used in a script of the same name (`convertToCluster.py`) that is available with the other scripts. Interestingly enough, in order to create a fairly complete script that performs a reasonable amount of error checking and verification doesn't require that many lines of code. At first glance, `convertToCluster.py` appears to have a little over 300 lines of code, but this is slightly misleading. There are lots of comment and empty (or blank) lines. When these are removed, it seems that approximately 75–80 lines of code were needed in order to provide a complete script that makes use of this **AdminConfig** method for converting an existing application server into a cluster member. We've found that quite powerful.

The latter is also demonstrated in a script of the same name as the **AdminConfig** method. It is a bit more complicated than the previous example. It also requires less than 200 lines of executable code and less than 350 total lines to have a reasonable script that includes command line parameter processing, script usage (documentation) information, error checking, exception handling, and numerous comments to explain how the script functions.

Two of the **AdminConfig** miscellaneous methods are related to Templates. The first of these, `listTemplates()`, is used in the `createClusterMember.py` example script to obtain a list of config IDs for templates of a given type. As it is used in that script, an optional parameter string is provided to identify text that must exist in each returned config ID (`'APPLICATION_SERVER'`). The other Template-related method is `createUsingTemplate()`, which can be used to create an object of a specified type in the configuration hierarchy. Another script is provided, `CreateServer.py`, that shows one way to use the `createUsingTemplate()` method.

The last of the paired miscellaneous **AdminConfig** methods are related to ResourceAdapters:

- `installResourceAdapter()`—Used to install a J2C resource adapter with the given .rar filename and an option string in the node.
- `uninstallResourceAdapter()`—Used to uninstall a J2C resource adapter with the given resource adapter config ID.

These methods are fairly well-documented in the online documentation. Unfortunately, we haven't had an opportunity to create scripts that use these methods. If you have need of scripts that make use of these methods, you might want to try modifying one of the available scripts to make use of these methods.

The final miscellaneous method is `getObjectName()`. It can be used to lookup and return the available MBean identifier for the specified object. For example, given the config ID of an application server, this method can be used to obtain the MBean identifier for an active instance of this application server. Remember, though, if the corresponding configuration object is not active, or if **wsadmin** is in local mode (that is, if **wsadmin** was started with the `-conntype none` command-line parameter), then either an exception will occur, or the result of the method call will be an empty string.

Summary

This chapter described the **AdminConfig** administrative scripting object, which deals with viewing and manipulating items in an application server configuration. We saw how objects can only be created when the config ID of an existing object of the appropriate type is specified. We also saw how some of the utility routines provided with this book can be used to make configuration viewing and manipulation easier.

## CHAPTER 9

The AdminControl Object

"...We will control the horizontal. We will control the vertical..."

—The Outer Limits

The **AdminControl** object is similar in many ways to the **AdminConfig** object. The primary difference between the two is that the **AdminConfig** object is used to manipulate configuration objects (represented using XML), and the **AdminControl** object is used to manipulate active application server objects (by interacting with managed beans—MBeans). One implication of this is that in order for this object to function, **wsadmin** must be connected to an active application server (the **AdminControl** object is not available when **wsadmin** is used in local mode).

Environment Information and Manipulation

As in previous chapters, the **AdminControl** methods here are grouped together to help you understand their respective roles. The first of these groups contains methods used to obtain information about the current environment. This group contains the following methods, each of which returns a string containing the specified value from the server to which **wsadmin** is connected:

- getCell()—Returns the cell name.
- getHost()—Returns the host name.
- getNode()—Returns the node name.
- getPort()—Returns the port number.
- getType()—Returns the type of connection being used.

A script that demonstrates the use of these **AdminControl** methods, named envInfo.py is available from the IBM Press® website for this book at http://www.ibmpressbooks.com/bookstore/product.asp?isbn=9780137009527.

The other methods in this group are as follows:

- reconnect()—Attempts to reconnect to the server.
- startServer()—Starts the specified server.
- stopServer()—Stops the specified server.

The last two methods in this group can only be used in a federated, or clustered, cell. Why is that? Well, unlike the startServer command script (for example, *.bat or *.sh), the AdminControl.startServer() method can only start a managed AppServer when **wsadmin** is connected to the Deployment Manager, and the managing node agent is also active. The AdminControl.stopServer() method, on the other hand is available, and can be used when **wsadmin** is connected to an unmanaged server. However, calling the AdminControl.stopServer() method when connected to an unmanaged node does not stop **wsadmin,** just the server. What happens about subsequent **wsadmin** requests? As shown in Listing 9.1, an exception is raised (lines 8–10).

Listing 9.1   Stopping and Reconnecting to an Unmanaged Server

```
 1|C:\IBM\WebSphere\AppServer70\bin>wsadmin -WAuJ
 2|WASX7209I: Connected to process "server1" ...
 3|wsadmin>node = AdminControl.getNode()
 4|wsadmin>print AdminControl.stopServer( 'server1', node )
 5|WASX7337I: Invoked stop for server "server1" Waiting for ...
 6|WASX7264I: Stop completed for server "server1" on node ...
 7|wsadmin>print AdminConfig.list( 'Server' )
 8|WASX7015E: Exception running command: ...
 9|... Connection refused: connect]
10|
11|wsadmin>print AdminControl.reconnect()
12|WASX7074I: Reconnect of SOAP connector to host localhost ...
13|
14|wsadmin>print AdminConfig.list( 'Server' )
15|server1(cells/ragibsonNode02Cell/nodes/ragibsonNode03/...
16|wsadmin>
```

When and why might you need to reconnect to the server? Consider the situation where you have a long running administrative script, and the server being administered becomes unavailable for one reason or another. AdminControl.reconnect() could be used to reestablish a connection to the server after it becomes available. Listing 9.1 shows how the unmanaged server is stopped using the `AdminControl.stopServer()` method. What you don't see is how, in a different command prompt, the `startServer` command script was used to restart the server before we were able to successfully reconnect to it (lines 11–13).

Anyway, let's get back to the `stopServer()` and `startServer()` methods. What can we do with these? One thing that came to mind while working with these methods was the usefulness of creating the following scripts, which are also available from the book's website:

- `StartServers.py`—Starts all managed application servers.
- `StopServer.py`—Stops all managed application servers.

The logic of each of these scripts is really straightforward. Each of them performs the following steps to start or stop all managed application servers:

1. Verify that the script was executed and not imported.
2. Verify that no user specified parameters were provided on the command line.
3. Verify that **wsadmin** has a connection to an active Deployment Manager (such as Network Deployment (ND) server).
4. Get the list of config IDs for all of the defined nodes.
5. For each non-ND node, obtain the list of application servers.
6. For each non-node agent, use the appropriate **AdminControl** method to either start or stop the server.

While writing and testing these scripts, we found that a little additional effort would allow these capabilities to be combined into a single script. This combined version, `StartOrStop.py`, which is also available from the book's website, can be used to start of stop all managed servers in a cell.

With a little more testing, we figured out that by adding some trivial checks we could look for an MBean for a particular application server before trying to start or stop it. If an MBean for a server exists, it doesn't make sense to try starting the server. Conversely, if an MBean for a server doesn't exist, it doesn't make sense to try stopping the server. The modified script that includes these checks is `SmartStartStop.py`. In addition to looking for an MBean before starting or stopping a server, this code also:

- Checks for the existence of extra application servers on the Deployment Manager node.
- Locates the node agent for each node and verifies that it is active before trying to start or stop the application servers on the node.

During the testing of this script, we found that we were frequently stopping every node in the cell, including all node agents and the Deployment Manager. It didn't take us long to realize that it would be fairly simple and more efficient to create a single script to do this for us. So the `StopCell.py` script was created.

One advantage of using a single **wsadmin** script to do this became clear once we realized how much overhead is associated with starting and initializing the Java Virtual Machine (JVM) to execute a **wsadmin** script. Consider for a moment an environment having a cell that has one Deployment Manager, two node agents, and two application servers. To use the command scripts provided with the product (for example, the `stopServer`, `stopNode`, and `stopManager` batch or script files) to stop the entire cell would require a JVM be started and initialized for each server instance. So this environment would require five JVM initializations to stop all of the servers. Using a single **wsadmin** script to do this means that only one JVM initialization occurs.

Are there any other advantages to having a script stop all of the servers in a cell? Sure. In fact, the one that leaps to mind is the fact that the servers are terminated gracefully in the proper order. You might not remember the appropriate order to terminate the servers in the cell. The script can do this for you, and you don't have to worry because the servers will always be terminated in the appropriate order.

What steps are used for `StopCell.py` to stop all of the servers in a cell?

1. Verify that the script was executed and not imported.

2. Verify that no user-specified parameters were provided on the command line.

3. Verify that **wsadmin** has a connection to an active Deployment Manager.

4. For each of the configured nodes, perform this for each server in the node:
   If the server is a node agent, save the server name; otherwise, stop the server
   Stop the node agent.

5. Stop the Deployment Manager.

After writing and testing this script did we learn anything? And as important a question, did we figure out any improvements? Certainly. One improvement would be to have the script check the status of the node agent before trying to stop its managed servers. Did we write this script and make it available on the book's website? Yes, it is named `SmartCellStop.py`.

After writing these scripts, it was pleasing to see how few **wsadmin** administrative objects and method calls were actually required to produce them. Each script needed at most the following objects and methods:

AdminConfig methods:

```
list()

getid()

getObjectName()

showAttribute()
```

AdminControl methods:

```
getAttribute()

getCell()
```

```
getNode()

completeObjectName()

startServer()

stopServer()
```

So using four **AdminConfig** and six **AdminControl** methods, some useful scripts can be developed. This is pretty neat!

Because many of these scripts are checking server status during the course of events, what is required to write a script to display the status of all application servers in the cell? The result can be found in CellStatus.py.

Before this script was available, in order to determine the status of the application servers on the machine, a batch file such as Listing 9.2 is necessary. Unfortunately, it is a very simple command script that generates multiple lines of output for each application server.

Of course, this script does have some limitations. Specifically, if the Deployment Manager is inactive, the script can't be used to gain any useful information. Additionally, if any node agents are inactive, the state of their managed servers are indeterminate. All the servers in the cell had to be on the same physical computer for this script to work. All the profiles had to be located in the <WAS_INSTALL_ROOT>/profiles directory. All the profiles are required to have the same name as the directory in which they are stored. Finally, the script in Listing 9.2 will only work if WebSphere Application Server is installed on a Windows computer. All of these restrictions are lifted if we write a **wsadmin** script. In addition, as described earlier, the performance gains obtained by using a single **wsadmin** script, and therefore a single JVM initialization, are significant especially for multiple node configurations.

Listing 9.2   Windows Status.bat File

```
@echo off
cd C:\IBM\WebSphere\AppServer\bin
for /d %%p in (..\profiles\*) do serverStatus -all -profileName %%~np
```

Besides generating lots of output, it can take a significant amount of time to complete, especially as the number of inactive servers increases. It appears that the serverStatus command[1] that is issued by this script has some kind of maximum time that is given for a server to respond to the "status" request. When a server is not active, the serverStatus command waits the entire time before deciding that an application server "appears to be stopped."

---

[1] The serverStatus command is provided with WebSphere Application Server product and is documented in the online documentation (e.g., http://publib.boulder.ibm.com/infocenter/wasinfo/v6r1/index.jsp).

So you have a trade-off. If your Deployment Manager and node agents are (mostly) active, the `CellStatus.py` script can be used. However, if you have unmanaged application servers, or if your node agents might be inactive, you may want to use something like the script shown in Listing 9.2.

Because some people don't like voluminous output like that generated by the `Status.bat` in Listing 9.2, we wrote a Python script that essentially performs the same action, filters the output of the `serverStatus` command to condense the information into something more usable. This script is called `wasStatus.py` and is available with the **wsadmin** script files for this chapter. Please note, however, that this Python script can't be run using **wsadmin**; it requires a Python interpreter to be executed. Listing 9.3 shows the output of a sample execution of this script.

Listing 9.3   Sample Output of `wasStatus.py`

```
C:\IBM\WebSphere\AppServer\bin>wasStatus ..
AppSrv00
  running: server1
AppSrv01
  stopped: nodeagent
  stopped: server1
AppSrv02
  stopped: nodeagent
  stopped: server1
Dmgr01
  stopped: dmgr
```

MBean Support Methods

The next methods to discuss are grouped together as a matter of convenience. The first of these, is the `help()` method, which was covered in Chapter 7, "Introduction to Admin Objects," in the "Help for Other Administrative Objects" section. There is no need for additional discussion here.

The next two methods (`getDefaultDomain()` and `getDomainName()`) return a string containing the domain name associated with the **wsadmin** environment (that is, WebSphere).

The next method, `getMBeanCount()`, can be used to determine the number of registered MBean types. It should not be confused with the number of MBean objects that have been instantiated. In fact, it returns the same value when connected to a Deployment Manager node with no node agents active as it did when the cell had the Deployment Manager, two node agents, and two managed application servers active.

The last method in this group, `queryMBeans()`, is unusual because unlike most of the Administrative object methods, which return a string to be processed, it returns a list of object instances. Unfortunately, this is not a Jython list; it is a Java list. This means that to use the result, it must be converted into something that the scripts can use. You can do this by invoking the `toArray()` method that exists for Java list objects. So instead of using `AdminControl.queryMBeans('type=Server,*')` to obtain the list of server MBeans to be used or processed by our script, remember to use something like `AdminControl.queryMBeans( 'type=Server,*' ).toArray()`.

Unfortunately, the discussion of working with Java objects within **wsadmin** Jython scripts is more aligned to the topic of a WebSphere Application Server Administration using JMX than it is to Jython. Therefore, the amount of discussion concerned with the use of Java-related objects is somewhat terse and abbreviated. There will be some discussion when other methods are encountered that return or require Java objects, but not much.

Objects, Names, and Instances

The next group of **AdminControl** methods deals more directly with MBeans. The first method, `completeObjectName()`, can be used to obtain a unique MBean object name string given the supplied information. If several MBean objects match the specified information, only the first is returned. Listing 9.4 shows an interactive session where **wsadmin** is connected to an unmanaged application server. When the `completeObjectName()` method is used (line 5) to retrieve an MBean string for an object of `type=Server` (only one exists in this environment), the method has no difficulty identifying the unique MBean being referenced.

Listing 9.4 makes use of two of the utility routines that are included in the `WAuJ_utilities` module. `MBnameAsDict()` (line 8) converts an MBean name string into a dictionary, and `displayDict()` (line 9) displays the contents of a dictionary in an easy to read format.

Listing 9.4 Use of `completeObjectName()`

```
 1|C:\IBM\WebSphere\AppServer70\bin>wsadmin -WAuJ
 2|...
 3|wsadmin>import WAuJ_utilities as WAuJ
 4|wsadmin>kind = 'type=Server,*'
 5|wsadmin>sBean = AdminControl.completeObjectName( kind )
 6|wsadmin>print sBean
 7|WebSphere:name=server1,process=server1,platform=proxy,...
 8|wsadmin>sDict = WAuJ.MBnameAsDict( sBean )
 9|wsadmin>WAuJ.displayDict( sDict )
10|          cell : ragibsonNode02Cell
11|       j2eeType : J2EEServer
12|mbeanIdentifier : cells/ragibsonNode02Cell/nodes/ragib...
13|          name : server1
14|          node : ragibsonNode03
15|       platform : proxy
```

```
16|        process : server1
17|    processType : UnManagedProcess
18|           spec : 1.0
19|           type : Server
20|        version : 7.0.0.3
21|wsadmin>
```

Should **wsadmin** be connected to a Deployment Manager with active node agents and possibly active managed application servers, the call to the `completeObjectName()` method will display a warning message (with message id of `WASX7026W`) indicating that only one of the matching MBean object name strings is being returned. Unfortunately, there is no way to tell from the result that the specified information matches multiple beans.

However, another option (method) exists that can resolve this situation. It is the `queryNames()` method. Passing this same search string to the `queryNames()` method returns all of the matching MBean string names. Again, it is best to use the `splitlines()` string method on this result in order to separate the lines of text into list elements. For example, this statement would look something like this:

```
serverBeans = AdminControl.queryNames( kind ).splitlines()
```

Here's a word of caution, though. Be sure that the search string used to find MBeans ends with a "wildcard" pattern (such as `'type=Server,*'`). Otherwise, the search string is interpreted as a complete MBean name string. It is much more likely that you will be supplying an incomplete MBean query and providing the wildcard asterisk to match the unspecified fields.

What other methods exist in this category, and what can they do for us? The `AdminControl.getConfigId()` method, for example, can be used to obtain the configuration ID for the specified MBean name string. This is the reciprocal of the `AdminConfig.getObjectName()` method discussed previously in Chapter 8, "The AdminConfig Object."

This leaves us with the `isRegistered()` method, which returns a 1 to indicate that the specified parameter identifies a registered object. Because the parameter is supposed to be an MBean name, it is hard for me to imagine how you might have an MBean name that wouldn't be registered.

Attribute-Related Methods

The next group or category of methods are related to retrieving (getting) and assigning (setting) the attribute values associated with MBeans. Here is the complete list of the regular methods:

- `getAttribute()`
- `setAttribute()`

- `getAttributes()`
- `setAttributes()`

Looking closely at this list of methods, you can see that there are singular and plural versions of getter and setter methods. What's the difference? Well, the singular version will either get or set a specific (singular) attribute value, whereas the plural may be used to get or set one or more attribute values all at the same time.

Is there any particular reason for using one form over the other? The singular methods tend to be a bit simpler, for example to get a single value, such as the processType, you could really use either form. All you would have to deal with would be the syntax of specifying the attribute to be retrieved and the value being returned. Listing 9.5 demonstrates this difference as well as shows another useful utility routine, `MBattrAsDict()`.

Listing 9.5 Example Use of `getAttribute()` and `getAttributes()`

```
 1|wsadmin>raw = AdminControl.queryNames( 'type=Server,*' )
 2|wsadmin>array = raw.splitlines()
 3|wsadmin>server = array[0]
 4|wsadmin>print AdminControl.getAttribute( server, 'processType' )
 5|UnManagedProcess
 6|wsadmin>print AdminControl.getAttributes( server, '[processType]' )
 7|[[processType UnManagedProcess] ]
 8|wsadmin>import WAuJ_utilities as WAuJ
 9|wsadmin>sAttrDict = WAuJ.MBattrAsDict( server )
10|wsadmin>sAttrDict[ 'processType' ]
11|'UnManagedProcess'
```

Table 9.1 explains this example in detail. From this, you might be able to decide whether (or if) you prefer the singular, `getAttribute()`, or plural, `getAttributes()`, version or if you might prefer the `MBattrAsDict()` utility routine.

Table 9.1 `getAttribute` versus `getAttributes` Explained

Line	Explanation
1	`AdminControl.queryNames()` obtains the names of all MBeans for all the active servers in the cell.
2	Convert the string into a list—one element for each Server MBean.
3	Select the first element of the list for use in this example.
4	`AdminControl.getAttribute()` is used to demonstrate how a single attribute value may be obtained.

5	The returned value is a simple string.
6	`AdminControl.getAttributes()` is used to demonstrate how one or more attribute values may be obtained.
7	The returned value is a list of strings. Note how the values are not quoted.
8	The `WAuJ_utilities` module is imported using an alias (`WAuJ`).
9	The `MBattrAsDict()` routine is used to retrieve all of the MBean attributes as a dictionary.
10	This demonstrates how easy it is to access a retrieved value from the returned dictionary.
11	The indexed value is a simple string.

Even though the help for the `getAttributes()` method doesn't show it, the list of attributes to be returned is optional. Be careful though. Should you try something as simple as `print AdminControl.getAttributes(server)`, you might be surprised by the amount of information that is returned (as a single string). When this was tested while connected to an unmanaged server, more than 20,000 characters of data were returned. If you are going to be dealing with multiple attributes, you are likely to prefer the `MBattrAsDict()` utility routine.

Given that the singular `getAttribute()` method can be used to retrieve a specific MBean attribute value, what steps are required to use this method? Fortunately, these steps are easy to describe:

1. Get the MBean for the object of interest (for example, a server).

2. Get the attribute name for this kind of object.

3. Use `AdminControl.getAttribute(mbean, attributeName)`.

The real question at this point is, "How do you know the names of the attributes that exist for a particular MBean?" In the "Help for MBeans" section of Chapter 7 you saw how the `Help.attributes()` method can be used obtain this information. In addition to providing the names and data types for each attribute, the returned string shows you whether or not each attribute can be modified. Is there an easy way to get the names of modifiable attributes? Well, as often is the case, there are a number of different ways to do this—some easier to understand than others. Let's take a look at some different approaches to the same problem.

Each of the following examples use the output of the `Help.attributes()` method to identify the modifiable attributes for a server MBean. The first, in Listing 9.6, uses a regular expression and list comprehension to perform this job. It could be written in fewer lines, but this would make the line too long to fit on one line in this book, and the explanation of this line would be harder to understand.

Listing 9.6   Extracting RW Attributes

```
1|wsadmin>import re
2|wsadmin>server = AdminConfig.list( 'Server' ).splitlines()[ -1 ]
```

```
 3│wsadmin>sBean   = AdminConfig.getObjectName( server )
 4│wsadmin>blanks = re.compile( ' +' )
 5│wsadmin>atStr   = Help.attributes( sBean )
 6│wsadmin>atStr   = blanks.sub( ' ', atStr ).splitlines()[ 1: ]
 7│wsadmin>modifiable = [ x for x in atStr if x.endswith( 'RW' ) ]
 8│wsadmin>print '\n'.join( modifiable )
 9│threadMonitorInterval int RW
10│threadMonitorThreshold int RW
11│threadMonitorAdjustmentThreshold int RW
12│wsadmin>
```

The explanation of this example can be found in Table 9.2. You might consider writing lines 4–6 in one statement. Before you do, think about how much harder a single line might be to understand (and maintain). And remember how hard a single statement might be for someone to read. Who knows, you could be the person who has trouble understanding it in six months or a year.

Table 9.2 RW Attribute Extraction Explained

Line(s)	Explanation
1	The regular expression (re) module is imported.
2	The config ID of the last server is retrieved using AdminConfig.list().
3	The server MBean (sBean) is obtained using AdminConfig.getObjectName().
4	A regular expression for matching one or more blanks is created.
5	The attributes for a server are obtained using Help.attributes().
6	All occurrences of multiple adjacent blanks are replaced by a single blank, and the result is converted to a list using splitlines(). The first line of the output of Help.attributes() has column headers, so this line is discarded.
7	This expression uses list comprehension to only keep those lines that end with "RW,", which indicates that the values are read-write.
8–11	The list of modifiable attributes is output with a newline character ('\n') between each attribute.

If you had any trouble understanding the example in Listing 9.6, you might prefer the example found in Listing 9.7. Granted, it might not be as efficient as the previous example, but whoever's responsible for the administrative scripts might understand this more easily.

Listing 9.7   Verbose Extraction of Modifiable Attributes

```
 1│wsadmin>cId = AdminConfig.list( 'Server' ).splitlines()[ -1 ]
 2│wsadmin>serverBean = AdminConfig.getObjectName( cId ) _
 3│wsadmin>attrText   = Help.attributes( serverBean )
 4│wsadmin>afterText  = attrText.replace( '  ', ' ' )
 5│wsadmin>while afterText != attrText :
 6│wsadmin>  attrText = afterText
 7│wsadmin>  afterText = attrText.replace( '  ', ' ' )
 8│wsadmin>
 9│wsadmin>attrLines = attrText.splitlines()[ 1: ]
10│wsadmin>modifiable = []
11│wsadmin>for attrLine in attrLines :
12│wsadmin>  if attrLine.endswith( ' RW' ) :
13│wsadmin>    modifiable.append( attrLine )
14│wsadmin>
15│wsadmin>print '\n'.join( modifiable )
16│threadMonitorInterval int RW
17│threadMonitorThreshold int RW
18│threadMonitorAdjustmentThreshold int RW
19│wsadmin>
```

The differences between the two listings are this: Lines 3–7 are used to obtain the text associated with the attributes for the specified MBean and replace all occurrences of multiple blanks with a single blank. Lines 9–13 are used to build the list of "read-write" attribute entries without using list comprehension. The two figures are extremes, though. You get to choose one technique over the other or something in the middle. In either case, remember to provide appropriate comments that explain the statements that you use and why.

Now that you've seen these two extremes, take another look at Listing 9.5. You might have missed it the first time through. Look how easy it was there to use the MBattrAsDict() utility routine to put all of the MBean attributes into a dictionary. Now think how easy it would be to combine this dictionary of server attributes with the list of modifiable attribute names generated to change their values. This is what setter methods are all about.

Having discussed the singular and plural getter methods for attributes, it's easy for us to understand that only some MBean attributes are (dynamically) modifiable. What does this mean? Can't we change everything? Well, sort of. The modifiable attributes are allowed to be changed on an active MBean. To change other attributes, you need to look at the configuration attributes that exist for this object. To change these attribute values requires a configuration change and a stop and restart of the appropriate resources (such as the application server):

```
att = 'threadMonitorInterval'
stringResult =  AdminControl.getAttribute( bean, att )
val = int( stringResult )
AdminControl.setAttribute( bean, att, str( val / 2 ) )
```

For the example shown in Listings 9.6 and 9.7, you can see that the modifiable attributes (for an application server) are those that have `threadMonitor` as a prefix. The singular form of the attribute setter method is pretty straightforward. For example, say you wanted to half the `threadMonitorInterval` attribute for the given application server. The first thing you must realize is that the data type returned by the `getAttribute()` method is a string and needs to be converted to a numeric type in order to perform the desired mathematical operation.

Note that by putting the name of the attribute to be modified into a variable makes the getting and setting a bit easier to read, as well as guaranteeing that the value being modified is the same one that was retrieved. You should also note that not only is the value returned by the getter a string, but the value to be modified needs to be a string as well.

What about the plural setter method (`AdminControl.setAttributes()`)? What does it look like?

```
result = AdminControl.setAttributes( bean, attributes )
```

What does `attributes` represent? Well, it can be either a string or a list of strings. If the string form is used, it should be a string representation of a list. For example, something like the following:

```
attributes = '[ [ name1 value1 ] [ name2 value2 ] ]'
```

The list of strings form would look very similar, e.g.,[2]

```
attributes = [ [ 'name1', 'value1' ], [ 'name2', 'value2' ] ]
```

Does it have to be used to modify a multiple values? No, you could use the singular form of the method for each attribute. Can it be used to modify a single value? Yes, it really doesn't matter how many attributes are specified, as long as each specified attribute is modifiable. You can even specify an empty string or list of attributes to be modified that changes the same value multiple times.[3] What is returned by the method? The result is a string list containing the attributes that were successfully modified by the call. Listing 9.8 shows a complete (interactive) example use of the `setAttributes()` method call that makes use of the `MBattrAsDict()` utility function described earlier. Some things to note from this example include the following:

1. The assignment of `"ts"` (the variable used to hold the `TraceService` configuration ID) and `"attr"` (the variable used to hold the attribute values to be modified) each uses two lines (lines 2–3 and 13–14, respectively) so that a long statement would not be wrapped across multiple lines.

2. The fact that the `MBattrAsDict()` utility function adds a `'Modifiable'` entry to the returned dictionary is very convenient (lines 5–8).[4]

---

[2] Note how the list form requires a comma delimiter between the list elements.

[3] If the same attribute name occurs multiple times, the last occurring value will be the one used.

[4] This attribute was specifically added because of the testing that was done related to the examples shown in Listings 9.6 and 9.7.

3. Even though the `'ringBufferSize'` attribute is "modifiable" (as seen by the list of modifiable attributes on line 10), and the modification was successfully made (as seen on line 16), the modification didn't really occur (as seen on line 18). Why? Because the current configuration of this `TraceService` is configured as `tracingToFile` and not to memory. So the request to modify the `'ringBufferSize'` was ignored.

4. Note that sometimes the value passed to the setter method may be "changed" when the actual attribute modification occurs. For example, when the application server `traceSpecification` value was set to `'com.ibm.*=all=disabled'`, the actual value saved was `'*=info'`.[5] Listing 9.8 not only demonstrates how to use the `setAttributes()` method call, it also shows that you might not actually be making the modifications that you think you are. Just be careful and test your scripts thoroughly. You may even consider having your script get the attribute that was just set and compare the two values.

Listing 9.8   Example Use of `setAttributes()`

```
 1|wsadmin>from WAuJ_utilities import MBattrAsDict
 2|wsadmin>ts = AdminControl.queryNames( 'type=TraceService,*' )
 3|wsadmin>ts = ts.splitlines()[ -1 ]
 4|wsadmin>tsDict = MBattrAsDict( ts )
 5|wsadmin>names  = tsDict[ 'Modifiable' ]
 6|wsadmin>width = max( [ len( x ) for x in names ] )
 7|wsadmin>for name in names :
 8|wsadmin>  print '%*s : %s ' % ( width, name, tsDict[ name ] )
 9|wsadmin>
10|    ringBufferSize : 0
11|traceSpecification : *=info
12|wsadmin>spec = names[ -1 ]
13|wsadmin>attr = [ [ spec, 'com.ibm.ws.*=all=enabled' ] ]
14|wsadmin>attr.append( [ 'ringBufferSize', '1' ] )
15|wsadmin>print AdminControl.setAttributes( ts, attr )
16|[ [ringBufferSize 1] [traceSpecification com.ibm.ws.*=all=e...
17|wsadmin>print AdminControl.getAttribute( ts,'ringBufferSize' )
18|0
19|wsadmin>print AdminControl.getAttribute( ts, spec )
20|*=info:com.ibm.ws.*=all
21|wsadmin>
```

---

[5] Why? Because the assigned trace string didn't match the expected and currently supported format.

What would a script look like that allowed all of the `TraceService` configuration settings to be viewed and optionally modified? The `TraceService.py` script does just this and is also available with from the book's website that appears to do the trick. One of the interesting things demonstrated by this script is the fact that configuration values that exist on multiple screens on the administrative console can, in fact, be modified by single execution of an administrative script.

Miscellaneous Methods

The penultimate group of methods cover some unrelated topics. This group of methods consists of the following:

- `invoke()`—Calls an MBean method.
- `testConnection()`—Tests the connection to a DataSource object.
- `trace()`—Sets the **wsadmin** trace specification.

Let's discuss these in reverse order, taking `AdminControl.trace()` first. The first time that we encountered this, we hoped that it would allow us to easily change the traceSpecification of an active application server. Unfortunately, that was not the case. For that, you need to use one of the setAttribute methods shown earlier. This method is used to change the trace settings for the **wsadmin** process. So a command like the following would be used to enable verbose tracing of **wsadmin**.[6]

```
AdminControl.trace( 'com.ibm.ws.scripting.*=all=enabled' )
```

This trace setting corresponds to the `com.ibm.ws.scripting.traceString` property found in the `wsadmin.properties` file.

Next, you can take a look at the `testConnection()` method. To use this method, you need to pass it the config ID of a `dataSource` object, for example, something trivial such as:

```
ds = AdminConfig.list( 'DataSource' ).splitlines()[ 0 ]
print AdminControl.testConnection( ds )
```

It is important to remember, however, that should the connection attempt fail, an exception is raised. So it is a good idea to remember to use a `try/except` error handler around this call.

The `invoke()` method can be used to execute MBean object methods. Chapter 7's "Help for MBean Operations" provided an example use of the `invoke()` method to obtain product version information. Let's take another look at this method in a bit more detail. When we say that the `invoke()` method can be used to execute MBean object methods, what does this really mean, and more importantly, how do you find out what kind of methods exist that can be called?

Let's start by looking at the online documentation:

1. Point your browser to the WebSphere Application Server Library page, http://www.IBM.com/software/webservers/appserv/was/library/.

---

[6] Most likely you would do this if requested to do so by IBM WebSphere Application Server technical support.

2. Select the tab for the version of the product being used (such as V 6.1).

3. Select the "View page" link for the product edition being used ("Network Deployment—distributed platforms").

4. Select the "View page" link for the product edition[7] ("WebSphere Application Server Network Deployment, Version 6.1").

5. In the left frame, expand the document of interest ("Network Deployment (Distributed platforms and Windows), Version 6.1").

6. Expand the "Reference" section.

7. Select the "MBean interfaces" section.

8. Scroll the "MBean Type List" selector to the MBean of interest and click a link (such as "Server").

9. Scroll the MBean details selector (the far right panel) to the "Operation Summary" to review the list of available methods for MBeans of this type.

We were surprised to find that one of the available methods for Server type MBeans is the `restart()` method. What is required to actually use this method?

You must obtain a MBname string for an object of the appropriate type and then use the `AdminControl.invoke()` method to call the method and pass it the necessary parameters.

Is that it? In a word, yes. So to execute the `restart()` method for an active application server, all you have to do is something like the following:

```
svr = AdminControl.queryNames('type=Server,* ' ).splitlines()[ -1 ]
AdminControl.invoke( svr, 'restart' )
# Give the new JVM time to initialize...
AdminControl.reconnect()
```

This even worked when **wsadmin** was connected to an unmanaged application server, which is pretty neat. So once you know how to find the MBean methods, it's pretty simple to have your scripts call them using `AdminControl.invoke()`.

What? You want another example? Oh, alright. Let's take another look at the TraceService mentioned earlier. In fact, in Listing 9.8 you saw how you could modify some attributes of a TraceService. What kinds of methods exist on the TraceService MBean that you can invoke? Well, from the online documentation, if you search for TraceService, one of the entries that is found is called the "TraceService MBean Definition Table." The list of methods that can be called can be found in the table labeled "Operation Summary." So to call or execute one of these methods you only need to:

---

[7] Why there are multiple layers of this variation, we do not know.

1. Obtain an MBean of the appropriate type.

```
ts = AdminControl.queryNames( 'name=TraceService,*' )
```

2. Use the documentation to identify the method to be executed.

3. Use the `AdminControl.invoke()` method to execute the MBean method.

```
print AdminControl.invoke( ts, 'listAllRegisteredGroups' )
```

Wow, this really doesn't look that bad. It does, however, require investigation into finding out what kinds of MBean methods exist to execute, but that really isn't too bad.

*_jmx Methods

We have seen and discussed singular and plural forms of attribute getter and setter methods. If you happened to look closely at the `AdminControl.help()` output, you would have seen some other methods having the same names, but with a "_jmx" suffix. What is this all about? Well, they are very similar to the methods described earlier, with the following differences:

1. Object names, and not object name strings, are used to identify the object instance to be manipulated. For example, instead of using something like this:

```
ts = AdminControl.queryNames( 'type=TraceService,*' )
ts = ts.splitlines()[ -1 ]
print AdminControl.getAttribute( ts, 'ringBufferSize' )
```

2. Scripts would need to use something along the lines of:

```
ts = AdminControl.queryNames( 'type=TraceService,*' )
ts = ts.splitlines()[ -1 ]
tsName = AdminControl.makeObjectName( ts )
print AdminControl.getAttribute_jmx( tsName, 'ringBufferSize' )
```

In this trivial example, it doesn't make much sense to have the additional conversion of the object name string value to an object string, just so that a different variant of the routine can be used. However, if your script is already using object names instead of object name strings, then it might make sense to use the `getAttribute_jmx()` method instead.

The `getAttributes_jmx()` method is a bit different. Earlier, we didn't see that the `getAttributes()` method has an optional second parameter that can be used to identify the attributes to be returned. For this method, the parameter is required, not optional. So instead of using something like:

```
ts = AdminControl.queryNames( 'type=TraceService,*' )
ts = ts.splitlines()[ -1 ]
attr = ['ringBufferSize', 'traceSpecification']
print AdminControl.getAttributes( ts, attr )
```

scripts would need to use something like:

```
ts = AdminControl.queryNames( 'type=TraceService,*' )
ts = ts.splitlines()[ -1 ]
attr = ['ringBufferSize', 'traceSpecification']
tsName = AdminControl.makeObjectName( ts )
print AdminControl.getAttribute_jmx( tsName, 'ringBufferSize' )
```

And another difference is what is returned. The non-*_jmx methods return a string that can be easily manipulated or parsed using Jython idioms. The *_jmx methods, on the other hand, might return Java management attribute object references, which are a bit more challenging to manipulate with Jython, but may be expected by other *_jmx methods.

An example script (setAttr_jmx.py) is provided that demonstrates the use of the setAttributes_jmx() method to modify the traceSpecification attribute of a selected TraceService MBean object instance. However, because the focus of this book is on Jython scripting and not on JMX programming using Jython, we won't discuss these JMX-related routines further.

Summary

This chapter has been all about the **AdminControl** scripting object. When you, as a WebSphere Application Server administrator, need to control or manipulate active resource objects, you will probably make use of this object and its methods. We have seen that some of these methods simply allow you to query the AppServer for information about its environment. There are some really valuable **AdminControl** methods, however, that are specifically related to the manipulation of MBean attributes. This allows us to dynamically change some of the AppServer environment without making a persistent configuration change. It also allows us to make changes to active MBean objects, which means that the AppServer or application doesn't have to be recycled (stopped and restarted) for these changes to take effect. This is what makes these methods really useful and worth learning.

## CHAPTER 10

The AdminApp Object

"Only one thing registers on the subconscious mind: repetitive application—practice. What you practice is what you manifest."

—Fay Weldon

The **AdminApp** object operates on applications. The following types of operations can be performed on an application:

1. Information
2. Install
3. Uninstall
4. Modify

AdminApp.help() provides the complete list of method calls, and the details about each method can be displayed by calling AdminApp.help('methodName').

Application Informational Methods

In this chapter, as in previous chapters, the **AdminApp** methods are grouped. The first group of methods provides information about applications. For example, the AdminApp.list() method can be used to obtain the list of deployed applications. If no parameters are specified, the complete list of deployed applications is returned as a text string. To separate these application names into elements of a list is as simple as using a statement such as the following:

```
apps = AdminApp.list().splitlines()
```

An optional scope parameter can be specified to filter or subset the list of applications returned. For example, if you have a number of applications deployed on individual servers, you might be interested in only those applications deployed upon a specific server.[1]

NOTE   The optional scope parameter must start with the `"WebSphere:"` domain name.

We find that the easiest way to provide a valid scope parameter to the `AdminApp.list()` method is to use the MBean for the particular resource. However, this requires that the resource be active. If that is not the case, the scope parameter should contain elements specified in the proper hierarchical order. For example:

```
WebSphere:cell=<cellName>
WebSphere:cell=<cellName>,node=<nodeName>
WebSphere:cell=<cellName>,node=<nodeName>,server=<serverName>
```

You can use the `AdminApp.isAppReady()` method to determine if an enterprise application is ready to execute. This method returns true if and only if 1) the server to which the application is deployed is ruming and 2) the enterprise application really is ready and able to start.

This method, as shown by the `AdminApp.help('isAppReady')` output, has a required and an optional parameter. The required parameter is the name of the application to be checked, and the optional parameter is allowed to be `'ignoreUnknownState'`. Listing 10.1 shows an excerpted interactive **wsadmin** session in which the use of the `AdminApp.isAppReady()` method is demonstrated.

Listing 10.1   Example Use of isAppReady()

```
 1|wsadmin>import WAuJ_utilities as WAuJ
 2|wsadmin>apps = AdminApp.list().splitlines()
 3|wsadmin>ready = {}
 4|wsadmin>for app in apps :
 5|wsadmin>ready[ app ] = AdminApp.isAppReady( app )
 6|wsadmin>
 7|...
 8|wsadmin>WAuJ.displayDict( ready )
 9|DefaultApplication : true
10| PlantsByWebSphere : true
11|    SamplesGallery : true
12|            ivtApp : true
13|             query : true
14|wsadmin>
```

---

[1] We'll see shortly that the complete server reference can be obtained by specifying '-server' for the optional second parameter to the `AdminApp.listModules()` method.

The following is an explanation of Listing 10.1:

- 1—Import utility library file (WAuJ_utilites) using an alias (WAuJ).
- 2—Build a list of deployed applications.
- 3—Initialize a dictionary variable to hold the ready state of each application.
- 4—Loop to iterate over each application name.
- 5—Assignment statement to save the current application status into the ready (dictionary) variable.
- 6—A blank line is required (by the interactive environment) to indicate the end of the `for` statement.
- 7—This line represents multiple output messages generated during the execution of the `for` loop.
- 8—Use the displayDict utility method to display the ready dictionary contents, which shows the ready status for each deployed application.

In a federated environment, you should note that by default if a nodeagent is unreachable, you will experience a delay while the `isAppReady()` method waits for the nodeagent to respond. If the optional `'ignoreUnknownState'` parameter is supplied, the `isAppReady()` method does not wait for the nodeagent to respond.

Another valuable piece of information about applications that is available via an **AdminApp** method is the list of modules that exist within an application. As shown in the help text for this method, it has a required and an optional parameter. As we have seen before, the required parameter is the name of an application about which information is being requested. If the optional `"-server"` parameter is also specified, then the result will include the information about the application servers on which each application is installed. Listing 10.2 provides an example for using `listModules()`.

Listing 10.2 Example Use of listModules()

```
 1|wsadmin>app    = AdminApp.list().splitlines()[ 0 ]
 2|wsadmin>mods   = AdminApp.listModules(app,'-server').splitlines()
 3|wsadmin>format = 'AppName: %s\n Module: %s\n Server: %s\n'
 4|wsadmin>for mod in mods :
 5|wsadmin>   ( name, module, server ) = mod.split( '#' )
 6|wsadmin>   print format % ( name, module, server )
 7|wsadmin>
 8|AppName: DefaultApplication
 9| Module: DefaultWebApplication.war+WEB-INF/web.xml
10| Server: WebSphere:cell=ragibsonCell01,node=ragibsonNode01,...
11|
12|AppName: DefaultApplication
```

```
13|  Module:  Increment.jar+META-INF/ejb-jar.xml
14|  Server:  WebSphere:cell=ragibsonCell01,node=ragibsonNode01,...
```

The following is an explanation of Listing 10.2:

- 1—Get the name of a deployed application using the `AdminApp.list()` method.
- 2—Get the list of modules for this application. By specifying the optional `"server"` parameter, each result identifies the server with which this application module is associated.
- 3—Define a format string so the formatted print statement won't be too long.
- 4—Process each module in the mods list using a `for` statement.
- 5—Extract the specified values from the result using `'#'` as a delimiter.[2]
- 6—Display the values using a formatted print statement.
- 7—Blank line to indicate the end of the `for` statement.
- 8—Start of the formatted output for each module.

The next useful **AdminApp** method, the `AdminApp.view()` method, can be used to display a great deal of information about an application or a module within an application. However, be aware that this method can easily generate lots of text. For example, the trivial script shown in Listing 10.3 generated about 300 lines of text for the `Default Application` and its associated modules. Yes, there is some overlap of information (details about the modules are also present in the containing application), but it is still a lot of information. We will see why shortly when we take a look at the options that exist for installing an application.

Listing 10.3   AdminApp.view() Example

```
1|( app, hr ) = AdminApp.list().splitlines()[ 0 ], '-' * 70
2|print 'Application: %s\n%s' % ( app, hr )
3|print AdminApp.view( app ) + '\n' + hr
4|for mod in AdminApp.listModules( app ).splitlines() :
5|   print 'Module: %s\n%s' % ( mod, hr )
6|   print AdminApp.view( mod ) + '\n' + hr
```

The information returned appears to be for human consumption. By that we mean it doesn't appear to be easily processed, or parsed, by a script. There's just so much of it and in various sections of the text.

One way to process the information from the `view()` method is to first separate the text into sections. To do so, identify the sections. Each section is associated with a specific, named

---

[2] If the `'-server'` option is not specified, only the application name and module information will be present on each line.

task. To obtain the task names for a deployed application, specify `'-tasknames'` as the second, optional parameter to the `view()` method. For example:

```
app = AdminApp.list().splitlines()[ 0 ]
taskNames = AdminApp.view( app, '-tasknames' ).splitlines()[3]
```

Given the task names that are listed for a deployed application, you can then view the information for a specific task by providing the task name as the second parameter to the `view()` method. For example:

```
for name in taskNames[ :-1 ] :
  print AdminApp.view( app, '-' + name )
  print '-' * 70
```

Another method you can use to help understand the installation of an enterprise application is the `AdminApp.options()` method. This method has a number of uses. The one just mentioned is obtained by providing a single parameter of an application name. For example:

```
opts = AdminApp.options( app )
```

The `options()` method returns a list of all the options available for editing the specified application. What other parameter choices exist for the `options()` method? Well, here is the complete list of parameter variations for it. If no parameters are specified, the `options()` method returns the list of "general" options that are available for every installable application.

- **Application Name**—If an application name is specified, the `options()` method returns information about all the modifiable options (that is, the ones available for editing) for the specified application.

- **Module Name**—If a module name is specified, the `options()` method returns information about the modifiable options for the specified module.

- **Filename**—If a filename is specified, the `options()` method returns information regarding the installation the specified file.

- **Filename, operation**—If a filename is specified with one of the following optional operations, the `options()` method returns information related to the installation of the specified file, and operation:

  - `installapp`
  - `updateapp`
  - `addmodule`
  - `updatemodule`

---

[3] There is an empty or blank line at the end of this call to the `view()` method. The result of this is that there is an empty entry at the end of the list that needs to be ignored.

The last of the methods in this category is the `AdminApp.getDeployStatus()` method. One interesting thing to note about this method is that unlike many of the others, it is not supported in local mode. So a connection to an active application server is required to use this method.

This method has one required parameter that must specify an existing application name. Unfortunately, like some of the other **AdminApp** methods, output is generated to the console that is used to indicate that the method process is occurring—for example, as shown in Listing 10.4.

Listing 10.4   getDeployStatus() Example

```
1|wsadmin>app = AdminApp.list().splitlines()[ 0 ]
2|wsadmin>result = AdminApp.getDeployStatus( app )
3|ADMA5071I: Distribution status check started for applicatio...
4|WebSphere:cell=ragibsonNode01Cell,node=ragibsonNode00,distr...
5|ADMA5011I: The cleanup of the temp directory for applicatio...
6|ADMA5072I: Distribution status check completed for applicat...
7|wsadmin>result
8| 'WebSphere:cell=ragibsonNode01Cell,node=ragibsonNode00,dist...
9|wsadmin>
```

Application Installation Methods

The next category of methods is the group you're most likely to use. The complete list of the methods in this group is as follows:

- `edit()`
- `editInteractive()`
- `install()`
- `installInteractive()`
- `uninstall()`
- `update()`
- `updateInteractive()`

Let's start by discussing the `installInteractive()` method. It has one "required" parameter, which is used to identify the fully qualified path of the file to be installed. The really neat thing about the "interactive" methods is that there is a built-in wizard to assist you with each phase, or task, associated with the process being performed (for example, edit, install, or update). As responses are provided to individual prompt, the wizard determines if some future tasks can be skipped based upon user input.

`AdminApp.installInteractive()` presents almost the exact same input screens in the same order as the administrative console. As a test, you can install an application once using the administrative console and once using `AdminApp.installInteractive()`. In almost every instance, you'll see that the default value shown on the administrative console agrees with the value shown during the execution of the interactive install method. The only exception is input validation. The interactive install defaulted to "`off`," and the administrative console default is "`warn`." You select "`warn`" for the value during the interactive install execution and let the install method run to completion. Both approaches can be made to show you the script you could have written to install the enterprise application without human intervention. You might want to save that script for future reference or for disaster recovery purposes. Remember to use the `AdminConfig.save()` method to copy the changes from the workspace to the application server configuration.

When the application server restarts and the Administrative console checks the status of the installed application, the newly installed application's status displays as "`started.`" This raises a question. How would you start a newly installed application within `wsadmin`?

For an unmanaged application server, this is as simple as the following:

1. Start the application server (if it is not already started) and start the `wsadmin` utility.

2. Get the MBean name of the application manager:

   ```
   AppMgr = AdminControl.queryNames( 'name=ApplicationManager,*' )
   ```

3. Invoke the `startApplication` method of the application manager:

   ```
   AdminControl.invoke( AppMgr, 'startApplication', appName )
   ```

How can the script tell if an application is currently started or stopped? By looking for an MBean associated with the specific application. If the MBean lookup returns an empty string, then no active MBean instance exists for the specified application, and the enterprise application is not started:

```
bean=AdminControl.queryNames('name=%s,type=Application,*' % appName)
```

If you happen to have "Command Assistance" enabled on your Administrative console[4] and you display information about the installed applications,[5] then "`View administrative scripting command for last action`" only shows that the last command executed as `AdminApp.list()`. It does not show each and every command or action performed to obtain all of the information currently displayed. However, it is a reasonable start.

You have probably been wondering if we were ever going to get around to explaining the actual options that can be used to install, edit, or update an application directly (that is, using the `install()`, `edit()`, or `update()` methods, instead of the interactive versions of these same methods). Well, the answer is yes...and no. There is a whole section of the online documentation related to this topic, entitled "Options for the **AdminApp** object install, installInteractive, edit, editInteractive, update, and updateInteractive commands." There is another related page entitled

---

[4] System administration-> Console Preferences-> Log command assistance commands.

[5] Applications-> Enterprise Applications.

"Usage table for the options of the **AdminApp** object install, installInteractive, update, updateInteractive, edit, and editInteractive commands," that also includes information to help us understand when different options should and should not be used.

A common "first impression," when these sections are encountered in the documentation is, "Oh, my goodness!" The list of options is huge. It's almost 100 options long, in fact.[6] It is no wonder people don't bother trying to remember all of these. This is exactly why wizards were developed, so that people like us don't have to spend time and energy trying to remember all of these things.

Let's start simple, though. Which scripting commands are required to install an application? Well, using nothing but the default installation settings, it is as simple as the following:

```
AdminApp.install( r'C:\temp\myApplication.ear' )
AdminConfig.save()
```

Turning these statements into a script file is pretty straightforward. An example script, named installApp.py, is available from the download page. It is slightly different from some of the other scripts in that it allows a parameter to be specified multiple times. This allows the script to be used to install multiple application EAR files with a single execution.

It also points out what happens when you pass a fully qualified[7] Windows filename to a script. Take a look at how the file name parameter was specified using a "raw string" (that is, using the r as a string prefix). If this isn't done, then every backslash would need to be specified using two backslashes ('\\').

What happens when a fully qualified Windows filename is passed into a script? Listing 10.5 shows what we're talking about. Lines 1–3 show a trivial script used to simply display the values passed into the script as command-line parameters. Line 4 shows how the script is executed by **wsadmin**, and line 7 shows the value of the filename parameter as it occurs when the script is executing.

Listing 10.5   Passing Filenames to Scripts

```
1|C:\IBM\WebSphere\AppServer\bin>type bob.py
2|for arg in sys.argv :
3|  print arg
4|...\WebSphere\AppServer\bin>wsadmin -f bob.py C:\temp\app.ear
5|WASX7209I: Connected to process "server1" on node ragibsonN...
6|WASX7303I: The following options are passed to the scriptin...
7|that are stored in the argv variable: "[C:\temp\app.ear]"
```

---

[6] A total of 94 options are listed in the version 6.1 of the documentation and 103 in 7.0 version of the documentation.

[7] A fully qualified filename is one containing the complete path to the file (e.g., 'C:\temp\filename.ext'), not just the name to the file, or a relative path and filename (i.e., containing '..' to refer to the parent directory).

```
 8|C:      emppp.ear
 9|
10|C:\IBM\WebSphere\AppServer\bin>
```

The value shown in line 8 is quite surprising. What happened to the nice fully qualified filename parameter? Well, what happened is that the '\t' and the '\a' were interpreted as string escape sequences. The '\t' was interpreted as a tab character (hence the space seen after the colon and before the emp and the '\a' as interpreted as an alarm character, that is, a beep will be sounded). So, what to do about this? A function named fixFileName() is provided in the WAuJ_utilities module that can help with this. This utility function is used in the installApp.py example script mentioned earlier. The trivial script shown in lines 2–3 of the following lines of code could be done using something simple such as the following:

```
from WAuJ_utilities import fixFileName
for arg in sys.argv :
  print fixFileName( arg )
```

As seen earlier, if no installation options are provided to the AdminApp.install() method, then each of the default values will be used. Unfortunately, the large number of installation options can be really difficult to display. Is there a way to determine how to specify non-default installation options? Yes, there is, and it involves using the installInteractive() method.

After using the installInteractive(), a message is logged to the **wsadmin** trace file,[8] which identifies the complete install() command that was used. The messageID for this message is WASX7278I, so it is easy to open the trace file (for example, wsadmin.traceout) in your favorite editor and search for this messageID. The good news is that all of the parameters are shown, so you can see what installation options were selected and how the values are specified. The bad news is that for version 6.1 of the WebSphere Application Server product, this message shows Jacl script instead of Jython. This has already been corrected in version 7.0 of the product and hopefully will be corrected in some future fix pack for version 6.1.

Regardless of whether the message in the trace file uses Jacl or Jython, it is quite easy to take the information from the message in order to build a complete parameter list for the install method. There are some things about the options, though, that you should realize:

- Some options have no value but have a positive and negative variation:

    "-preCompileJSPs" and "-nopreCompileJSPs"

- Some options have a single, simple value:

    "-appname myApp" and "-reloadInterval 10"

---

[8] The property that is labeled "com.ibm.ws.scripting.traceFile" in the wsadmin.properties file.

- Some options have specific allowed values:

   ```
   "-asyncRequestDispatchType DISABLED" and "-validateinstall fail"
   ```
- Some options are regular expressions:

   ```
   "-filepermission",  ".*\\.jsp=777#.*\\.xml=755"
   ```
- Some options require a list of lists:

   ```
   "-JSPCompileOptions", [["MyApp", "MyApp.war,WEB-INF/web.xml",
   "jspcp", "AppDeloymentOption.Yes", 15,
   "AppDeploymentOption.No"]]
   ```

One thing to note from these examples is the fact that option names have a hyphen or dash prefix. This allows the **AdminApp** method to distinguish between option names, and their values. So, what's the best way to list the options needed to install an application, and how should those options should be specified? Take advantage of the assistance provided by the installInteractive() method to list what options can, and should, be specified. Then, you can use the information from the trace file to find out how to specify the options you wish to use. From this, you can write scripts that can install your applications.

Edit, Update, and Uninstall

What about the other frequently used **AdminApp** methods in this category? The only parameter that needs to be specified for the **uninstall()** method is the name of the application to be removed. For example:

```
AdminApp.uninstall( 'myApp' )
AdminConfig.save()
```

The question that remains is, "What's the difference between the edit() and update() methods?" You can distinguish them in this way: To change the options associated with an installed application, use either the AdminApp.edit() or the AdminApp.editInteractive() method. To change the contents of the application (that is, to add to, replace, or remove application sub-components), the AdminApp.update() or AdminApp.updateInteractive() method should be used.

As with the installInteractive() method, you can use the editInteractive() method to make changes to the configuration settings associated with an installed application. Once all of the prompt answers have been provided, an edit() operation is performed, and a message is written to the trace file with the messageID of WASX7278I to show the options that were specified. You can use the same technique recommended here to locate these options and write a script to perform this same type of edit command on the application of your choosing.

The AdminApp.updateInteractive() method, unlike the installInteractive() and editInteractive() methods, requires more than the application name to be specified. The second parameter to this method is used to identify the content type to be updated. The available values for the content type parameter are as follows:

- `app`—Indicates that the application is to be updated, with the "operation" option identifying the kind of operation to be performed on the application.

- `file`—Indicates that a single file is to be added, removed, or updated at any scope within the deployed application.

- `modulefile`—Indicates that a module is to be updated.

- `partialapp`—Indicates that a partial application is to be updated.

In addition to the application name and the content type, you will need additional options. The exact options you need will vary depending on the specifics of your enterprise architecture. This is where the online documentation mentioned earlier comes in very handy. You will need the online Information Center to find the subset of options that your organization needs.

Let's work through an example to better understand how to make use of the information that exists. Looking at the "Usage table..." page in the online documentation, you see that almost every option is allowed to be specified while using either the `updateInteractive()` or `update()` methods and specifying a content type of `"app"`. One of the important options to be specified while using either of the `update()` methods is the operation option. The allowed values of the operation option are as follows:

- `add`—Adds new content.

- `addupdate`—Adds or updates content based on the existence of content in the application.

- `delete`—Deletes content.

- `update`—Updates existing content.

So a reasonable starting place would be to build the list of options to be used for the application's update. First, however, it is best to find out which of the options, if any, are required. Reviewing the "Options for the AdminApp object..." page, you find that only the following options are required, and each has an associated caveat:

- `contents`—Required unless the `delete` operation is specified.

- `contenturi`—Required if the content type is `file` or `modulefile`.

- `operation`—Required if the content type is `file` or `modulefile`. If the content type is `app`, the operation type must be `update`.

Because we have chosen the content type to be `app`, this means that the `-operation` option must be `update`. So now you can start building the list of options:

```
options = '-operation update'
```

Then the type of update to be performed will help in defining additional values. For example, if the application has been revised and you want to update the deployed application using a newly built EAR file, it could be as simple as follows:

```
app     = AdminApp.list().splitlines()[ -1 ]
ear     = r'C:\temp\myApplication.ear'
```

```
options = '-operation update -content ' + ear
AdminApp.updateInteractive( app, 'app', [ options ] )
```

This causes the interactive update operation to be executed, which prompts you for the allowed update options and executes the update of the specified application using the contents of the indicated file and the options you supplied. Should the update be successful, a message is logged to the trace file using the same messageID as mentioned earlier (that is, WASX7278I), containing the complete update request. It is a simple matter to extract the information from this update request and to build a script to perform this type of update on your deployed application using these options.

Keep in mind that if an application is active (that is, it is running), then changing any application setting causes the application to be stopped and restarted. On an unmanaged application server, the application will restart after the configuration has been saved. For a deployment manager environment, the application restart will occur after the save and after file synchronization for the associated node completes.

Miscellaneous AdminApp Methods

The remainder of the AdminApp methods can be grouped together as a matter of convenience. They are the following:

- `deleteUserAndGroupEntries()`—This method is used to remove all of the user and group information for all of the roles, including RunAs roles, for a given application. Only one parameter exists, and it is required. It is the name of the application from which the user and group information are to be removed. The following code snippet demonstrates one way to use this method:

```
AdminApp.deleteUserAndGroupEntries( 'myApp' )
AdminConfig.save()
```

- `export()`—This method can be used to copy the contents of a deployed application to a user-specified file. The two required parameters are the application name and the fully qualified output file name. The following code snippet demonstrates how this method might be used:

```
AdminApp.export( 'myApp', r'C:\temp\bob.zip' )
```

An optional parameter, `-exportToLocal`, exports the file to the client machine:

```
AdminApp.export( 'myApp', '/home/me/bob.zip', \
                              [-exportToLocal] )
```

- `exportDDL()`—This method can be used to copy the Data Definition Language (DDL) files from the EJB modules of an application to a user-specified directory. The two required parameters are the application name and the fully qualified directory name.

  The following code snippet demonstrates how this method might be used:

```
AdminApp.exportDDL( 'myApp', r'C:\temp\myApp' )
```

There is an optional parameter that can be used to specify a specific subset of DDL values to be exported. Valid options include `ddlprefix`.

- `publishWSDL()`—The purpose of publishing the Web Services Description Language (WSDL) file for an application is to provide clients with the description of the Web service.[9] This includes identifying the location information for it. So this method can be used to provide the WSDL information after modifying the endpoint values.

There are two required and one optional parameter allowed for this method. The required parameters are the application name and the fully qualified output file name. The following code snippet demonstrates how this method might be used while specifying only the required parameters:

```
AdminApp.publishWSDL( 'myApp', r'C:\temp\myWSDL.zip' )
```

If no WSDL exists in the specified application, an exception is raised. To cover that eventuality, it would probably be best to include a try/except statement, something like the following:

```
try :
  AdminApp.publishWSDL( 'myApp', r'C:\temp\myWSDL.zip' )
except :
  print 'No WSDL exists'
```

The optional parameter is used to specify the partial URL information for each binding on a per-module basis for the application. The format of this parameter is as follows:

```
[ [ module [ binding [ partial-URL ] ] ] ]
          An example for which might be
[ [ 'myApp.war' [ ['http' 'http://localhost:9080' ] ] ] ]
```

- `searchJNDIReferences()`—This method is used to identify the applications that exist on a specific node that refer to a particular Java Naming and Directory Interface (JNDI) name. The configuration ID of the node to be searched and the options parameter are the two required parameters that exist for this method.

The options parameter must include the `-JNDIName` option with an associated value that identifies the name of the JNDI resource to be located. An optional value of `'-verbose'` might also be specified that requests additional information about the lookup be provided. For example:

```
opts = [ '-JNDIName', 'eis/myName', '-verbose' ]
node = AdminConfig.list( 'Node' )
data = AdminApp.searchJNDIReferences( node, opts )
```

---

[9] See Chapter 15, "Administering Web Services," for a discussion of Web services-related **AdminTask** methods. See "Exporting the WSDL for a Web Service" in that chapter for additional details.

- `taskInfo()`—This method can be used to obtain information about a specific task for a specified application file. There are two required parameters:
  - The application file name
  - The task name

  An example use of this method would be as follows:

  ```
  earFile = r'C:\temp\myApp.ear'
  print AdminApp.taskInfo( earFile, 'ActSpecJNDI' )
  ```

  If an invalid task name is provided, a ScriptingException occurs. Interestingly enough, the exception text includes a list of valid task names, should you be interested in extracting this information. Perhaps using something like the following:

  ```
  result = AdminApp.taskInfo( earFile, 'unknown' )
  except :
    ( kind, info ) = sys.exc_info()[ :2 ]
    ( kind, info ) = str( kind ), str( info )
    left  = info.rfind( '"[' )
    taskNames = info[ left + 2 : -2 ].split(', ' )
    for task in taskNames :
      print AdminApp.taskInfo( earFile, task )
      print '-' * 70
  ```

- `updateAccessIDs()`—This method is used to update the application binding file for a deployed application using access IDs for all of the users and groups that are defined to various roles in the application. There are two required parameters: the application file name and a Boolean value.

  Specifying true (that is, any non-zero numeric value) for the second parameter will cause all of the access IDs for the users and groups to be updated in the application binding file, even if access IDs exist.

Summary

AdminApp allows you to install, uninstall, and modify enterprise applications, as well as query them for information.

You have many options for administering enterprise applications using the **AdminApp** scripting object. In the chapters that follow, we explore the hundreds of methods available from the **AdminTask** scripting object, many of which are related to enterprise applications.

## CHAPTER 11

The AdminTask Object—Server Management

Introduction

WebSphere Application Server is not a monolithic piece of code but instead consists of many discrete parts, such as application components, Java EE-specified containers, connectors, managers, service providers, and much more. There are many complex relationships between these parts, as well as products built on top of WebSphere Application Server, such as WebSphere Enterprise Service Bus, WebSphere Process Server, or even just Feature Packs, that add even more parts. The modular and inter-related nature of WebSphere Application Server made maintaining its administrative infrastructure challenging, and it cried out for a change. The **AdminTask** object, introduced in WebSphere Application Server V6, addresses the needs of this modular approach.

Prior to WebSphere Application Server V6, the primary administrative objects were the ones that have been covered so far in the book:

- **AdminConfig**—For managing the XML configuration repository
- **AdminControl**—For managing the runtime state of WebSphere
- **AdminApp**—A specialized object for managing applications

WebSphere Application Server V6 introduced a crucial change and improvement to WebSphere Administration: As new functional components are added to the codebase, companion administrative components can be added, too. In the case of the scripting interface, this change appears as the **AdminTask** object. But what you might not realize is that the **AdminTask** object is a façade whose perceived abilities are assembled dynamically at runtime. Just as new functional components can be added, so too can new administrative commands be registered,[1] which are presented via the **AdminTask** object.

Although the **AdminTask** object has been described by some sources as being a higher level alternative to **AdminConfig**, it is capable of being used across all administrative categories. To quote the architects, "The WebSphere command framework lets developers implement more end-user-friendly and high-level task-oriented commands for common—yet complex—administrative tasks, such as configuration and application management service functions, execution of JMX MBeans, and so on." Whenever you can, you are urged to use **AdminTask** instead of the more primitive administrative objects. For one thing, an **AdminTask** command might be authored to maintain consistency across inter-related configuration and runtime states—a problem that the primitive administrative objects cannot manage.

This chapter is the first of a series, running from this point through the end of the book, which largely makes use of the **AdminTask** object and specific commands. The examples and the methods discussed in this chapter come from the following **AdminTask** command groups:

- AdminReports
- ClusterConfigCommands
- ConfigArchiveOperations
- CoreGroupManagement
- GenerateSecurityConfigCommand
- NodeGroupCommands
- PortManagement
- ServerManagement

For the purposes of this chapter's discussion, it is assumed that several steps have already been completed, as well as that you have installed WebSphere Application Server version 6.1 or later and have created a deployment manager profile and two managed profiles. Finally, it is assumed that you have federated both profiles to create a cell that has a deployment manager and two nodes. It is not assumed that you have created any application servers.

Starting from this point, we use **AdminTask** methods to create and delete some servers, modify some configuration parameters, create and delete clusters and gather information about the servers in the cell.

---

[1] The details of this capability are described in the IBM WebSphere Technical Journal Article, "Administrative command framework programming guide for WebSphere Application Server," at (http://www.ibm.com/developerworks/websphere/techjournal/0610_chang/0610_chang.html), which explains it in detail and provides instructions for writing your own **AdminTask** commands.

Simple One-Line Examples

Open a command prompt, and change to the `"bin"` directory beneath the Deployment Manager's profile directory. If the Deployment Manager is started, type the following command line:[2,3]

```
wsadmin -c "print AdminTask.reportConfiguredPorts()"
```

Otherwise, type the following command line:

```
wsadmin -conntype none -c "print AdminTask.reportConfiguredPorts()"
```

The information displayed shows the following for every server in your cell:

- The name of each server
- The name of the node containing the server
- The port number of each port used by the server
- The name associated with each port

This is very useful information. Make a note of the name of each node. You will need this information when you create servers and cluster members. If you would like to see the same information returned in a slightly different way and limited to only one server, say only the Deployment Manager, type the following command line:

```
wsadmin -c "print AdminTask.listServerPorts( 'dmgr' )"
```

Here is yet another useful method, especially when you are troubleshooting your configuration:

```
print AdminTask.reportConfigInconsistencies()
```

On a production cell, you want this report to say that there are no items. This method does not send its output to the screen. Instead, it sends its output to a file. The name and location of this file are specified in the `wsadmin.properties` file in each profile directory. The `com.ibm.ws.scripting.validationOutput` property controls this.

If you would like a verbose checklist of security-related items, this command line can suffice:

```
print AdminTask.generateSecConfigReport()
```

You will likely want to redirect the output from this method to a file. The output is voluminous. However, this output does not take the place of having a genuine security audit performed by professionals. On the other hand, it does list many configuration items that affect

---

[2] Because the `'-c'` **wsadmin** option is specified, the **wsadmin** tool will return to the command prompt after the specified task is completed.

[3] Please note that we assume that you have set `jython` as the default language using `wsadmin.properties`.

the security of your cell and is a good place to start. The output of this method shows the following information:

- The name that the Admin Console uses for this setting
- The attribute name the Admin Console uses for this setting
- The current value of this setting
- The breadcrumb path in the Admin Console for viewing this value

While this output is very much Admin Console-focused, it is still provides a very helpful checklist of things to examine. Again, a real security audit would include many things that are not provided in the output of this method.

ServerType-Related Methods

In this section, let's examine a few more **AdminTask** methods that deal with ServerTypes. These methods are as follows:

```
createServerType()

getServerType()

listServerTypes()

showServerTypeInfo()
```

The following realizations, or conclusions, were drawn after investigating these **AdminTask** methods:

- Logically associated methods are not always in the same group. For the list shown here, the createServerType() method is not in the same (ServerManagement) group as are the other ServerType methods, at least not in the version 6.1 product.[4] This issue has been corrected in the version 7.0 product.

- Grouping and listing methods together in this way can show that something is missing. For example, no methods exist that allow ServerType entries to be removed or modified.[5] This emphasizes how important it is that the user of the createServerType() method understand what this method does and why it exists.

- Just because a method exists does not mean that WebSphere Application Server administrators are expected to, or should, use it. This is particularly true for the createServerType() method. This method is intended to be used by developers who need to create a new ServerType. In general, this would only occur for a product that

---

[4] In fact, in version 6.1, the createServerType() command isn't in any commandGroup. This oversight has been corrected in version 7.0 of the WebSphere Application Server product.

[5] A product request for these commands has been added to the product.

needs to include and make use of a WebSphere Application Server environment. So the users of this method are not going to be "normal" administrators of, or application developers for, the WebSphere Application Server product.

- Occasionally, the output of some methods will surprise you. For example, while executing an interactive **wsadmin** session using an Unmanaged node configuration (wsadmin -conntype none -profileName AppSrv00), the output of the AdminTask.listServerTypes() method is identical to the output received when the **wsadmin** tool is working with a Deployment Manager configuration (wsadmin -conntype none -profileName Dmgr01), as shown in Listing 11.1.

Listing 11.1   AdminTask.listServerTypes()

```
wsadmin>print AdminTask.listServerTypes()
PROXY_SERVER
APPLICATION_SERVER
WEB_SERVER
GENERIC_SERVER
```

What is surprising about this list is the lack of entries for the DEPLOYMENT_MANAGER and NODE_AGENT server types. At least we were surprised until it occurred to us that creating a Deployment Manager or Node Agent server using scripting may have been considered "potentially dangerous." But this means that in order to create a Deployment Manager, an administrator must use either the manageprofiles command or, if it is available for the environment, the profile management tool.

Predefined items might not match the required and optional values defined for creation methods. For example, the help text for the createServerType() method, as seen in Listing 11.2, identifies the required and optional attributes.[6]

Listing 11.2   createServerType Arguments

```
*version - The Product Version
*serverType - The ServerType (e.g.: APPLICATION_SERVER)
*createTemplateCommand - The Command used to create a Server Template
*createCommand - The Command used to create a Server
 defaultTemplateName - The name of the default Template (non-z/OS)
 defaultzOSTemplateName - The name of the default z/OS Template (non-
z/OS)
*configValidator - The name of the Config Validator class
```

Listing 11.3, on the other hand, shows the output of the ServerTypes.py script, available from the book's companion website, which shows that not every "required" parameter is present

---

[6] The createServerType() argument names do not exactly match the attribute names that actually exist.

in every predefined ServerType. It uses the listServerTypes() method to determine the kinds of servers for which information exists. It then uses the showServerTypeInfo() method to obtain the list of name/value pairs of attributes for each server type.

One interesting thing to note is that the ServerType named PROXY_SERVER has many additional attributes that could not be provided within a createServerType() method invocation. This leads us to believe that the createProxyServer() method could not have been used to create this default Proxy Server.

Listing 11.3　Output of ServerTypes.py

```
             createCommand : createApplicationServer
     createTemplateCommand : createApplicationServerTemplate
       defaultTemplateName : default
    defaultzOSTemplateName : defaultZOS
                      name : APPLICATION_SERVER
                   version : 6.0
             createCommand : createGenericServer
     createTemplateCommand : createGenericServerTemplate
       defaultTemplateName : default
    defaultzOSTemplateName : defaultZOS
                      name : GENERIC_SERVER
                   version : 6.0
           configValidator: com.ibm.websphere.server.config.validator
             createCommand : createProxyServer
     createTemplateCommand : createProxyServerTemplate
 defaultHTTPSIPTemplateName : http_sip_proxy_server
defaultHTTPSIPzOSTemplateName : http_sip_proxy_server_zos
    defaultSIPTemplateName : sip_proxy_server
 defaultSIPzOSTemplateName : sip_proxy_server_zos
       defaultTemplateName : proxy_server
    defaultzOSTemplateName : proxy_server_zos
                      name : PROXY_SERVER
                   version : 6.0
             createCommand : createWebServer
       defaultTemplateName : IHS
    defaultzOSTemplateName : HTTPSERVERZOS
                      name : WEB_SERVER
                   version : 6.0
```

At this point, the only unexplained method is `getServerType()`. So let's take a look at how you can take the information from the help text and use it to create a trivial script that uses this method. The required and optional parameters for the `getServerType()` method are as follows:

- `serverName`—The Server Name
- `nodeName`—The Node Name

From this, you can build an example `getServerType()` method call:

```
getServerType( '[ -serverName server1 -nodeName myNode01 ]' )
```

More importantly, a trivial script that includes this method, as well as the output of executing this script, is shown in Listing 11.4. Why take the time to do this? So you can see how easy it is to go from the help text to a working script that uses the parameters identified in the help text for the specific method.

Listing 11.4 `getServerType.py` and Output

```
...\bin>type getServerType.py
from WAuJ_utilities import ConfigIdAsDict
for server in AdminConfig.list( 'Server' ).splitlines() :
  sDict  = ConfigIdAsDict( server )
  server = sDict[ 'servers' ]
  node   = sDict[ 'nodes' ]
  parms  = '[-serverName %s -nodeName %s]' % ( server, node )
  sType  = AdminTask.getServerType( parms )
  print '%10s : %21s : %s' % ( server, node, sType )


...\bin>wsadmin -conntype none -f getServerType.py
...
      dmgr : ragibsonCellManager01 : DEPLOYMENT_MANAGER
 nodeagent :           ragibsonNode01 : NODE_AGENT
 nodeagent :           ragibsonNode02 : NODE_AGENT
   server1 :           ragibsonNode01 : APPLICATION_SERVER
   server1 :           ragibsonNode02 : APPLICATION_SERVER
```

Creating Servers and Clusters

In this section, we create an application server and a cluster with two member servers. We also create a core group and a node group. We then explore the issues involved in deleting everything we created. Listing 11.5 shows the variables used in this section.

Listing 11.5   Variables for the Examples

```
 1| import AdminConfig
 2| import AdminTask
  |
 3| NameOfSomeNode = "ExamplesNode01"
 4| NameOfAnotherNode = "ExamplesNode02"
 5| AppSrvName = "happy"
  |
 6| Cluster01Name = "group01"
  |
 7| Cluster01Member01 = "left"
 8| Cluster01Member02 = "right"
  |
 9| CoreGroupName = "nassau"
10| NodeGroupName = "financial"
```

The examples shown in Listings 11.6 and 11.7 use the variables shown in Listing 11.5. You should be able to modify the code for your environment just by changing their values.

Listing 11.6   Creating Servers

```
21| def createServers():
22|   """Create some servers and clusters"""
23|   print AdminTask.createCoreGroup( '[-coreGroupName ' +        \
  |   CoreGroupName + ' ]' )
24|   print AdminTask.createNodeGroup( NodeGroupName,              \
  |   '[-description "Servers used by accounting" ]' )
25|   print AdminTask.createApplicationServer( NameOfSomeNode,    \
  |   '[-name ' + AppSrvName + ' -templateName default]' )
26|   print AdminTask.addNodeGroupMember( NodeGroupName, '[ ' +   \
  |   '-nodeName ' + NameOfSomeNode + ' ]' )
27|   print AdminTask.addNodeGroupMember( NodeGroupName, '[ ' +   \
  |   '-nodeName ' + NameOfAnotherNode + ' ]' )
28|   print AdminTask.createCluster(                              \
  |   '[-clusterConfig [-clusterName ' + Cluster01Name + ' ] ' + \
  |   ' -replicationDomain [-createDomain true ] ]' )
29|   print AdminTask.createClusterMember('[-clusterName ' +      \
  |   Cluster01Name + ' -memberConfig [-memberNode ' +           \
  |   NameOfAnotherNode + ' -memberName ' + Cluster01Member01 +  \
  |   ' -replicatorEntry true] -firstMember ' +                  \
  |   '[-templateName default ' +                                \
```

```
    |      ' -nodeGroup ' + NodeGroupName +                    \
    |      ' -coreGroup ' + CoreGroupName + ' ] ]')
30|     print AdminTask.createClusterMember('[-clusterName ' +   \
    |     Cluster01Name + ' -memberConfig [-memberNode ' +       \
    |     NameOfSomeNode + ' -memberName ' +                      \
    |     Cluster01Member02 + ' -replicatorEntry true]]')
```

Line 25 creates an application server called 'happy' on one of the nodes. The only mandatory parameters are the name you choose to call the server and the name of the node where the server will be located. AdminTask.createApplicationServer() returns the configuration ID of your new server. That is why the print statement is included.

Now let's create a cluster. You should think of a cluster as nothing more than a list of lists. The first list is a list of zero or more servers. The second list is one of zero or more applications deployed to all of those servers simultaneously. The third is a list of zero or more messaging buses delivering messages to the cluster.

We created a node group and a core group for the server because some advanced WebSphere Application Server configurations allow administrators to create policies that determine how traffic is routed among servers to minimize response time and policies that determine how WebSphere Application Server reacts to certain server failures. Node groups and core groups become useful in those advanced topologies. If you are scripting for one of those advanced topologies, you get a chance to walk through some issues you may encounter when you create and delete node groups, core groups, and clusters later in this chapter. If you are not scripting for one of those advanced topologies, you can ignore node groups and core groups and safely remove them from the samples.

If you are using node groups and core groups, you should create them and populate them before you try to create a cluster that makes use of them. Lines 23 and 24 create a node group and a core group. Lines 26 and 27 populate the node group and the core group. If you are not using an advanced topology, you can safely delete these four lines.

Line 28 creates a cluster and performs two steps:

1. The clusterConfig step gives the cluster its name. This step is mandatory.

2. The replicationDomain step is optional. If you want to enable automatic failover from one cluster member to another and do not want to lose any session information when that failover takes place, perform this step; otherwise, omit it.

At this point, you have a cluster. If you were to print out the list of configured ports again, you would see that there are no new servers and no new ports in the cell. A cluster is just an empty list. By deciding to create a replication domain, you are making session failover possible when and if you add more than one member server to your cluster. Lines 29 and 30 add some member servers to the cluster.

Listing 11.7　Deleting Servers

```
40| def deleteServers():
41|   """Delete the servers and clusters we created earlier"""
42|   s = AdminConfig.getid( '/Node:' + NameOfSomeNode +    \
   |   '/Server:' + AppSrvName + '/' )
43|   print AdminConfig.remove( s )
   |
44|   print "About to delete all members of a cluster..."
45|   array = AdminConfig.getid( '/ServerCluster:' + \
   |   Cluster01Name + '/ClusterMember:/' ).splitlines()
46|   counter = 1
47|   for m in array:
48|     print "About to delete member",counter
49|     print AdminTask.deleteClusterMember( m , \
   |     ' -replicatorEntry [-deleteEntry true ] ' )
50|     counter += 1
   |
51|   id = AdminConfig.getid( '/ServerCluster:' + Cluster01Name + \
   |   '/' )
52|   print "About to delete the cluster itself..."
53|   print AdminTask.deleteCluster( id ,                  \
   |   '-replicationDomain [-deleteRepDomain true ] ' )
   |
54|   array = AdminConfig.getid( '/NodeGroup:' + NodeGroupName + \
   |   '/NodeGroupMember:/' ).splitlines()
55|   for m in array:
56|     n = AdminConfig.showAttribute( m, 'nodeName' )
57|     print AdminTask.removeNodeGroupMember( NodeGroupName, \
   |     '[-nodeName ' + n + ' ]' )
58|     print "Removed " + n + " from " + NodeGroupName
59|   print AdminTask.removeNodeGroup( NodeGroupName )
60|   print "Deleted " + NodeGroupName
   |
61|   array = AdminConfig.getid( '/CoreGroup:' + \
   |   CoreGroupName + '/CoreGroupServer:/' ).splitlines()
62|   for m in array:
63|     s = AdminConfig.showAttribute( m, 'serverName' )
64|     n = AdminConfig.showAttribute( m, 'nodeName' )
65|     print AdminTask.moveServertoCoreGroup(              \
   |     '[-source ' + CoreGroupName +                      \
```

```
   |       ' -destination DefaultCoreGroup -nodeName ' + n + \
   |       ' -serverName ' + s + ' ]' )
66 |     print "Removed " + n + " from " + NodeGroupName
67 |     print AdminTask.deleteCoreGroup( '[-coreGroupName ' +       \
   |     CoreGroupName + ']' )
68 |     print "Deleted " + CoreGroupName
```

Deleting servers is straightforward (see line 43). When you have created clusters, replication domains, messaging buses, core groups and node groups, you might have to delete some items in a particular order.

If you want to delete an entire cluster, you do not have to remove individual cluster members first. Deleting the cluster on line 53 will also delete all member servers. If you created a replication domain when you created your cluster, you can delete the replication domain, all the entries in the replication domain, and the cluster at the same time. This is what was done on line 53.

If you only want to delete one cluster member, use line 49 as an example. Because an entry for these members was created in the replication domain when the members were created, it was necessary to clean up that entry when deleting the cluster member. This is why you have a replicatorEntry step on line 49. If you do not use replication domains, you don't need this step.

The other thing you should note about line 49 is the configuration ID. Cluster members are servers. You can get at least two different configuration IDs for them:

1. A configuration ID as a Server

2. Another configuration ID as a ClusterMember

Remember to use the ClusterMember configuration ID as was done on line 45.

You cannot delete a node group until you remove all nodes that are members of the node group. And you cannot do that until you delete any cluster members that happen to belong to those nodes (see lines 54 through 59).

A similar rule applies to core groups. Every server must belong to some core group. You cannot delete a core group that has members. To delete a core group, you must first move its servers to a different core group. In this example, the DefaultCoreGroup (see lines 50 to 67) was used.

Server-Related Commands

Let's continue looking at the commands in the ServerManagement group. This time, we delve into the Server-related commands in this group, specifically:

```
createApplicationServer()

createGenericServer()

createProxyServer()

createWebServer()
```

```
deleteServer()

deleteWebServer()

listServers()

showServerInfo()

showServerInstance()
```

Starting with the `listServers()` command, you find that the supported arguments are `serverType` and `nodeName`, which are both optional. This means that the simplest call would be as follows:

```
print AdminTask.listServers()
```

So what? The output looks like the list of configuration IDs produced by this call, seen previously in Chapter 8, "The AdminConfig Object":

```
print AdminConfig.list( 'Server' )
```

Doesn't it? This output is similar, yes, but not identical. Don't be confused. The values returned by the `AdminConfig.list()` call are configuration identifiers, whereas the values returned by the `AdminTask.listServers()` call are the list of server files (fully qualified paths to server.xml files) that match the specified arguments.

What about the parameters, or arguments, for the `listServers()` command? Looking at the command help text shows that the following optional values can be specified:

1. `serverType`—The type of Server (for example, `APPLICATION_SERVER`)

2. `nodeName`—The name of the node on which the server exists

This means that in addition to the empty parameter list shown here, the following kinds of calls are also valid:

```
print AdminTask.listServers( '[-serverType APPLICATION_SERVER]' )
print AdminTask.listServers( '[-nodeName %s]' % myNodeName )
```

The valid server types are displayed by calling the `AdminTask.listServerTypes()` command. Unfortunately, this means that neither `DEPLOYMENT_MANAGER` nor `NODE_AGENT` are valid server types for this command.

Next, let's take a look at the `AdminTask.create*Server()` commands, specifically:

```
createApplicationServer()

createGenericServer()

createProxyServer()

createWebServer()
```

Why it was decided that separate `create` commands should be used for each of these server types, I do not know. It is especially difficult to justify when we look at the help text for each of these commands. In the help text, we find that the only differences between these commands are the unique steps that exist to specify values to be configured for each specific server type.

So what parameters exist for these create commands? The first parameter is required[7] and is called the *target object*. It specifies the name of the node on which the server is to be created.

The target object parameter for the create server commands identifies the name of the target node, not the configuration ID of the parent object, as was seen with the `AdminConfig.create()` method.

The remaining parameters are "named" and must be specified as a string list. This means that these parameters can be specified either as a list of strings or as a string containing a list. The former would be specified in this manner:

```
[ '-name1', 'value1', '-name2', 'value2' ... ]
```

And the latter would be specified this way:

```
'[ -name1, value1, -name2, value2 ... ]'
```

The latter requires less typing, so the examples herein use this convention. If, however, you prefer the former, you are encouraged to use the form that you find the easiest to use (or that has been required by your particular organization).

The names and descriptions of the parameters that exist for these `server creation` commands are shown in Table 11.1.

Table 11.1 `createServer` Command Parameters

Name	Description
`*name`	The only other "required parameter" specifies the name of the server to be created.[8]
`templateName`	The name of the template to be used during the creation process.
`genUniquePorts`	Indicates whether unique http ports should be generated for the generated server (`true` or `false`).[9]
`template Location`	The location (directory) where the specified template is located. If this value is not provided, it defaults to the system defined location, which is recommended.

---

[7] It's required but only if the `-interactive` option isn't specified.

[8] The online documentation contains a list of characters that are not allowed in object names on a page entitled "Object names include information that the name string cannot contain."

[9] The default value is `true`, which is a reasonable default given that it is unlikely that you are going to want conflicting ports to be configured for your environment.

Table 11.1   `createServer` Command Parameters

Name	Description
specificShortName	The server-specific short name is applicable only on z/OS platforms. All servers should have a unique specific short name comprised of eight or fewer characters, all uppercase. This parameter is optional, and when it is not specified, a unique specific short name is automatically assigned.
genericShortName	The server-generic short name is applicable only on z/OS platforms. All members of a cluster should share the same generic short name, and all individual servers should have unique generic short name. The short name is comprised of eight or fewer characters, all uppercase. This optional parameter, if not specified, causes a unique generic short name to be automatically assigned.
clusterName	This name indicates the name of an existing cluster with which this server is to be created.

create*Server Optional and Required Steps

In addition to the named parameters shown, the `create` server commands support the following steps, which allow one or more additional values to be provided to the command. These values are positional in nature and are specific for each particular step. The details about these steps and their values are shown and described in Table 11.2.

Table 11.2   Required and Optional `create*Server` steps

Step Name	Description
ConfigCoreGroup	This optional step is valid for either the `createApplicationServer` and `createProxyServer` commands and is used to specify the name of the core group with which the created server is to be associated.
ConfigProcDef	This optional step is valid for the `createGenericServer` command and is used to provide the following configuration values for the server being created: • `startCommand`—The command to run when the generic server is started. • `startCommandArgs`—The command-line arguments that will be passed to the start command. • `executableTargetKind`—Specifies whether a Java classname (use `JAVA_CLASS`) or the name of an executable Jar file (use `EXECUTABLE_JAR`) will be used as the executable target for this process. This field should be left blank for binary executables.

Table 11.2 Required and Optional `create*Server` steps

Step Name	Description
	• `executableTarget`—The name of the executable target (a Java class containing a `main()` method or the name of an executable Jar), depending on the executable target type. This field should be left blank for binary executables. • `workingDirectory`—The working directory that will be used for this generic server. • `stopCommand`—The command to run when the generic server is stopped.
`serverConfig`	This required step is valid for the `createWebServer` command and is used to provide the following configuration values for the server being created: • `webPort`—Web server Port. • `webInstallRoot`—Install Root for Web server. • `pluginInstallRoot`—Plugin Install Root. • `configurationFile`—configurationFileDesc_2.[10] • `serviceName`—Windows `ServiceName` for starting IHS Web server as a Service. • `errorLogfile`—errorLogfileDesc_2. • `accessLogfile`—accessLogfileDesc_2. • `webProtocol`—Web server protocol. • `webAppMapping`—Web server application mapping.
`remoteServer Config`	This required step is valid for `createWebServer` command and is used to provide the following configuration values for the administrative server being created: • `adminPort`—Port Number. • `adminUserID`—Administrator userID. • `adminPasswd`—Administrator password. • `adminProtocol`—Administration protocol.

---

[10] Don't you just love this wonderful description? A product defect has been opened to get this corrected.

Server Template-Related Commands

The next subgroup of commands is closely related to the group we just saw. They are associated with server templates:

```
createApplicationServerTemplate()

createGenericServerTemplate()

createProxyServerTemplate()

createWebServerTemplate()

deleteServerTemplate()

listServerTemplates()

showTemplateInfo()
```

Let's start with the easiest of these methods, that is, the `listServerTemplates()` method, which can be used to display the current list of configured Server Templates or a subset of this based on specific values. The help for the `listServerTemplates()` method indicates that all of the parameters are optional. So to get a complete list of the configured server templates, you only have to `print AdminTask.listServerTemplates()`.

You can use the optional parameters to return server templates that match specific characteristics. For example, if you need a list of server templates that are related to Application Servers, then you could use something like the following:

```
print AdminTask.listServerTemplates('[-serverType APPLICATION_SERVER]').
```

Or if you needed the complete configuration identifier associated with the server template named IHS, you could simply:

```
print AdminTask.listServerTemplates('[-name IHS]')[11]
```

Why do this? Well, the next method (`showTemplateInfo()`) has a single parameter that identifies the server template about which information is being requested, and this target object is a server template configuration identifier. This might not be intuitively obvious the first time you read it, so an example might help make things more clear. Listing 11.8 shows an example use of the `listServerTemplates()` and `showTemplateInfo()` methods.

Another example script (`TemplateInfo.py`) is available from the book download page that uses these same methods and formats the output for all of the configured server templates. A portion of the formatted output can be seen in Listing 11.9. The complete output, at least for the environment on which the script was executed, was more than 250 lines long and therefore too long to be included herein.

---

[11] The value of the name must match an existing server template name exactly, so `'[-name ihs]'` is not the same as `'[-name IHS]'` and will return an empty string.

Listing 11.8 Example Use of `showTemplateInfo()`

```
wsadmin>from WAuJ_utilities import nvTextListAsDict, displayDict
wsadmin>ihs = AdminTask.listServerTemplates('[-name IHS]')
wsadmin>sDict = nvTextListAsDict( AdminTask.showTemplateInfo( ihs ) )
wsadmin>displayDict( sDict )
com.ibm.websphere.baseProductMajorVersion : 6.1
com.ibm.websphere.baseProductMinorVersion : 0.0
    com.ibm.websphere.baseProductVersion : 6.1.0.0
    com.ibm.websphere.nodeOperatingSystem :
                          description : The IHS Web Server Template
                     isDefaultTemplate : true
                      isSystemTemplate : true
                                  name : IHS
wsadmin>
```

Listing 11.9 Example `TemplateInfo.py` Output

```
com.ibm.websphere.baseProductMajorVersion : 6.1
com.ibm.websphere.baseProductMinorVersion : 0.0
    com.ibm.websphere.baseProductVersion : 6.1.0.0
    com.ibm.websphere.nodeOperatingSystem :
                          description : The APACHE Web Server
                                        Template
                     isDefaultTemplate : false
                      isSystemTemplate : true
                                  name : APACHE

com.ibm.websphere.baseProductMajorVersion : 6
com.ibm.websphere.baseProductMinorVersion : 0.0
    com.ibm.websphere.baseProductVersion : 6.0.0
    com.ibm.websphere.nodeOperatingSystem :
                          description : The APACHE Web Server
                                        Template
                     isDefaultTemplate : false
                      isSystemTemplate : true
                                  name : APACHE_60X
```

The next set of methods in the subgroup that need to be discussed are `create*Template()` methods. These methods can be used should you need to create a new server template from which servers could be easily created. The complete list of these methods is the following:

```
createApplicationServerTemplate()

createGenericServerTemplate()

createProxyServerTemplate()

createWebServerTemplate()
```

Each of these methods has the same required and optional parameters, specifically:

- `templateName`—The name of the server template being created (which should be unique).

- `serverName`—The name of the Server from which the template values should be obtained.

- `nodeName`—The name of the Node on which the specified Server exists.

- `description`—Optional descriptive text to be associated with this template.

- `templateLocation`—Optional location (fully qualified directory and filename) where the template should be stored.[12]

How would any of these `create*Template()` methods be used then? First, create a server of the desired type and modify the server configuration attributes to suit your specific need. Then use the specific `create*Template()` method to create an appropriate template based on this existing server configuration.

The last method in this subgroup is the `deleteServerTemplate()` method, which can be used to remove a user-created template. It cannot be used to remove a template that has an `isSystemTemplate` value of true.

JVM-Related Methods

The next methods to be discussed are all related, in some way, to the Java Virtual Machine (JVM):

```
getJVMMode()

setGenericJVMArguments()

setJVMDebugMode()
```

---

[12] If the `templateLocation` is not specified, a default system location is used. This is the recommended practice.

```
setJVMInitialHeapSize()
setJVMMaxHeapSize()
setJVMMode()
setJVMProperties()
setJVMSystemProperties()
showJVMProperties()
showJVMSystemProperties()
```

When first looking at this collection of methods, you might be initially surprised by the fact that there is only one getter method, (`getJVMMode()`); all of the others are either setter methods or show methods.

Looking a little deeper, you find that the `getJVMMode()` and `setJVMMode()` methods are specific to the z/OS environment and are used to determine, or change, whether the JVM should be executing in 31 or 64 -bit mode.

JVM System Properties

The next pair of methods is made up of the `setJVMSystemProperties()` and `showJVMSystemProperties()` methods. What, exactly, are JVM System Properties? Well, using the graphical administrative console, you can take the following actions to traverse down to the corresponding screen, which displays the items that the **AdminTask** object identifies as JVM System Properties. The resulting screen also enables you to manipulate the items identified.

1. Log into the Administrative console.
2. Expand the "Servers" section of the left frame.
3. Select the "Application servers" link.
4. Select the specific application server in question (`server1`, in this case).
5. Select the "Java and Process Management" section under "Server Infrastructure."
6. Select the "Process Definition" link.
7. Select the "Java Virtual Machine" link.
8. Select the "Custom Properties" link.

So what the **AdminTask** object identifies as JVM System Properties are identified as "Custom Properties" by the graphical administrative console. This is one of many instances where some variation exists in how items, properties, or attributes have different names depending on how they are being accessed.

An astute observer might ask some questions at this point. The administrative console includes a way to delete a custom property,[13] but we haven't seen a way to do this with the **AdminTask** object. In fact, if you use the setJVMSystemProperties() method, it appears to add a new property, even if a property of the same name already exists!

Let's take a closer look. While having **wsadmin** connected to an unmanaged application server, you can use the following command to assign a value of '1' to a new "custom property" named a:

```
AdminTask.setJVMSystemProperties('[-propertyName a -propertyValue 1]')
```

However, if you change your mind and decide that the value for this property should actually be '2', you could execute this command to make this happen:

```
AdminTask.setJVMSystemProperties('[-propertyName a -propertyValue 2]')
```

After making these changes, you need to have the changes made to the configuration files by calling AdminConfig.save(). Interestingly enough, when you restart **wsadmin** and connect to this same application server, you can use the showJVMSystemProperties() method to display the current "custom" or "system" properties:

```
print AdminTask.showJVMSystemProperties()
```

Unfortunately, the output is somewhat deceiving. For this specific scenario, the output would be '[a 2]', which is what you would expect. If you use the graphical administrative console to view the custom properties for this same application server, you find two entries. The first is '[a 1]', and the second is '[a 2]'.

Can you create duplicate entries using the graphical administrative console? No, the mechanism for adding a new property using the console verifies that the property name is unique. However, if duplicates exist, you can use the console to remove or modify the extra values. You are cautioned, though, to remove duplicates using the console rather than leaving them around.[14]

JVM Properties

In addition to the JVM System Properties, methods exist to display and manipulate the general settings for a specific JVM. Using the console, you can use the same sequence of steps shown earlier to display the custom properties. By leaving off the last two steps ("Select the Custom Properties link" and "Select the Java Virtual Machine link"), we find ourselves at the "Process Definition" page, which displays most of the items the **AdminTask** object defines as JVMProperties. Listing 11.10 shows some steps you can use to display these properties in a more readable form.

---

[13] Simply select a particular property checkbox and click the delete button.

[14] A defect has been opened for this issue, so hopefully it will be resolved soon.

Listing 11.10   Formatted JVM Properties

```
wsadmin>from WAuJ_utilities import nvTextListAsDict, displayDict
wsadmin>sDict = nvTextListAsDict( AdminTask.showJVMProperties() )
wsadmin>displayDict( sDict.keys )
                bootClasspath :
                    classpath :
                    debugArgs : -Djava.compiler=NONE -Xdebug -Xnoagent ...
                    debugMode : false
                   disableJIT : false
          executableJarFileName :
           genericJvmArguments : -Xquickstart
               hprofArguments :
              initialHeapSize : 0
       internalClassAccessMode : ALLOW
              maximumHeapSize : 0
                       osName :
                      runHProf : false
             verboseModeClass : false
  verboseModeGarbageCollection : false
               verboseModeJNI : false
wsadmin>
```

OK, so that demonstrates how you can determine the collection of JVM property settings using the showJVMProperties() method. Interestingly enough, there is also a setJVMProperties() method that allows you to change any and all of these properties with one call. For example, you could use it to set the osName property to any value you choose:

```
AdminTask.setJVMProperties( '[-osName "Dos 1.0"]' )
```

And should you decide to remove this attribute value, you can use the same kind of call and omit the value:

```
AdminTask.setJVMProperties( '[-osName]' )
```

If you use the setJVMProperties() method to provide values for any of the JVM properties, why bother with these other methods that only allow us to modify a specific JVM property value? If you want to change more than one JVM property at the same time, setJVMProperties() is the way to go. Also if there is ever a JVM property that does not have a specific method, you can still set it using the setJVMProperties() method. Otherwise, it is whichever you prefer.

```
setGenericJVMArguments()

setJVMDebugMode()

setJVMInitialHeapSize()

setJVMMaxHeapSize()
```

Each of these methods has optional parameters to identify the server (`serverName`) and node (`nodeName`)—and for z/OS Application Servers, the process type (`processType`). Then there is a required parameter for the specific JVM Property being set. So you can just as easily use the `setJVMProperties()` method as any of these to set any of these properties:

```
AdminTask.setJVMProperties('[-genericJVMArguments [-Xquickstart]]')
```

z/OS-Specific Methods

The following methods are only appropriate for on the z/OS version of the product, so they won't be discussed here:

```
changeClusterShortName()

changeServerGenericShortName()

changeServerSpecificShortName()

setServerInstance()
```

Miscellaneous ServerManagement Methods

The following are the remaining methods in this group:

```
getDmgrProperties()

getJavaHome()

isFederated()

setProcessDefinition()

setTraceSpecification()

showProcessDefinition()
```

Let's discuss the `isFederated()` method first. If the configuration profile being processed by **wsadmin** is that of a Deployment Manager server, a federated Application Server, or a cluster member, then the result of calling the `isFederated()` method will be `true`; otherwise, it will be `false`. This method could be used instead of checking the process type (for example, using something like `AdminConfig.getObjectName()` or `AdminControl.getAttribute()`).

If your script works with a type of managed profile (such as Deployment Manager, Federated Application Server, or cluster member), it might want to call the `getDmgrProperties()` method to get the following values as a list in text string format:

- Hostname
- Profile name
- Port number

What does the result of this call look like? That's easy enough to find out. You simply have to test it using an interactive **wsadmin** session that is working with the Deployment Manager profile. For this environment, the output looks like the following:

```
wsadmin>print AdminTask.getDmgrProperties()
[ [port 8879] [name dmgr] [host ragibson] ]
```

What would you need to do if your script needed to know the port number used to connect to the Deployment Manager? Using one of the utility methods in WAuJ_utilities, it would be as easy as:

```
from WAuJ_utilities import nvTextListAsDict
print nvTextListAsDict( AdminTask.getDmgrProperties() )[ 'port' ]
```

Say what? How does this work? Remember that the nvTextListAsDict() method expects a list in text string format and returns a dictionary. And you can access an element of a dictionary using the key, or index, value. All this second line does it create the dictionary and access an individual element to get a particular value. If the script needed to work with any of the other values, then it is likely that the result of calling the nvTextListAsDict() utility method would be stored in a variable for later processing.

We can't speak for you, but we're getting to like these utilities. They make WebSphere administrative scripts easier to write and a lot easier to understand.

What's next? Let's take a look at the getJavaHome() method, which seems to be pretty straightforward. Wait a minute. Why would the serverName and nodeName parameters be required? Think about it for a moment. In a federated (or cluster) environment, you need to uniquely identify the server for which you want to obtain the value of JavaHome, which means that both the server name and the node name need to be specified. So finding out the Java Home directory for a particular application server is as easy as[15]

```
args = '[-serverName server1 -nodeName ragibsonNode01]'
print AdminTask.getJavaHome( args )
```

---

[15] Generally, it is not recommended to hard-code the server and node name in a script. Nor should this be done in two steps. However, the line to use to build the argument string to this call would be much longer than would fit on a single line for this book.

The `showProcessDefinition()` and `setProcessDefinition()` methods fit the same kind of pattern that seen previously. Listing 11.11 shows how to display the process definitions should you be working with a configuration for which only a single application server exists.[16]

Listing 11.11   Example Use of `showProcessDefinition()`

```
wsadmin>from WAuJ_utilities import nvTextListAsDict, displayDict
wsadmin>sDict = nvTextListAsDict( AdminTask.showProcessDefinition() )
wsadmin>displayDict( sDict )
executableArguments   :
       executableName :
      executableTarget : com.ibm.ws.runtime.WsServer
executableTargetKind : JAVA_CLASS
          processType :
         startCommand :
      startCommandArgs :
          stopCommand :
       stopCommandArgs :
      terminateCommand :
terminateCommandArgs :
      workingDirectory : ${USER_INSTALL_ROOT}
wsadmin>
```

And from this, you can see that setting one or more process definitions would be as easy as:

```
AdminTask.setProcessDefinition( '[-interactive]' )
```

Of course, this particular call would prompt you for each of the argument values.

The last method in this group is `setTraceSpecification()` and is one of the most useful seen so far. It can be used to dynamically change the trace specification for an application server. If you have ever had to work with IBM WebSphere Application Server technical support to perform problem determination, it is quite likely that you would have been asked to change the tracing level for your application servers. Without scripting, this requires you to use the administrative console to change the tracing and recycle the application server for the modified tracing to take effect. Unfortunately, this means that when the application server is started, the modified tracing will be

---

[16] Otherwise, the `-serverName` parameter would be required, and the `-nodeName` parameter as well, if the `-serverName` were not unique within the configuration.

in place, and all of the application server initialization processing will generate significantly more messages. If the issue being worked is unrelated to the startup of your application server, then this additional tracing is of no use.

Now, with this method you can use a simple script to dynamically enable or disable the tracing you need at any time! This is wonderful. So what is required to set a new trace string? Nothing more than this:

```
traceString = '[-traceSpecification com.ibm.*=all]'
AdminTask.setTraceSpecification( traceString )[17]
```

This is pretty neat. In fact, we're sure some people will take a look at this and say something like, "Why didn't they tell me that it was this easy to change the tracing dynamically?"

Reference Section

This section provides detailed information about the **AdminTask** methods that configure servers. Of the more than 100 methods in this category, detailed information about the methods you will likely use most often is included. The methods are divided into categories based on **AdminTask** groups, and within those categories, the methods are presented in the order in which you might have to use them. Numerous sources were drawn from for the information presented in this section, and we drew on the most recent version of the help that IBM provides within the **AdminTask** scripting object itself, as well as details from several sources within the InfoCenter. There are also some details that folks from the IBM support staff were kind enough to provide, which were supplemented with things we learned from our own experiences.

Finally, the arguments to each method are divided into groups. The first group is the **Required arguments**. The second group is arguments that are not required, but you are very likely to have to use. The third group is made up of arguments that are optional and are seldom used. The fourth group is arguments that you will have to supply if you are configuring a secure environment.

The general pattern for calling **AdminTask** methods is as follows:

```
AdminTask.methodName( target,                          \
          '[ -argument value -nextArgument value2  ' \
     + '-stepName [ -arg01 val01 -arg02 val02 ] ' \
     + '-nextStepName [ -arg03 val03]  -yetAnotherStep ]' )
```

There might or might not be a target. If there is, it might be a configuration ID or a name. There might or might not be arguments as well. Arguments are name/value pairs. There might or might not be steps, and there might be more than one step. Think of steps as arguments that take either a list of name/value pairs as their value or no argument at all. Bundle all the arguments and all the steps into one big list and pass it to the method.

---

[17] Again, it is not normally recommended to do this call on multiple lines. However, even a simple trace string makes this line too long for the width of this page.

Node Group Command Group and Core Group Command Group

The methods that create, delete, modify, and display Core Groups and Node Groups are in these two **AdminTask** command groups. All servers must belong to some core group. Unless you specify the core group, servers belong to the DefaultCoreGroup. It is not a good idea to delete the DefaultCoreGroup even if you remove all servers from it. All nodes must belong to some node group. Unless you specify a node group, nodes belong to the DefaultNodeGroup. It is not a good idea to delete the DefaultNodeGroup.

createCoreGroup

Creates a core group.

> **Required argument:**
>
> • coreGroupName—The name of the new core group.

createNodeGroup

Creates a node group.

> **Target (Mandatory):**
>
> The name of the new node group.
>
> **Optional arguments that you are likely to use:**
>
> • description—Any text you might want to add to describe this part of your bus topology.
>
> **Optional arguments that you are less likely to use:**
>
> • shortName—Only z/OS uses short names.

addNodeGroupMember

Add a node to the node group.

> **Target (Mandatory):**
>
> The name of the node group.
>
> **Required argument:**
>
> • nodeName—The name of the node that will join this group.

removeNodeGroupMember

Remove a node group member from the node group.

Target (Mandatory):

The name of the node group.

Required argument:

- `nodeName`—The name of the node to remove from the group.

removeNodeGroup

Delete a node group. The node group must be empty before it can be deleted.

Target (Mandatory):

The name of the node group.

moveClusterToCoreGroup

Moves all the member servers from one core group to another.

Required arguments:

- `source`—The name of the core group the server is to be moved from.
- `target`—The name of the core group the server is to be moved to.
- `clusterName`—Move all members of this cluster from the source to the target.

Optional argument that you are less likely to use:

- `checkConfig`—You would only specify this argument on the advice of IBM support. By default, it is set to `true`. All member servers of a cluster must belong to the same core group. By default, this method throws an exception if that rule is violated. If you set this argument to `false`, you are disabling that configuration check. You would only do this if you were trying to fix a corrupted configuration.

moveServerToCoreGroup

Moves the specified server from one core group to another.

Required arguments:

- `source`—The name of the core group the server is to be moved from.
- `target`—The name of the core group the server is to be moved to.
- `nodeName`—The name of the node containing the server.
- `serverName`—The name of the server to move from the source to the destination.

deleteCoreGroup

Deletes a core group. This method will fail unless you first remove all member servers. If any member servers belong to a cluster, you must either delete those member servers or move them to a different core group before calling this method.

> **Required argument:**
>
> • `coreGroupName`—The name of the core group you wish to delete.

AdminReports Command Group

The methods in this command group generate useful reports about the configuration of the servers in the cell.

reportConfigInconsistencies

Checks the configuration repository and reports any structural inconsistencies. Writes any inconsistencies to whatever file you specify using the `com.ibm.ws.scripting.validationOutput` property in the `wsadmin.properties` file. This file is found in the properties directory of each profile.

ReportConfiguredPorts

Lists every port configured for every server in the entire configuration repository in the profile from which the command executes. This method works even if no servers are started.

> **Occasionally used optional argument:**
>
> • `node`—Limit the report to a node.

ClusterConfigCommands Command Group

The methods in this command group create, delete, modify, and display configuration information about clusters in the cell.

createCluster

Creates a new cluster with no server members, no deployed applications, and no messaging buses. You can create a cluster of any application servers, a cluster of proxy servers, or a cluster of OnDemand routers. All members of the cluster will be the same server type. The number of steps and the names of the steps vary depending on the version of WebSphere Application Server and the product enhancements you have purchased. The additional steps that are available only on WebSphere Process Server prepare the messaging buses and messaging databases that Process Server requires.

> **Steps:**
>
> • `clusterConfig`—This step is required.
>
> **Required argument:**
>
> • `clusterName`—The name for this cluster.

Occasionally used optional arguments:

- `preferLocal`—The default value of `true` is what you normally want.

- `shortName`—This argument is only used on z/OS systems.

- `clusterType`—Specifies the type of server that is created every time you add a new cluster member. The legal values are `APPLICATION_SERVER` or `PROXY_SERVER` or `ONDEMAND_ROUTER`. An apparent bug in this method causes exceptions any time this argument is specified. If you do not specify this argument, your new cluster is created with a `clusterType` of `APPLICATION_SERVER`.

- `replicationDomain`—This step is probably a good idea.

Frequently used optional arguments:

- `createDomain`—Set this argument to `true` if you want WAS to back up the HTTP session data of each member server. You would do this if you want to preserve this session data in the event of the failure of a member server.

- `convertServer`—This step is only necessary if you are trying to convert an existing server into a cluster of servers.

Frequently used optional arguments: (There is no way to perform this step without specifying the following arguments.)

- `serverNode`—Name of node with the existing server to convert to first member of the cluster.

- `serverName`—Name of existing server to convert to first member of the cluster.

- `replicatorEntry`—Enable this member to use data replication service for HTTP session persistence. It is probably a good idea to set this value to `true`.

Occasionally used optional arguments:

`nodeGroup`—Name of node group that all cluster member nodes must belong to. In advanced WAS topologies, it makes sense to create a node group that holds the servers in one or more clusters.

`memberWeight`—Weight value of cluster member. As a rule, you don't want to change this value from its default unless you know that you will have cluster members deployed on servers with significantly different processing power.

`promoteProxyServer`—This step configures the event service configuration of the new server cluster. There are no arguments for this step.

`eventServiceConfig`—This step configures the event service configuration of the new server cluster. There are no arguments for this step.

`BPCCreateCluster`—Only available and only necessary on WebSphere Process Server. There are no arguments for this step.

`SOACoreCreateClusterStep`—Only available and only necessary on WebSphere Process Server. There are no arguments for this step.

SCACreateClusterStep—Only available and only necessary on WebSphere Process Server. There are no arguments for this step.

wpsndCreateClusterStep—Only available and only necessary on WebSphere Process Server. There are no arguments for this step.

createClusterMember

Creates a new server and makes it a member of a cluster.

Target:

Configuration ID of the server cluster. You must supply either this or a clusterName argument (see next item).

Frequently used optional argument:

• clusterName—The name of the server cluster. You must supply either this or a configuration ID target (see target just described).

Steps:

• memberConfig—This step specifies some basic configuration settings for the new member of the cluster.

Required arguments:

• memberNode—The new server will be a part of this node.

• memberName—The new server will have this name.

Frequently used optional arguments:

• replicatorEntry—Enable this member to use data replication service for HTTP session persistence.

• memberWeight—Weight value of new cluster member. You would only specify this value if you know that some of your cluster members will execute on more powerful hardware than others. In that case, you would assign the members that execute on the more powerful hardware higher weights and the members that execute on less powerful hardware lower weights.

Occasionally used optional arguments:

• genUniquePorts—Generates unique port numbers for HTTP transports defined in the server. The default value is true. None of the authors can think of a reason why you would ever set this value to false.

• specificShortName—Specific short name of cluster member for z/OS platforms. This argument is only used by cluster members that execute on z/OS platforms.

• memberUUID—UUID of new cluster member. By default, a unique identifier is automatically assigned to the cluster member that you are creating. You should probably not use this argument.

- `firstMember`—This step specifies additional information required to configure the first member of a cluster. On more advanced topologies, this step performs some specialized configuration. For example, under Process Server, this step creates some messaging buses that the cluster member will need in order to execute correctly.

Frequently used optional arguments: (The word "optional" is a little misleading here. You must use at least one and possibly two of the following arguments.)

- `templateName`—Name of server template to use as a model for new cluster member. This could be the name of one of the IBM-supplied server templates or a server template you create. If you do not supply this argument, you must identify a configured server in your cell that you wish to use as a model for every server member you ever create in this cluster.

- `templateServerName`—Name of server to use as a template for the new cluster member. If you do not supply a server template name, then you must identify a server in your cell to serve as a model for every server member you ever create for this cluster. If the server name you specify is unique within the entire cell, you do not have to supply a node name.

- `templateServerNode`—Name of node with existing server to use as template for new cluster members. If you do not supply the name of a server template as the model for every member server you create for this cluster, and the server name you supply is not unique throughout the cell, then you must supply the name of the node that contains the server that you wish to use as a model.

Occasionally used optional arguments:

- `nodeGroup`—Name of node group that all cluster member nodes must belong to. This node group must exist before you try to create your first server member of this cluster. In advanced topologies, node groups are a useful tool for deciding how to deal with things like high request volumes, network congestion, network latency, and server failures.

- `coreGroup`—Name of core group that all cluster members must belong to. This core group must exist before you try to create your first server member of this cluster. In advanced topologies, core groups are a useful tool for deciding how to deal with things like high request volumes, network congestion, network latency, and server failures.

- `remoteProxyServer`—If a proxy server was specified and no other servers exist in the cluster, apply its proxy settings to the cluster.

- `eventServiceConfig`—This step specifies the event service configuration of a new member of the cluster. There are no arguments for this step.

- `BPCCreateClusterMember`—Only available and only necessary on WebSphere Process Server. There are no arguments for this step.

- `SCACreateClusterMemberStep`—Only available and only necessary on WebSphere Process Server. There are no arguments for this step.

deleteClusterMember

Deletes one cluster member from a cluster.

Target:

Configuration ID of the cluster member. You must supply either the configuration ID or the arguments listed here.

Frequently used optional arguments: (These arguments are only optional if you choose to supply the configuration ID target just described.)

- `clusterName`—Name of server cluster that the cluster member to be deleted belongs to.
- `memberNode`—Name of node where the cluster member resides.
- `memberName`—Name of cluster member to be deleted.

Steps:

- `replicatorEntry`—This step specifies the removal of a replicator entry for this cluster member.

Frequently used optional arguments:

- `deleteEntry`—Deletes the replicator entry that has the server name of this cluster member from the cluster's replication domain.
- `eventServiceConfig`—This step specifies the event service configuration when a member is deleted from the cluster.
- `WebsvcsConfigCoreGroup`—Frequently used optional argument.
- `coregroupName`—The name of the core group.

deleteCluster

Deletes the selected cluster and all members of the cluster.

Target:

Configuration ID of the cluster you want to delete. You must supply either this target or the argument `clusterName` (see next item).

Frequently used optional argument:

- `clusterName`—Name of server cluster to delete. You must supply either this argument or the target configuration ID (see target just described).

Steps:

- `replicationDomain`—This step specifies the removal of the replication domain for this cluster.

Frequently used optional arguments:

- `deleteRepDomain`—Deletes the replication domain for this cluster.

- `CleanupSIBuses`—This step deletes any messaging bus resources that are part of this cluster's configuration. It takes no arguments.

ConfigArchiveOperations Command Group

The methods in this group either back up an existing configuration or restore some previous configuration.

exportServer

Export the configuration information of a server to a ZIP file.

Required arguments:

- `serverName`—The name of the server whose configuration will be archived.

- `archive`—The fully qualified name of the archive file. Given that the archives are stored in ZIP format, it is a good idea to end the archive file name in `.zip`. Regardless of what the underlying operating system uses for path delimiters in a file name, you must use forward slashes (`'/'`) to separate path names from each other and from the file name.

Frequently used optional argument:

- `nodeName`—The name of node that contains the server you want to export. This argument is optional if the name of the server is unique within the cell. It becomes a mandatory argument if two or more servers have serverName.

importServer

Import a server configuration from a configuration archive. This command creates a new server based on the server configuration defined in the archive.

Required arguments:

- `archive`—The fully qualified name of the zip file that holds archive information for a server.

- `nodeName`—This is the name of the node where you want to create a new server using the archived configuration (the zip file) as a model.

Frequently used optional argument:

- `serverName`—By default, the server you create will have the same name as the server in the archive. If you supply a `serverName` argument, you can have any name you want.

Occasionally used optional arguments:

- `coreGroup`—The name of the core group to which the new server will be assigned. If this parameter is not specified, the newly created server is assigned to the `DefaultCoreGroup`. For simple topologies, this is what you want. For complex topologies, this might not be acceptable, and you should assign the new server to a core group of your choosing. The core group must exist before you call this method.
- `nodeInArchive`—The name of a node defined in the config archive (the zip file). This parameter becomes optional if there is only one node in the archive.
- `serverInArchive`—The name of a server defined in the config archive (the zip file). This parameter becomes optional if there is only one server in the archive.

GenerateSecurityConfigCommand Command Group

There is only one method in this group.

generateSecConfigReport

Creates a report listing the current setting of dozens of configuration items that are known to have security implications. The entire configuration repository of the profile in which this command executes is examined. This method does *not* take the place of a real security audit done by experienced professionals.

PortManagement Command Group

The methods in this group either modify or display the configuration of ports on servers throughout the cell.

listApplicationPorts

Displays a list of ports that is used to access the specified application, including the name of every node and server that has any web module from this application mapped to its web container. For each of those servers, this method displays the named endpoint the host and the port value of each virtual host mapped to that web container.

Target (Mandatory):

The name of the application. This must be the display name of the enterprise application as returned by `AdminApp.list()`.

listServerPorts

Target (Mandatory):

The name of the server.

Frequently used optional argument:

- node—The node that contains the server. If the server name is not unique within the cell, this argument is mandatory.

ServerManagement Command Group

The bulk of the methods that configure the configuration of the process in which a server executes are in this group. It is a very important **AdminTask** group. Methods in this group are among the most frequently used **AdminTask** methods.

listServer

Returns configuration IDs for one or more servers. Lists servers of specified server type and node name. If node name is not specified, whole cell is searched. If the server type is not specified servers of all types are returned. You can use these configuration IDs anywhere you would use a configuration ID from `AdminConfig.getid()` or from `AdminConfig.list()`.

Frequently used optional arguments:

- serverType—Any of the types that `AdminTask.listServerTypes()` returns are legal values here.
- nodeName—If you supply this optional argument, you limit the search to servers that are part of the node you specify.

getServerType

Returns the type of the specified server.

Required arguments:

- serverName—The name of the server.
- nodeName—The name of the node that contains this server.

listServerTypes

Lists the available server types. If you call this method without any target, you will get all the available server types in the entire cell.

Target:

Configuration ID of a node. If you supply this optional target, you will learn what server types you can create in that particular node. Without a target, you discover what server types you can create anywhere in the cell.

showServerInfo

Shows some simple information about a given server. Information includes cell name, node name, server name, server type, and product version.

Target (Mandatory):

Configuration ID of a server.

showServerTypeInfo

Shows some simple information about a server type. Server type must be one of the types returned by `AdminTask.listServerTypes()`. Information includes the name of the template used to create this type of server, the name of the Java class that validates the configuration of this type of server, and the product version of this type of server.

Target (Mandatory):

The name of a server type.

createApplicationServer

Creates a new application server. The **AdminTask** methods that create a proxy server, a web server, and a generic server are similar.

Target (Mandatory):

The name of the node that will contain the new server. Notice that this is a node name rather than a configuration ID.

Required argument:

- `name`—The name of the new server. There are restrictions on the characters that you can use for the name of a server.[18]

Frequently used optional arguments:

- `templateName`—The name of the template that describes how to create the new application server. Although this is an optional argument, it is an extremely good idea to supply this information. The authors strongly recommend it. Although there are default values that WAS is supposed to apply, in some versions and some configurations, this is not done correctly.

Occasionally used optional arguments:

- `specificShortName`—The server-specific short name is applicable only on z/OS platforms. This represents the specific short name of the server. All servers should

---

[18] See the online information for a list of characters that are not allowed. The page is titled "Object names: What the name string cannot contain."

have a unique specific short name. This parameter is optional, and when it is not specified, a unique specific short name is automatically assigned. The value should be eight characters or less and all uppercase.

- `genericShortName`—The server-generic short name is applicable only on z/OS platforms. This represents the generic short name of the server. All members of a cluster should share the same generic short name. Individual servers should have unique generic short name. This parameter is optional, and when it is not specified, a unique generic short name is automatically assigned. The value should be eight characters or less and all uppercase.

- `templateLocation`—The location where the template is stored. WAS uses the system-defined location if it is not specified. Using the system-defined location is recommended. It is not suggested that you supply this argument.

- `genUniquePorts`—Parameter to generate unique http ports for a server. The default value for this argument is `true`. The authors cannot think of any reason for setting it to `false`.

Steps:

- `ConfigCoreGroup`—By default, all servers are part of the `DefaultCoreGroup` unless you create a different core group and move the server from the `DefaultCoreGroup` to the core group you created. In advanced topologies, core groups are a useful tool for deciding how to deal with things like high request volumes, network congestion, network latency, and server failures.

Frequently used optional arguments:

- `coregroupName`—The name of the core group that you want this server to belong to. The core group must exist before you attempt to execute this step.

createApplicationServerTemplate

Creates a new application server template using the specified server as a model. Creating templates for a proxy server, a generic server, or a web server is similar.

Required arguments:

- `templateName`—The name that this template will be called.

- `serverName`—The name of the server that will serve as the model for this template.

- `nodeName`—The node that contains the server that will serve as the model for this template.

Frequently used optional argument:

- `description`—Any text that you choose to describe this part of your configuration.

Occasionally used optional arguments:

- `templateLocation`—This is where the template will be stored. If you do not supply this information, the template will be stored in the default system location with the other templates. Typically, this would be in `config/templates` directory of the profile.

Steps:

- `DeleteSIBEngines`—Do not use any configured `SIBEngines` as part of this template.

deleteServer

Deletes any server.

Required arguments:

- `serverName`—The name of the server you wish to delete.

- `nodeName`—The node that contains the server you wish to delete.

setJVMProperties

Set multiple JVM configuration values in one method call. All of these properties are vendor-independent. All Java virtual machines support them.

Frequently used optional arguments:

- `serverName`—The name of the server whose process definition is modified. If there is only one server in the entire configuration, then this parameter is optional.

- `nodeName`—The name of the node. This is only needed for the server scopes that do not have a unique name across nodes.

- `verboseModeGarbageCollection`—Specifies whether to use verbose debug output for garbage collection. The default is not to enable verbose garbage collection.

- `initialHeapSize`—Specifies the initial heap size available to the JVM code in megabytes.

- `maximumHeapSize`—Specifies the maximum heap size available to the JVM code in megabytes.

- `genericJvmArguments`—Specifies command-line arguments to pass to the Java virtual machine code that starts the application server process.

Occasionally used optional arguments:

- `disableJIT`—Specifies whether to disable the just in time (JIT) compiler option of the JVM code.

- `verboseModeClass`—Specifies whether to use verbose debug output for class loading. The default is not to enable verbose class loading.

- `verboseModeJNI`—Specifies whether to use verbose debug output for native method invocation. The default is not to enable verbose Java Native Interface (JNI) activity.

- `runHProf`—This setting applies to base WebSphere Application Server only. It specifies whether to use HProf profiler support. To use another profiler, specify the custom profiler settings using the HProf arguments setting. The default is not to enable HProf profiler support.

- `classpath`—The standard class path in which the Java virtual machine code looks for classes.

- `executableJarFileName`—Specifies a full path name for an executable Jar file that the JVM code uses.

- `debugMode`—Specifies whether to run the JVM in debug mode. The default is not to enable debug mode support.

- `processType`—The process type of the server. This is for z/OS only.

setJVMSystemProperties

If you need to set some nonstandard JVM property, this is the method that lets you do it.

Required arguments:

- `propertyName`—The name of the JVM system property.

- `propertyValue`—The value you want to assign to that property.

Frequently used optional arguments:

- `serverName`—The name of the Server whose process definition is modified. If there is only one server in the entire configuration, then this parameter is optional.

- `nodeName`—The name of the node. This is only needed for the server scopes that do not have a unique name across nodes.

Occasionally used optional argument:

- `processType`—The process type of the server. This is for z/OS only.

setProcessDefinition

If you have to integrate a JBoss server (or any other non-IBM product) into your cell, this is the method you can call to set the commands that start and stop the non-IBM server. You can also use it to set the working directory of a WAS server to some non-standard directory. All of the arguments are optional because IBM has no way of knowing what attributes you will have to set in order to integrate that non-IBM server.

Frequently used optional arguments:

* `serverName`—The name of the Server whose process definition is modified. If there is only one server in the entire configuration, then this parameter is optional.

* `nodeName`—The name of the node. This is only needed for the server scopes that do not have a unique name across nodes.

* `workingDirectory`—The file system directory that the process uses as its current working directory.

Occasionally used optional arguments:

* `executableName`—The executable name that is invoked to start the process. This parameter is only applicable to WebSphere Application Server.

* `executableArguments`—The arguments that are passed to the process when it is started. This parameter is applicable to WebSphere Application Server only.

* `processType`—The process type of the server. This is for zOS only.

* `startCommandArgs`—This command applies to the z/OS platform only. It specifies any additional arguments required by the start command.

* `stopCommandArgs`—This parameter applies to the z/OS platform only. It specifies any additional arguments required by the stop command.

* `terminateCommandArgs`—This parameter only applies to the z/OS platform. It specifies any additional arguments required by the terminate command.

* `executableTarget`—The name of the executable target (a Java class containing a `main()` method or the name of an executable Jar), depending on the executable target.

* `executableTargetKind`—The type of the executable target (`JAVA_CLASS` | `EXECUTABLE_JAR`).

Server Management Methods that Do Not Belong to Any Command Group

The method below is not part of any command group. This could well be an oversight on the part of IBM. This method might migrate into the `ServerManagement` command group in some future release.

createServerType

This method is intended to be used by developers that need to create a new `ServerType`. In general, this would only occur for a product that needs to include and make use of a WebSphere Application Server environment. So the users of this method are not going to be "normal" administrators of or application developers for the WebSphere Application Server product.

Required arguments:

* `version`—Product version.

- serverType—What kind of server will this be called?

- createTemplateCommand—This is the command that creates a server template.

- createCommand—This is the command that will create a new server of this type.

- configValidator—This is the class that will validate the configuration for this server type.

Summary

This chapter began our exploration of the complex world of the **AdminTask** scripting object. We explored a subset of the methods that manage server configuration. In the chapters that follow, we explore the methods of **AdminTask** that control security configuration, database configuration, and messaging configuration.

Scripting and Security

The **AdminApp**, **AdminConfig**, and **AdminTask** scripting objects are all useful in configuring Web-Sphere security. In this chapter, we consider the following security items and present examples of scripted administration of these issues:

- Create / List / Modify / Remove JAAS (J2C) Aliases
- Enable / Disable Administrative Security
- Enable / Disable Application Security
- Map Java EE Roles to Users and/or Groups
- Enable / Disable Java 2 Security
- Configure Additional LDAP Hosts for Failover
- Federated Registries
- Configure Multiple Security Domains

WebSphere Security Basics

Addressing security is essential when administrating an application server. Your enemy does exist and is well trained, well funded, well equipped, and highly motivated. Moreover the economic costs incurred from having an improperly secured environment can be staggering, both to the company and to its clientèle. To be sure, security is not just a WebSphere configuration issue. Security must be addressed pervasively and systemically.

Even within the realm of WebSphere, this book can touch on only a few common security concerns, so please be sure to read the appropriate WebSphere Application Server Security Handbook for your version of WebSphere. For details on WebSphere V6.1 security, this would be the

IBM WebSphere Application Server V6.1 Security Handbook (SG246316)—a volume equal in size to this entire book. In this book, we focus on some of what you, the WebSphere Administrator, can do to configure WebSphere security using scripting.

Loosely speaking, security within WebSphere is manifested in several ways, including the following:

- **Authentication:** Used to establish an identity
  - User Registry, which is used to establish user identity.
  - JAAS (J2C) Authentication Data, which is used with Datasources, SIB resources, and other JCA-managed resources.
- **Authorization:** Used to establish permissions or rights
  - Role-based Authorization, which assigns permissions to an entity to access Java EE resources such as Web URLs and EJB methods.
  - Java 2 Security, which assigns permissions to Java code to access controlled resources, such as files, sockets, and so on.

We use **AdminApp**, **AdminConfig**, and **AdminTask** as appropriate to manipulate these security aspects. By now we assume that you are familiar with `AdminConfig.save()` and `AdminConfig.reset()` and know when to use each, so we will leave them out of our examples.

JAAS (J2C) Aliases

Whether alternately referred to in WebSphere as Authentication Aliases, JAAS Authentication Data, J2C Authentication Data, or Authentication Data Entries (depending on where you are in the product and what documentation you are reading), these configuration items consist of an alias name, a user name, a password, and an optional description. The term "J2C" is IBM-specific and appears to be in the process of being phased out. You will still find it in the Integrated Solutions Console and in the scripting documentation, where it refers to "J2EE Connector Architecture (J2C)" authentication data. The standard name for the latter is Java Connector Architecture, and the acronym is JCA. Whatever we call them, these are important configuration items.

In this section, we take a look at creating these reusable items. In the sections on JDBC and SIB, we present examples using them. We also examine the standard CRUD operations: create, retrieve, update and delete. To do so, we start with **AdminConfig**. WebSphere V7 does add new **AdminTask** commands for these items, which we also review.

All of the current, real code is on the book's FTP site. The files are `JAASAliases.py` and `JAASAliasTasks.py`. Here, we look at the key segments.

Create a J2C (JAAS) Alias

Prior to WebSphere 7, **AdminConfig** was used to create a `JAASAuthData` configuration object. As you will see, this may continue to be your method of choice when working with WebSphere 7, as well. The only real trick to creating a `JAASAuthData` object is knowing its parent, which is the Security configuration object.

Listing 12.1 shows a simple method for creating a JAASAuthData object. As a reminder, the '\' character at the end of a line is the standard "continuation character" and is used when text that should logically be treated as one line does not fit on one line. Remember that AdminConfig.create() can take a list of lists specifying the creation parameters for the item being constructed. The parameter list is constructed by listing all of the possible parameters in the form of nested [key, value]-pairs, and then using a list comprehension to eliminate any for which the value is None. There are other means by which to construct variable parameter lists, but you may find this one more concise and clear once you understand the idiom.

Listing 12.1 Method for Creating a JAASAuthData Object[1]

```
def createJAASAlias(alias, userid, password, description=None):
    securityConfigID = AdminConfig.getid("/Security:/")
    opt = [ item for item in ['alias', alias], \
                ['description', description], \
                ['userId', userid],          \
                ['password',password] if item[1] ]
    return AdminConfig.create( 'JAASAuthData', securityConfigID, opt )
```

In Listing 12.1, this crucial configuration object was created using **AdminConfig**. But as discussed in the previous chapter, you are urged to use **AdminTask** instead of the more primitive administrative objects whenever you can. If nothing else, with **AdminConfig**, you need to know the internal name for what you want to create and have no interactive help in creating it. With **AdminTask**, you just need to know what values you want and can have interactive help in building the command.

WebSphere V7 introduced a new **AdminTask** command, createAuthDataEntry, for performing the same task just completed using **AdminConfig**. The parameters for it are the same as for **AdminConfig**: an alias, a description, a password, and a user. There is also an optional security domain name for working with the new security domains feature of WebSphere 7.

Listing 12.2 presents a simple method of invoking createAuthDataEntry. Again, you make use of a list comprehension to construct a list of lists containing the parameters. However, this time, you need a flat list for **AdminTask**. The denest utility method, which is on the FTP site, takes a list of lists and returns a de-nested list, e.g., converting [["key1", "value1"], ["key2", "value2"]] to ["key1", "value1", "key2","value2"]. This provides the necessary parameter for createAuthDataEntry. Note that although you have to provide the parameters for the actual configuration item (see Listing 12.1 for a full set), you no longer need to know details about its parent or its internal type.

---

[1] This is the one time that we will show you the full options list if it extends over a line of text, because we want you to understand the Python idiom being used. In other cases, if the code does not fit, we'll elide it, which means using "..." in place of the full text. See the companion web site for full listings.

Listing 12.2   Using **AdminTask** to Create an Authentication Data Entry

```
def createJAASAlias_Task(alias, user, pwd, desc=None, domain=None):
    params = denest([ i for i in ['-alias', alias], ... if item[1] ])
    return AdminTask.createAuthDataEntry(params)
```

So let's go ahead and use these methods in a **wsadmin** session connected to a WebSphere
V7 deployment manager. Listing 12.3 shows a **wsadmin** session loading the code using
execfile and then executing the methods to test them.

Listing 12.3   Testing the createJAASAlias* Methods

```
wsadmin>execfile("JAASAliases.py")
wsadmin>execfile("JAASAliasTasks.py")
wsadmin>id1 = createJAASAlias("myAlias", "me", "pwd")
wsadmin>id2 = createJAASAlias_Task("yourAlias", "you", "pwd")
```

Viewing JAAS Aliases

OK, well, they're now created, so let's now take a look at them. You can use AdminConfig
.show() with the configuration ID that was just returned from creating the JAAS Aliases, as is
done in Listing 12.4, or you can use AdminConfig.list("JAASAuthData") to retrieve them.
In WebSphere V7, you can also use AdminTask.listAuthDataEntries():

```
wsadmin>print AdminTask.listAuthDataEntries()
[[alias myAlias] [userId me] [description ] ... ]
[[alias was7host01CellManager01/yourAlias] [userId you] ... ]
```

Listing 12.4   Viewing the JAAS Aliases

```
wsadmin>print AdminConfig.show(id1)
[alias myAlias]
[password *****]
[userId me]
wsadmin>print AdminConfig.show(id2)
[alias was7host01CellManager01/yourAlias]
[password *****]
[userId you]
```

However, there is an issue here. The AdminTask.createAuthDataEntry()
command—and the WebSphere V6.1 (prior to FixPack 23) and V7.0 Integrated Solutions
Console—implicitly prefix the alias with the node name of the current administrative service

(*q.v.,* `AdminControl.getNode()`). You will not find this in the **AdminTask** documentation; it just does it, leading to problems when trying to manipulate JAAS Aliases via scripting. For example, in the `JAASAliases.py` file, you will find code for finding an authentication entry by its alias name, which can be used to view it, as shown in Listing 12.5.

Listing 12.5   Viewing JAAS Aliases by Name

```
wsadmin>showJAASAlias("myAlias")
[alias myAlias]
[password *****]
[userId me]
wsadmin>showJAASAlias("yourAlias")
wsadmin>showJAASAlias("was7host01CellManager01/yourAlias")
[alias was7host01CellManager01/yourAlias]
[password *****]
[userId you]
```

Notice that the second call failed because `yourAlias` does not exist, even though that was the name used when it was created.

It would be a bad idea to modify the code for locating an entry by alias to strip off the prefix because there is no guarantee that the un-prefixed aliases are unique. It would be potentially devastating to change (or delete, as in section 12.2.4) the wrong authentication entry. If you consider using `AdminControl.getNode() + "/" + alias"`, keep in mind that if the entry were created in a pre-federated node, you would have an unresolvable mismatch post-federation, due to the runtime value of `AdminControl.getNode()`. **AdminConfig** does not implicitly prefix, which is why you might prefer to use it, even with WebSphere V7, until this naming issue is resolved. This way, you can maintain control over the exact alias name used.

Modify a JAAS Alias

Having created (and viewed) our authentication aliases, we might need to change them in the future, for example if the credentials used to access a database change. You can do this is with `AdminConfig.modify()`, which you can see in Listing 12.6, just as you would for other configuration items.

Listing 12.6   Modifying a JAAS Alias

```
def changeJAASAlias(alias,userid=None,password=None,description=None):
    e = getJAASByAlias(alias)
    if e:
        opt = [ i for i in ['description', desc], ... if item[1] ]
        AdminConfig.modify(e, opt )
```

Once again, you use the list comprehension idiom to populate the necessary list regardless of which set of attributes you wish to modify; any for which the value is None will be left out of the list and thus unmodified. You could use changeJAASAlias or one of the several convenience methods, such as changeJAASPassword—all of these are in JAASAliases.py.

Listing 12.7 shows a **wsadmin** session, where you can view the contents of a JAAS alias, modify it, and view the modified result.

Listing 12.7   Testing the Ability to Modify a JAAS Alias

```
wsadmin>showJAASAlias("myAlias")
[alias myAlias]
[password *****]
[userId me]
wsadmin>changeJAASAlias("myAlias", userid="newuser",
password="newpassword", description="Use me!")
wsadmin>showJAASAlias("myAlias")
[alias myAlias]
[description "Use me!"]
[password *****]
[userId newuser]
```

Delete a JAAS Alias

We complete our tour of the CRUD operations by deleting JAAS Aliases. Both AdminConfig.remove() and AdminTask.deleteAuthDataEntry() provide the necessary means.

In the case of AdminConfig.remove(), you need the configuration ID, so once again you need to use the utility code to delete it by alias name. Listing 12.8 shows the solution, and Listing 12.9 illustrates it being used.

Listing 12.8   Delete a JAAS Entry by Name

```
def deleteJAASAlias(alias):
    "Delete a named JAAS entry by alias"
    id = getJAASByAlias(alias)
    if id:
        AdminConfig.remove(id)
```

Listing 12.9   Testing the Ability to Delete a JAAS Entry

```
wsadmin>showJAASAlias("myAlias")
[alias myAlias]
```

```
[description "Use me!"]
[password *****]
[userId newuser]
wsadmin>deleteJAASAlias("myAlias")
wsadmin>showJAASAlias("myAlias")
wsadmin>
```

The `AdminTask.deleteAuthDataEntry` command makes the coding a bit easier because you don't have to search for the configuration ID. You do have to properly format the parameter, so once again you can turn to de-nesting a list comprehension to do the preparation. Listing 12.10 shows that implementation. A coding advantage here is that you did not need to look up the configuration ID.

Listing 12.10   Deleting a JAAS Entry by Name Using AdminTask

```
def deleteJAASAlias_Task(alias, domain=None):
    "Delete a named JAAS entry by alias"
    params = denest([ i for i in ['-alias', alias], ... if i[1] ])
    AdminTask.deleteAuthDataEntry(params)
```

But what about the prefixing issue? Let's take a look at some examples. First, looking at the short example in Listing 12.11, notice that `AdminTask.deleteAuthDataEntry` deleted the JAAS Alias regardless of whether or not there was a prefix. This is not necessarily a good thing, as you can see from the longer example in Listing 12.12.

Listing 12.11   Experimenting with Deleting JAAS Aliases

```
wsadmin>showJAASAlias("myAlias")
[alias myAlias]
[password *****]
[userId me]
wsadmin>deleteJAASAlias_Task("myAlias")
wsadmin>showJAASAlias("myAlias")
wsadmin>showJAASAlias("yourAlias")
wsadmin>showJAASAlias("was7host01CellManager01/yourAlias")
[alias was7host01CellManager01/yourAlias]
[password *****]
[userId you]
wsadmin>deleteJAASAlias_Task("yourAlias")
wsadmin>showJAASAlias("was7host01CellManager01/yourAlias")
wsadmin>
```

Listing 12.12   A Longer Example

```
wsadmin>showJAASEntries()
- - - - - - -
[alias was7host01CellManager01/myAlias]
[password *****]
[userId user2]
- - - - - - -
[alias myAlias]
[password *****]
[userId me]
- - - - - - -
wsadmin>deleteJAASAlias_Task("myAlias")
wsadmin>showJAASEntries()
- - - - - - -
[alias myAlias]
[password *****]
[userId me]
- - - - - - -
wsadmin>createJAASAlias_Task("myAlias", "otherUser", "somepwd")
wsadmin>showJAASEntries()
- - - - - - -
[alias myAlias]
[password *****]
[userId me]
- - - - - - -
[alias was7host01CellManager01/myAlias]
[password *****]
[userId otherUser]
- - - - - - -
wsadmin>deleteJAASAlias_Task("myAlias")
wsadmin>showJAASEntries()
- - - - - - -
[alias was7host01CellManager01/myAlias]
[password *****]
[userId otherUser]
- - - - - - -
```

Whoa! What just happened?! Listing 12.12 started with two aliases, in order:
was7host01CellManager01/myAlias and myAlias. We deleted myAlias and found that

the first one, with the prefix, was deleted. We then recreated it, which put the prefixed entry after the non-prefixed entry and did the delete again. This time the non-prefixed entry was removed. In both cases, `AdminTask.deleteAuthDataEntry()` deleted the first `JAASAuthData` item whose alias matched after stripping off the prefix, if any. According to Murphy's Law, the `JAASAuthData` item removed would have been the one you can least afford to lose and would have been crucial to the runtime behavior of your enterprise. And Murphy was an optimist.

Perhaps for now we can agree that it might be a best practice to stick with **AdminConfig** for working with `JAASAuthData` items until this naming issue can be resolved and documented.

Configuring Application Security

The Java EE specification allows enterprise applications to declare security constraints on Web and EJB resources. This is why WebSphere forces you to login when you attempt to access certain URLs (and why you are denied access if you don't have the rights). This specification also allows WebSphere to enforce who can and cannot invoke various EJB methods. For WebSphere to enforce those constraints, application security must be enabled and configured.

Prior to WebSphere V6.1, Administrative and application security were conflated into a single switch, known as *global security*. That changed with WebSphere V6.1. By default, new cells (Deployment Manager and Standalone Server profiles) are created with Administrative security enabled and Application security disabled. The name global security still exists but now refers to Administrative security.

For the moment, let's assume that you have configured your cell's registry the way you need it and will look at the security configuration required to be able to enforce Java EE application security.

Enabling/Disabling Administrative and Application Security

For application security to work, you must first enable administrative security. That is normally the case, so let's just verify that is enabled.

```
wsadmin> print AdminTask.isGlobalSecurityEnabled()
true
```

If it were off, you would turn it on with the following:

```
wsadmin> AdminTask.setGlobalSecurity ('[-enabled true]')
```

This example presumes that your registry is properly configured, which you can assume at this point. Now you can turn on application security, which requires knowledge of the proper attribute of the Security object. Listing 12.13 illustrates testing, setting, and verifying the setting.

Listing 12.13 Enabling Application Security

```
wsadmin>print AdminTask.isAppSecurityEnabled()
false
```

```
wsadmin>securityConfigID = AdminConfig.getid("/Security:/")
wsadmin>AdminConfig.modify(securityConfigID,[['appEnabled','true']])
''

wsadmin>print AdminTask.isAppSecurityEnabled()
true
```

Don't forget that in order for these settings to take effect, you must save them, synchronize, and restart the cell. After you've enabled application security, you can move on to mapping users and/or groups to the security roles defined by each application.

As an aside, we find that Administrators working with WebSphere security for the first time often need to disable Administrative security because they have locked themselves out for one reason or another. Should this happen to you, use what is possibly the world's most common single-line **wsadmin** command:

```
$ wsadmin -conntype NONE -c "securityoff"
```

Yes, it does exactly what you think it does. If the user executing that command has file system write access to the profile's config/directory, security will be turned off.

Mapping Java EE Roles

Once application security is enabled, a common administrative activity is mapping users or groups to application roles. This must be done for each application that you want secured, so a common question is how to handle that via scripting. Let's now look at how to do that using the **AdminApp** scripting object.

As a reminder, the basic idea is that the Java EE application can define various named roles. A *role* is nothing more than a label. EJB modules can declare that in order to invoke a given method, the requesting user must have a particular role. Likewise, Web modules can declare that to access a URL, the user must have a particular role. These constraints are enforced by the Web container for Web modules and the EJB container for EJB modules.

The roles and constraints are defined by deployment descriptors in the application, which can be modified and redeployed, but the mapping of actual users and/or groups to roles is maintained by WebSphere itself. This leads us to the mention of a best practice. Please be sure to always map only groups to roles. There are multiple reasons for this:

- The volume of user to role mappings would be exceedingly onerous in most production environments. Consider: Would you rather have WebSphere maintain in its XML files a few groups mapped to various roles or thousands of entries for users mapped to those roles?

- The corporate role of administrating users is generally assigned to someone other than a WebSphere Administrator—generally it is performed by LDAP Administrators using interfaces more suitable to the task than the WebSphere Integrated Solutions Console.

So what you want to do consistently is map users to groups in the user registries and then map groups to roles within WebSphere. For now, having expressed that best practice, let's focus on the mechanics of performing the mappings via scripting. You have the choice of following that practice or not.

The actual mapping of roles to users and/or groups is provided by the `MapRolesToUsers` task of **AdminApp**, which is available in three contexts: installing, editing, and updating applications. The content of the `MapRolesToUsers` is the same for all three, so we're going to just work with `AdminApp.edit()` in this chapter. You can take the same nested list structure and add it as an option when installing or updating an application.

Review the Current and Available Mappings

Before you begin mapping roles, you might want to view the current assignments. This is not something you are likely to do in an automated situation, and it can easily be done in the Integrated Solutions Console. But you will still want to know how to query it in a script, and you will certainly want to do it when debugging your scripts—particularly if you ever want to author scripts that modify existing mappings, given that `MapRolesToUsers` *replaces* the existing mappings, rather than modifies them.

The **AdminApp**.`view()` method provides the means for viewing the current assignments:

```
wsadmin>print AdminApp.view("ivtApp", "-MapRolesToUsers")


MapRolesToUsers: Mapping users to roles
. . .
```

In `MapRoles.py`, you find convenience methods for displaying the roles of a single application or all the applications in your installation.

Mapping Roles to Users and/or Groups

So now we come down to actually performing the mapping. Despite all of the inquiries from people about how to do this, the only real "trick" to performing this task is formatting the option parameter. So that's what we'll look at, and then you'll see how easy it is to actually perform the mappings via scripting. The basic structure is as follows:

```
["-MapRolesToUsers", roleMappings]
```

This is pretty easy, just a list consisting of the task name and a parameter. The `roleMappings` item itself is just a list of lists. Each inner list consists of the following five `String` entries, in order, and each must be present:

1. Role Name
2. Everyone? ("yes" | "no")
3. All Authenticated? ("yes" | "no")

   4. Mapped Users ("user1|user2|...userN")

   5. Mapped Group ("group1|group2|...groupN")

You can construct the entire list structure for a single role with the code shown in Listing 12.14.
The `mapOneRoleToUsersOrGroups` function in `MapRoles.py` puts that all together.

Listing 12.14   Mapping to a J2EE Role

```
# role     is the name of the role
# everyone is "yes" or "no" to say if everyone has the role
# allAuth  is "yes" or "no" to say if every authenticated
#          user has the role
# users    is a LIST of strings, one for each user
# groups   is a LIST of strings, one for each group

# create a single role mapping
roleMapping = [role, everyone, allAuth, \
               '|'.join(users), '|'.join(groups)]

# The construct '|'.join(list) converts the list of Strings
# into the single '|' separated string we need.

# put that role within a list.
roleMappings = [rolemapping]

# If we had multiple roles, we would create
# additional roleMapping values, and append
# them to roleMappings, e.g.
# roleMappings = [role1Mapping role2mapping ... roleNmapping]

# finally, create the list the defines the task
options=["-MapRolesToUsers", roleMappings]

# All that remains is to apply this to the application
AdminApp.edit(application, options)
```

   Listing 12.15 shows multiple experiments using the `mapOneRoleToUsersOrGroups`
function. Each invocation would replace the settings made by the preceding invocation.

Listing 12.15   Mapping J2EE Roles

```
# Clear any existing assignments for the Admin role on MyApp
mapOneRoleToUsersOrGroups("MyApp", "Admin")
```

```
# Give everyone the Admin role on MyApp
mapOneRoleToUsersOrGroups("MyApp", "Admin", everyone="yes")

# Give every (and only) authenticated user the Admin role on MyApp
mapOneRoleToUsersOrGroups("MyApp", "Admin", allAuth="yes")

# Give wasadmin the Admin role on MyApp
mapOneRoleToUsersOrGroups("MyApp", "Admin", users=["wasadmin"])

# Give me and you the Admin role on MyApp
mapOneRoleToUsersOrGroups("MyApp", "Admin", users=["me", "you"])

# Give members of wasadmins the Admin role on MyApp
mapOneRoleToUsersOrGroups("MyApp", "Admin", groups=["wasadmins"])

# Give members of us and them the Admin role on MyApp
mapOneRoleToUsersOrGroups("MyApp", "Admin", groups=["us", "them"])
```

Remember that these Java EE roles are not global to WebSphere. Each application has its own roles and mappings, even if the role names are the same across multiple applications. So someone might be an Admin for MyApp but not an Admin for YourApp.

Enable/Disable Java 2 Security

In the preceding section, Java EE application security was enabled, and groups (or users if you insist) were mapped to Java EE security roles. There is another type of security defined within the Java runtime environment, known as "Java 2 security." This is a totally different type of security. Where the Java EE role-based security is permissive by default, until a deployment descriptor defines role-based constraints, once Java 2 security is turned off, it denies by default.

Java 2 security is embedded within Java classes themselves and protects access to resources such as files, network sockets, and so on. Java 2 Security determines which bits of code will have access to which resources. The decision is governed by the presence of "policy" files. WebSphere provides policy files for itself and some general basics for applications. But unless they don't need access to protected resources, applications must be prepared for Java 2 security by providing an application-specific policy file, which is was.policy in the EAR file. For this reason, Java 2 security defaults to being off. This default setting, however, is undesirable from a security perspective, and IBM recommends that you enable Java 2 security.

From a security and WebSphere Administration perspective, there is a lot that we could discuss about Java 2 security. Consider this: Are you running third-party software without Java 2 security? How many of your developers are building with software modules of, quite frankly, unknown provenance that have been automatically downloaded from repositories, for example, by Maven?

If you are running without Java 2 security enabled, you are permitting whatever code is installed in your JVM to do whatever it wants. And once you have enabled Java 2 security, someone should review the security policy for each and every installed application to ensure that rogue permissions are not present.

Sound paranoid? Well, this *is* a chapter about security, and paranoia is a positive, adaptive trait in a security person. It is not a question of whether or not there are people who want what you have; it is simply a question of stopping them.

From a scripting perspective, however, there is relatively little for us to do with Java 2 security. Basically, it is a matter of enabling or disabling it and perhaps manipulating the was.policy file.

The steps to enable or disable Java 2 security are quite straightforward and can be performed with either **AdminConfig** or **AdminTask**. To enable Java 2 security, enter the following:

```
wsadmin> param = '-enforceJava2Security true'
wsadmin> AdminTask.setAdminActiveSecuritySettings(param)
```

or to disable Java 2 security, change the assignment to use `false`:

```
wsadmin> param = '-enforceJava2Security false'
```

The **AdminConfig** alternative is:

```
wsadmin> securityConfigID = AdminConfig.getid("/Security:/")
wsadmin> param = [['enforceJava2Security', 'true']]
wsadmin> AdminConfig.modify(securityConfigID, param)
```

Again, to disable Java 2 security, change the assignment to use `false`:

```
wsadmin> param = [['enforceJava2Security','true (or false)']]
```

The steps to manipulate the was.policy file are to extract it to a known location, modify it, and then update the file. The **AdminConfig** object provides the necessary means for "extracting" and "checking in" the file, as is shown later in the chapter. What you do for manipulating it is up to you. The fact that you can do this on the fly, rather than via an application update, is arguably of questionable value, but you might have some emergent need.

With both `AdminConfig.extract()` and `AdminConfig.checkin()`, you need the path to the file in the application. The format of this is as follows:

```
cell/cellname/applications/app_ear/deployments/app_name/META-
INF/was.policy
```

An example of using this with the default application is shown in Listing 12.16.

Listing 12.16   Accessing an Application's was.policy

```
wsadmin> p =  "cells/was7host01Cell101/applications/"
wsadmin> p += "DefaultApplication.ear/deployments/"
```

```
wsadmin> p += "DefaultApplication/META-INF/was.policy"
wsadmin> digest = AdminConfig.extract(p, "/tmp/was.policy")
... at this point in time, make some change to the file and then ...
wsadmin> AdminConfig.checkin(p, "/tmp/was.policy", digest)
```

You can extract the was.policy file to /tmp/was.policy, make some changes (in this case, just adding a comment to indicate that it has been approved), and replace it. Then you simply need to restart the application for the new Java 2 security policy to take effect. The *digest* is simply a token provided when you extract the file that you must provide back when replacing the file.

LDAP Failover

If you have configured WebSphere to use LDAP for authentication, you might have asked what would happen if that were to fail. The answer, of course, is that if the repository is not available, it cannot authenticate. In case you are wondering—no, a federated registry is not a solution to this problem.

If anything, a federated registry actually makes the situation more precarious. Consider the following scenario: In a federated registry, you have an LDAP managed by Human Resources for employees, another LDAP managed by the Business Partner Liaison office for Business Partners, and a third LDAP for web customers. Remember that WebSphere enforces unique user identity across the entire federated space, therefore if any one of those LDAP registries is not available, WebSphere will not permit login from the others because it cannot ensure that even though an ID is found in the one registry, that the same ID does not exist in one that failed.

The solution to the problem of LDAP availability is to establish a cluster of (usually replicated) LDAP servers whenever you use LDAP. But having done that, how do you tell WebSphere to use it? That depends on whether you are working with a standalone LDAP repository or a federated registry.

For a federated registry, the WebSphere V7 Integrated Solutions Console allows you to add multiple servers to an LDAP repository, as does the **AdminTask**.addIdMgrLDAPServer() scripting command. More on that in the next section. For the remainder of this section, we discuss the standalone LDAP repository case.

The WebSphere Integrated Solutions Console allows you to enter a single LDAP host in the form of a host address and port. You could add a load balancer in front of the LDAP cluster, at the expense of additional hardware, complexity, and network latency—or, if all you need is failover support, you could simply tell WebSphere about the additional LDAP servers.

Scripting allows you to add as many LDAP hosts as you want, and there is even an example in the InfoCenter that makes it all seem rather straightforward. But as simple as it seems on the surface, you are going to find out that things are not quite so simple when working with the hosts attribute of LDAPUserRegistry. And because this is hardly the only place where this lack of simplicity can raise its head, we might as well examine the issues. For example, the

InfoCenter shows that you modify the `hosts` attribute with a list of lists that you can describe as follows:

```
[[["host" <ip>]["port" <port>]]+]
```

But let's start by seeing what there is before making any changes:

```
wsadmin>AdminConfig.showAttribute(myLDAP, "hosts")
'[(cells/was7host01Cell01|security.xml#EndPoint_1)]'
```

Hello! That doesn't look like a list of lists containing `[["host" <ip>]["port" <port>]]` pairs. And even though that appears to be a list of something, it is actually a string. Converting the full range of JACL-formatted strings that smell like a list (which is what **wsadmin** too often provides, even though JACL has been deprecated) can be quite a chore, but in this particular case, it will turn out to be fairly straightforward. You can convert from this string to a list of configuration ids by the simple expedient of:

```
hosts=AdminConfig.showAttribute(myLDAP, "hosts")[1:-1].split(' ')
```

Now that you have it, what exactly *is* it? You can discover that in two ways—first by looking at the attributes of `LDAPUserRegistry` and second by looking at what type is associated with the configuration id that was just isolated. Those are checked in Listing 12.17, and you can see what attributes that particular type has.

Listing 12.17   Exploring `LDAPUserRegistry`

```
wsadmin>print AdminConfig.attributes("LDAPUserRegistry")
...
hosts EndPoint*
...
wsadmin>print AdminConfig.getObjectType(hosts[0])
EndPoint
wsadmin>print AdminConfig.attributes("EndPoint")
host String
port int
wsadmin>AdminConfig.show(hosts[0])
'[host []]\n[port 389]'
```

As shown in Listing 12.17, the `hosts` attribute is (logically) a list of configuration ids, each of which is an `EndPoint`, each of which has a host and port attribute. Showing the `EndPoint` gives us a string, not an interesting data structure to work with. So although adding LDAP servers is a simple matter of properly formatting a list of lists, doing anything else with them would be a bit more work. We're going to show you how to add, set, remove and view the hosts. All of the code is in the `LDAP.py` file available from the companion website.

Viewing the Hosts

Because it will be useful to have as you develop the other capabilities, the first thing that to look at is how to view the hosts. Remember that what you're going to get is a long string that looks like a list of configuration ids. Not very useful to us humans. Believe it or not, though, you can generate a human readable list of `[["host" <ip>]["port" <port>]]` pairs with precisely one line of Python code. For purpose of fitting on this page, the code is formatted a bit differently, using two helpful functions to help format the code, in Listing 12.18, to fit the page width.

Listing 12.18   Generating a List of `host:port` Pairs for an LDAP Registry

```
def h(e):
    return AdminConfig.showAttribute(endpoint, "host")

def p(e):
    return int(AdminConfig.showAttribute(endpoint, "port"))

def showLDAPHosts(id):
    "For an LDAP registry, show all the hosts"

    eps = AdminConfig.showAttribute(id, "hosts")[1:-1].split(" ")
    print [[["host", h(e)], ["port", p(e)]] for e in eps]
```

First there's that long string containing configuration ids. We removed the surrounding brackets and made a list from it, splitting at the spaces. That provided a list of configuration ids for `EndPoint` objects. And then the fun began. If you haven't yet realized the power of Python list comprehensions, you should start to do so now. In one concise statement that clearly illustrated the desired format, a list comprehension was used to iterate over the list of Endpoint configuration ids and produce the desired list of `[["host" <ip>]["port" <port>]]` nested lists. This problem of having to convert from a string formatted data structure that was originally designed to work with the TCL language to a format you can conveniently use with Python is so common in WebSphere scripting that such examples are important to understand and study. And the difference between having this code and not?

```
wsadmin>AdminConfig.showAttribute(myLDAP, "hosts")
'[(cells/was7host01Cell01|security.xml#EndPoint_1)]'
wsadmin>showLDAPHosts(myLDAP)
[[['host', ''], ['port', 389]]]
```

This will become useful as you start to manipulate the list of LDAP hosts.

Adding Additional LDAP Hosts

The key to adding additional hosts is the proper formatting of the hosts attribute of an `LDAPUserRegistry` configuration object, which you can see in Listing 12.19.

Listing 12.19   Adding a Failover LDAP Host

```
def addLDAPHosts(ldapID, hosts):
  "For an LDAP registry (configID) add hosts [[ip,port]+]"

  p = [["hosts", []]]
  p[0][1].extend([[["host",h[0]],["port",h[1]]] for h in hosts])
  AdminConfig.modify(ldapID, p)
```

The `addLDAPHosts` method in Listing 12.19 expects us to pass a nested list of ip-address and port pairs, and modifies the `hosts` attribute. But please note that although it uses **AdminConfig**.`modify`, it is called `add`, a point that is illustrated in Listing 12.20.

Listing 12.20   Adding LDAP Hosts

```
wsadmin>addLDAPHosts(myLDAP, [["127.0.0.1", 389],["127.0.0.2", 389]])
wsadmin>AdminConfig.showAttribute(myLDAP, "hosts")
'[(cells/was7host01Cell01|security.xml#EndPoint_1243664679144)
(cells/was7host01Cell01|security.xml#EndPoint_1243664679145)
(cells/was7host01Cell01|security.xml#EndPoint_1243664679146)]'
wsadmin>showLDAPHosts(myLDAP)
[[['host', ''], ['port', 389]],
 [['host', '127.0.0.1'], ['port', 389]],
 [['host', '127.0.0.2'], ['port', 389]]]
```

Remember that when using **AdminConfig**.`modify()` to modify something that is a list, the effect is to append the items to the existing list. The single existing entry on the original list consisted of an empty host address and the standard LDAP port 389. That single existing entry is the default value for the hosts attribute of a `LDAPUserRegistry` object. You can see how to view the actual host information, rather than the configuration ids for the `EndPoint` objects.

Setting the Host List

As you saw in the preceding section, when using **AdminConfig**.`modify()` to modify something that is a list, the effect is to append the items to the existing list. Even experienced scripting programmers get burned by this behavior. When you need to replace a list, the pattern for dealing with it is to call **AdminConfig**.`modify()` twice. First set the list to `[]` (an empty list). Then set the desired values. The `setLDAPHosts()` function in Listing 12.21 uses this pattern to make its implementation very simple. Recall that addLDAPHosts() prepares the necessary parameter and calls AdminConfig.modify() to modify the list, setLDAPHosts() just calls addLDAPHosts() twice: once with an empty list to clear the value and the other with the desired replacement list.

Listing 12.21   Setting a New Host List for an LDAP Registry

```
def setLDAPHosts(ldapID, hosts):
    "For an LDAP registry (configID) set the hosts [[ip,port]+]"

    # first reset the list so that we can add to it anew
    addLDAPHosts(ldapID, [])
    addLDAPHosts(ldapID, hosts)
```

The fact that calling something called add with an empty list actually deletes the entire value is certainly a semantically odd side-effect, so if it offends you, you would want to check that the list is not empty and report an error if an empty list is passed. This would apply not only to this code, but to any code of your own authorship that similarly modifies a list attribute.

Removing LDAP Hosts

Remember that even though you set the hosts attribute by providing actual address and port settings, under the covers those are used to create EndPoint configuration items, whose configuration ids are the actual content of the hosts attribute. This means that selectively removing LDAP hosts from an existing LDAP server ought not be addressed by constructing the nested list of current hosts, removing the ones you want removed, and setting the revised list back to the LDAPUserRegistry. Instead, you should realize that an EndPoint configuration item is an entity in its own right, which you can modify and/or remove using the **AdminConfig** administrative object. In this case, use **AdminConfig**.remove() to delete the EndPoint object, as illustrated in Listing 12.22.

Listing 12.22   Removing a Host from an LDAP Registry

```
def removeLDAPHosts(id, hosts):
    eps = AdminConfig.showAttribute(id, "hosts")[1:-1].split(" ")
    for endpoint in eps:
        eph = AdminConfig.showAttribute(endpoint, "host")
        epp = int(AdminConfig.showAttribute(endpoint, "port"))
        for host in hosts:
            if (eph == host[0] and epp == host[1]):
                AdminConfig.remove(endpoint)
                break
```

First you get the list of `EndPoint` configuration ids, just as you've done before. Then for each `EndPoint` configuration object, you get its host and port values, converting the latter to an integer. Finally, you loop through the same sort of nested list of hosts that you've been using as a parameter in this section, and if you find a match against an `EndPoint`, you remove that `EndPoint`. And since you have found that host, you can break out of the inner loop and immediately proceed to compare other `EndPoint` objects.

This concludes our look at working with multiple LDAP hosts for failover. In addition to being a practical topic, this example also explores various issues that often come up when working with a WebSphere configuration, such as:

- What happens when you modify a list?

- How do you handle asymmetric write and read operations (referring to the situation when you provide data in one form to modify a value, and WebSphere creates and uses a different type of configuration object instead of the form you provide)? In this case, a nested list of host values was provided, and thereafter you would need to work with `EndPoint` objects created from that data by WebSphere.

Federated Registries (and Other Essentially Undocumented Scripting Areas)

WebSphere V6.1 and V7 default to using a Federated registry, initially consisting of a file-based repository containing Administrator credentials. Once you have created your Deployment Manager profile, one of your next steps will be to add one or more LDAP repositories to the Federated registry.

At present, you would be hard-pressed to find documentation on how to perform this configuration via scripting. The capability exists, but even the necessary **AdminTask** command group is sparsely documented. So instead of going through this in great detail, we'll accept the situation, and discuss how to address it pragmatically. It might not be the ideal solution, but it can get the job done.

A scripting purist might ignore that the Integrated Solutions Console exists. That would be a mistake. Although in WebSphere V6.1 relatively few commands generated command assistance, in WebSphere V7 over 750 tasks generate command assistance.

To address the problem at hand—adding LDAP repositories to a Federated Registry—first ensure that Command Assistance logging is enabled and then perform the tasks using the Integrated Solutions Console. Next, review the `commandAssistanceJythonCommands_<user>.log` file, which you will find in the deployment manager's log directory, for the commands. What you will find, in this case, are various **AdminTask** commands from the `IdMgrRepositoryConfig` command group. Amongst the **AdminTask** steps you will find is that for each LDAP repository you add to the Federated Registry:

- An LDAP repository is created using **AdminTask**.createIdMgrLDAPRepository().

- One or more LDAP Servers are added to that LDAP repository using **AdminTask**.addIdMgrLDAPServer(). This is analogous to what we did in the preceding section for standalone LDAP repositories.

You can take those commands and use them to build a script so that you can reproduce this configuration, or ones like it, in the future. This approach will also provide you a basis for exploring and scripting other largely undocumented features.

Multiple Security Domains (WebSphere V7)

WebSphere V7 introduces the concept of multiple security domains. Heretofore with WebSphere, you configured one registry (federated or otherwise), Java 2 security was either on or off for the entire cell, application security was on or off for the entire cell, and so on. Security domains changed that and allow you much more flexibility.

A security domain lets you configure it pretty much the same as you would the Security object that we looked at earlier in this chapter. But first you need to create it. You create a security domain with one of several **AdminTask** commands from the SecurityDomainCommands command group, either by creating it anew or copying from an existing security domain. You can create a new one with the following:

```
opts = ['-securityDomainName', 'newDomain']
opts +=['-securityDomainDescription', 'new security domain']
secdomain = AdminTask.createSecurityDomain(opts)
```

For our example, let's stipulate that global security domain is configured the way you want the new security domain to be, except that you want to turn on Java 2 security. You can create a new security domain by copying the global security domain:

```
opt = ["-securityDomainName", "mySecurityDomain"]
opt += ["-securityDomainDescription", "Global Security Copy"]
secdomain = AdminTask.copySecurityDomainFromGlobalSecurity(opt)
```

Having done that, you can modify the security domain. But there are some nuances here. What the documentation does not tell you is that when you create a security domain, the code creates a Security Domain object but returns the configuration id for an AppSecurity configuration object that was also created for the new security domain.[2] So at the time you create a new security domain, you can use **AdminConfig** to manipulate the associated AppSecurity object. To do this easily is essentially a one-time opportunity. After this, if you want to modify the security domain, you would use **AdminTask** to do so by name. Listing 12.23 illustrates this point and the equivalence.

---

[2] In WebSphere 7.0.0.0, all of the methods for creating and copying security domains have an apparent defect. They return the configuration id without the necessary () characters around it—you have to add them in order to use the configuration id.

Listing 12.23   Cloning and Modifying a New Security Domain

```
id = '('+AdminTask.copySecurityDomainFromGlobalSecurity(opt)+')'
print AdminConfig.showAttribute(id, "enforceJava2Security")
AdminConfig.modify(id, [['enforceJava2Security','true']])
print AdminConfig.showAttribute(id, "enforceJava2Security")
AdminConfig.modify(id,[['enforceJava2Security','false']])
AdminConfig.showAttribute(id, "enforceJava2Security")
p = ["-securityDomainName", "mySecurityDomain"]
p += ["-enforceJava2Security", "true"]
AdminTask.setAppActiveSecuritySettings(p)
print AdminConfig.showAttribute(id, "enforceJava2Security")
```

How do you add applications or other resources to a security domain? Well, it does not work quite that way. You can assign the cell to the security domain, but more likely you will assign a cluster, server, or bus to the security domain.

In Listing 12.24, we have mapped a cluster, and therefore all of the applications in that cluster, to a new Java 2 security-enabled clone of global security. We also mapped a bus. If you want to remove a resource from the security domain, it is just as simple, but you invoke AdminTask.removeResourceFromSecurityDomain instead:

```
AdminTask.removeResourceFromSecurityDomain(domain + resource)
```

Listing 12.24   Adding Resources to a Security Domain

```
domain = ["-securityDomainName", "mySecurityDomain"]
resource = ["-resourceName", "Cell=:ServerCluster=TradeCluster"]
AdminTask.mapResourceToSecurityDomain(domain + resource)
resource = ["-resourceName", "Cell=:SIBus=msgBus"]
AdminTask.mapResourceToSecurityDomain(domain + resource)
```

Listing 12.25 shows you how you can discover which domain is responsible for a resource or which resources are in a given domain.

Listing 12.25   Identifying Resource / Security Domain Mappings

```
d = ['-securityDomainName', "mySecurityDomain"]
print AdminTask.listResourcesInSecurityDomain(d).splitlines()

r = ["-resourceName", "Cell=:ServerCluster=TradeCluster"]
print AdminTask.getSecurityDomainForResource(r)
```

```
r = ["-resourceName", "Cell=:SIBus=msgBus"]
print AdminTask.getSecurityDomainForResource(r)
```

Additional Security Topics

Hopefully we have given you a feel for security-related topics and the kinds of things that you can script in WebSphere. There are many more things that you can do with security and scripting than we can cover in this chapter. Some are covered in more detail elsewhere in this book, such as Bus security and Datasources. The following sections contain brief overviews of some of those items.

Bus Security

In Chapter 14, "Messaging," you go through the detailed steps[3] to secure a messaging bus. Here is an overview of these steps:

- Enable administrative security for the cell.
- Enable security for the bus.
- Create (or use an existing) authentication alias to use between messaging engines.
- Create (or use an existing) secure transport chain to use between messaging engines.
- Disable (or delete) insecure messaging transport chains.
- Remove default authorization policies.
- Secure the Distribution and Consistency Service (DCS).
- Secure each messaging engine on the messaging bus.
- Secure any data stores used by the members of the messaging bus.
- Create (or use an existing) authentication alias for transaction recovery.
- Create (or use an existing) authentication alias for mediation.

Datasources

A Datasource will generally need to be configured with one or more of the JAAS aliases created earlier in this chapter. This is detailed in Chapter 13, "Databases and Authorization."[4] The JCA manager, or more specifically the underlying Relational Resource Adapter, uses that credential

---

[3] See the topic, "Enabling Bus Security" in Chapter 14 for extensive details.

[4] See the discussion of `AdminTask.createDataSource()` in the reference section of Chapter 13. In particular, take note of two arguments—the `xaRecoveryAuthAlias` and the `componentManagedAuthentication Alias`.

when interacting with the database server (see Chapter 17 of the *IBM WebSphere Application Server V6.1 Security Handbook*).

Web Services

Web services can be secured in multiple ways, some of which are covered in Chapter 15, "Administering Web Services."

AdminTask Security Reference

The **AdminTask** methods that control security are spread over some obvious and some not so obvious command groups. A subset of all those methods is presented here. No matter what the details of your enterprise security, you are very likely to need the details consolidated here.

- SecurityConfigurationCommands
- SecurityDomainCommands
- SecurityRealmInfoCommands
- WIMManagementCommands
- WizardCommands
- JACCUtilityCommands
- IdMgrRepositoryConfig

The general pattern for calling **AdminTask** methods is:

```
AdminTask.methodName( target,                              \
          '[ -argument value -nextArgument value2  ' \
    + '-stepName [ -arg01 val01 -arg02 val02 ] ' \
    + '-nextStepName [ -arg03 val03]  -yetAnotherStep ]' )
```

There might or might not be a target. If there is, it might be a configuration ID or it might be a name. Targets are usually containment parents. There might or might not be arguments. Arguments are almost always names followed by values. There might or might not be steps. Think of steps as arguments that require either a list of names followed by values or nothing at all. Bundle all the arguments and steps into one big list and pass it to the method as shown previously and in the code samples in this book.

SecurityConfigurationCommands Group

Methods in this command group create, delete, display, and modify many aspects of administrative security. This command group is new with version 7. In many ways, the methods in this group simplify security configuration. Prior to this version, you must navigate your own way through WebSphere Application Server's configuration tree and use the equivalent **AdminConfig** commands.

createAuthDataEntry

The `createAuthDataEntry` command creates an authentication data entry for a J2EE Connector architecture (J2C) connector. The `AuthDataEntry` that you create can either be part of the global security or it can be part of a security domain. Although at a later time you can *copy* this authentication data entry from global security to a security domain, it cannot be *created* in both. Which of these two behaviors it exhibits depends on whether you choose to pass a `securityDomainName`.

Required argument:

- `alias`—The alias of the authentication data. Think of this alias as the key that WebSphere uses to find the user name and password. This eliminates the need to have user names and passwords hard-coded into application code or files.
- `user`—The user name part of the authentication data.
- `password`—The password part of the authentication data.

Frequently used optional arguments:

- `securityDomainName`—Name used to uniquely identify the security domain within the cell. If you wish the `AuthDataEntry` to be part of a security domain rather than being part of global security, pass this argument and the authentication data entry will be part of the security domain that you specify. If you omit this argument, the `AuthDataEntry` will be part of global security.
- `securityDomainDescription`—Description of the function this security domain plays in your topology.

deleteAuthDataEntry

Delete an authentication data entry in the administrative security configuration or in a security domain.

Required argument:
`alias`—The alias of the auth data.

Frequently used optional argument:
`securityDomainName`—This argument is only optional if this authentication entry is part of the global domain rather than a security domain. It is mandatory if the `AuthDataEntry` is part of a security domain.

listAuthDataEntries

List authentication data entries in the administrative security configuration or a in a security domain.

Frequently used optional argument:

securityDomainName—This argument is optional, but it is really a switch. If you omit this argument, you get all the AuthDataEntries from global security. If you pass the name of a security domain, you get the AuthDataEntries from that domain.

getActiveSecuritySettings

This command returns the active security settings for the security domain of interest or the global security configuration, which includes the following settings:

enableGlobalSecurity (global security only)

adminPreferredAuthMech (global security only)

activeAuthMechanism (global security only)

dynUpdateSSLConfig (global security only)

cacheTimeout

issuePermissionWarning

activeAuthMechanism

enforceJava2Security

appSecurityEnabled

activeUserRegistry

enforceFineGrainedJCASecurity

useDomainQualifiedUserNames

customProperties

Frequently used optional argument:

securityDomainName—This argument is optional, but it is really a switch. If you omit this argument, you get all the settings from global security. If you pass the name of a security domain, you get the settings from that domain.

setAdminActiveSecuritySettings

Sets the security attributes on the global security configuration. Starting in version 6, global security is called administrative security. This method does not return anything.

Frequently used optional arguments:

- enableGlobalSecurity—Specifies whether to enable global security. Specify true to enable global security or specify false to disable global security. (Boolean)

- cacheTimeout—Specifies the amount of time, in seconds, before authentication data becomes invalid. (Integer)

- `issuePermissionWarning`—Specifies whether to issue a warning during application installation if the application requires security permissions. Specify `true` to enable the warning notification or specify `false` to disable the warning notification. (Boolean)

- `enforceJava2Security`—Specifies whether to enable Java Platform, Enterprise Edition (Java EE) security. Specify `true` to enable Java EE security permissions checking or specify `false` to disable Java EE security. (Boolean)

- `enforceFineGrainedJCASecurity`—Specifies whether to restrict application access. Specify `true` to restrict application access to sensitive Java EE Connector Architecture (JCA) mapping authentication data. (Boolean)

- `appSecurityEnabled`—Specifies whether to enable application-level security. Specify `true` to enable application level security or specify `false` to disable application-level security. (Boolean)

- `dynUpdateSSLConfig`—Specifies whether to dynamically update SSL configuration changes. Specify `true` to update SSL configuration changes dynamically or specify `false` to update the SSL configuration when the server starts. (Boolean)

- `activeAuthMechanism`—Specifies the active authentication mechanism. Specify `LTPA` for LTPA authentication, `KRB5` for Kerberos authentication, or `RSAToken` for RSA token authorization. (String)

- `adminPreferredAuthMech`—Specifies the preferred authentication mechanism. Specify `LTPA` for LTPA authentication, `KRB5` for Kerberos authentication, or `RSAToken` for RSA token authorization. (String)

- `activeUserRegistry`—Specifies the active user registry for the server. (String)

- `useDomainQualifiedUserNames`—Specifies the type of user name to use. Specify `true` to use domain-qualified user names or specify `false` to use the short name. (Boolean)

- `customProperties`—Specifies a comma-separated list of quoted attribute and value pairs that the system stores as custom properties on the user registry object. For example, use the format: `"attr1=value1","attr2=value2"` (String)

setAppActiveSecuritySetting

Sets the active security settings on a security domain. This method does not return anything.

Required argument:

`securityDomainName`—Name used to uniquely identify the security domain.

Frequently used optional arguments:

- `cacheTimeout`—Specifies the amount of time in seconds before authentication data becomes invalid. (Integer)

- `issuePermissionWarning`—Specifies whether to issue a warning during application installation if the application requires security permissions. Specify `true` to enable the warning notification or specify `false` to disable the warning notification. (Boolean)

- `enforceJava2Security`—Specifies whether to enable Java Platform, Enterprise Edition (Java EE) security. Specify `true` to enable Java EE security permissions checking or specify `false` to disable Java EE security. (Boolean)

- `enforceFineGrainedJCASecurity`—Specifies whether to restrict application access. Specify `true` to restrict application access to sensitive Java EE Connector Architecture (JCA) mapping authentication data. (Boolean)

- `appSecurityEnabled`—Specifies whether to enable application-level security. Specify `true` to enable application-level security or specify `false` to disable application-level security. (Boolean)

- `activeUserRegistry`—Specifies the active user registry for the server. (String)

- `useDomainQualifiedUserNames`—Specifies the type of user name to use. Specify `true` to use domain-qualified user names or specify `false` to use the short name. (Boolean)

- `customProperties`—Specifies a comma-separated list of quoted attribute and value pairs that the system stores as custom properties on the user registry object. For example, use the format: `"attr1=value1"`, `"attr2=value2"` (String)

unsetAppActiveSecuritySettings

Removes the specified attribute from the security setting.

Required argument:

`securityDomainName`—Name used to uniquely identify the security domain.

Frequently used optional arguments:

- `unsetCacheTimeout`—Specifies the amount of time in seconds before authentication data becomes invalid. (Integer)

- `unsetIssuePermissionWarning`—Specifies whether to issue a warning during application installation if the application requires security permissions. Specify `true` to enable the warning notification or specify `false` to disable the warning notification. (Boolean)

- `unsetEnforceFineGrainedJCASecurity`—Specifies whether to enable Java Platform, Enterprise Edition (Java EE) security. Specify `true` to enable Java EE security permissions checking or specify `false` to disable Java EE security. (Boolean)

- `unsetAppSecurityEnabled`—Specifies whether to enable application-level security. Specify `true` to enable application level security or specify `false` to disable application-level security. (Boolean)

- `unsetActiveUserRegistry`—Specifies the active user registry for the server. (String)

- `unsetUseDomainQualifiedUserNames`—Specifies the type of user name to use. Specify `true` to use domain-qualified user names or specify `false` to use the short name. (Boolean)

getSingleSignon

Returns information about the single signon settings for global security. This method takes no arguments.

configureSingleSignon

Configures single signon.

Frequently used optional arguments:

- `enable`—Set to enable or disable single signon.

- `requiresSSL`—Set if SSL is required.

- `interoperable`—Set the single signon interoperability mode.

- `attributePropagation`—Configures single signon attribute propagation.

- `domainName`—Configures the domain for single signon.

getUserRegistryInfo

Returns information about a user registry from the administrative security configuration or an application security domain.

Frequently used optional arguments:

- `securityDomainName`—Think of this argument as a switch. If you supply the name of a security domain, you get information about the user registry for that security domain. Otherwise, you get information about the user registry for global security.

- `userRegistryType`—The type of the user registry values include `LDAPUserRegistry`, `WIMUserRegistry`, `CustomUserRegistry`, and `LocalOSUserRegistry`.

listInterceptors

List interceptors from the global security configuration or from a security domain.

> **Frequently used optional argument:**
>
> `securityDomainName`—Think of this argument as a switch. If you supply the name of a security domain, you get information about the user registry for it. Otherwise, you get information about the user registry for global security.

SecurityDomainCommands Group

Prior to WebSphere Application Server version 7, security domains did not exist. Therefore, this command group is new in version 7. Methods in this group give you the ability to create, delete, display, and modify security domains. These methods give you the ability to add and remove resources from a given security domain.

createSecurityDomain

Create an empty security domain from scratch.[5]

> **Required argument:**
>
> `securityDomainName`
>
> **Frequently used optional argument:**
>
> `securityDomainDescription`—Text to describe the purpose of this security domain in your topology.

copySecurityDomainFromGlobalSecurity

Creates a security domain by copying the global administrative security configuration.[6]

> **Required argument:**
>
> `securityDomainName`
>
> **Frequently used optional argument:**
>
> - `securityDomainDescription`—Text to describe the purpose of this security domain in your topology.
> - `realmName`—If an active user registry is defined then a new realm name must be used in the new security domain.

---

[5] This is the first of three ways to create a security domain.

[6] This is the second of three ways to create a security domain.

copySecurityDomain

Creates a security domain by copying some other security domain's configuration.[7]

Required argument:

`securityDomainName`

Frequently used optional argument:

- `securityDomainDescription`—Text to describe the purpose of this security domain in your topology.

- `realmName`—If an active user registry is defined, then a new realm name must be used in the new security domain.

deleteSecurityDomain

Deletes a security domain.

Required argument:

`securityDomainName`—Name used to uniquely identify the security domain.

Frequently used optional argument:

- `force`—When force is set to true, the security domain is deleted without checking if any resources exist in the domain. This option can be used when the resources in the security domains are not valid resources.

listSecurityDomains

Returns the names and possibly the descriptions of security domains.

Frequently used optional arguments:

- `listDescription`—Specify `true` to include the description of each security domain in the list returned and `false` to just return the names of the security domains.

- `doNotDisplaySpecialDomains`—Specify `true` to not include the special domains in the list of security domains returned and `false` to display the special domains.

---

[7] This is the third of three ways to create a security domain.

SecurityRealmInfoCommands

Prior to WebSphere Application Server version 7, security domains did not exist. Therefore, this command group is new in version 7. Methods in this group give you the ability to add, remove, and display registry groups and trusted realms.

listRegistryUsers

Returns a list of users in a security realm, security domain, or resource. All the arguments are optional. If you do not pass any arguments, you get all the users in the global security. You have the choice of seeing the users with or without their access IDs.

Frequently used optional arguments:

- `displayAccessIds`—Specify `true` to return the list of user IDs and access IDs and `false` just to return a list of user IDs.
- `resourceName`—Specifies the name of the resource for which a user list will be returned.
- `securityDomainName`—Specifies the name of the security domain for which a user list will be returned.
- `securityRealmName`—Specifies the name of the security realm for which a user list will be returned.
- `numberOfUsers`—Specifies the maximum number of users to return.
- `userFilter`—Specifies a filter to be used to get the list of users.

listRegistryGroups

Returns a list of groups in a security realm, security domain, or resource. All the arguments are optional. If you do not pass any arguments, you get all the groups in the global security. You have the choice of seeing the groups with or without their access IDs.

Frequently used optional arguments:

- `displayAccessIds`—Specify `true` to return the list of group IDs and access IDs, and `false` just to return a list of group IDs.
- `resourceName`—Specifies the name of the resource for which a group list will be returned.
- `securityDomainName`—Specifies the name of the security domain for which a group list will be returned.
- `securityRealmName`—Specifies the name of the security realm for which a group list will be returned.
- `numberOfGroups`—Specifies the maximum number of groups to return.
- `groupFilter`—Specify a filter to be used to get the list of groups.

listSecurityRealms

List all security realms in the configuration from global security and the security domains. Requires no parameters.

WIMManagementCommands

This group of methods manipulate WebSphere Application Server's virtual member manager and the default user repository that sits behind it. These methods exist in both version 6 and version 7 of WebSphere Application Server.

createUser

Creates a `PersonAccount` in the default realm.

> **Required arguments:**
> - `cn`—The common name of the entity.
> - `password`—The password of the user.
> - `sn`—The surname of the entity.
> - `uid`—The UID of the `PersonAccount`.
>
> **Occasionally used optional arguments:**
> - `confirmPassword`—Used to guarantee and confirm that the `confirmPassword` is the same as the password.
> - `parent`—The parent of the entity.

createGroup

Creates a group in the default realm.

> **Required argument:**
>
> `cn`—The common name of the entity.
>
> **Frequently used optional arguments:**
> - `description`—A description of a group.
> - `memberUniqueName`—The `uniqueName` of the member to add or remove.
>
> **Occasionally used optional argument:**
>
> `parent`—The parent of the entity.

deleteUser

Deletes a `PersonAccount` from the default realm.

> **Required argument:**
>
> `uniqueName`—The name that uniquely identifies an object of a virtual member manager entity.

deleteGroup

Deletes a group from the default realm.

> **Required argument:**
>
> uniqueName—The name that uniquely identifies an object of a virtual member manager entity.

duplicateMembershipOfUser

Makes a user a member of the same groups as another user.

> **Required arguments:**
>
> - copyFromUniqueName—The uniqueName of the virtual member manager entity from which the membership is copied.
>
> - copyToUniqueName—The uniqueName of the virtual member manager entity to add to the same groups as the specified copyFromUniqueName entity.

duplicateMembershipOfGroup

Makes a group a member of the same groups as another group.

> **Required arguments:**
>
> - copyFromUniqueName—The uniqueName of the virtual member manager entity from which the membership is copied.
>
> - copyToUniqueName—The uniqueName of the virtual member manager entity to add to the same groups as the specified copyFromUniqueName entity.

WizardCommands

These methods report or modify the same security properties as the admin console security wizard. The methods in this command group are present in both WebSphere Application Server version 6 and version 7.

isGlobalSecurityEnabled

Returns either true or false depending on whether the administrative security setting is currently enabled. Requires no parameters.

setGlobalSecurity

Turns administrative security on or off.

Required argument:

enabled—If this argument is `true`, turn administrative security on. If this argument is `false`, turn administrative security off.

isAppSecurityEnabled

Returns the current application security setting of `true` or `false`. Requires no parameters.

JACCUtilityCommands

isJACCEnabled

Returns either `true` or `false` depending on whether the Java Authorization Contract for Containers is enabled. Requires no parameters.

isSingleSecurityDomain

Checks if the current runtime is a single security domain. Returns `true` or `false`. Requires no parameters.

IdMgrRepositoryConfig

addIdMgrLDAPServer

Adds an LDAP server to the LDAP repository configuration.

Required arguments:

- `host`—The host name for the LDAP server.
- `id`—The unique identifier of the repository.

Frequently used optional arguments:

- `authentication`—The authentication method to use.
- `bindDN`—The binding distinguished name for the LDAP server.
- `bindPassword`—The LDAP server binding password.
- `certificateFilter`—If you specify the certificate map mode, use this property to specify the LDAP filter, which maps attributes in the client certificate to entries in LDAP.
- `certificateMapMode`—Specifies whether to map X.509 certificates into an LDAP directory by exact distinguished name or certificate filter. Specify the certificate filter to use the specified certificate filter for the mapping.
- `connectTimeout`—Connection timeout (in seconds).

- `connectionPool`—LDAP connection pool.
- `derefAliases`—Controls how aliases are de-referenced. Possible values are always (default), never, finding, and searching.
- `ldapServerType`—The type of LDAP server used.
- `port`—The port number for the LDAP server.
- `referral`—LDAP referral.
- `sslConfiguration`—Secure Sockets Layer (SSL) configuration.
- `sslEnabled`—Enable Secure Sockets Layer (SSL) for the LDAP server.

Databases and Authorization

The **AdminTask** scripting object has several groups of methods that directly or indirectly support data access. In this chapter, we explore the methods from the JDBCProviderManagement and VariableConfiguration groups.

We use a subset of the commands in these groups to present an example that is not well-documented elsewhere. Afterward, we list the other commands in these groups, along with a brief explanation of each.

Database Basics

Any serious enterprise application requires interaction with a database. Given that WebSphere Application Server is really a network of centrally managed servers, this presents a few interesting issues:

- How do you connect to the database in the first place?
- How do you pool connections to the database for efficiency and performance?
- How do you effectively manage what could be a complex configuration?

The database vendor, or some third-party vendor, supplies a jar file that contains a database driver, and that database driver allows database connections to the defined. Application modules deployed to the containers of an application server use that connection to query the database, get result sets from those queries, and update tables in the database. We, as systems administrators, create pools of database connections that applications ultimately use. We decide how big those pools are and how big they will get, and we configure security credentials that allow applications to access the database.

Terminology

DataSource—Creates a pool of database connections and shares that pool among applications on the same server.

J2C Authentication Alias—A flexible data structure that holds a user ID, password, and possibly other data as well. All of this is accessible using an alias. The purpose of this data structure is to enable access to Enterprise Information Systems of all kinds.

JDBC™ Provider—Supplies the actual code that establishes communications between an application and a database.

A Simple Example

An example script file, named database.py, is available from the book website and contains the functions shown in this chapter that can be used to create some basic but useful plumbing to support database connections. If you want to use this script, there are some things you will have to change:

- You will have to change the example node name to a node name that exists in your cell.

- You will have to change the example server name to the name of a server that exists within that node in your cell.

- If your cell already has any of the JNDI names that we use in the sample script, you will have to edit these names so that they do not conflict with your existing JNDI names.

- You may have to make some other changes depending on the specifics of the database you want to use.

You will need some variables for this simple example and will use them throughout it. If your database requires any kind of security credentials, you will need to create a JAAS Authentication Alias.[1]

```
uid = "KevinsDataSource-User"
pwd = "SuperTopSecret"
desc = "This is an example of a JAAS Authentication Alias"
DataBaseAccessAlias = "Boss/KevinsDatabaseCredentials"
```

Notice that the name of the alias is prefixed with the name of one of the nodes, specifically the Deployment Manager's node's name. The reason for this has to do with the way the **AdminTask** SecurityConfiguration command group creates and deletes JAAS Authentication Aliases.[2]

```
    secMgrID = AdminConfig.list( 'Security' )
```

This line of script is used to obtain the configuration ID of WebSphere Application Server's security manager. You see sample code like this on many official IBM websites. This code assumes that there is exactly one Security object in your cell.[3] There is more than one way to

---

[1] We cover JAAS Authentication Alias extensively in Chapter 12, "Scripting and Security."

[2] See the discussion about creating a JAAS alias in Chapter 12.

[3] That assumption might not always be true. For a discussion of more advanced security configurations, see the "Multiple Security Domains" section in Chapter 12.

create a JAAS Authentication Alias. This is simply one way. Other choices are discussed in Chapter 12, "Scripting and Security."[4]

```
jaasID = AdminConfig.create( 'JAASAuthData', secMgrID, \
                    [ ['alias', DataBaseAccessAlias], \
                    ['description', desc],           \
                    ['userId', uid],                 \
                    ['password',pwd]  ] )
```

The first piece of real database-related work is creating a JDBCProvider. The JDBCProvider supplies the database driver class that actually talks to the database. The two things you absolutely must provide to create a JDBCProvider are the name of a JDBCProvider and the name of the driver class. Although that satisfies the bare bones minimum application server configuration syntax, it is not enough information to do useful work with a database.

The **AdminTask** scripting object has a method called createJDBCProvider that provides a useful configuration environment for a supported database driver. This method requires more information than the bare bones minimum for a JDBCProvider,[5] but it produces a configuration that does useful work. In the next example, we supply some optional arguments in addition to the required arguments:

```
p = AdminTask.createJDBCProvider('[-scope Node=Node01 '              \
    + '-databaseType DB2 -providerType "DB2 Using IBM JCC Driver" '\
    + '-implementationType "XA data source"  '                      \
    + '-name KevinsBrandNewProvider '                               \
    + '-description "This is a fairly simple thing to create" ]')
```

This JDBCProvider is created at the node scope.[6] Once the database type, the provider type, and the implementation type are specified, if you also specify one of the supported databases, AdminTask.createJDBCProvider() uses the default JDBCProvider template for that database to fill in some default information about your database driver. The description you specify will appear in the Administrative Console.

There are two possible choices for implementationType: "XA data source" and "Connection pool data source". You must specify one of these case sensitive strings.[7] The first string specifies a driver class that gives your JDBCProvider the ability to perform a two-phase

---

[4] See the discussion about creating a JAAS alias in Chapter 12.

[5] For a complete list of the attributes of JDBCProvider, type **print AdminConfig.attributes ('JDBCProvider')**.

[6] See the reference section at the end of this chapter. Our discussion of the scope parameter of AdminTask.createJDBCProvider() has examples of how to specify each scope.

[7] See the reference section at the end of this chapter for a more complete discussion of the arguments for AdminTask.createJDBCProvider().

commit. This allows your driver class to participate in transactions that span multiple databases. The second string specifies a driver class that lacks this ability. Both strings result in a JDBCProvider that can support pools of connections.

Once you have a JDBCProvider, you can create a DataSource, which manages a pool of connections to a database. The DataSource created here is as follows:

```
d = AdminTask.createDataSource( p,                                              \
     '[-name KevinsDataSource -jndiName jdbc/kevinsData '                       \
   + '-description "This DataSource pools connections" '                        \
   + '-category "classroom exercise" '                                          \
   + '-dataStoreHelperClassName '                                              \
   + ' com.ibm.websphere.rsadapter.DB2UniversalDataStoreHelper '               \
   + '-componentManagedAuthenticationAlias '                                   \
   + DataBaseAccessAlias                                                        \
   + ' -xaRecoveryAuthAlias ' + DataBaseAccessAlias                            \
   + ' -configureResourceProperties [ '                                        \
   + '[databaseName java.lang.String KevinsToyClassroomDatabase] '  \
   + '[serverName java.lang.String host01.ibm.com] '                           \
   + '                                            ]   '                         \
   + ']'   )
```

The name, description, and category of the DataSource are purely descriptive. You can specify any value you'd like for them. They are there for your benefit and for your documentation. The componentManagedAuthenticationAlias[8] and the xaRecoveryAuthAlias provide the credentials that the database requires to access data in the database and to roll back failed transactions. The list of lists that follows configureResourceProperties is database-specific and arbitrary. You can see what you need to supply here, either by examining the documentation that comes with the database driver class for your database or by calling AdminTask .createDataSource('-interactive').

Troubleshooting Configuration Problems

Once you have created a JDBCProvider and a DataSource, you can test that connection with one or two lines of script. In the code that follows, assume that d holds the configuration ID of a DataSource that you would like to test:

```
print AdminControl.testConnection( d )
```

---

[8] Some versions of IBM help documents fail to mention this argument. See the reference section at the end of this chapter for a description of all arguments for this method.

In order for this connection test to work, you might have to configure either the `preTestConfig` attribute[9] of this `DataSource` configuration or some attributes of the `DataSource` MBean[10] for this `DataSource` or both.

Testing the connection[11] verifies that the drivers you installed work properly, that the network between your server and the database works, and that your security credentials work on the database. The only thing that `AdminControl.testConnection()` ignores is the JNDI name that you specified in your `JDBCProvider`. If your connection passes `AdminConfig` `.testConnection()` but you cannot connect to the database, check the spelling of the JNDI name and the scope in which you installed that JNDI name. These are the problems you are most likely to encounter when you try to create `JDBCProvider`s and `DataSource`s:

- Failure to install JDBC driver jar files or installing files in the wrong place
- Specifying an incorrect path to JDBC driver jar files
- Misspelling the names of WebSphere variables in various configurations
- Misspelling the values mapped to WebSphere variables

These problems occur when you create a `JDBCProvider`, but you won't see them until you create a `DataSource` and try to test the connection. If your connection fails, make sure the driver files are where you specified. You should also examine the `classpath` attribute of your `JDBCProvider` and compare that with your file system. If there are any WebSphere variables in your `classpath`, print out those variables, too, and make sure that there are no typos. Typos occur in both the variable names and the variable values. In addition, WebSphere variables and their values are case-sensitive. The data type of a WebSphere variable is `VariableSubstitutionEntry`. You can look at all the `VariableSubstitutionEntry`s in your cell or just the `VariableSubstitutionEntry`s at a particular scope.

```
print AdminConfig.list( 'VariableSubstitutionEntry' )
n = AdminConfig.getid( '/Node:nameOfSomeNode/' )
print AdminConfig.list( 'VariableSubstitutionEntry',n )
```

Each `VariableSubstitutionEntry` has a description, a symbolic name, and a value. Check that the symbolic name attribute matches the case-sensitive spelling of any variable in your classpath. Then check that the value attribute matches the case-sensitive spelling of your file system.

---

[9] This attribute holds a `ConnectionTest` object. Its `preTestConnection` attribute must be set to "true" and both its retryInterval attribute and its retryLimit attribute must be nonzero integers.

[10] See the comments for the `testConnection` attribute and the `testConnectionInterval` attribute of the `DataSource` MBean under "Useful MBeans" in the reference section at the end of this chapter.

[11] For detailed information about this test and the actual SQL query used for this test, see Listing 13.8.

Keep in mind, there was also a bug on some versions of WebSphere Application Server that caused misinterpretation of `classpath` if a `VariableSubstitutionEntry` in a different scope had an identical symbolic name and a value less than one character long. You might consider removing any `VariableSubstitutionEntry` that has a value less than one character long. In the code here, assume that `v` holds the configuration ID of a `VariableSubstitutionEntry`:

```
if len( AdminConfig.showAttribute( v, 'value' ) ) < 1:
    AdminConfig.remove( v )
```

If you know the symbolic name of the variable and the scope in which it lives, you can use the methods in the `VariableConfiguration` command group of `AdminTask`. If you have a node named `Node01` and a variable in that scope with a symbolic name of `LOG_ROOT`, the following line of script displays its value:

```
print AdminTask.showVariable(
             '[-scope Node=Node01 -variableName LOG_ROOT ]' )
```

If you know the `symbolicName` of the `VariableSubstitutionEntry` that you want to change, you can use the following:

```
AdminTask.setVariable(
             '[-variableName x -scope Node=Node01 -variableValue Ding ]' )
```

In general, if you know the `symbolicName` of the `VariableSubstitutionEntry` that you want to manipulate, it is easier to use the **AdminTask** methods. If you have to search for variables, **AdminConfig** is easier albeit a bit more cryptic and circumspect.

Let's say that you create a `JDBCProvider` and a `DataSource`. Let's also say that you test the connection, and your test fails. Now, let's say you look in your `SystemOut` log file and see text similar to this:

```
DSRA8040I: Failed to connect to the DataSource.  Encountered "":
java.lang.ClassNotFoundException: com.ibm.db2.jcc.DB2XADataSource
```

That `ClassNotFoundException` speaks for itself. For one reason or another, the application server cannot find your jar file, or the jar file is corrupted. When you check the `classpath` attribute of the `JDBCProvider`, you can see that the `classpath` contained a WebSphere variable called `UNIVERSAL_JDBC_DRIVER_PATH`:

```
print  AdminTask.showVariables(                                           \
             '[ -variableName UNIVERSAL_JDBC_DRIVER_PATH ' + \
             ' -scope Node=Node01 ]' )
```

The preceding code showed that the WebSphere variable had no value. After checking the file system, we found the jar file and fixed the problem with the following code:

```
AdminTask.setVariable( '[-variableName
UNIVERSAL_JDBC_DRIVER_PATH ' \
```

```
+ ' -scope Node=Node01 ' \
+ ' -variableValue /opt/ibm/db2/V9.5/java ]' )
```

The most common configuration problems involving databases are variables with incorrect values and missing jar files. Both problems are easy to fix.

Many times, your DataSource might work, but the response might be slow. Check the IBM Documentation[12] for procedures to troubleshoot[13] slow response and for performance tuning[14] information. Common attributes that need modification include minimum and maximum connections, various timeouts, and various trace strings. Most of these settings involve modifying attributes of the ConnectionPool that belongs to the DataSource. Assuming that ds[2] holds the configuration ID of a DataSource, the following script changes the values of minimum and maximum connections and various timeouts.[15] If you are setting the maximum number of connections for a server that is part of a cluster, remember to add the maximum connection number from each server in the cluster and to make sure that your database can handle that number of connections.

```
cp = AdminConfig.showAttribute( ds[2], 'connectionPool' )
AdminConfig.modify( cp, [ ['minConnections', 3],['maxConnections',
8] ] )
AdminConfig.modify( cp, [ ['connectionTimeout', 360] ] )
AdminConfig.modify( cp, [ ['reapTime', 90],['agedTimeout', 2400] ] )
```

Remember that none of these modifications to configuration take effect until you synchronize the nodes in your cell and restart your servers. If you would like to test the modifications you are about to make without restarting servers, you can change the appropriate attributes of the DataSource MBean. Changes to MBeans take effect immediately. They disappear when you stop the server. Keep in mind that you modify the *configuration* for things like minimum and maximum connections and various time outs by modifying attributes of a ConnectionPool configuration object. But you modify the *runtime behavior* by modifying the attributes of a DataSource MBean.

In addition to modifying various attributes on the ConnectionPool and the DataSource, you can also specify the amount of tracing and what components will be traced. Tracing is done on a per server basis. The trace service controls tracing. You can make permanent changes to the things you trace by changing the configuration of the trace service.

---

[12] http://www.IBM.com/support/docview.wss?rs=180&uid=swg21247168.

[13] For specific troubleshooting techniques, consider the IBM redbook, *WebSphere Application Server v6.1 Problem Determination* (SG247461).

[14] For concepts and topics that affect system performance, consider Chapter 7 of the IBM redbook, *WebSphere Application Server v7.0: Concepts, Planning and Design* (SG247708).

[15] The description of the DataSource MBean in the reference section in the back of this chapter has an extensive discussion of all of these values and their implications.

Permanent changes do not take effect until you save your configuration and reboot the server in question. In a network deployment environment, you will have to synchronize your nodes before you restart your server(s). You can make immediate but temporary changes to the trace service by calling operations or changing attributes of the TraceService MBean. These changes disappear when you stop the server. Or you can make immediate changes that survive server restart by changing both the trace service configuration and the TraceService MBean.

If you need to trace a connection leak, you can use one of the following trace strings:

- ConnLeakLogic=finest
- WAS.j2c=finest

Assume that ts[1] is a string containing the name of an MBean that controls the trace service on the server of interest to you. The code that follows will append our string to the existing trace specification. Modifying the traceSpecification attribute directly causes your modification to be appended to any existing trace specification. Notice that you should save the old trace specification before making any modifications.[16]

```
oldSpec = AdminControl.getAttribute( ts[1], 'traceSpecification' )
AdminControl.setAttribute( ts[1],
                    'traceSpecification', 'ConnLeakLogic=finest' )
```

As soon as this code executes, the application server starts using the new trace specification. At some point, you will want to go back to your original trace specification. To do that, you need the following code:[17]

```
AdminControl.invoke( ts[1], 'setTraceState', oldSpec )
```

Advanced Settings

In the following code examples, the more advanced settings of JDBCProvider, DataSource, and ConnectionPool are modified. You might do this because you have complex database needs, you have to integrate an arcane version of an unsupported database, you are troubleshooting a database problem, or you are trying to tune database performance. If you have to integrate an old version of a database driver class or if you have to integrate some exotic and possibly unsupported database, you might experience problems with the database driver class that appears to be class loader-related. One option to consider is isolating the database driver class by loading it from its own class loader. You can do this as long as you (or the default template that creates your JDBCProvider) do not set a value for the nativepath attribute of your JDBCProvider.

---

[16] Changing the trace specification does not work exactly as you might expect. See the description of the TraceService MBean in the reference section at the end of this chapter for the different operations that modify the traceSpecification.

[17] Changing the trace specification does not work exactly as you might expect. See the description of the TraceService MBean in the reference section at the end of this chapter for the different operations that modify the traceSpecification.

In previous code examples, you saw a `JDBCProvider` for IBM's DB2® database. The default template for DB2 sets a value for `nativepath`. Therefore, you cannot set the `isolatedClassLoader` attribute of our `JDBCProvider` to true. But if you could, this would be the line of script to do it:

```
AdminConfig.modify( p, [ ['isolatedClassLoader', 'true'] ] )
```

The `DataSource` object has an interesting attribute called `propertySet`, which holds a config-uration ID. If you pass that configuration ID to `AdminConfig.show()`, you will see what is effectively a list of configuration IDs. Examining the attributes of each of these configuration IDs tells you a lot about the tunable features of your database driver. The code in Listing 13.1 shows you how to find the configuration ID of the list of property sets for a given `DataSource`. These features can change from version to version of the driver and from version to version of the product.

Listing 13.1   Show `propertySet` Configuration IDs

```
array = AdminConfig.list( 'DataSource' ).splitlines()
ps = AdminConfig.showAttribute( array[0], 'propertySet' )

print ps
#   produces a line that looks like:
# (cells/McG/nodes/N1|resources.xml#J2EEResourcePropertySet_9)

stuff = AdminConfig.show( ps )
print stuff
#    prints a list of configuration IDs of property sets
```

Listing 13.2 shows a dump utility method that displays the data to which each configuration ID points. The `propertySet` attribute of a `DataSource` is a Jacl list. To do anything useful with that list, you have to write some code to parse a Jacl list. Use the code from Listing 13.1 to display the raw Jacl list of property sets. Line 04 in Listing 13.2 shows you where in that Jacl list to find the property set name. Line 07 of Listing 13.2 modifies the Jacl list so that Jython can easily parse it. And the loop starting on line 10 of Listing 13.2 prints each property set from the list.

Listing 13.2   Parse a Jacl List in Order to Display a `DataSource` `propertySet`

```
1|  def dumpPropertySet( setName, jaclList ):
2|    delimeter = '`'
3|    # remove distractions
4|    jaclList = jaclList.replace( '[' + setName + ' [', '' )
5|    jaclList = jaclList.replace( ']]', '' )
6|    #create a reliable delimiter
7|    jaclList = jaclList.replace( ') ', ')' + delimeter )
8|    listOfProperties = jaclList.split( delimeter )
```

```
 9|    print "There are",len(listOfProperties), "properties\n"
10|    for p in listOfProperties:
11|      print AdminConfig.showAttribute( p, 'name' ) \
12|             + "     " + AdminConfig.showAttribute( p, 'type' ) \
13|             + "     " + AdminConfig.showAttribute( p, 'value' )
14|      print AdminConfig.showAttribute( p, 'description' ) + '\n'
```

What you see when you run the dumpPropertySet method will vary depending on the DataSource propertySet you are exploring. Some excerpts from the printout are displayed in Listing 13.3. This is the propertySet from the DataSource for the DB2 provider that was installed earlier in this chapter.

The top line of each paragraph of the dump will tell you the following:

- The name of the property
- The type of data it expects
- The current value (if any)

The rest of each paragraph of the dump is a description of the property. These descriptions are exactly what is provided by either the JDBCProvider template or by whoever installed the JDBCProvider.

Listing 13.3   First Four Properties from a propertySet

```
There are 64 properties

databaseName    java.lang.String    KevinsToyClassroomDatabase
This is a required property. This is an actual database name, not the
locally cataloged database name. The IBM Data Server driver does not
rely on information catalogued in the DB2 database directory.


driverType    java.lang.Integer    4
The JDBC connectivity type of a data source. If you want to use a type
4 driver, set the value to 4. If you want to use a type 2 driver, set
the value to 2. On WebSphere Application Server for Z/OS, driverType 2
uses RRS and supports 2-phase commit processing.


serverName    java.lang.String    was7host01.ibm.com
The TCP/IP address or host name for the DRDA server. If custom property
driverType is set to 4, this property is required.


portNumber    java.lang.Integer    50000
The TCP/IP port number where the DRDA server resides. If custom
property driverType is set to 4, this property is required.
```

As you can see, there are 64 properties in this particular `propertySet`. The Derby `DataSource` has a `propertySet` with only eight. The properties just listed are pretty straightforward; however, Listing 13.4 shows some other properties that shed some light on less clearly understood driver behavior.

Listing 13.4   Three Arcane Properties from a `propertySet`

```
deferPrepares     java. lang.Boolean     true
This property provides a performance directive that affects the
internal semantics of the input data type conversion capability of the
driver. By default the IBM Data Server driver defers 'internal prepare
requests'. In this case, the driver works without the benefit of
described parameter or result set meta data until execute time. So
undescribed input data is sent 'as is' to the server without any data
type cross-conversation of the inputs.


queryCloseImplicit    java.lang.Integer
Specifies whether cursors are closed immediately after all rows are
fetched. queryCloseImplicit applies only to type 4 connectivity to DB2
for z/OS database servers. Possible values are
DB2BaseDataSource.QUERY_CLOSE_IMPLICIT_YES (1) and
DB2BaseDataSource.QUERY_CLOSE_IMPLICIT_NO (2). The default is
DB2BaseDataSource.QUERY_CLOSE_IMPLICIT_YES. A value of
DB2BaseDataSource.QUERY_CLOSE_IMPLICIT_YES can provide better
performance because this setting results in less network traffic.


useJDBC4ColumnNameAndLabelSemantics     java.lang.Boolean
Specifies how the JDBC driver handles column labels in
ResultSetMetaData.getColumnName, ResultSetMetaData.getColumnLabel, and
ResultSet.findColumn method calls. Possible values are: 0, 1, 2. Please
see the JDBC driver documentation for details.
```

Other properties illuminate the various ways we impact the security of the communication between the driver and the database, as shown in Listing 13.5.

Listing 13.5   Some Properties That Configure Communications Security

```
sslConnection    java.lang.Boolean
Specifies whether the JDBC driver uses an SSL socket to connect to the
DB2 server. If sslConnection is set to true, the connection uses an SSL
socket. If sslConnection is set to false, the connection uses a plain
socket.


securityMechanism     java.lang.Integer
Specifies the DRDA security mechanism. Possible values are: 3
(CLEAR_TEXT_PASSWORD_SECURITY), 4 (USER_ONLY_SECURITY), 7
```

(ENCRYPTED_PASSWORD_SECURITY), 9
(ENCRYPTED_USER_AND_PASSWORD_SECURITY), or 11 (KERBEROS_SECURITY). If
this property is specified, the specified security mechanism is the
only mechanism that is used. If no value is specified for this
property, 3 is used.

kerberosServerPrincipal   java.lang.String
For a data source that uses Kerberos security, specifies the name that
is used for the data source when it is registered with the Kerberos Key
Distribution Center (KDC). It should be of the format user@realm.

And yet other properties have implications for debugging problems, as shown in Listing 13.6.

Listing 13.6   Properties That Aid Debugging

sysSchema   java.lang.String
Specifies the schema of the DB2 shadow catalog tables or views that are
searched when an application invokes a DatabaseMetaData method. The
sysSchema property was formerly called cliSchema.

traceLevel   java.lang.Integer   -1
Specifies the level of trace, determined by a bitwise combination of
constants: TRACE_NONE=0, TRACE_CONNECTION_CALLS=1,
TRACE_STATEMENT_CALLS=2, TRACE_RESULT_SET_CALLS=4,
TRACE_DRIVER_CONFIGURATION=16, TRACE_CONNECTS=32, TRACE_DRDA_FLOWS=64,
TRACE_RESULT_SET_META_DATA=128, TRACE_PARAMETER_META_DATA=256,
TRACE_DIAGNOSTICS=512, TRACE_SQLJ=1024, TRACE_META_CALLS=8192,
TRACE_DATASOURCE_CALLS=16384, TRACE_LARGE_OBJECT_CALLS=32768,
TRACE_SYSTEM_MONITOR=131072, TRACE_TRACEPOINTS=262144, TRACE_ALL=-1.

traceFile   java.lang.String
The file to store the trace output. If you specify the trace file, the
DB2 JCC trace will be logged in this file. If this property is not
specified and the WAS.database or com.ibm.ws.db2.logwriter trace group
is enabled, then both WebSphere Application Server trace and DB2 trace
will be logged into the WebSphere Application Server trace file.

traceFileAppend   java.lang.Boolean   false
Specifies whether to append to or overwrite the file specified by the
traceFile property. The default is false, which means the file
specified by the traceFile property is overwritten.

traceDirectory   java.lang.String
Specifies the directory where the trace file will be created.

Still other properties have implications for performance, as shown in Listing 13.7. These properties and their values vary from database vendor to database vendor.

Listing 13.7   Properties That Fine-Tune Performance

```
streamBufferSize      java.lang.Integer
```
Specifies the size, in bytes, of the JDBC driver buffers for chunking LOB or XML data. The JDBC driver uses the streamBufferSize value regardless of whether it uses progressive streaming. The data type of streamBufferSize is int. The default is 1048576. If the JDBC driver uses progressive streaming, LOB or XML data is materialized if it fits in the buffers, and the driver does not use the fullyMaterializeLobData property.

```
xaNetworkOptimization     java.lang.Boolean
```
Specifies whether the XA network optimization is enabled for type 4 connectivity. You might need to disable the XA network optimization in an environment in which XA Start and XA End are issued from one Java process, and XA Prepare and XA Commit are issued from another Java process. With XA network optimization, the XA Prepare can reach the DB2 server before the XA End, which results in an XAER_PROTO error. To prevent the XAER_PROTO error, disable the XA network optimization. The default is true, which means the XA network optimization is enabled. If xaNetworkOptimization is false, which means the XA network optimization is disabled, then the driver closes any open cursors at XA End time.

```
fullyMaterializeInputStreams     java.lang.Boolean
```
Indicates whether streams are fully materialized before they are sent from the client to a database server. The default is false.

```
fullyMaterializeLobData     java.lang.Boolean     true
```
This setting controls whether or not LOB locators are used to fetch LOB data. If enabled, LOB data is not streamed, but is fully materialized with locators when the user requests a stream on the LOB column. The default value is true.

The default values for all of these properties work well for the vast majority of situations. The debugging properties are very useful when things go wrong. The optimizing properties should not be adjusted until all the traditional optimizations (setting the number of connections, setting various timeouts, and so on) have been performed. Because all of these settings are a part of server configuration, none of them take effect until you save the configuration, synchronize all your affected nodes, and restart the affected servers.

Someday, for whatever reason, you might need to pass specialized, driver-specific values to the driver. You would do this by creating an entire `propertySet` for the `JDBCProvider` or by

modifying one or more existing values in the `propertySet`. One value you might choose to modify is the test query. The `preTestSQLString` holds the SQL query that `AdminControl.testConnection()`[18] sends to your database. If `AdminControl`
`.testConnection()` receives a result set in response to this query, it reports that your server can connect to your database. If it receives any other response or no response at all, `AdminControl`
`.testConnection()` reports that your server cannot connect to your database. That query is one of the properties you can expect to find in the `JDBCProvider`'s `propertySet`. Listing 13.8 shows the description of the `preTestSQLString` from one database vendor.

Listing 13.8   Property That Specifies the SQL Test Query

```
preTestSQLString     java.lang.String
                     SELECT CURRENT SQLID FROM SYSIBM.SYSDUMMY1
This SQL statement is used for pre-test connection function. For
example, SELECT 1 FROM [TESTTABLE]. If pre-testing of connection is
enabled for the connection pool, this SQL statement will be executed to
the connection to make sure the connection is good. If you leave this
field blank, the default SQL statement, SELECT CURRENT SQLID FROM
SYSIBM.SYSDUMMY1, will be used at runtime. This will slow down the
execution because of the exception handling if table SYSIBM.SYSDUMMY1
is not defined in the database. Users are recommended to provide their
own SQL statement to improve the performance.
```

You can execute any SQL query you choose, but you want to make sure that the query will work when you first configure your system. You probably want a query that does not take long to execute and does not return a lot of data. Listing 13.9 shows how to change one property within a `propertySet`. The changes do not take effect until you save your changes, synchronize any affected nodes, and restart the affected servers.

Listing 13.9   Code That Modifies Values in a `propertySet`

```
1| def changePropertySet( setName, jaclList,     \
                   propertyName, propertyValue ):
2|    delimeter = '`'
3|    # remove distractions
4|    jaclList = jaclList.replace( '[' + setName + ' [', '' )
5|    jaclList = jaclList.replace( ']]', '' )
6|    #create a reliable delimiter
7|    jaclList = jaclList.replace( ') ', ')' + delimeter )
8|    listOfProperties = jaclList.split( delimeter )
```

[18] Be aware that you might have to do some additional configuration to make this test work. See the footnotes at the beginning of "Troubleshooting Configuration Problems" in this chapter.

```
 9|    for p in listOfProperties:
10|      if AdminConfig.showAttribute( p, 'name' ) == propertyName:
11|        if propertyValue == "[]":
12|          AdminConfig.modify( p, [[ 'value', [] ]] )
13|        else:
14|          AdminConfig.modify( p, [[ 'value', propertyValue ]] )
15|        print AdminConfig.queryChanges()
16|        break
```

Databases Reference Section

This section provides detailed information about the **AdminTask** methods that configure all aspects of database connectivity. You need two groups of **AdminTask** methods and two MBeans any time one of your scripts creates the "plumbing" to interact with databases. **AdminTask** methods from the JDBCProviderManagement group and the VariableConfiguration group, as well as from the DataSource MBean and the TraceService MBean will all be documented.

Finally, the arguments to each method have been divided into groups. The first group contains the required arguments. The second group is made up of arguments that are not required, but that you are very likely to have to use. The third group is comprised of arguments that are optional and seldom used. The fourth group is arguments that you will have to supply if you are configuring a secure environment. The general pattern for calling **AdminTask** methods is

```
AdminTask.methodName( target,                                    \
          '[ -argument value -nextArgument value2  ' \
    + '-stepName [ -arg01 val01 -arg02 val02 ] ' \
    + '-nextStepName [ -arg03 val03 ]  -yetAnotherStep ]' )
```

There might or might not be a target. If there is, it might be a configuration ID or it might be a name. Targets are usually containment parents. There might or might not be arguments. Arguments are almost always names followed by values. There might or might not be steps as well. Think of steps as arguments that require either a list of names followed by values or nothing at all. Bundle all the arguments and steps into one big list and pass it to the method.

JDBCProviderManagement Group

This section details the JDBCProviderManagement Group methods.

createJDBCProvider

This method creates a new JDBCProvider that is used to connect with a relational database for data access. It uses the default JDBCProvider template for the database in question on the environment in which the application server lives to create a useful working installation and configuration for a supported database driver.

Required arguments:

- `scope`—Scope for the new `JDBCProvider`. Must be one of the following:

  `Cell`=nameOfYourCell

  `Node`=nameOfSomeNode

  `Node`=nameOfSomeNode,`Server`=nameOfSomeServer

  `Cluster`=nameOfSomeCluster

  `Application`=displayNameOfSomeApplication

- `databaseType`[19]—The type of database used by this `JDBCProvider`.
- `providerType`—The `JDBCProvider` type used by this `JDBCProvider`.
- `implementationType`—The implementation type for this `JDBCProvider`. Use `'Connection pool data source'` if your application runs in a single phase or local transaction. Use `'XA data source'` to run in a global transaction. You must use one of those two case-sensitive strings.

Frequently used optional arguments:

- `name`—The name of the `JDBCProvider`.
- `description`—Text to describe the part that this `JDBCProvider` plays in your topology.
- `implementationClassName`—The name of the Java class for the JDBC driver implementation.
- `classpath`—Specifies a list of paths or jar file names that together form the location for the resource provider classes. The `classpath` can contain multiple elements provided that they are separated with a colon, semicolon, or comma.
- `nativePath`—Specifies a list of paths that forms the location for the resource provider native libraries. The native path can contain multiple elements provided that they are separated with a colon, semicolon, or comma.

createDataSource

This method creates a new `DataSource` to access the backend data store. Application components use the `DataSource` to connect to a database. Each `DataSource` has a connection pool. This allows connections to be shared.

Target:

The configuration ID of the `JDBCProvider` that will provide the actual connections to the database. This target is required.

---

[19] Print `AdminConfig.listTemplates('JDBCProvider')` in order to see both `providerType` and `databaseType` available to you.

Required arguments:

- `name`—The name of the `DataSource`.
- `jndiName`—The Java Naming and Directory Interface (JNDI) name for this `DataSource`.

Optional arguments that matter if you enable security:

- `componentManagedAuthenticationAlias`—The alias used for database authentication when querying or updating the database.
- `xaRecoveryAuthAlias`—The alias used for database authentication during transaction recovery processing.

Frequently used optional arguments:

- `description`—Some text to describe the purpose this `DataSource` plays in your topology.
- `category`—The category that can be used to classify or group the resource. Although this argument is optional, it is very useful for documentation purposes.

Occasionally used optional arguments:

- `acknowledgeMode`—How the session acknowledges any messages it receives.

Steps:

- `configureResourceProperties`—Configures the resource properties for the `DataSource`. These are required properties specific to the type of `DataSource` being configured. This is a required step. The arguments below are part of a collection. In addition, each of these arguments is read-only. Once they are passed to the `DataSource`, they cannot be modified or deleted. If you need to change them, you must create another `DataSource`. Required arguments for this step:

You need a set of these arguments for each resource property, which are resource-specific. The documentation for the names and legal values of these properties comes from whoever provides the resource:

- `Name`—The name of the resource property. This is a read-only parameter.
- `Type`—The resource property type. This is a read-only parameter.
- `Value`—The resource property value. This is a required parameter.

listJDBCProviders

This method returns the configuration ID of each `JDBCProvider` in the specified scope. If you do not provide a scope argument, you get a list of the configuration IDs of all `JDBCProviders`.

Frequently used optional arguments:

- `scope`—Scope for the `JDBCProviders` that are to be listed. If you do not supply this argument, the default result is to return the configuration IDs of all `JDBCProviders`. Permitted values are as follows:

    `Cell`=nameOfYourCell

    `Node`=nameOfSomeNode

    `Node`=nameOfSomeNode,Server=nameOfSomeServer

    `Cluster`=nameOfSomeCluster

    `Application`=displayNameOfSomeApplication

listDataSources

This method returns the configuration ID of each `DataSource` in the specified scope. If you do not provide a scope argument, you get a list of the configuration IDs of all `DataSources`.

Frequently used optional arguments:

- `scope`—Scope for the `DataSources` that are to be listed. If you do not supply this argument, the default result is to return the configuration IDs of all `JDBCProviders`. Permitted values are as follows:

    `Cell`=nameOfYourCell

    `Node`=nameOfSomeNode

    `Node`=nameOfSomeNode,Server=nameOfSomeServer

    `Cluster`=nameOfSomeCluster

    `Application`=displayNameOfSomeApplication

VariableConfiguration Group

You can create, modify, and display WebSphere variables in one of two ways. You can use the three methods in this group, or you can call `AdminConfig.create()`, `AdminConfig.modify()`, and `AdminConfig.show()`. The methods in this group are much easier to use. The **AdminConfig** methods require you to traverse WebSphere's configuration tree to the correct scope, then find the `VariableMap` within that scope, then find the correct `VariableSubstitutionEntry` in that `VariableMap`. The methods in this group do that search for you.

showVariables

This method displays the name of one or more variables and the values of those variables. It can be limited to a certain scope, a certain variable name, or both.

Frequently used optional arguments:

- `scope`—Specifies the location of the variable.xml file you want to search. If you omit this argument, `Cell` scope is displayed. Scope can be specified in one of the following ways:

  `Cell`=nameOfYourCell

  `Node`=nameOfSomeNodeInYourCell

  `Server`=nameOfSomeServer. If you have more than one server with the same name, you must specify both the node name and the server name. For instance: `Node=Node15,Server=server1`

  `Cluster`=nameOfCluster

  `Application`=nameOfApplication

- `variableName`—The name of the variable. You get the value of this variable as defined in the variable.xml file in the scope you specify. If you omit this argument, you get the name and value of every variable defined in the variable.xml within the scope you specify.

setVariable

This method assigns a value to a variable. If the variable does not yet exist, it will be created. If the variable does exist, any value it currently holds will be changed.

Required arguments:

- `variableName`—The name of the variable to be created or changed.

Frequently used optional arguments:

- `scope`—Specifies the location of the variable.xml file you want to search. If you omit this argument, `Cell` scope is displayed. Scope can be specified in one of the following ways:

  `Cell`=nameOfYourCell

  `Node`=nameOfSomeNodeInYourCell

  `Server`=nameOfSomeServer. If you have more than one server with the same name, you must specify both the node name and the server name. For instance: `Node=Node15,Server=server1`

  `Cluster`=nameOfCluster

  `Application`=nameOfApplication

- `variableValue`—The value of the variable.

- `variableDescription`—Use this field to describe the role this variable plays in your topology.

removeVariable

This method deletes a variable.

Required arguments:

- `variableName`—The name of the variable to be created or changed.

Frequently used optional arguments:

- `scope`—Specifies the location of the variable.xml file you want to search. If you omit this argument, Cell scope is displayed. Scope can be specified in one of the following ways:

  `Cell`=nameOfYourCell

  `Node`=nameOfSomeNodeInYourCell

  `Server`=nameOfSomeServer. If you have more than one server with the same name, you must specify both the node name and the server name. For instance: `Node=Node15,Server=server1`

  `Cluster`=nameOfCluster

  `Application`=nameOfApplication

Useful MBeans

In addition to the **AdminTask** methods that manipulate `DataSources` and `JDBCProviders`, it is sometimes useful to work directly with several MBeans. For each MBean, a subset of its attributes and a subset of its operations are described. These subsets are the attributions and operations that are the most useful for debugging and fine-tuning database access.

DataSource MBean

This MBean, as its name implies, controls and reports on the operation of a `DataSource`. It also controls and reports on the operation of the connection pool that each `DataSource` contains. Each `DataSource` has its own MBean. Many of the attributes of this MBean are also attributes of the `DataSource` configuration item. If you want to change the runtime behavior of a `DataSource` without stopping the server that hosts the `DataSource`, you can change the modifiable attributes of the `DataSource` MBean. That allows you to experiment and do some troubleshooting without having to synchronize nodes and restart servers.

Interesting Read/Write attributes:

- `reapTime - java.lang.Integer`—The thread that enforces all the other timeouts runs once each time this number of seconds expire. All other timeouts are effectively rounded up to the next even multiple of `reapTime`.

- `minConnections - java.lang.Integer`—Once this number of connections has been opened, the `DataSource` always keeps at least this number of connections open.

- `maxConnections - java.lang.Integer`—The `DataSource` will never open more than this number of connections.

- testConnection - java.lang.Boolean—If this value is set to true and testConnectionInterval is greater than zero, you can call the testConnection method of **AdminControl** to send a test query over a connection from the free pool.

- testConnectionInterval - java.lang.Integer—This must be set to a value greater than zero in order to call the testConnection method of **AdminControl**. This value is the number of seconds that the DataSource will wait for a response from the database before failing the connection test.

- stuckTime - java.lang.Integer—Any active connection that does not respond and does not return to the connection pool within this number of seconds is considered "stuck." It is strongly recommended that stuckTime be at least four times as long as the stuckTimerTime.

- stuckTimerTime - java.lang.Integer—How many seconds before the thread that looks for stuck connections runs. This thread marks connections as stuck or as unstuck. It is strongly recommended that this value be less than one fourth as long as stuckTime.

- stuckThreshold - java.lang.Integer—Once this number of connections are judged to be stuck, any request for a new connection from this pool generates a resource exception. Applications can trap this exception and continue processing if they so choose. One possible remediation available to administrators would be to call the purgePoolContents() method of this MBean. Another possible remediation would be to contact the administrator of the back-end resource.

- surgeThreshhold - java.lang.Integer—When there are more than this number of simultaneous[20] requests for connections, each simultaneous request above the number specified here is forced to wait for surgeCreationInterval number of seconds. If your application(s) exhibit spikey, bursty traffic patterns that momentarily overload back-end resources, you might consider adjusting this attribute. The default value is -1. Any value below zero turns off surge protection. A value of zero delays every connection request.

- surgeCreationInterval - java.lang.Integer—See surgeThreshhold. The number of seconds that excessive simultaneous connection requests are forced to wait to give the back-end resource time to catch up.

- connectionTimeout - java.lang.Integer—Length of time in seconds before a connection request times out and throws an exception.

- unusedTimeout - java.lang.Integer—Interval in seconds after which an unused connection is discarded by the connection pool maintenance thread.

- agedTimeout - java.lang.Integer—Interval in seconds after which an unused aged connection is discarded by the connection pool maintenance thread.

---

[20] Note that surgeThreshold deals with simultaneous requests, not total requests for connections.

- `holdTimeLimit - java.lang.Integer`—`diagnosticMode` 1 and 2 track the connection hold time by an application. If the hold time is greater than the `holdTimeLimit`, it is reported in the `getPoolContents` information. If the `diagnosticMode` is 2, it also collects the callstack at the time of the `getConnection` request for those connections exceeding the `holdTimeLimit`.

Interesting operations: (All of these operations have interesting potential for debugging or for performance tuning.)

- `getRegisteredDiagnostics`—Returns a list of all diagnostic information available from this MBean. This information varies from version to version of WebSphere Application Server. It can also vary based on any enhancements you purchase and based on your database vendor and version.

- `getJndiName`—Returns the JNDI name for this `DataSource`. This can be useful for either documentation reasons or troubleshooting reasons.

- `showPoolContents`—Dumps all the connections in the pool.

- `purgePoolContents`—Closes all the connections in the pool.

- `getStatementCacheSize`—The size of the statement cache affects performance.

TraceService MBean

This MBean controls the amount of debugging and performance information that an individual server records. The records could be stored in a file or held in memory. If held in memory, you can control the size of the memory buffer. Indirectly, that determines the number of events your server remembers. Although this MBean reports the name of the file used to hold trace results, this MBean cannot permanently change the name, location of the trace file, or the decision to store trace results in memory versus in a file. It can, however, do all of that on a temporary basis. None of these changes will survive a server stop.

Interesting Read / Write attributes:

- `ringBufferSize - int`—The size of the ring buffer that holds trace events if tracing is done in memory as opposed to dumping the trace data to a file.

- `traceSpecification - java.lang.String`—This string determines what the trace service traces and how much information it captures. If you directly manipulate the value of this string, your modification is processed by the `appendTraceString` operation of this MBean. Your modifications are appended to the existing `traceSpecification`. They do not replace the existing `traceSpecification`. Call the `setTraceState` operation if you want to replace the entire `traceSpecification`. The tracing is based on Log4J. You can trace IBM Java code and third-party Java code. You can also trace certain standard events depending on any combination of:

  - Which Java package(s) you choose to trace

- Which groups of Java packages you choose to trace
- Which individual Java classes you choose to trace
- What level of information you choose to extract from each thing you choose to trace

Interesting operations: (All of these operations have interesting potential for debugging or for performance tuning.)

- `checkTraceString`—Tells you if the string you pass in conforms to TraceString grammar.
- `setTraceOutputToRingBuffer`—Make the ring buffer the active trace destination to which trace is routed. If trace is currently being routed to the ring buffer, the existing ring buffer is simply resized. If trace is currently being routed to a file, the file is closed, and the listener that wraps it is removed from the listener list. This operation requires the following two arguments:
  - `ringBufferSize - int`—The size in kilobytes for the ring buffer.
  - `traceFormat - java.lang.String`—Must be one of the following case-sensitive strings:
    - `basic`—Preserves only basic trace information. Select this option to minimize the amount of space taken up by the trace output.
    - `advanced`—Preserves more specific trace information. Select this option to see detailed trace information for use in troubleshooting and problem determination.
    - `logicanalyzer`—Preserves trace information in the same format as produced by Showlog tool.
- `setTraceOutputToFile`—Makes the specified file the active trace destination to which trace is routed. If trace is currently being routed to the ring buffer, the existing ring buffer is discarded. If trace is currently being routed to a file, the file is closed and a new one opened. Caution: The results could be unpredictable if the filename is the same as the name of the file currently in use. Requires the following arguments:
  - `nameOfFile - java.lang.String`—Gets the trace output.
  - `rolloverSize - int`—When the file grows to this size, it is renamed by adding the current timestamp to the end of the filename, and a new output file is opened. The number must be greater than zero. The number is the limit expressed in megabytes.
  - `numberOfBackups - int`—This number must be zero or higher.
  - `format - java.lang.String`—Must be one of the following case-sensitive strings:
    - `basic`—Preserves only basic trace information. Select this option to minimize the amount of space taken up by the trace output.
    - `advanced`—Preserves more specific trace information. Select this option to see detailed trace information for use in troubleshooting and problem determination.
    - `logicanalyzer`—Preserves trace information in the same format as produced by Showlog tool.

- `rolloverLogFileImmediate`—If you have to troubleshoot a busy server, this operation can be a godsend. It immediately rolls over either the `SystemOut` or the `SystemErr` file. You pick the name of the backup file. Requires the following arguments:

  - `streamName - java.lang.String`—Must be one of the following case-sensitive choices: `SystemOut` or `SystemErr`.

  - `backUpFileName - java.lang.String`—The name of the file used to archive the contents of the chosen stream. May be null. If null is specified, the system generates a file name.

- `setTraceState`—Replaces the current trace specification with the string you supply. Requires the following argument:

  - `replacementSpecification - java.lang.String`—The new trace specification.

- `appendTraceString`—Adds the string you supply to any existing trace specification. Note: If any part of this string duplicates an existing portion of a trace string, that portion is replaced rather than duplicated. If you directly manipulate the `traceSpecification` attribute of this MBean, this is the method that processes your new trace string. Requires the following argument:

  - `additionalSpecification - java.lang.String`—This string will be appended to any existing trace string.

- `dumpRingBuffer`—Dump the contents of the ring buffer to a file of your choice. This only works if you are tracing to a ring buffer instead of tracing to a file. WebSphere Application Server must have operating system permission to write to the file you specify. Requires the following argument:

  - `nameOfFile - java.lang.String`—The file name. Can be fully qualified. Use forward slashes to delimit directory names regardless of what the underlying operating system uses.

- `listComponentsInGroup`—Given the name of a trace group, it returns the names of all the packages that make up that group. Requires the following argument:

  - `nameOfGroup - java.lang.String`—The trace group; can also be given as an array of strings containing multiple groups.

Summary

Database access is very important to almost every serious enterprise application. In this chapter, you learned how to manage database connectivity on the WebSphere Application Server platform. We explored the **AdminTask** methods you are most likely to need, as well as some MBeans that figure prominently in database connectivity. We explored ways to troubleshoot database connectivity and performance issues, and we provided both online and print references for further study. In the next chapter, we explore messaging on the WebSphere Application Server platform.

## CHAPTER 14

Messaging

The **AdminTask** scripting object has several groups of methods that support messaging. In this chapter, we explore some useful methods from the following groups:

```
SIBAdminCommands
SIBJMSAdminCommands
SIBAdminBusSecurityCommands
```

Depending on your version of the product, there are 125 to 175 methods in the command groups that deal with messaging. Nobody uses all of those methods every day. We have selected a manageable subset of the methods in these groups to illustrate the main tasks that have to be performed any time you configure a messaging bus. We also give information that is not well-documented elsewhere and illustrate our points with a simple example. We then list the other commands in these groups at the end of this chapter along with a brief explanation of each.

An Introduction to Messaging

Messaging can be used to integrate legacy applications, to combine existing applications to serve new business needs, and to add a façade to an existing application. It is a very loosely coupled method of performing system integration. Messaging requires you to configure two distinct pieces of plumbing within an application server.

You have to configure some plumbing that prepares the application server with other application servers. The **AdminTask** methods that configure this plumbing are all part of the SIBAdminCommands command group.

You have to configure some additional plumbing that allows an application to be deployed to that server to send messages and retrieve messages.[1] The **AdminTask** methods that configure this plumbing are all part of the SIBJMSAdminCommands command group and the SIBAdminBusSecurityCommands command group.

Messaging Basics

Let's use email as an example to walk through basic messaging. The sender must know the recipient's address, but the recipient does not have to be online when the message is sent. Messaging builds on this pattern.

First, however, let's get rid of one requirement: The sender does not have to know the recipient's address information. So when the sender "sends" a message, you can just append that message to the end of a table in a database. You can configure[2] that imaginary database to be either a file or real database. Either way, that imaginary database always isolates sender from receiver. When a recipient wants to "receive" a message, the recipient reads the last row in the data table and marks it for deletion.

Second, you can hide all of the details from any applications that use messaging. An application will ask a factory to provide it with access to a messaging resource. The application will then either send a message or retrieve a message. The sender can determine whether a message was delivered, but the sender will not know who retrieved the message or whether the same recipient received two consecutive messages.

Messaging can be set up to deliver a message several ways. It can deliver the message to the first recipient who retrieves that message; messaging set up in this fashion is called a *queue*. Messaging can also be set up to retain a message until all registered listeners have acknowledged receipt of the message; messaging set up in this fashion is called a *topic*.

In its simplest form, configuring messaging requires you to perform the following configuration steps on the application server:

1. Create the messaging bus itself.

2. Add one or more members to the bus.

3. Create either a queue or a topic.

4. Create a connection factory.

5. Create either a JMSQueue or a JMSTopic.

We explore this in a simple example and then discuss ways in which you might need to improve this example for your environment.

---

[1] A discussion of the Java Message Service is beyond the scope of this book. For a good introduction, consider Chapter 33 of http://java.sun.com/j2ee/1.4/docs/tutorial/doc/index.html.

[2] See AdminTask.createSIBEngine(). The decision to use a database versus a filestore must be made when the messaging engine is created.

Terminology

The messaging scheme described in the previous section is called a *messaging bus*. The queue or the topic that holds messages for a bus is called a *destination*. It is convenient to think of a queue or a topic as a table in an imaginary database. It is convenient also to think of sending a message as appending a row to that table, as it is convenient to think of retrieving a message as selecting a row from that table and then marking that row for deletion. There is a lot of complexity hidden under all that convenient thinking.[3] But that metaphor exposes just enough of the details to allow us to configure a simple messaging bus.

Each application server and each cluster that communicates on the messaging bus is called a *bus member*. Each bus member has a messaging engine. The messaging engine gets created automatically when a server or a cluster is added as a member of a messaging bus. Messaging engines talk to our imaginary database. The IBM InfoCenter calls this imaginary database a *message store*. This message store can either be a real database or a file in the file system. You create this message store whenever you do something that creates a messaging engine.[4] Messaging engines also talk to each other.

Example: Creating a Bus

In this very simple example, we create a simple but useful messaging queue. If you want to use this script, there are some things you will have to change:

- You will have to change the node name to a node name that exists in your cell.

- You will have to change the server name to a server that exists on that node in your cell.

- If your cell already has an SIBus with the same name used, you will have to use a different name. Each SIBus in a cell must have a unique name.

- If your cell already has any of the JNDI names that are used in this sample script, you will have to edit the names so that they do not conflict with your existing JNDI names.

- If your cell already has a queue or a connection factory or a J2C administrative object with a name used here, you will have to change the names.

The variables in Listing 14.1 are used in this example code. You should be able to download this file and adapt this sample to your environment by just changing the values assigned to the variables in lines 01 through 18.

---

[3] For a lot more formal detail, consider the IBM Redbook SG247297, "Experience J2EE! Using WebSphere Application Server V6.1," section 15.1. The additional resources listed in that chapter are also quite helpful.

[4] See `AdminTask.addSIBusMember()` and `AdminTask.createSIBEngine()` for additional details.

Listing 14.1   Variables for Sample Code

```
 1|  #messagingBus.py

 2|  import AdminConfig
 3|  import AdminTask

 4|  # You should be able to modify this example pretty extensively
 5|  # just by changing the values of the following variables
 6|  nameOfBus = "VerySimpleBus"
 7|  oneNodeName = "Node01"
 8|  oneServerName = "Q01Srv"
 9|  nameOfFactory = "SimpleSIBFactory"
10|  jndiNameOfFactory = "jms/simpleSIB01"
11|  connectionFactoryScope = "/Cell:Cell01/"
12|  connectionFactoryDescription = "\"The factory for our " + \
  |  nameOfBus + "\""

13|  nameOfQueue = "SimpleBusDestination-AQueue"
14|  sibDestinationDescription =                              \
  |  "\"Just some tables in a database that supports our " \
  |  + nameOfBus + "\""

15|  actualLocationOfQueue = ' -node ' + oneNodeName + \
  |  ' -server ' + oneServerName

16|  nameOfJMSQueue = "SimpleQueueJMSWrapper"
17|  jndiNameOfJMSQueue = "jms/simpleQueueWrapper"
18|  jmsQueueDescription = \
  |  "\"This wrapper allows an application to use our " \
  |  + nameOfQueue + \
  |  " queue even if we change messaging software in the future\""
```

The following lines create the messaging bus[5] and display any messaging buses[6] that exist in a cell.

```
    print AdminTask.createSIBus('[-bus ' + nameOfBus + ' ]')
    print AdminTask.listSIBuses()
```

What you see of a bus in the configuration files at this point is nothing more than a few elements in a file called `sib-bus.xml`. This file lives in your configuration repository. You will find this

---

[5] See `AdminTask.createSIBus()` in the reference section of this chapter.

[6] See `AdminTask.listSIBuses()` in the reference section of this chapter.

file under cells/buses/nameOfBus. Although this line is necessary for every line of script that follows, it does not really add any functionality to any server in the cell. Until you add bus members and destinations, the messaging bus itself is nothing more than a name.

The following code configures some plumbing for one particular application server[7] and displays[8] the plumbing you configured.

```
print AdminTask.addSIBusMember('[-bus ' + nameOfBus +                \
    ' -node ' + oneNodeName + '  -server ' + oneServerName + \
    ' -fileStore ]')
print AdminTask.listSIBusMembers( '[-bus ' + nameOfBus + ' ]' )
```

The code here does several things. It adds a busMembers element to the sib-bus.xml file. Adding a bus member creates configuration for a messaging engine inside the server or inside the cluster[9] you added to the bus. A messaging engine knows how to talk to the imaginary database that will act as the middle man standing between message producer and message consumer. In this example, the imaginary database is actually a file store. If you change one argument and supply a JNDI name, you can use either an embedded database called Derby or an industrial strength database such as DB/2 or Oracle.

You could easily modify the code here slightly to configure messaging plumbing for a cluster instead of a server. All you would have to do is provide the name of a cluster instead of the names of a node and server.[10] Although it is easy to add a cluster as a messaging bus member, it is important to understand the default behavior of a cluster that becomes a member of a messaging bus.

By default, if you create a cluster with five member servers[11] and you make that cluster a member of a messaging bus, only one server out of the entire cluster will actually send and receive messages on the messaging bus. This is because, by default, the application server only activates one messaging engine[12] no matter how many servers there are in the cluster. Therefore, in this

---

[7] See AdminTask.addSIBusMember() in the reference section of this chapter.

[8] See AdminTask.listSIBusMembers() in the reference section of this chapter.

[9] This book assumes that the reader is already familiar with clusters and the reasons for creating and using clusters. For a good discussion of the fundamentals of clusters, see the WebSphere Application Server documentation at http://publib.boulder.ibm.com/infocenter/wasinfo/v7r0/index.jsp?topic=/com.ibm.websphere.pmc.nd.iseries.doc/concepts/cjn_mdb_endpt_overview.html. For a discussion about how a cluster interacts with a messaging bus, see http://publib.boulder.ibm.com/infocenter/wasinfo/v7r0/index.jsp?topic=/com.ibm.websphere.pmc.nd.iseries.doc/concepts/cjn_mdb_endpt_overview.html. The subtopics on this page explain in detail what it means to add a cluster as a bus member.

[10] See AdminTask.addSIBusMember() in the reference section of this chapter.

[11] There is nothing magical about the choice of five servers. The point is that no matter how many servers you create in the cluster, only one will get an active messaging engine. The other servers will be on hot standby, doing nothing but waiting for the active server's messaging engine to fail.

[12] See "Adding a cluster to a bus" in the WebSphere Application Server documentation at http://publib.boulder.ibm.com/infocenter/wasinfo/v6r1/index .jsp?topic=/com.ibm.websphere.pmc.nd.doc/concepts/cjt0005_.html.

sample cluster with five member servers, one server is actively communicating on the messaging bus, and the other four are on hot standby. It is possible to activate more than one messaging engine per cluster. Administratively, it is easy to do. It is just a matter of writing policies for the messaging engines in the cluster. There are side effects to doing this that include possible loss of message order and stranded messages. Make sure you read and understand the WebSphere Application Server documentation article on "Workload sharing with queue destinations"[13] and *all* articles mentioned on that page before proceeding.

Given that we often use clusters to provide workload balancing for applications and (by default) clusters provide high availability, not load balancing, for messaging engines, it makes sense to create one cluster to support messaging buses and additional clusters to support applications. This is especially true for WebSphere Application Server v6.1, since v7 adds additional messaging topology options. This is called the remote messaging pattern. There are two diagrams and a short section of text that describe this pattern in an IBM Redbook®.[14] Make sure you understand this material before you attempt to workload balance the messaging engines in a messaging bus.

So far, there are no tables that you need to care about in this imaginary database. That will change in the following code sample that creates a queue[15] and displays the queue[16] after you create it:

```
options  = '[-bus' + nameOfBus + ' -name ' + nameOfQueue
options += '-type Queue' + actualLocationOfQueue
options += ' ' -description ' + sibDestinationDescription + ' ]'
print AdminTask.createSIBDestination( options )
id = AdminConfig.getid( '/Node:%s/Server:%s/' %  \
   ( oneNodeName, oneServerName ) )
print AdminTask.listSIBJMSQueues( id )
```

When the `AdminTask.createSIBDestination()` method is executed, code in the application server creates the necessary tables in this imaginary database. The same method can be used to create either a queue or a topic space simply by changing the value of the "-type" option. Please note though that a separate set of methods are used to display the configuration information about queues,[17] topic spaces, and any topics they might contain. Remember too that topics are hierarchical creatures that live inside a topic space. Topic spaces and topics[18] have their own display methods.

After you create those tables, you have configured all the plumbing needed for the server or cluster to act as a part of the messaging bus you created. It is that easy. So far, we have not yet

---

[13] See http://publib.boulder.ibm.com/infocenter/wasinfo/v6r1/index.jsp?topic=/com.ibm.websphere.pmc.nd.doc/concepts/cjt0014_.html.

[14] See IBM Redbook SG247776, "Leading Practices for WebSphere Dynamic Process Edition v6.2," section 7.2.2, *Remote Messaging Topology Pattern*. In particular, notice Figures 7-2 and 7-3.

[15] See `AdminTask.createSIBDestination()` in the reference section of this chapter.

[16] See `AdminTask.listSIBJMSQueues()` in the reference section of this chapter.

[17] See `AdminTask.listSIBJMSQueues()` and `AdminTask.showSIBJMSQueue()`.

[18] See `AdminTask.listSIBJMSTopics()` and `AdminTask.showSIBJMSTopic()`.

given any application the ability to use any of that plumbing. The following code changes that. Start by creating[19] a connection factory and then displaying[20] the newly created connection factory's attributes, as shown in the following code lines:

```
factoryVisibility = AdminConfig.getid(connectionFactoryScope)
srvCfgID = AdminConfig.getid( '/Node:' + oneNodeName + \
                              '/Server:' + oneServerName + '/' )

factoryID = AdminTask.createSIBJMSConnectionFactory(           \
factoryVisibility, '[-name ' + nameOfFactory +                 \
                ' -jndiName ' + jndiNameOfFactory +            \
                ' -busName ' + nameOfBus +                     \
                ' -category Experiment01 -description ' +  \
                connectionFactoryDescription + ' ]')
print AdminTask.showSIBJMSConnectionFactory( factoryID )
```

A connection factory gives an application a way to find your messaging plumbing and retrieve a piece of code that will actually ask the messaging bus to send and receive messages on behalf of the client application. Think of a connection factory as something that maps the industry standard Java Messaging Service (JMS) façade to the underlying proprietary Service Integration Bus implementation. Applications use components of the Java Messaging Service. You configure service integration buses (SIB) to integrate components of your enterprise architecture. You must specify the following in order for the connection factory to do its job:

- How visible the connection factory should be. You can make a connection factory that an entire cell and an entire node can use. You can restrict the visibility of your connection factory to just one server or one cluster of servers.

- The name of the bus that will hold the queue or the topic that applications will ultimately use.

- A JNDI name that applications will use when they want to talk to a queue or a topic that this connection factory knows about. The mapping of the JNDI name to a queue or a topic on a specific bus is the glue that connects JMS to SIB.

NOTE   The description and the category are optional arguments that help you document your configuration decisions. Any text you supply for these arguments will also be visible to anybody who uses the Admin Console.

---

[19] See `AdminTask.createSIBJMSConnectionFactory()` in the reference section of this chapter.

[20] See `AdminTask.showSIBJMSConnectionFactory()` in the reference section of this chapter.

The following code shows how to have a connection factory create a code object—an
SIBJMSQueue—that allows an application to use the messaging bus to send and receive messages.[21]
The line displays[22] attributes of the SIBJMSQueue that was configured.

```
jmsQueueWrapper = AdminTask.createSIBJMSQueue( srvCfgID,              \
'[-name ' + nameOfJMSQueue + ' -queueName ' + nameOfQueue  +          \
' -busName ' + nameOfBus + ' -jndiName ' + jndiNameOfJMSQueue +  \
' -description ' + jmsQueueDescription + '  ]')
print AdminTask.showSIBJMSQueue( jmsQueueWrapper )
```

You've just completed everything necessary to create the simplest possible messaging queue. All
you needed to accomplish this task were the following **AdminTask** methods:

- createSIBus
- addSIBusMember
- createSIBDestination
- createSIBJMSFactory
- createSIBJMSQueue

There are a few things you might want to change depending on the needs of your system and the
needs of your customers. We used the file system for our imaginary database. You might choose
to change that to a commercial database product. Extremely demanding security requirements
might require additional constraints. We enable security later in this chapter.

Example: Deleting a Bus

Deleting a bus is very important during development and debugging. Very often, it is easier to
start from scratch than to figure out which setting is incorrectly configured and what side effects
that might have caused. To delete a messaging bus, as shown in Listing 14.2, you need to delete:

- The bus itself
- The SIBJMSQueue
- The SIBJMSConnectionFactory

If you have enabled security, you might have to delete some authentication artifacts as well. If you
are using an external database, you might have to delete some DataSources and JDBC artifacts.
Again, sometimes it is easier to delete the incorrect configuration, correct your create method, and
recreate a configuration than it is to locate all the side effects of an improper configuration.

---

[21] See AdminTask.createSIBJMSQueue() in the reference section of this chapter.

[22] See AdminTask.showSIBJMSQueue() in the reference section of this chapter.

Listing 14.2 shows some code that deletes this sample bus. Notice that to find the `SIBJMSQueue` you created, you have to look for a `J2CAdminObject`, which is on line 50. Also worth noting is that to find `SIBJMSConnectionFactory`, you have to look for a `ConnectionFactory`—on line 55. In both cases, you also have to know the name of the object you want. You can see that while `AdminTask.deleteSIBus()`[23] takes the name of a bus as its parameter, both `AdminTask` `.deleteSIBJMSQueue()`[24] and `AdminTask.deleteSIBJMSConnectionFactory()`[25] require configuration IDs. Unfortunately, we don't currently have an easy way to locate the configuration ID, given the name attribute of the configuration item. Therefore, you will see a `findIDbyName()` method here.

Listing 14.2   Delete Our Sample Messaging Bus

```
40| def delete():
41|    """Delete all the artifacts of our messaging queue"""
42|    print "About to delete " + nameOfBus
43|    # This deletes:
44|    #    the bus itself
45|    #    all bus members
46|    #    the messaging engines
47|    AdminTask.deleteSIBus( '[-bus ' + nameOfBus + ' ]' )

48|    #  Delete the SIBJMSQueue (really a J2CAdminObject)
49|    print "Trying to find " + nameOfJMSQueue + \
       " so we can delete it"
50|    q = findIDbyName( 'J2CAdminObject', nameOfJMSQueue )
51|    print "About to delete " + nameOfJMSQueue
52|    AdminTask.deleteSIBJMSQueue(q)

53|    #  Delete the ConnectionFactory
54|    print "Trying to find " + nameOfFactory + \
       " so we can delete it"
55|    c = findIDbyName( 'ConnectionFactory', nameOfFactory )
56|    print "About to delete " + nameOfFactory
57|    AdminTask.deleteSIBJMSConnectionFactory( c )
58|    print "Deleted everything"
```

---

[23] See `AdminTask.deleteSIBus()` in the reference section of this chapter.

[24] See `AdminTask.deleteSIBJMSQueue()` in the reference section of this chapter.

[25] See `AdminTask.deleteSIBJMSConnectionFactory()` in the reference section of this chapter.

```
59|  def findIDbyName( wasType, name ):
60|    """Search all the ConfigIDs of given type for name"""
61|    array = AdminConfig.list( wasType ).splitlines()
62|    for t in array:
63|      if AdminConfig.showAttribute( t, 'name' ) == name:
64|        return t
65|    return None
```

If you delete a messaging bus that uses either a filestore or a Derby database or a Cloud-scape® database, you might want to make sure you delete the file system directory that contains that datastore or filestore. If you recreate the messaging bus with the same bus name as a messaging bus you deleted and the new messaging bus refuses to start, check your logs for error messages that mention a common mode error.[26] If you find such an error, delete the directory that contained the database or filestore for the messaging bus. This is an operating system task. There are no scripting objects that do this for you. These databases can be found in the profile that holds the configuration information for your deployment manager. In the root of that profile, look for a directory that has a name such as `databases` or `devicestores`. The directory you need to delete will be one of the directories under that. The exact names might be version-dependent. See the WebSphere Application Server documentation for details.

Security

It is difficult to find any resource that concisely delineates the steps you must take to secure a messaging bus. Because of this, we created an administrative checklist for you. This checklist is not a substitute for a security audit by a qualified professional. To secure a messaging bus, you must

- Enable administrative security for the cell.
- Enable security for the bus.
- Create (or use an existing) authentication alias to use between messaging engines. This step becomes unnecessary beginning with WebSphere Application Server version 7.
- Create (or use an existing) secure transport chain to use between messaging engines.[27]
- Disable (or delete) insecure messaging transport chains.

---

[26] See details in the WebSphere Application Server documentation at http://publib.boulder.ibm.com/infocenter/wasinfo/v6r1/index.jsp?topic=/com.ibm.websphere.pmc.nd.doc/ref/rjk_prob0.html. Page down to the section titled "Problems when you re-create a service integration bus."

[27] Setting up SSL from scratch can involve some work. Depending on how much has already been done and how much of that you are allowed to reuse, the work could include generating digital certificates, copying those certificates to appropriate computers, creating keystores, and configuring servers to use those keystores. Additional details can be found in the WebSphere Application Server documentation under the topic "Creating a Secure Sockets Layer configuration" at http://publib.boulder.ibm.com/infocenter/wasinfo/v7r0/index.jsp?topic=/com.ibm.websphere.nd.multiplatform.doc/info/ae/ae/tsec_sslconfiguration.html.

- Remove default authorization policies.
- Secure the Distribution and Consistency Service (DCS).
- Secure each messaging engine on the messaging bus.
- Secure any data stores used by the members of the messaging bus.
- Create (or use an existing) authentication alias for transaction recovery. This step becomes unnecessary beginning with WebSphere Application Server version 7.

When securing a messaging bus, the word "security" really means two categories of things:

- Restricting access to the messaging bus. This is often called *bus security*.
- Encrypting the communications involving the various components. This is often called *transport security*.

Enabling Bus Security

Messaging bus security is enabled by default. However, if you ever disable administrative security, you will also be disabling messaging bus security. Also if you have not yet enabled administrative security, enabling messaging bus security will have no effect. WebSphere Application Server versions 6.1 and later enable administrative security by default. Earlier versions disable it by default. Before version 6.1, administrative security was called *global security*.

There are five security roles that apply to messaging buses:

- **Connector**—This role allows you to connect to the bus.
- **Browser**—This role type applies to alias, port, and queue destinations.
- **Receiver**—This role type applies to alias, port, queue, and `topic space` destinations.
- **Sender**—This role applies to alias, `foreignDestination`, port, queue, and `topicSpace` destinations.
- **Creator**—This role applies to temporary destinations only.

Two special groups apply to messaging buses as well:

- **AllAuthenticated**—Any entity that successfully logs in belongs to this group.
- **Everyone**—As the name implies, all entities, whether authenticated or not, belong to this group. Giving this group access to any resource is the same as turning security off for that resource.

If you ignore the two special groups, in order to do anything useful, an application must belong to a group that has the following roles to use the following types of messaging bus components:

- Queue, port, or Web service requires sender, receiver, browser, creator roles.
- Alias requires sender, receiver, browser roles.
- Topic Space requires sender, receiver roles.
- Foreign Destinations require sender role.

By default, messaging engines communicate over the `InboundBasicMessaging` transport chain. Change this by specifying a secure transport chain[28] as your inter-engine transport chain. In addition, you have to specify a secure transport chain for your Distribution and Consistency Services communications. By default, Distribution and Consistency Services use the DCS transport chain.

There is an `InboundSecureMessaging` transport chain that you can use to secure communications between messaging engines and a `DCS-Secure` transport chain that you can use to secure Distribution and Consistency Services communications.

You should specify user groups with appropriate role permissions as authorized users of your messaging bus. While there is no mutual authentication, the receiving messaging engine authenticates incoming messages against the user registry. It checks to see that the user name specified on the incoming message matches a user name it is authorized to serve. You should not use default authorization policies in a secure environment.

Example: Enabling Bus Access Security

In the following code, you're creating a secure messaging bus. Notice that this code depends on variables defined in Listing 14.1. A number of the settings you need in order to secure a messaging bus are, in fact, the default settings. In those cases, you do nothing to change those defaults. If, by chance, your system has different values for these attributes, you will have to write some code to change those values. If you do have to write code to change the values of attributes of the messaging bus or any of its component parts, it is extremely important to make those changes using the `AdminTask.modifySIB*` methods documented in the "Modifying a Bus and Bus Components" section of this chapter. Under no circumstances should you ever use **AdminConfig** to modify an attribute of any messaging bus component. Some of those attributes have values that are dynamically generated. The appropriate **AdminTask** methods respect those dynamically generated values. **AdminConfig** does not.

When you execute the following lines of script on your system, it should tell you that bus security is enabled.[29] If not, you must set the secure attribute of your `SIBus` to `true`.

```
print AdminTask.showSIBus('[-bus ' + nameOfBus + ' ]')
```

After you execute this line, look for `secure=`. Right after that, you should see `true`. Then look for `permittedChains=`. Right after that, you should see `SSL_ENABLED`. If not, you have to modify some attributes of the messaging bus.[30]

---

[28] Setting up SSL from scratch can involve some work. Depending on how much has already been done and how much of that you are allowed to reuse, the work could include generating digital certificates, copying those certificates to appropriate computers, creating keystores, and configuring servers to use those keystores. Additional details can be found in the WebSphere Application Server documentation under the topic "Creating a Secure Sockets Layer configuration" at http://publib.boulder.ibm.com/infocenter/wasinfo/v7r0/index.jsp?topic=/com.ibm.websphere.nd.multiplatform.doc/info/ae/ae/tsec_sslconfiguration.html.

[29] See `AdminTask.showSIBus()` in the reference section of this chapter.

[30] See `AdminTask.modifySIBus()` in the reference section of this chapter.

```
print AdminTask.modifySIBus( '[ -bus ' + nameOfBus +          \
          ' -busSecurity true -permittedChains SSL_ENABLED ]'  )
```

Any time you enable or disable bus security, be careful to modify the `busSecurity` argument rather than the `secure` argument. The names are very similar. To make matters even more confusing, the attribute name that is displayed is `secure`. Nevertheless, the `secure` argument is deprecated.

For security reasons, it is very important to remove the default authorizations for the messaging bus. You do not want to provide any known vectors of attack to an intruder.

```
print AdminTask.removeDefaultRoles( '[-bus ' + nameOfBus + ' ]'  )
```

After you remove the default authorizations,[31] you need to create authorized groups and/or users for your installation,[32] as shown in Listing 14.3.

Listing 14.3 Creating New Authorized Users for Secure Messaging Bus

```
01|   secMgrID = AdminConfig.list( 'Security' )
02|   # create JAAS authentication identity data
03|   desc = 'for users of ' + nameOfBus
  |   # create an arbitrary name for a user ID
04|   uid = nameOfBus + '-User'
05|   pwd = 'TopSecretPassword'
06|   print "In WAS Version 5, user names had to be less",    \
07|   "than 12 characters"
08|   print "The same restriction applies to WebSphere MQ"
09|   print uid,"is",str( len(uid)    ),"characters long"
  |
10|   jaasID = AdminConfig.create( 'JAASAuthData', secMgrID,  \
  |   [ ['alias', 'SimpleBusAuthenticationAlias'],            \
  |   ['description', desc],                                  \
  |   ['userId', uid], ['password',pwd]   ] )
12|   print jaasID
```

The code in Listing 14.3 assumes that there is a user in your user registry with a user ID and a password that matches information supplied when you created the `JAASAuthData`. If this is not true, you will not get any errors when you run the code in Listing 14.3. Your `JAASAuthData`

---

[31] See `AdminTask.removeDefaultRoles()` in the reference section of this chapter.

[32] See the `AdminTask.addGroupTo*Role()` and `AdminTask.addUserTo*Role()` sections of the reference portion of this chapter.

won't get you access when you try to use it. It will fail authentication by your user registry.[33] The code in Listing 14.4 sets the correct permissions for your new user. Be aware that you can set permissions for a group instead of a user. There is a parallel series of **AdminTask** methods, each of which perform the same functions on a group instead of a user. You have to add a user or group to the bus connector role to allow that entity to connect to the bus at all. If you enable security for a bus and it stops working, this is something you should check. You should also check to make sure that your user is in your user registry.

Listing 14.4   Setting Permissions for Users

```
21|   # authorize the new identity to access the bus
22|   print AdminTask.addUserToBusConnectorRole(         \
      '[ -bus ' + nameOfBus + ' -user ' + uid + ' ]' )
23|   print AdminTask.addUserToDefaultRole(              \
      '[ -bus ' + nameOfBus + ' -role Sender ' +        \
      '-user ' + uid + ' ]' )
24|   print AdminTask.addUserToDefaultRole(              \
      '[ -bus ' + nameOfBus + ' -role Receiver ' +      \
      '-user ' + uid + ' ]' )
25|   print AdminTask.addUserToDefaultRole(              \
      '[ -bus ' + nameOfBus + ' -role Browser ' +       \
      '-user ' + uid + ' ]' )
26|   print AdminTask.addUserToDefaultRole(              \
      '[ -bus ' + nameOfBus + ' -role Creator ' +       \
      '-user ' + uid + ' ]' )
```

Example: Enabling Transport Security

Secure chains should be enabled. Insecure transport chains must be disabled. It is not enough just to specify SSL_ENABLED chains. If lines 28 through 42 in Listing 14.5 show the wrong value, you will have to set the enabled attribute to the correct value for that chain.

There is nothing **AdminTask** specific in the code that inspects transport chains in Listing 14.5. The code just searches the entire configuration repository for every Chain[34] that has a name that includes either the text SecureMessag, BasicMessag, DCS, or DCS-Secure. Any transport chain that was created by IBM to support a message bus will have the text Messag as part of its name. Because this code depends on undocumented naming conventions, you might want to print out a list of every Chain in your configuration and confirm the naming conventions that

---

[33] See the WebSphere Application Server documentation for all the administrative steps to enable administrative security.

[34] Chain is a WebSphere Application Server data type. Its name is case-sensitive. Notice in the example code, we search for Chain, not TransportChain.

IBM used on your version of the product. Alternatively, you are free to create your own secure transport chains and use them for message bus communications.

Message buses also communicate with Distribution and Consistency Services (DCS). This communication contains the location of messaging resources. By default, DCS requires a valid LTPA token from any entity that attempts communications with DCS, but the communications themselves are unencrypted. Thus, anybody with a network sniffer (and a lot of patience) could discover the location of all of your allegedly secure messaging resources. This would be an unacceptable security hole in many enterprises.

To close this hole, create another core group (which is described in Chapter 11, "The AdminTask Object—Server Management.") Make any server or cluster member that will use your secure message bus a member of that core group. Specify the DCS-secure transport chain as the transport chain between that core group and DCS.

Listing 14.5   Finding Secure and Insecure Transport Chains

```
27|    # all insecure chains should be DISabled
28|    insecure = getBasicMessagingChains()
29|    print str( len(insecure) ),"INsecure chains"
30|    for c in insecure:
31|      enabled = AdminConfig.showAttribute( c, 'enable' )
32|      if enabled != 'false':
33|        print c
34|        print "Enabled is ",enabled
35|    # all secure chains should be ENabled
36|    secure = getSecureMessagingChains()
37|    print str( len(secure) ),"SECURE chains"
38|    for c in secure:
39|      enabled = AdminConfig.showAttribute( c, 'enable' )
40|      if enabled == 'false':
41|        print c
42|        print "Enabled is ",enabled


50| def getBasicMessagingChains():
  |    """Find all the INsecure transport chains"""
51|    messagingChains = []
52|    srvCfgID = AdminConfig.getid( '/Node:' + oneNodeName +      \
  |      '/Server:' + oneServerName + '/' )
53|    raw = AdminConfig.list( 'Chain', srvCfgID )
54|    array = raw.splitlines()
55|    for c in array:
56|      chainName = AdminConfig.showAttribute( c, 'name' )
```

```
57|     if chainName.find( 'BasicMessag' ) > -1:
58|       messagingChains.append( c )
59|       continue
60|     if chainName.find( 'DCS(' ) > -1:
61|       messagingChains.append( c )
62|       continue
63|   return messagingChains


70| def getSecureMessagingChains():
  |   """Find all the SECURE transport chains"""
71|   messagingChains = []
72|   srvCfgID = AdminConfig.getid( '/Node:' + oneNodeName +       \
  |     '/Server:' + oneServerName + '/' )
73|   raw = AdminConfig.list( 'Chain', srvCfgID )
74|   array = raw.splitlines()
75|   for c in array:
76|     chainName = AdminConfig.showAttribute( c, 'name' )
77|     if chainName.find( 'SecureMessag' ) > -1:
78|       messagingChains.append( c )
79|       continue
80|     if chainName.find( 'DCS-Secure' ) > -1:
81|       messagingChains.append( c )
82|       continue
83|   return messagingChains
```

Finally, you have to provide the configuration ID of your JAAS authentication alias to two attributes of the ConnectionFactory -authDataAlias and xaRecoveryAuthAlias. This is done in the following sample code:

```
c = findIDbyName( 'ConnectionFactory', nameOfFactory )
AdminConfig.modify( c, [ [ 'authDataAlias', jaasID ], \
  [ 'xaRecoveryAuthAlias', jaasID ]  ] )
```

Here are two separate authentications that happen on the messaging bus and its assorted components. When you send a message, you are really inserting a row into an imaginary database table. If you configure your messaging bus to use a real database,[35] then sending a message might well require authentication by the database. Any real database used to support messaging is required to support transactions. When a transaction fails and it needs to be rolled back, there is a separate

---

[35] As opposed to an imaginary database like a filestore.

authentication required by the database. You are free to use the same credentials for both authentications. You just have to remember to configure for both authentications.

Reference Section

In this section, we provide detailed information about the **AdminTask** methods that configure messaging buses. Of the hundreds of methods in this category, detailed information is provided about the methods you will likely use most often. The methods are divided into categories. Within those categories, we present the methods in the order in which you might have to use them. We drew on numerous sources for the information we present in this section, as well as the most recent version of the help that IBM provides within the **AdminTask** scripting object itself. We added details from several sources within the WebSphere Application Server documentation and that folks from the IBM support staff were kind enough to provide. We also supplemented this with things we learned from our own experience.

Finally, the arguments to each method are divided into groups. The first group is made up of the required arguments. The second group are arguments that are not required but that you are very likely to have to use. The third group is comprised of arguments that are optional and are seldom used. The fourth group are arguments that you will have to supply if you are configuring a secure environment.

The general pattern for calling **AdminTask** methods is:

```
AdminTask.methodName( target,                              \
        '[ -argument value -nextArgument value2  ' \
    + '-stepName [ -arg01 val01 -arg02 val02 ] ' \
    + '-nextStepName [ -arg03 val03]  -yetAnotherStep ]' )
```

There might or might not be a target. If there is one, it might be a configuration ID, or it might be a name. Targets are usually containment parents of whatever the method touches. There might or might not be arguments. Arguments are almost always name/value pairs. And there might or might not be steps—and there might be more than one step. Think of steps as arguments that take either a list of name/value pairs as their value or no argument at all. Bundle all the arguments and all the steps into one big list and pass it to the method.

Creating Message Buses

createSIBus

This method creates a messaging bus.

Required argument:

- bus—Every bus has to have a name. This is where you specify the name of the bus you are about to create.

Optional arguments you might need if you want to secure the bus:

- busSecurity—The default value true enables messaging bus security. Change this to false to disable bus security. This argument has no effect unless you have already enabled administrative security.

- InterEngineAuthAlias—For authenticating communications between messaging engines (used by complex topologies).

- mediationsAuthAlias—For authenticating a message to a mediation layer. Only needed if you are doing mediations within your SIBus and then only in secure environments.

Optional arguments that you are likely to use:

- description—Any text you might want to add to describe this part of your bus topology.

- discardOnDelete—The default value is false. This argument decides whether messages should be deleted from the database that supports a queue if and when a queue gets deleted.

- HighMessageThreshold—The default is 50,000.

Optional arguments that you are less likely to use:

- configurationReloadEnabled—The default is true. Set this to false if you do not want to allow bus configuration information to be dynamically reloaded.

- ScriptCompatibility—Default of 6.1 works unless you have version 6 (or earlier) servers as bus members. In that case, set this value to 6.

- secure—You are not likely to use this argument because it has been deprecated. Use busSecurity instead.

addSIBusMember

This method configures the plumbing that a server uses to become a member of a bus.

Required argument:

- bus—The name of the bus that this server or cluster will join.

Although the following arguments are not marked "mandatory," you are required to use some of them. You have to specify either the server or cluster or WebSphere MQ server that will receive the extra plumbing that will make it a member of a messaging bus. If you want to add an individual server to a messaging bus, you must specify the server name and the node name of that server. If you want to add an entire cluster to the messaging bus, you must specify the name of the cluster, and you cannot specify a node name or a server name. If you want a WMQ server to host this destination, supply a WebSphere MQ server name. Omit node, server, and cluster arguments.

- node—The name of the node that contains the server you want to add to the messaging bus.

- server—The name of the server you want to add to the messaging bus.

- `cluster`—The name of the cluster that you want to add to the messaging bus.

- `wmqServer`—The name of a WebSphere MQ server that you want to add to the messaging bus

- `port`—Required if you are adding a WebSphere MQ server to the messaging bus

- `channel`—Required if you are adding a WebSphere MQ server to the messaging bus

- `securityAuthAlias`—Required if you are adding a WebSphere MQ server to the messaging bus

Frequently used optional arguments:

- `fileStore`—Store messages in the file system instead of in the file system. Do not use this argument and the `dataStore` argument.

- `dataStore`—Store messages in a database instead of in a database. Do not use this argument and the `dataStore` argument.

- `trustUserIds`—You might choose to use this argument if you are making a WMQ server a bus member.

- `transportChain`—You might choose to override the default transport chain that communicates with an WMQ server.

Occasionally used optional arguments:

- `logSize`—The size, in megabytes, of the log file.
- `logDirectory`—The name of the log files directory.
- `minPermanentStoreSize`—The minimum size, in megabytes, of the permanent store file.
- `maxPermanentStoreSize`—The maximum size, in megabytes, of the permanent store file.
- `unlimitedPermanentStoreSize`—`true` if the permanent file store size has no limit; `false` otherwise.
- `permanentStoreDirectory`—The name of the store files directory for permanent data.
- `minTemporaryStoreSize`—The minimum size, in megabytes, of the temporary store file.
- `maxTemporaryStoreSize`—The maximum size, in megabytes, of the temporary store file.
- `unlimitedTemporaryStoreSize`—`true` if the temporary file store size has no limit; `false` otherwise.
- `temporaryStoreDirectory`—The name of the store files directory for temporary data.
- `schemaName`—The name of the database schema used to contain the tables for the data store. This only matters if you are creating data tables, and then it only matters if you have some special schema that you want to substitute for the standard schema that IBM uses.
- `createDefaultDatasource`—When adding a server to a bus, set this to `true` if a default `datasource` is required. When adding a cluster to a bus, this parameter must not be supplied.

- `datasourceJndiName`—The JNDI name of the datasource to be referenced from the datastore created when the member is added to the bus. You will only need to supply this value if you are using an external database.

- `authAlias`—The name of the authentication alias used to authenticate the messaging engine to the data source. You will only need to supply this value if you are using an external database.

createSIBDestination

This method creates either a queue or a topic or a link on an existing bus member to some other bus.

Required arguments:

- `bus`—The name of the bus that this destination will serve.

- `name`—Destination name.

- `type`—Destination type must be one of the following (`Alias|Foreign|Port|Queue|TopicSpace|WebService`).

Although the following arguments are not marked "mandatory," you are required to use some of them. You have to specify either the server or the cluster or WebSphere MQ server that will host this destination. If the destination is really a link to some other bus, there are several additional arguments you must supply. If you want to an individual server to host this destination, you must specify the server name and the node name of that server. If you want an entire cluster to host this destination, you must specify the name of the cluster and you may not specify a node name or a server name. If you want to add a WMQ server as a bus member, supply a WebSphere MQ server name, a WMQ queue name, and whether or not to use RFH2. Omit node, server, and cluster arguments. If this destination will be an alias for another `SIBus`, then `aliasBus`, `targetBus`, and `targetName` must also be supplied. If this destination will be a link to a foreign bus (such as MQ Series), then `foreignBus` must also be supplied.

- `node`—To assign the destination to a server, supply node name and server name but not cluster name or WebSphere MQ server name.

- `server`—To assign the destination to a server, supply node name and server name but not cluster name or WebSphere MQ server name.

- `wmqServer`—To assign the destination to a WebSphere MQ server, supply a WebSphere MQ server name but not node, server name, or cluster name.

- `wmqQueueName`—The name of the WebSphere MQ queue for messages. This must be specified with the WebSphere MQ server name but not node, server name, or cluster name.

- `useRFH2`—Determines if messages sent to the WebSphere MQ destination have an RFH2 header or not. This must be specified with the WebSphere MQ server name but not node, server name, or cluster name.

Frequently used optional arguments:

- `description`—Any text you want to add to document your topology decision. This description will show up in the Admin Console.

- `defaultPriority`—The default priority for message flows through this destination, in the range 0 (lowest) through 9 (highest). This default priority is used for messages that do not contain a priority value.

- `maxReliability`—The maximum reliability quality of service that is accepted for values specified by producers.

- `maxFailedDeliveries`—The maximum number of times that service tries to deliver a message to the destination before forwarding it to the exception destination.

- `persistentReliability`—The quality of service used for inbound messages that WebSphere MQ regards as being persistent. Allowable values are (BEST_EFFORT_ NONPERSISTENT | EXPRESS_NONPERSISTENT | RELIABLE_NONPERSISTENT | RELIABLE_PERSISTENT | ASSURED_PERSISTENT).

- `overrideOfQOSByProducerAllowed`—Controls the quality of service for message flows between producers and the destination. Select this option to use the quality of service specified by producers instead of the quality defined for the destination.

Occasionally used optional arguments:

- `exceptionDestination`—The name of another destination to which the system sends a message that cannot be delivered to this destination within the specified maximum number of failed deliveries. By default, messages that cannot be delivered go to the system exception destination.

- `delegateAuthorizationCheckToTarget`—Indicates whether the authorization check should be delegated to the alias or target destination.

- `replyDestination`—The name of the destination for reply messages.

- `replyDestinationBus`—The name of the bus on which the reply destination is configured.

- `maintainStrictMessageOrder`—Select this option (setting it to `true`) to enforce message order for this destination.

- `receiveExclusive`—Select this option (setting it to `true`) to allow only one consumer to attach to a destination.

- `receiveAllowed`—Clear this option (setting it to `false`) to prevent consumers from being able to receive messages from this destination.

- `sendAllowed`—Clear this option (setting it to `false`) to stop producers from being able to send messages to this destination.

Steps:

- `defaultForwardRoutingPath`—You normally don't have to set this unless you have a complex bus topology. If you do have to perform this step, these are the arguments you will have to supply. These arguments are passed as a collection.
- `Destination`—Destination name. This argument is mandatory.
- `bus`—Bus name.

createSIBEngine

This method creates a messaging engine for the specified bus member. Normally, you do not need to call this method because a messaging engine gets created when you add a member to a bus.

Required argument:

- `bus`—The name of the bus to which the bus member belongs.

Although the following arguments are not marked "mandatory," you are required to use some of them. You must use at least one, and possibly two, of the next three arguments in order to properly identify the bus member that will contain this `SIBEngine`:

- `node`—To create a messaging engine on a server, supply node and server name but not cluster name.
- `server`—To create a messaging engine on a server, supply node and server name but not cluster name.
- `cluster`—To create a messaging engine on a cluster, supply cluster name but not node and server name.

Frequently used optional arguments:

- `description`—Use this text to describe the messaging engine.
- `fileStore`—Indicates that a file store is to be created. No value is needed.
- `dataStore`—Indicates that a data store is to be created. No value is needed.

Argument that affects bus security:

- `authAlias`—The name of the authentication alias used to authenticate the messaging engine to the database.

Occasionally used optional arguments:

- `initialState`—Whether the messaging engine is started or stopped when the associated application server is first started. Until started, the messaging engine is unavailable (`Stopped`|`Started`).
- `highMessageThreshold`—The maximum total number of messages that the messaging engine can place on its message points.
- `logSize`—The size, in megabytes, of the log file.

- `minPermanentStoreSize`—The minimum size in megabytes of the permanent store file.

- `maxPermanentStoreSize`—The maximum size, in megabytes, of the permanent store file.

- `unlimitedPermanentStoreSize`—`true` if the permanent file store size has no limit; `false` otherwise.

- `permanentStoreDirectory`—The name of the permanent store files directory.

- `temporaryStoreDirectory`—The name of the temporary store files directory.

- `unlimitedTemporaryStoreSize`—`true` if the temporary file store size has no limit; `false` otherwise.

- `minTemporaryStoreSize`—The minimum size in megabytes of the temporary store file.

- `maxTemporaryStoreSize`—The maximum size, in megabytes, of the temporary store file.

- `logDirectory`—The name of the log files directory.

- `schemaName`—The name of the database schema used to contain the tables for the data store.

- `createTables`—Select this option if the messaging engine creates the database tables for the data store. Otherwise, the database administrator must create the database tables.

- `createDefaultDatasource`—When adding a server to a bus, set this to `true` if a default data source is required. When adding a cluster to a bus, this parameter must not be supplied.

- `datasourceJndiName`—The JNDI name of the data source to be referenced from the datastore created when the member is added to the bus.

createSIBJMSConnectionFactory

This method creates an SIB JMS connection factory at the scope identified by the target object. Applications need this factory to obtain an `SIBJMSQueue` object or an `SIBJMSTopic` object.

Target (mandatory):

The management scope at which this factory is visible. This scope must be a configuration ID.

Required arguments:

- `busName`—The bus name.

- `name`—The name of the SIB JMS connection factory.

- `jndiName`—The JNDI name of the SIB JMS connection factory.

Optional arguments you might need if you want to secure the bus:

- `xaRecoveryAuthAlias`—The authentication alias used during XA recovery processing.

- `userName`—The user name that is used to create connections from the connection factory.

- `password`—The password that is used to create connections from the connection factory.

- `targetTransportChain`—The name of the protocol that should be used to connect to a remote messaging engine.

Frequently used optional arguments:

- `description`—Any text you might use to describe the connection factory. This description will show up in the Admin Console.
- `category`—Arbitrary text you might choose to use to classify or group the connection factory.
- `persistentMapping`—When a message specifies persistent mapping, what should our bus do? Must be one of (`BestEffortNonPersistent` | `ExpressNonPersistent` | `ReliableNonPersistent` | `ReliablePersistent` | `AssuredPersistent` | `AsSIBDestination` | `None`). Note that this value can overrule the value specified in the message and, in fact, make the message non-persistent.
- `target`—The name of a target that resolves to a group of messaging engines.
- `targetType`—Specifies the type of the name in the target parameter. Legal values are (`BusMember` | `Custom` | `ME`).
- `targetSignificance`—This property specifies the significance of the target group.

Occasionally used optional arguments:

- `manageCachedHandles`—Whether cached handles (handles held in instance variables in a bean) should be tracked by the container.
- `logMissingTransactionContext`—Whether or not the container logs that there is a missing transaction context when a connection is obtained.
- `connectionProximity`—The proximity of acceptable messaging engines. Legal values are (`Bus` | `Host` | `Cluster` | `Server`). The default value is `Bus`.
- `tempQueueNamePrefix`—Temporary queue name prefix.
- `tempTopicNamePrefix`—Temporary topic name prefix.
- `shareDataSourceWithCMP`—Used to control how data sources are shared.
- `shareDurableSubscriptions`—Used to control how durable subscriptions are shared. Legal values are (`InCluster` | `AlwaysShared` | `NeverShared`).

createSIBJMSQueue

This method creates the JMS wrapper object that applications use in order to interact with a queue on the bus.

Target (mandatory):
The management scope at which this queue is visible. This value must be a configuration ID.

Required arguments:

- `busName`—The bus name.
- `name`—The name of the SIB JMS queue.
- `jndiName`—The JNDI name of the SIB JMS queue.
- `queueName`—The name of the underlying SIB queue to which the queue points.

Frequently used optional arguments:

- description—Any text that describes this queue for the purpose of documenting this part of your topology. This description will show up in the Admin Console.

- priority—The priority for messages. Whole number in the range 0 to 9.

- deliveryMode—The delivery mode for messages. Legal values are (Application | NonPersistent | Persistent).

Occasionally used optional argument:

- timeToLive—The time in milliseconds to be used for message expiration.

createSIBJMSTopic

This method creates the JMS wrapper object that applications use in order to interact with a topic on the bus.

Target (mandatory):

The management scope at which this topic is visible. This scope must be a configuration ID.

Required arguments:

- busName—The bus name.

- name—The name of the SIB JMS topic.

- jndiName—The JNDI name of the SIB JMS topic.

Frequently used optional arguments:

- topicSpace—The name of the underlying SIB topic space to which the topic points.

- topicName—The topic to be used inside the topic space (for example, books/scripting/ WebSphere).

- description—Any text that describes this topic for the purpose of documenting this part of your topology. This description will show up in the Admin Console.

- priority—The priority for messages. Whole number in the range 0 to 9.

- deliveryMode—The delivery mode for messages. Legal values are (Application | NonPersistent | Persistent).

Occasionally used optional argument:

- timeToLive—The time in milliseconds to be used for message expiration.

createSIBJMSActivat ionSpec

This method creates the plumbing that activates a Message Driven Bean when an appropriate message arrives.

Target (mandatory):

Scope of the SIB JMS resource adapter to which the activation specification will be added. This scope must be a configuration ID.

Required arguments:

- `name`—Any arbitrary name you would like to call this activation specification.
- `jndiName`—JNDI name of the activation specification.
- `destinationJndiName`—JNDI name of an `SIBDestination`.

Optional arguments you might need if you want to secure the bus:

- `authenticationAlias`—Security credentials. The configuration ID of a `JAASAuthData` object.
- `userName`—User name.
- `password`—Password.
- `targetTransportChain`—The name of the protocol that should be used to connect to a remote messaging engine.

Frequently used optional arguments:

- `busName`—Name of the bus to connect to.
- `subscriptionDurability`—Whether a JMS topic subscription is durable or nondurable.
- `subscriptionName`—The subscription name needed for durable topic subscriptions.
- `clientId`—Client identifier. Required for durable topic subscriptions.
- `durableSubscriptionHome`—Name of the durable subscription home. This identifies the messaging engine where all durable subscriptions accessed through this activation specification are managed.
- `shareDurableSubscriptions`—Used to control how durable subscriptions are shared.
- `shareDataSourceWithCMP`—Used to control how data sources are shared.

Occasionally used optional arguments:

- `acknowledgeMode`—How the session acknowledges any messages it receives.
- `maxBatchSize`—The maximum number of messages received from the messaging engine in a single batch.
- `maxConcurrency`—The maximum number of endpoints to which messages are delivered concurrently.
- `target`—The SIB JMS activation specification new target value.
- `targetType`—The SIB JMS activation specification new target type value. Legal values are (`BusMember` | `Custom` | `ME`).
- `targetSignificance`—This property specifies the significance of the target group.

Deleting a Bus and Bus Components

Keep in mind that deleting a bus itself will not delete the JMS components associated with that bus. You must delete each of these separately. Deleting a messaging bus requires you to delete the bus itself, the related JMS artifacts, and possibly some JAASAuthData artifacts. The two groups of **AdminTask** methods that you will need any time one of your scripts deletes a messaging buses and their component parts are as follows:

```
SIBAdminCommands
SIBJMSAdminCommands
```

Of the 70+ methods[36] in these two groups, the methods you are most likely to need are the following when you delete a bus or any of its components.

deleteSIBJMSActivationSpec

This method deletes an SIBJMSActivationSpec.

> **Target (mandatory):**
> The configuration ID of theactivation spec to be deleted.

deleteSIBJMSQueue

This method deletes an SIBJMSQueue.

> **Target (mandatory):**
> The configuration ID of the JMS queue to be deleted.

deleteSIBJMSTopic

This method deletes an SIBJMSTopic.

> **Target (mandatory):**
> The configuration ID of the topic to be deleted.

deleteSIBJMSConnectionFactory

This method deletes an SIBJMSConnectionFactory.

> **Target (mandatory):**
> The configuration ID of the connector factory to be deleted.

deleteSIBus

This method both the bus and all of the SIB components that make up the bus. Thus, bus members, messaging engines, aliases, and foreign buses get deleted. This command also deletes the new artifacts that are created when queues are assigned or mediated to a WebSphere MQ server bus member, including the WebSphere MQ server bus members. However, none of the JMS plumbing that sits on top of the bus gets deleted. Each of the JMS components must be deleted separately. You must also separately delete queue managers that are associated with the bus using WebSphere MQ server definitions (if applicable), messages residing on WebSphere MQ queue managers (if applicable), or WebSphere MQ queues (if applicable).

---

[36] The exact number will depend on your version of WebSphere Application Server and whether you have licensed any of the more advanced product offerings.

Required argument:

- `bus`—The name, not the configuration ID, of the bus you wish to delete. Deleting any SIB component requires a name rather than a configuration ID.

removeSIBusMember

Remove the configuration for the plumbing that makes a server a member of a messaging bus. Use this method only if you are trying to remove one bus member. If you want to delete an entire bus, it is not necessary to call this method. `AdminTask.deleteSIBus()` will delete all bus members.

Required argument:

- `name`—The name, not the configuration ID, of the bus this member belongs to.

Frequently used optional arguments:
(You must supply at least one and possibly two of the following optional arguments.)

- `node`—If the bus member is an individual application server, supply the name of the node and the name of the server. Do not supply any of the other optional arguments.
- `server`—If the bus member is an individual application server, supply the name of the node and the name of the server. Do not supply any of the other optional arguments.
- `cluster`—If the bus member is a cluster, supply cluster name. Do not supply any of the other optional arguments.
- `wmqServer`—If the bus member is a WebSphere MQ server bus member, supply the name of the WebSphere MQ server. Do not supply any of the other optional arguments.

deleteSIBDestination

Deletes a bus destination. Use this method only if you are trying to remove one bus destination. If you want to delete an entire bus, it is not necessary to call this method. `AdminTask.deleteSIBus()`[37] deletes all bus destinations.

Required arguments:

- `bus`—The name of the bus.
- `name`—The name of the destination.

Frequently used optional arguments:
(You only need these arguments if the destination you are deleting is a foreign destination or an alias destination.)

- `aliasBus`—If the destination to be deleted is an alias destination, then the `aliasBus` parameter must be supplied if the alias bus for the destination is not the local bus.

---

[37] See `AdminTask.deleteSIBus()` in this reference for details.

- `foreignBus`—If the destination to be deleted is a foreign destination, then name of the foreign bus must be supplied.

Modifying a Bus and Bus Components

Again, the methods in this section come from two **AdminTask** groups:

```
SIBAdminCommands
SIBJMSAdminCommands
```

modifySIBus

This method modifies one or more items that are part of the configuration for a bus.

Required argument:

- `bus`—The name of the bus that will be modified.

Optional arguments that affect security:

- `interEngineAuthAlias`—Name of the authentication alias used to authorize communication between messaging engines on the bus.

- `mediationsAuthAlias`—Name of the authentication alias used to authorize mediations to access the bus.

- `busSecurity`—Enables or disables bus security. This argument has no effect unless you have already enabled administrative security.

- `permittedChains`—The permitted transport chains value can be set to one of the following: (ALL | SSL ENABLED | LISTED).

Frequently used optional arguments:

- `highMessageThreshold`—The maximum number of messages that any queue on the bus can hold.

- `description`—Use this field to describe the role this bus plays in your topology.

Occasionally used optional arguments:

- `protocol`—The protocol used to send and receive messages between messaging engines and between API clients and messaging engines.

- `discardOnDelete`—Indicate whether or not any messages left in a queue's data store should be discarded when the queue is deleted.

- `configurationReloadEnabled`—Indicate whether configuration files should be dynamically reloaded for this bus.

- `secure`—You are not likely to use this argument because it has been deprecated. Use `busSecurity` instead.

modifySIBEngine

This method modifies an SIBEngine. Notice that this method cannot change the decision to use a filestore versus a database. That decision is made when the messaging engine is created.[38]

Required argument:

- bus—The name of the bus that will be modified.

Although the following arguments are not marked "mandatory," you are required to use some of them depending on whether you are modifying the SIBEngine of a bus member that is a server, a cluster, or a WebSphere MQ server. If the SIBEngine belongs to a server and that server's name is not unique within the cell, then you must specify the node name as well. Remember, all of the following are names, not configuration IDs:

- node—To specify a server bus member, supply node and server name but not cluster name or WebSphere MQ server name.

- server—To specify a server bus member, supply node and server name but not cluster name or WebSphere MQ server name.

- cluster—To specify a cluster bus member, supply cluster name but not node name, server name, or WebSphere MQ server name.

- wmqServer—To specify an WebSphere MQ server bus member, supply WebSphere MQ server name but not node name, server name, or cluster name.

Frequently used optional arguments:

- initialState—Whether the messaging engine is started or stopped when the associated application server is first started. Until started, the messaging engine is unavailable (Stopped | Started).

- highMessageThreshold—The maximum total number of messages that the messaging engine can place on its message points.

- defaultBlockedRetryTimeout—The default blocked retry interval for destinations owned by this messaging engine.

modifySIBDestination

This method modifies either a queue or a topic or a link to some existing bus member or a link to some other bus. Notice that these arguments all modify transport aspects of the bus destination.

Required arguments:

- bus—The name, not the configuration ID, of the bus that this destination belongs to.

- name—The name, not the configuration ID, of the destination that is being modified.

---

[38] See AdminTask.createSIBEngine() in this reference for details.

Frequently used optional arguments:

- `description`—A description of the role this destination plays in your topology.

- `defaultPriority`—The default priority for message flows through this destination, in the range 0 (lowest) through 9 (highest). This default priority is used for messages that do not contain a priority value.

- `maxReliability`—The maximum reliability quality of service that is accepted for values specified by producers.

- `overrideOfQOSByProducerAllowed`—Controls the quality of service for message flows between producers and the destination. Select this option to use the quality of service specified by producers instead of the quality defined for the destination.

- `maxFailedDeliveries`—The maximum number of times that service tries to deliver a message to the destination before forwarding it to the exception destination.

- `exceptionDestination`—The name of another destination to which the system sends a message that cannot be delivered to this destination within the specified maximum number of failed deliveries.

Arguments that affect bus security:

- `delegateAuthorizationCheckToTarget`—Indicates whether the authorization check should be delegated to the alias or target destination.

- `topicAccessCheckRequired`—Topic access check required.

Occasionally used optional arguments:

- `sendAllowed`—Clear this option (by setting it to `false`) to stop producers from being able to send messages to this destination.

- `receiveAllowed`—Clear this option (by setting it to `false`) to prevent consumers from being able to receive messages from this destination.

- `receiveExclusive`—Select this option (by setting it to `true`) to allow only one consumer to attach to a destination.

- `maintainStrictMessageOrder`—Select this option (by setting it to `true`) to enforce message order for this destination.

- `replyDestination`—The name of the destination for reply messages.

- `replyDestinationBus`—The name of the bus on which the reply destination is configured.

Steps:

- `queuePoints`—This step specifies a list of the queue points that will be used by users of the alias destination. The arguments for this step are passed as a collection.

Required arguments:

- `identifier`—The queue point identifier.

- mediationPoints—This step specifies a list of the mediation points that will be used by users of the alias destination. The arguments for this step are passed as a collection.

Required arguments:

- identifier—The identifier for the mediation point to be used. There will be one of these for each mediation point in the list.
- defaultForwardRoutingPath—This step specifies a default forward routing path. The arguments that follow form a collection. The arguments for this step are passed as a collection.
- destination—The name, not the configuration ID, of the destination where messages get forwarded.

Optional argument:

- bus—The name, not the configuration ID, of the bus where messages get forwarded.

modifySIBJMSQueue

Modify the attributes of the supplied SIB JMS queue using the supplied attribute values. Notice that the arguments to this method pretty much focus on modifying the mapping from the JMS queue facade[39]—an SIBJMSQueue—to the underlying SIB queue, an SIBQueue. Contrast this method with AdminTask.modifySIBDestination().

Target (mandatory):
The configuration ID, not the name, of the SIB JMS queue to be modified.

Frequently used optional arguments:

- busName—The name of the bus on which the queue resides.
- name—If you are changing the name of the queue, this is the SIB JMS queue's new name.
- jndiName—If you are changing the JNDI name for the queue, this is the SIB JMS queue's new JNDI name.
- description—If you are changing the description of the queue, this is some text to explain the purpose of this item in your topology.
- queueName—If you are changing the mapping from the JMS queue to the underlying SIB queue, this is the name of the underlying SIB queue to which the queue will point.
- deliveryMode—The new delivery mode for messages. Legal values are (Application|NonPersistent|Persistent).
- timeToLive—The new time in milliseconds to be used for message expiration.

---

[39] A discussion of the Java Message Service is beyond the scope of this book. For a good introduction, consider Chapter 33 of http://java.sun.com/j2ee/1.4/docs/tutorial/doc/index.html.

- priority—The new priority for messages. Whole number in the range 0 to 9.

- scopeToLocalQP—Indicates if the underlying SIB queue destination should be scoped to a local queue point when addressed using this JMS queue.

- producerBind—Indicates how JMS producers should bind to queue points of the clustered queue. true indicates that a queue point should be chosen when the session is opened and should never change; false indicates that a queue point should be chosen every time a message is sent.

- producerPreferLocal—Indicates whether queue points local to the producer should be used.

- gatherMessages—Indicates whether JMS consumers and browsers should be given messages from any queue points, rather than the single queue point that they are attached to.

modifySIBJMSTopic

Modify the attributes of the supplied SIB JMS topic using the supplied attribute values. Notice that this method focuses on modifying both the mapping from the JMS topic facade[40] to some underlying SIB topic, and the structure of a topic space and the topics that are part of that topic space. Contrast this method with AdminTask.modifySIBDestination(). The JMS topic façade is an SIBJMSTopic. The underlying SIB topic is part of a SIBTopicSpace.

Target (mandatory):
The configuration ID, not the name, of the SIB JMS topic space or topic to be modified.

Frequently used optional arguments:

- busName—The name of the bus on which the topic resides.

- name—If you are changing the name of the topic, this is the SIB JMS topic's new name.

- jndiName—If you are changing the JNDI name for the topic, this is the SIB JMS topic's new JNDI name.

- description—If you are changing the description of the topic, this is some text to explain the purpose of this item in your topology.

- topicSpace—If you are changing the hierarchy of topics in an SIB topic space or if you are changing the mapping of a JMS topic to an SIB topic, this is the name of the underlying SIB topic space.

- topicName—If you are changing the hierarchy of topics in an SIB topic space or if you are changing the mapping of a JMS topic to an SIB topic, this is the SIB topic to be used inside the SIB topic space (for example, stock/IBM or stock/IBM/common or

---

[40] A discussion of the Java Message Service is beyond the scope of this book. For a good introduction, consider Chapter 33 of http://java.sun.com/j2ee/1.4/docs/tutorial/doc/index.html.

stock/IBM/preferred). In this example, stock would be the topic space. Everything below that topic space is a hierarchical list of topics.

- `deliveryMode`—The new delivery mode for messages. Legal values are (`Application`|`NonPersistent`|`Persistent`).
- `timeToLive`—The new time in milliseconds to be used for message expiration.
- `priority`—The new priority for messages. Whole number in the range 0 to 9.

Displaying Buses and Bus Components

There are two groups of methods—one that starts with `list` and one that starts with `show`. The methods that start with list just displays a list of names or configuration IDs of items in a cell. The methods that start with show provides more detailed information about one named item. The methods in this section come from two **AdminTask** groups:

```
SIBAdminCommands
SIBJMSAdminCommands
```

listSIBuses

This method lists the configuration ID of every bus in a cell. It requires no arguments. If you ever have to write code to change the values of attributes of the messaging bus or any of its component parts, it is extremely important to make those changes using the `AdminTask.modifySIB*` methods we document in the "Modifying a Bus and Bus Components" section of this chapter. Even though this method returns configuration IDs, under no circumstances should you ever use **AdminConfig** to modify an attribute of any messaging bus component. Some of those attributes have values that are dynamically generated. The appropriate **AdminTask** methods respect those values. **AdminConfig** does not. Extract the name attribute from the configuration ID and use the **AdminTask** methods.

showSIBus

This method displays some of the attributes of one particular bus.

Required argument:

- `bus`—The name, not the configuration ID, of the bus.

listSIBusMembers

This method lists the configuration ID of every member of a bus unless you limit the scope of this query. In spite of the fact that this method returns a configuration ID, IBM strongly discourages the use of **AdminConfig** methods on any part of a messaging bus configuration. You should use the various **AdminTask** methods to display or modify messaging bus components:

Required argument:

- `bus`—The name, not the configuration ID, of the bus.

showSIBusMember

This method displays selected information about a particular bus member.

Required argument:

- `bus`—The name, not the configuration ID, of the bus.

Frequently used optional arguments:

(These are not really optional arguments. You must use either one or two of them depending on whether you want an individual server or a cluster or an MQ server.)

- `node`—To specify a server bus member, supply node, and server name but not cluster name or WebSphere MQ server name

- `server`—To specify a server bus member, supply node, and server name but not cluster name or WebSphere MQ server name.

- `cluster`—To specify a cluster bus member and supply cluster name, but not node name, server name, or WebSphere MQ server name.

- `wmqServer`—To specify an WebSphere MQ server bus member and supply WebSphere MQ server name but not node name, server name, or cluster name.

listSIBEngines

This method lists the configuration IDs of all the messaging engines within the scope you specify. The argument(s) you must supply depend on the scope of your query. Acceptable scopes are either an entire bus, a server in a given node, or a cluster.

Frequently used optional arguments:

(These are not really optional arguments. You must use either one or two of them depending on whether you want an individual server or a cluster or an MQ server.)

- `bus`—The bus whose engines are to be listed. You do not have to supply a bus name unless you want to limit your query to engines that belong to one particular bus. Servers and clusters can host more than one message bus.

- `node`—To list messaging engines on a server, supply node and server name but not cluster name.

- `server`—To list messaging engines on a server, supply node and server name but not cluster name.

- `cluster`—To list messaging engines on a cluster, supply cluster name but not node and server name.

showSIBEngine

This method displays some attributes of one particular messaging engine. Unlike the `listSIBEngines` method shown earlier, you cannot request attributes from more than one messaging engine at a time. Thus, you must provide enough scoping information to narrow the search to one particular messaging engine.

Required argument:

- `bus`—The name, not the configuration ID, of the bus that contains the messaging engine you wish to query.

Frequently used optional arguments:

(Even though these are optional arguments, you must supply either one or two of them.)

- `node`—To show a messaging engine that belongs to a server, supply node, and server name but not cluster name.

- `server`—To show a messaging engine that belongs to a server, supply node, and server name but not cluster name.

- `cluster`—To show a messaging engine that belongs to a cluster and supply cluster name but not node and server name.

- `engine`—The name of the engine to show.

showSIBJMSConnectionFactory

Return a list containing the SIB JMS connection factory's attribute names and values.

Target (mandatory):
The configuration ID of the SIB JMS connection factory whose attributes are required.

listSIBJMSQueues

List all SIB JMS queues at the specified scope.

Target (mandatory):
The configuration ID of the server (the scope) at which to find the SIB JMS queues to list.

showSIBJMSQueue

Return a list containing the SIB JMS queue's attribute names and values.

Target (mandatory):
The configuration ID of the SIB JMS queue whose attributes are required.

listSIBJMSTopics

List all SIB JMS topics at the specified scope.

Target (mandatory):
The configuration ID of the server (the scope) at which to find the SIB JMS topics to list.

showSIBJMSTopic

Return a list containing the SIB JMS topic's attribute names and values.

Target (mandatory):
The configuration ID of the SIB JMS topic whose attributes are required.

listSIBMediations

This method lists the configuration IDs of all the mediations of a given bus.

Required argument:

- bus—The name, not the configuration ID, of the bus that contains the messaging engine you wish to query.

showSIBMediation

This method displays some attributes of a given mediation of a given bus.

Required arguments:

- bus—The name, not the configuration ID, of the bus that contains the messaging engine you wish to query.
- mediationName—The name, not the configuration ID, of the mediation.

Bus Security

The methods in this section come from the SIBAdminBusSecurityCommands group.

removeDefaultRoles

This method is pretty much the first step in securing a bus. As the name implies, it removes all default authorizations for a given bus.

Required arguments:

- bus—The name, not the configuration ID, of the bus that contains the messaging engine you wish to query.

removeGroupFromAllRoles

This method does just what the name implies. It revokes all permissions for a given group on a given bus.

Required arguments:

- bus—The name, not the configuration ID, of the bus.
- group—The name of the group that will be denied all access to the bus.

removeUserFromAllRoles

This method does just what the name implies. It revokes all permissions for a given user on a given bus.

Required arguments:

- bus—The name, not the configuration ID, of the bus.
- user—The name of the user that will be denied all access to the bus.

addGroupToBusConnectorRole

This method gives a group permission to connect to a bus. Without this permission, no member of this group will be able to do anything on this bus.

Required arguments:

- `bus`—The name, not the configuration ID, of the bus.
- `group`—The name of the group that will be allowed to connect to the bus.

addUserToBusConnectorRole

This method gives a user permission to connect to a bus. Without this permission, this user will not be able to do anything on this bus.

Required arguments:

- `bus`—The name, not the configuration ID, of the bus.
- `user`—The name of the user that will be allowed to connect to the bus.

addGroupToDefaultRole

This method gives a group permission to act in some role on a given a bus. Typically, you will have to call this method several times to give a particular group enough permissions to be useful.

Required arguments:

- `bus`—The name, not the configuration ID, of the bus.
- `group`—The name of the group that will be allowed to perform some role on the bus.
- `role`—The role name. Allowable values are (`Sender` | `Receiver` | `Browser` | `Creator` | `IdentityAdopter`).

addUserToDefaultRole

This method gives an individual user permission to act in some role on a given a bus. Typically, you will have to call this method several times to give a particular group enough permissions to be useful.

Required arguments:

- `bus`—The name, not the configuration ID, of the bus.
- `user`—The name of the user that will be allowed to perform some role on the bus.
- `role`—The role name. Allowable values are (`Sender` | `Receiver` | `Browser` | `Creator` | `IdentityAdopter`).

addGroupToDestinationRole

This method grants a group access to a destination for the specified destination role. This method is not necessary unless you are trying to implement some very fine-grained access control scheme. It will probably be necessary to call this method several times in order to grant a meaningful set of permissions.

Required arguments:

- `bus`—The name, not the configuration ID, of the bus.
- `destination`—The name, not the configuration ID, of the destination.
- `type`—The destination type. Allowable values are (`Queue` | `Port` | `Webservice` | `TopicSpace` | `ForeignDestination` | `Alias`).
- `group`—The name of the group that will receive this access.
- `role`—The role name. Allowable values are for Queues/Ports/WebServices (`Sender` | `Receiver` | `Browser` | `Creator` | `IdentityAdopter`), for TopicSpaces (`Sender` | `Receiver` | `IdentityAdopter`), for Aliases (`Sender` | `Receiver` | `Browser` | `IdentityAdopter`), and for Foreign (`Sender` | `IdentityAdopter`).

Occasionally used optional argument:

- `foreignBus`—Foreign bus name. This is only necessary if you are granting permissions on the foreign bus itself.

addUserToDestinationRole

This method grants a user access to a destination for the specified destination role. This method is not necessary unless you are trying to implement some very fine-grained access control scheme. It will probably be necessary to call this method several times in order to grant a meaningful set of permissions.

Required arguments:

- `bus`—The name, not the configuration ID, of the bus.
- `destination`—The name, not the configuration ID, of the destination.
- `type`—The destination type. Allowable values are (`Queue` | `Port` | `Webservice` | `TopicSpace` | `ForeignDestination` | `Alias`).
- `user`—The name of the user that will receive this access.
- `role`—The role name. Allowable values are for Queues/Ports/WebServices (`Sender` | `Receiver` | `Browser` | `Creator` | `IdentityAdopter`), for TopicSpaces (`Sender` | `Receiver` | `IdentityAdopter`), for Aliases (`Sender` | `Receiver` | `Browser` | `IdentityAdopter`), and for Foreign (`Sender` | `IdentityAdopter`).

Occasionally used optional argument:

- `foreignBus`—Foreign bus name. This is only necessary if you are granting permissions on the foreign bus itself.

addGroupToTopicRole

This method gives a group permission to access the topic for the specified role. This method is not necessary unless you are trying to implement some very fine-grained access control scheme.

Required arguments:

- bus—The name, not the configuration ID, of the bus.
- group—The name of the group that will receive this access.
- role—The role name. Allowable values are (Sender|Receiver|IdentityAdapter).
- topic—The name of the topic.
- topicSpace—The name of the topic space that contains this topic.

addGroupToTopicSpaceRootRole

This method gives a group permission to access a given topic space root for the specified role. This method is not necessary unless you are trying to implement some very fine-grained access control scheme.

Required arguments:

- bus—The name, not the configuration ID, of the bus.
- group—The name of the group that will receive this access.
- role—The role name. Allowable values are (Sender|Receiver|IdentityAdapter).
- topicSpace—The name of the topic space that contains this topic.

addUserToTopicRole

This method gives a user permission to access the topic for the specified role. This method is not necessary unless you are trying to implement some very fine-grained access control scheme.

Required arguments:

- bus—The name, not the configuration ID, of the bus.
- user—The name of the user that will receive this access.
- role—The role name. Allowable values are (Sender|Receiver|IdentityAdapter).
- topic—The name of the topic.
- topicSpace—The name of the topic space that contains this topic.

addUserToTopicSpaceRootRole

This method gives a user permission to access a given topic space root for the specified role. This method is not necessary unless you are trying to implement some very fine-grained access control scheme.

Required arguments:

- bus—The name, not the configuration ID, of the bus.
- user—The name of the user that will receive this access.
- role—The role name. Allowable values are (Sender|Receiver|IdentityAdapter).
- topicSpace—The name of the topic space that contains this topic.

listAllDestinationsWithRoles

This method lists all destinations that have roles defined for them on a given bus.

Required arguments:

- `bus`—The name, not the configuration ID, of the bus.
- `type`—The destination type. Allowable values are (`Queue` | `Port` | `Webservice` | `TopicSpace` | `ForeignDestination` | `Alias`).

listAllForeignBusesWithRoles

This method lists all foreign buses that have roles defined for them on a given bus.

Required argument:

- `bus`—The name, not the configuration ID, of the bus.

listAllTopicsWithRoles

This method lists all topics within a given topic space that have roles defined on them for a given bus.

Required arguments:

- `bus`—The name, not the configuration ID, of the bus.
- `topicSpace`—The name of the topic space to search.

listAllRolesForGroup

This method lists all roles defined on a given group on a given bus.

Required arguments:

- `bus`—The name, not the configuration ID, of the bus.
- `group`—The name of the group.

listAllRolesForUser

This method lists all roles defined on a given user on a given bus.

Required arguments:

- `bus`—The name, not the configuration ID, of the bus.
- `user`—The name of the user.

listGroupsInBusConnectorRole

This method lists all groups that have permission to connect to this bus.

Required argument:

- `bus`—The name, not the configuration ID, of the bus.

listGroupsInDefaultRole

This lists all groups in a given role on a given bus.

Required arguments:

- bus—The name, not the configuration ID, of the bus.
- role—The role name. Allowable values are (Sender | Receiver | Browser | Creator | IdentityAdopter).

listGroupsInDestinationRole

This method lists the groups in the specified role in the destination security space role for the given destination on a given bus.

Required arguments:

- bus—The name, not the configuration ID, of the bus.
- destination—The name of the destination.
- type—The destination type. Allowable values are (Queue | Port | Webservice | TopicSpace | ForeignDestination | Alias)
- role—The role name. Allowable values are for **Queues/Ports/WebServices** (Sender | Receiver | Browser | Creator | IdentityAdopter), for **TopicSpaces** (Sender | Receiver | IdentityAdopter), for **Aliases** (Sender | Receiver | Browser | IdentityAdopter), and for **Foreign** (Sender | IdentityAdopter).

Occasionally used optional arguments:

- foreignBus—If you want to list groups that have privileges on the foreign bus that lives behind a given destination, name that bus.

listGroupsInTopicRole

This method lists the groups who have a given role in a given topic in a given topic space on a given bus.

Required arguments:
- bus—The name, not the configuration ID, of the bus.
- topicSpace—The name of the topic space that contains the topic.
- topic—The name of the topic.
- role—The role name. Allowable values are (Sender | Receiver | IdentityAdopter).

listGroupsInTopicSpaceRootRole

This method lists the users who have a given role in a given topic space on a given bus.

Required arguments:

- bus—The name, not the configuration ID, of the bus.

- `topicSpace`—The name of the topic space that contains the topic.
- `role`—The role name. Allowable values are (`Sender`|`Receiver`|`IdentityAdopter`).

listUsersInBusConnectorRole

This method lists all users that have permission to connect to this bus.

Required argument:

- `bus`—The name, not the configuration ID, of the bus.

listUsersInDefaultRole

This lists all users in a given role on a given bus.

Required arguments:

- `bus`—The name, not the configuration ID, of the bus.
- `role`—The role name. Allowable values are (`Sender` | `Receiver` | `Browser` | `Creator`|`IdentityAdopter`).

listUsersInDestinationRole

This method lists the users in the specified role in the destination security space role for the given destination on a given bus.

Required arguments:

- `bus`—The name, not the configuration ID, of the bus.
- `destination`—The name of the destination.
- `type`—The destination type. Allowable values are (`Queue` | `Port` | `Webservice` | `TopicSpace`|`ForeignDestination`|`Alias`).
- `role`—The role name. Allowable values are for Queues/Ports/WebServices (`Sender` | `Receiver`|`Browser`|`Creator`|`IdentityAdopter`), for TopicSpaces (`Sender` |`Receiver`|`IdentityAdopter`), for Aliases (`Sender` |`Receiver`|`Browser`| `IdentityAdopter`), and for Foreign (`Sender`|`IdentityAdopter`).

Occasionally used optional argument:

- `foreignBus`—If you want to list groups that have privileges on the foreign bus that lives behind a given destination, name that bus.

listUsersInTopicRole

This method lists the users who have a given role in a given topic in a given topic space on a given bus.

Required argument:

- `bus`—The name, not the configuration ID, of the bus.

- `topicSpace`—The name of the topic space that contains the topic.
- `topic`—The name of the topic.
- `role`—The role name. Allowable values are (`Sender`|`Receiver`|`IdentityAdopter`).

listGroupsInTopicSpaceRootRole

This method lists the users who have a given role in a given topic space on a given bus.

Required arguments:

- `bus`—The name, not the configuration ID, of the bus.
- `topicSpace`—The name of the topic space that contains the topic.
- `role`—The role name. Allowable values are (`Sender`|`Receiver`|`IdentityAdopter`).

Summary

Conceptually, messaging is simple. It is just an architecture for passing an arbitrary sized message from a sender (the producer) to a recipient (the consumer). There are many ways to customize[41] that simple architecture. That means your configuration for messaging can be simple or complex according to the needs or your enterprise. We gave you some simple code that you can extend and enhance according to your needs, and we showed you how to secure a messaging bus. In the next chapter, we cover Web services.

---

[41] For many useful details about both messaging architecture and configuration, see "WebSphere Application Server V7 Messaging Administration Guide," SG247770.

CHAPTER 15

Administering Web Services

The **AdminApp**, **AdminConfig**, and **AdminTask** scripting objects are all useful in configuring Web services in WebSphere. In this chapter, we consider the following topics:

What are Web services?

- The Java standards, JAX-RPC (JSR-101) and JAX-WS (JSR-224), used to author Java-based Web services.
- The Web service for Java EE (JSR-109) specification, which dictates how Java-based Web services run in environments such as WebSphere.

The WSEE (JSR-109) Deployment models supported by WebSphere:

- SOAP/HTTP using a "Plain Old Java Object" (POJO)
- SOAP/HTTP using a Stateless Session EJB
- SOAP/JMS using a Stateless Session EJB

WebSphere scripting support for Web services:

- The introduction of Web service policies, which can simplify almost inherently complex administrative tasks related to Web services.

The WS-Security specification, which covers such things as authentication, non-repudiation, confidentiality, and integrity for Web services and presents examples of scripted administration of these issues.

Web Services Basics

Web services are at the core of the Service-Oriented Architecture approach to application development that is increasingly being deployed within and between enterprises. But while a Web service application is installed just like any other application, after it is deployed, there are several possible administrative activities. To understand those activities, it helps to know a bit about what Web services are and how they work.

The idea of a Web service is fairly simple; the majority of Web services look like Remote Procedure Calls. To use Web services terminology, they use one of two "Message Exchange Patterns": Request-Response and One-Way.

Because Web services are essentially providing Remote Procedure Call behavior, you might ask what makes them special and worth the hype. In one word, the answer is interoperability.

To ensure interoperability—the raison d'être of Web services—they should adhere to the Web Services Interoperability Organization (WS-I—http://www.ws-i.org) profiles. These profiles ensure that regardless of whether a Web service is written using the following:

- C#® on Microsoft® .NET platform
- C# on Novell's Mono platform
- Java on WebSphere
- Java on WebLogic
- Python using any of a number of libraries, such as
    - SUDS—Arguably the best for WSDL-based clients
    - soaplib—Possibly the easiest for SOAP-based Web services

or any other combination programming language, runtime environment, operating system, hardware platform, and so on, the Web services can all communicate and interact with each other. In other words: interoperate. This can be even more challenging than might appear at first because even seemingly simple things like dates and times can be problematic. Fortunately, these issues are in the hands of developers, so you can focus on the problems that present themselves to administrators.

WS-I Profiles

A WS-I profile is basically a standard that lists other existing standards and explains how to use them in combination to achieve interoperability—across all languages, operating systems, and hardware platforms. There are many (some would argue far too many) additional specifications. Only a very few, such as WS-Security, are true standards. And even amongst those, interpretation varies because in the real world specifications are not unambiguous.

The WS-I profiles dictate which of the myriad WS-* specifications are actually to be considered interoperable standards—therefore permissible to use—and how to use them in the appropriate manner. The WS-I also provides conformance testing tools to help ensure that interoperability is achieved.

The key profiles from the WS-I are as follows:

Basic Profile

- Fundamental profile that permits us to build interoperable Web services.
- Covers SOAP, WSDL, and (in recent revisions) WS-Addressing and MTOM (attachments).
- Bans the use of Section 5 (SOAP Encoding) of the SOAP specification in its entirety.
- Mandates the use of HTTP as the transport and details how to do so.

Basic Security Profile

- Adds support for WS-Security with a specific set of security tokens, such as user name and password and X.509 certificates. You would add this profile when implementing:
  - Authentication
  - Integrity
  - Confidentiality

Reliable Secure Profile (RSP)

- Adds support for WS-ReliableMessaging and WS-SecureConversation. You would generally use either the Basic Profile or the Basic Security Profile with most Web services, although the use of the RSP profile is gaining adoption, now that more Web services runtime environments offer support for it. This is one of the challenges: Even with WS-I profiles, there's no guarantee which profiles your partners will use. Someone will need to tell you which ones—which *policy*—to administratively apply to any given Web service, based on business requirements.

WSDL and SOAP

The WS-I mandates that Web services are described using the Web Services Definition Language (WSDL) and that they exchange SOAP messages. It is helpful to know something about these fundamental specifications.

A WSDL document is an XML document that describes the interface to a Web service. The essential structure of a WSDL document is as follows:

- **Data Types**—This section uses XML Schema to define the types of data that is exchanged between the Web service requester and Web service provider.
- **Messages**—Web services work by exchanging messages. This section describes the messages that will be exchanged. The messages contain the data types previously defined.
- **Service Interface**—This is known as a Port Type in the currently mandated version of WSDL and describes the interface to the Web service.

- **Operations**—The service interface consists of defined operations. Each operation is defined in terms of messages:

- **Input**[required]—This is the message sent to the Web service to initiate the request.

- **Output**[optional]—This is the message sent by a Web service if it follows a request-response (RPC) pattern.

- **Fault**[optional]—This is the message sent by a Web service to indicate some sort of exception, a.k.a., fault.

- **Binding**—This section describes how to map the generic definition of the Web service (bullets 1–3 in this list) to a specific transport, such as HTTP and formatting.

- **Service**—This section describes the location (endpoint) of the Web service, such as an HTTP URL or JMS queue.

The WSDL could be generated for developers if they had started by writing a Web service using some tooling environment, or they could have received the WSDL from some standards body or from you if they are writing code to match an existing Web service already deployed in the environment. In the later case, developers can start from a WSDL document and generate the necessary code to begin implementing a Web service client or a similar Web service provider.

A SOAP document is also an XML document and is the data format used for all messages between Web service requesters and providers. The essential format of a SOAP document is as follows:

- **Envelope**[required]—This wraps the entire SOAP message.

  - **Headers**[optional]—This can contain all sorts of metadata about the message and is used extensively when using specifications such as WS-Security.

  - **Body**[required]—This contains the payload—the message—being exchanged.

A Web Service Example

To put some of what we've covered so far in perspective, let's take a quick look at a very simple Web service. Don't worry if you are not a Java programmer; the operative word here is "simple."

The Web service provider is implemented as a single Java class, `PingService`, with a single operation (`ping`) that takes a string as a parameter and returns the same string. The class implementation is represented in Listing 15.1.

Listing 15.1   `ping` Service Java Code

```
package com.wasscripting.services;
import javax.jws.WebService;

@WebService
public class PingService {
  public String ping(String request) {
```

```
    return request;
  }
}
```

Developers can implement the class in Rational® Application Developer or other similar tooling, along with client code, and deliver the resulting EAR file(s) to the administrator for deployment and administration.

A Java client might be as simple as the code in Listing 15.2.

Listing 15.2 `ping` Client Java Code

```
package com.wasscripting.serviceclients;
import com.wasscripting.services.PingService;
import com.wasscripting.services.PingServiceProxy;

public class PingServiceClient {
  public static void main(String[] args) {
    PingService ping = new PingServiceProxy();
    String result = ping("Hello");
    System.out.println("Ping result: " + result);
  }
}
```

The sole purpose for showing you these trivial examples is to emphasize the point that there is nothing magical happening in the programs themselves. Other than an annotation, @WebService, in the service and the use of PingServiceProxy in the client, there was nothing "Web service-ish" in either of them. The essential magic to make them Web service providers and Web service requesters, respectively, happens within vendor-provided code generators or within WebSphere Application Server[1] itself. And that's the catch and the reason for the code just shown. Administrators configure the magic (a.k.a., the Web services runtime environment) to make interesting things, such as WS-Security or other non-default behaviors, happen. A sample partial WSDL[2] for this Web service is shown in Listing 15.3.

Listing 15.3 Partial WSDL Document for the `ping` Web Service

```
<message name="ping">
    <part type="xsd:string" name="request"/>
</message>
```

---

[1] WebSphere Application Server provides the underlying Web service runtime environment.

[2] Web Services Descriptor Language. This document tells clients of the service how to request your service and what, if anything, will return to them when they make a request. For extensive details, see http://www.w3.org/TR/wsdl20/.

```
<message name="pingResponse">
    <part type="xsd:string" name="return"/>
</message>

<portType name="PingService">
  <operation name="ping">
    <input message="ping"/>
    <output message="pingResponse"/>
  </operation>
</portType>
```

A pre-existing XML type was used here, so there is no section for defining types, and the binding and service sections are not shown. The resulting messages would be similar to what is presented in Listing 15.4.

Listing 15.4   SOAP Messages Exchanged Between Client and `ping` Service

```
Request message from client:
<soap:Envelope>
  <soap:Headers/>
  <soap:Body>
    <ping>
     <request>Hello</request>
    </ping>
  </soap:Body>
<soap:/Envelope>

Response message from Ping service:
<soap:Envelope>
  <soap:Headers/>
  <soap:Body>
    <pingResponse>
     <return>Hello</return>
    </pingResponse>
  </soap:Body>
<soap:/Envelope>
```

Again, this is nothing fancy. But, it gets a lot more complicated when you want to take advantage of additional capabilities, such as digitally signing the messages and encrypting the messages.

When that happens, the code stays the same, and the WSDL stays the same. However, the way you configure the Web services runtime environment will have to change. The information in the message headers will explode in size and complexity. In this example, those headers are empty now. As you add features to the Web service, the runtime environment must add quite a bit of information to the header section of each message. The Web services runtime environment decides what to put in various headers based on configuration data that the administrator's supply. Much of Web services' flexibility comes directly from configuration decisions that the administrators make.

Web Services Runtimes

WebSphere ships with and supports more than one Web services runtime environment. The two that are of importance to us are as follows:

- **JAX-RPC** (JSR-101)—This is the first specification for writing Web services in Java.
- **JAX-WS** (JSR-224)—This was initially called JAX-RPC v2 and is the second and current specification for writing Web services in Java. It is supported only by WebSphere V7 (or WebSphere V6.1 with the Web services Feature Pack).

It is important for you to know that these specifications exist and are supported. For one thing, many of the new administrative capabilities for managing Web services in WebSphere V7, including the related **AdminTask** command groups, work only with Web services implemented using JAX-WS and not those written using JAX-RPC.

Another vital specification is *Web Services for Java EE* (JSR-109) *a.k.a.,* WSEE, which specifies how to deploy Web services written using either JAX-RPC or JAX-WS in a Java EE application server (which is what WebSphere provides).

WSEE defines a few different approaches to deploying Web services. In summary, these are:

- A "Plain Old Java Object" (POJO) using SOAP over HTTP. This is the kind of Web service implemented earlier. It is deployed as part of a web module into the web container. The web container is responsible for implementing all of the technology necessary for the Web service to work properly. Authorization is at the level of the Web service interface, not individual operations.
- An EJB using SOAP over HTTP. Developers write a normal Stateless Session Bean—a type of Enterprise Java Bean (EJB). That EJB is deployed as part of an EJB module into the EJB container. Because the EJB container does not handle HTTP traffic—that's the job of the web container—it is typical to see a companion web module automatically generated to match the Web service and deployed in the EAR file along with it. The web module deploys to the web container and routes the Web service request to the EJB in the EJB container. There are several advantages to this type of Web service implementation:

  - The Web service runs in a transactional environment (the EJB container).

- Individual Web service methods can be restricted so that only authorized users can invoke them.

- An EJB using SOAP over JMS. Developers write a normal Stateless Session Bean—a type of Enterprise Java Bean (EJB). That EJB is deployed as part of an EJB module into the EJB container. Because the EJB exposes the Web service interface and does not natively communicate with JMS, the Web service runtime is responsible for making the connection. IBM's JAX-RPC runtime, for example, provides a Message-Driven Bean (MDB) to help bridge the gap between JMS and the Web service.

  - As an administrator, there is more work to do here because you need to create the JMS resources, that is, JMS queues for exchanging messages and an Activation Specification to link our request queue to the MDB.

  - This model includes the advantages of the EJB using SOAP over HTTP approach and others, such as: The Web service requester and provider are decoupled in time. At the time that the request is made, the requester only needs to be able to post to a queue. Messages from the queue can be delivered when the Web service provider is available.

  - Because this deployment model does not use HTTP, it is not WS-I–compliant. The reason for this is that there is not an accepted standard for SOAP over JMS across all of the Java EE vendors. But work is progressing rapidly on such a standard, and WebSphere V7 has support for the current draft.

Irrespective of the ability to interoperate with other JMS providers, JMS is still not interoperable with non-Java platforms. Again, the mandate for HTTP is to ensure interoperability between Web services, regardless of programming language, operating system, or hardware platform.

Managing Web Services

The examples in this chapter use the **AdminApp, AdminConfig, and AdminTask** administrative objects, as appropriate, to manage Web services. As noted earlier, many of the **AdminTask** commands discussed do not exist in WebSphere V6.1. You must be using WebSphere V7 (or WebSphere V6.1 with the Web services Feature Pack). For purposes of this chapter, it is assumed that you are using WebSphere V7.

It is also assumed that by now you are familiar with AdminConfig.save() and AdminConfig.reset() and know when to use each,[3] so they have been left out of the given examples. The complete code examples can be found on the book's FTP site. The following sections cover key segments.

---

[3] See the "Create and Modify Methods" section in Chapter 8, "The AdminConfig Object," for details.

Exploring Web Services

First, let's look at how to explore the Web services that might already be installed in your WebSphere environment. The interactive mode of **wsadmin** will be used for this exploration.

For purposes of illustrating the scripts, we have already created and deployed our Web service (described previously) in the following applications:

- [JAX-WS] PingServiceApplication
- [JAX-WS] PingServiceClientApplication
- [JAX-RPC] PingServiceJAXRPCApplication
- [JAX-RPC] PingServiceJAXRPCClientApplication

The code for the Web service requester and Web service provider is essentially identical in all cases. They differ only in the use of JAX-RPC or JAX-WS.

Listing Web Services

In preparation, you might want to simply list the applications that are installed, as in Listing 15.5.

Listing 15.5   List Applications

```
wsadmin>print AdminApp.list()
PingServiceApplication
PingServiceClientApplication
PingServiceJAXRPCApplication
PingServiceJAXRPCClientApplication
```

In Listing 15.5, you can see four applications: two Web service requesters and two Web service providers. The method named and the documentation for AdminTask.listWebServices() and related methods might lead you to believe that you can use these methods to investigate the Web services, but look closely at the results in Listing 15.6.

Listing 15.6   List (JAX-WS) Web Services

```
wsadmin>print AdminTask.listWebServices()

[[application PingServiceApplication] [module PingService.war]
[service {http://services.wasscripting.com/}PingServiceService]
[client false] [type JAX-WS] ]
```

As seen in Listing 15.6, there is a surprise: Where is the service for PingServiceJAXRPCApplication? It is not there because not only are these **AdminTask** commands new for WebSphere V7, but they only work for new, JAX-WS-based, Web services.

Note, too, that in Listing 15.6, `AdminTask.listWebServices()`[4] only listed the service provider. If you want to see the client(s), you have to add a parameter as shown in Listing 15.7:

Listing 15.7   List (JAX-WS) Web Services Clients

```
wsadmin>print AdminTask.listWebServices("-client true")

[[application PingServiceClientApplication] [module
PingServiceClient.war] [service
{http://services.wasscripting.com/}PingServiceService] [client true] ]
```

In Listing 15.7, the command has only provided information about JAX-WS clients. If you are using JAX-RPC-based Web services, these commands provide no information. The **AdminTask** methods only provide information for JAX-WS web services and their clients.

Listing Web Services Information

Two other useful commands are `AdminTask.listWebServicesEndpoints`[5] and `Admin Task.listWebServicesOperations`.[6] From `AdminTask.listWebServicesEndpoints`, you can get the endpoints as defined in WebSphere, as shown in Listing 15.8.

Listing 15.8   Listing (JAX-WS) Web Service Endpoints

```
wsadmin>print AdminTask.listWebServiceEndpoints("[-application
PingServiceApplication -module PingService.war -service
{http://services.wasscripting.com/}PingServiceService]")

[[logicalEndpoint PingServicePort] ]
```

This might not seem useful, but that `logicalEndpoint` attribute is necessary for the `AdminTask.listWebServicesOperations` command, as shown in Listing 15.9.

Listing 15.9   Listing (JAX-WS) Web Service Operations

```
wsadmin>print AdminTask.listWebServiceOperations("[-application
PingServiceApplication -module PingService.war -service
{http://services.wasscripting.com/}PingServiceService -logicalEndpoint
PingServicePort]")
```

---

[4] See details in the reference section of this chapter.

[5] See details in the reference section of this chapter.

[6] See details in the reference section of this chapter.

```
[[operation ping] ]
```

This section has listed the available Web service operation(s), but not sufficiently enough for the developers to understand nor in sufficient detail to understand the SOAP messages that might be exchanged. For that, you need the WSDL for the Web services.

Exporting the WSDL for a Web Service

There is an **AdminApp** command to export the WSDL for a Web service, which also works for JAX-RPC-based Web services.

```
wsadmin>AdminApp.publishWSDL("PingServiceJAXRPCApplication",
  "/tmp/PingWSDL.zip")
```

The WSDL related for the Web service will be written to the specified location. The .zip is not really optional. You can specify whichever filename you want, but the result will still be a ZIP-formatted archive, no matter what you call it. One reason is that WSDL documents support an import operation. The document can be broken into multiple parts that are reusable components. For example, the data types might be used in many different Web services using different messages. So WebSphere writes a ZIP-formatted archive to hold the possibly multiple parts that makeup the logical document.

Web Service Policy Sets

WebSphere V7 introduces the administrative notion of *policy sets*. Policy sets allow you to declare Qualities of Service (QOS) for Web services, store them separately, and apply them to various Web services. The overall structure surrounding policy sets is fairly simple:

- **Policy Set**—A collection of policies. WebSphere V7 comes with a number of preconfigured policy sets.
  - Policy[7]—A collection of QoS attributes defined in general terms.
- **Policy Set Bindings**—Mapping between general terms, used in policies and actual values. These allow policies to be defined fairly generically and then reused with specific values for such types of information as the following:
  - Keys and keystores, which are used for signature and encryption
  - Authentication information
  - Persistent information

---

[7] See details at http://www.w3.org/Submission/WS-Policy/.

- **Policy Set Attachment**—Associates a Web service with a policy set. Attachments can be made at any of the following four levels:
  - Application
    - Web service
      - Endpoint
        - Operation

WebSphere V7 comes with sample policy set bindings, which you can use as examples for the ones created here. You can list the available policy sets with `AdminTask.listPolicySets()`[8] as in Listing 15.10.

Listing 15.10   Application Level Policy Sets

```
wsadmin>print AdminTask.listPolicySets()
Username SecureConversation
Kerberos V5 HTTPS default
WSAddressing default
LTPA WSSecurity default
WS-I RSP
Username WSSecurity default
WSHTTPS default
SSL WSTransaction
WSReliableMessaging persistent
```

Those are not all of the available policy sets. `AdminTask.listPolicySets()` takes a parameter, `policySetType`, which can have one of several values: `application`, `system`, `system/trust`, `default`, and `application`. The default is `application` (yes, despite the seeming oddity, `default` is not the default). Regardless, the default does not show all available policies, so you have to loop through them, as shown in Listing 15.11.

Listing 15.11   All Policy Sets

```
for type in ["application", "system", "system/trust", "default"]:
    print type + ":";
    print AdminTask.listPolicySets(["-policySetType", type])

result:
application:
    Username SecureConversation
```

---

[8] See details in the reference section of this chapter.

```
    Kerberos V5 HTTPS default
    WSAddressing default
    LTPA WSSecurity default
    WS-I RSP
    Username WSSecurity default
    WSHTTPS default
    SSL WSTransaction
    WSReliableMessaging persistent
system:
    SystemWSSecurityDefault
system/trust:
    TrustServiceSymmetricDefault
    TrustServiceSecurityDefault
default:
```

You can now use `AdminTask.getPolicySet()`[9] to get more information on any of these policy sets. You will find it is easier to use a Python list as the parameter rather than a string due to the presence of spaces in the policy set names. Without proper formatting, you would receive a `CWPST0055E: The {} policy set is not found` exception. You could use nested quotes to work around that issue, but a Python list is used here, instead, which also makes it easier to vary the parameter list.

Please note the technique used to build these parameter lists. With it a list is prepared in which some number of list members are of the form `"%(variableName)s"`, and then a list comprehension is used along with the python construct `string % locals()` to create a new list in which all of the `"%(variableName)s"` entries have been replaced with the current value of those variables in the local scope. This can be a very nice technique for preparing and reusing parameter lists when working with scripting objects. Listing 15.12 shows one policy set.

Listing 15.12   The `SecureConversation` Policy Set

```
# Prepare argument list
# This argument list will be used in other listings
args=[]
args.append("-policySet")
args.append("%(policySet)s")

# List Information About Policy Set
# The data in this variable will change
```

---

[9] See details in the reference section of this chapter.

```
# in each listing
policySet="Username SecureConversation"
print \
AdminTask.getPolicySet([item % locals() for item in args])


result:
[
   [version 7.0.0.0]
   [name [Username SecureCon6yy4Z hyrgmhdti89iiiiiiiiooiOoo8mj
hi888535tversation]]
   [default true]
   [type application]
   [description [This policy set provides message integrity
by digitally signing the body, the time stamp, and the
WS-Addressing headers. Message confidentiality is provided
by encrypting the body and the signature. Message
authentication is provided by using the Username Token.
This policy set follows the WS-SecureConversation and
WS-Security specifications.]]
]
```

Listing 15.13 shows that you can obtain details about a different policy set simply by changing the name that is passed to **AdminTask**.getPolicySet().

Listing 15.13   The WSSecurity Policy Set

```
policySet="Username WSSecurity default"
print AdminTask.getPolicySet([item % locals() for item in args])


result:
[
   [version 7.0.0.0]
   [name [Username WSSecurity default]]
   [default true]
   [type application]
   [description [This policy set provides message integrity
by digitally signing the body, time stamp, and
WS-Addressing headers using RSA encryption.
Message confidentiality is provided by encrypting the body
and signature using RSA encryption. Message authentication
is provided by using the Username Token. This policy set
```

```
follows the WS-Security specifications.]]
]
```

These two seem pretty similar when you look at the descriptions, except for the comment about WS-SecureConversation. So what is the difference? There are different ways to explore that topic, but a quick way to do so is to export the two policy sets,[10] as shown in Listing 15.14, and then view the results in an editor.

Listing 15.14   Exporting Policy Sets

```
# Prepare argument list
args=[]
args.append("-policySet")
args.append("%(policySet)s")
args.append("-pathName")
args.append("%(pathName)s")

# Export Policy Sets
policySet="Username SecureConversation"
pathName="/tmp/UsernameSecureConversation.zip"
AdminTask.exportPolicySet([item % locals() for item in args])

policySet="Username WSSecurity default"
pathName="/tmp/UsernameWSSecuritydefault.zip"
AdminTask.exportPolicySet([item % locals() for item in args])
```

As it turns out, there are two policies in each of these policy sets: WS-Security and WS-Addressing. By looking at the XML files for their WS-Addressing policies, you can immediately see that they are identical, so these two policy sets differ only in their WS-Security policy configuration.

Alternatively, in Listing 15.15, you can see which policies are contained in a policy set by using the **AdminTask**.listPolicyTypes()[11] command.

Listing 15.15   Policy Types

```
# Prepare Argument List
args=[]
args.append("-policySet")
```

---

[10] See the details of **AdminTask**.exportPolicySet() in the reference section of this chapter.

[11] See the details of **AdminTask**.listPolicyTypes() in the reference section of this chapter.

```
args.append("%(policySet)s")

# List Policy Types
AT=AdminTask
print AT.listPolicyTypes([item % locals() for item in args])

result (for policySet="Username WSSecurity default"):
WSSecurity
WSAddressing

result (for policySet="" or print AdminTask.listPolicyTypes()):
SSLTransport
WSSecurity
WSAddressing
HTTPTransport
WSReliableMessaging
JMSTransport
WSTransaction
```

And Listing 15.16 lists the attributes of the policy via the **AdminTask**. `getPolicyType()`[12] command.

Listing 15.16   Policy Attributes

```
# Prepare Argument List
args=[]
args.append("-policySet")
args.append("%(policySet)s")
args.append("-policyType")
args.append("%(policyType)s")
policyType="WSSecurity"

# Display Policy Information
print         \
AdminTask.getPolicyType([item % locals() for item in args])
```

But, there is a reason why you won't see the voluminous output in this book. It is far easier to view the XML representation of the policy than to view the response from that command. In

---

[12] See details in the reference section of this chapter.

fact, although there are commands for setting the policy attributes, if you need to modify a policy, you might well want to export[13] the policy set, edit the WS-Policy files (those XML files in the archive), and import[14] the modified policy set.

Another important reason for exporting policy sets is that the Rational Application Developer (RAD) tool used by your programmers can *use* but cannot *create* policy sets (as of RAD 7.5.2), so the pattern of use is to export policy sets from WebSphere and import them into RAD.

As you've seen, a policy set describes a set of policies for how to apply various Web service capabilities, such as WS-Security and WS-Addressing, to Web services. They are sharable and reusable. In fact, given that you want Web services to be able to interoperate, the requester and the provider need compatible policies. When they are installed in WebSphere, you would use the same policy set with each.

Rather than use the default policy sets that come with WebSphere, we recommend you make a copy. That way, you can avoid accidentally impacting other Web services when you modify a policy set. A couple of **AdminTask** commands can help here: **AdminTask**. listAttachmentsForPolicySet()[15] and AdminTask.copyPolicySet().[16] Both are shown in Listing 15.17.

Listing 15.17   List Attachments and Copy Policies

```
# Prepare Argument List
# to show policy set attachments
args=[]
args.append("-policySet")
args.append("%(policySet)s")


# List Attachments for a Policy Set
arg=[item % locals() for item in args]
print AdminTask.listAttachmentsForPolicySet(arg)


# Prepare Argument List
# to copy a policy
args=[]
args.append("-sourcePolicySet")
args.append("%(sourcePolicySet)s")
args.append("-newPolicySet")
```

---

[13] See details of **AdminTask**.exportPolicySet() in the reference section of this chapter.

[14] See details of **AdminTask**.importPolicySet() in the reference section of this chapter.

[15] See details in the reference section of this chapter.

[16] See details in the reference section of this chapter.

```
args.append("%(newPolicySet)s")
args.append("-newDescription")
args.append("%(newDescription)s")
args.append("-transferAttachments")
args.append("%(transferAttachments)s")

sourcePolicySet="Username WSSecurity default"
newPolicySet="PingServicePolicySet"
newDescription="Policy for Working with the Ping Service"
transferAttachments="false"


AdminTask.copyPolicySet([item % locals() for item in args])
```

The attachments (uses) of the policy set have been listed and copied, as well as a copy made without copying any attachments so that there would be no worry about future change(s) unintentionally impacting unrelated Web services.

Policy Set Bindings

The policy set that created here can be attached to the Web service requester(s) and provider(s), but the policies are general and need to be bound to specific resources, such as the specific keys and keystores to use for cryptography with the WS-Security policy. Typically, bindings are specific to the application and/or platform. In this example, the bindings are specific to the platform—keys and keystores—but not to the application. Don't be confused by the names chosen for the keys and keystore files—such things *could* be specific to an application, but in this case they are not.

To perform a binding, you need something to bind to, and for WS-Security, you need such things as keys and keystores. Before creating the bindings, you need to prepare some resources. For the purposes of this example and for reference, these were the commands used:

Create Server Key Pair

```
$ keytool -genkey -v -alias server1 -keyalg RSA              \
  -keystore pingServiceKeys.jks -storepass storew0rd          \
  -dname "cn=server1,O=wasscripting,C=US" -keypass keyw0rd
```

Create Client's Key Pair

```
$ keytool -genkey -v -alias client -keyalg RSA               \
  -keystore pingClientKeys.jks -storepass storew0rd           \
  -dname "cn=client,O=wasscripting,C=US" -keypass keyw0rd
```

Export Server's Public Key

```
$ keytool -export -v -alias server1 -file /tmp/server1.cert \
 -rfc -keystore pingServiceKeys.jks -storepass storew0rd
```

Export Client's Public Key

```
$ keytool -export -v -alias client -file /tmp/client.cert \
 -rfc -keystore pingClientKeys.jks -storepass storew0rd
```

Import Client's Key Into the Server's Keystore

```
$ keytool -import -v -noprompt -alias client                 \
 -file /tmp/client.cert -keystore pingServiceKeys.jks        \
 -storepass storew0rd
```

Import Server's Key Into the Client's Keystore

```
$ keytool -import -v -noprompt -alias server1               \
 -file /tmp/server1.cert -keystore pingClientKeys.jks        \
 -storepass storew0rd
```

As indicated, these commands have created the necessary messaging resources used with WS-Security using the standalone *keytool* provided with WebSphere's implementation of Java.[17] Because this is using platform-specific bindings, rather than application-specific, let's start by copying one of the default bindings provided with WebSphere. You can query the default bindings with **AdminTask**.getDefaultBindings().[18]

```
wsadmin>print AdminTask.getDefaultBindings()
[ [client [Client sample]] [provider [Provider sample]] ]
```

And you can easily copy the binding. In this case, you see the provider binding completed in Listing 15.18, but we're leaving the consumer binding as an exercise for you.

Listing 15.18   Copy Provider Bindings

```
args=[]
args.append("-sourceBinding")
args.append("%(sourceBinding)s")
args.append("-newBinding")
```

---

[17] It is located in ${INSTALL_ROOT}/java/bin/keytool[.exe].

[18] See details in the reference section of this chapter.

```
args.append("%(newBinding)s")
args.append("-newDescription")
args.append("%(newDescription)s")

sourceBinding="Provider sample"
newBinding="PingProviderBindings"
newDescription="Bindings for WS-Security w/ the Ping service."

AdminTask.copyBinding([item % locals() for item in args])
```

Now you need to bind the physical keys and keystores to logical references that are used by the WS-Security policy in our policy set. And this is where things get rather tricky. This is where things get...ugly, to be honest. The WebSphere Application Server V7 Information Center topic, *Enabling secure conversation using wsadmin scripting*, provides an example of what you need to do. For all intents and purposes, it is presented without any explanation at all. You need to set properties on the bindings, and there is basically no documentation on what those properties are and how they need to be set. In cases such as this, once again, you can and should turn to the Command Assistance feature of the Integrated Solutions Console to see the commands that it generates. It does not generate optimal commands, but it does provide the necessary properties.

You can also query the current set of properties using **AdminTask**.getBindings().[19] Listing 15.19 shows the code.

Listing 15.19   Getting Binding Information

```
args=[]
args.append("-policyType")
args.append("%(policyType)s")
args.append("-bindingLocation")
args.append("%(bindingLocation)s")
args.append("-bindingName")
args.append("%(bindingName)s")

policyType="WSSecurity"
bindingLocation=""
bindingName="PingProviderBindings"

AdminTask.getBinding([item % locals() for item in args])
```

We'll spare you the page or two of output that this emits.

---

[19] See details in the reference section of this chapter.

To bind the keys and keystores, the **AdminTask**.setBinding() command is used to modify the policy set binding's contents. The **AdminTask**.setBinding() command is also used to associate the policy set binding with a policy set attachment, as you will see later on, as well as to delete the binding from the system.

To delete a binding, you use the -remove parameter with **AdminTask**.setBinding().[20] See the example in Listing 15.20.

Listing 15.20   Delete Binding

```
args=[]
args.append("-bindingLocation")
args.append("%(bindingLocation)s")
args.append("-bindingName")
args.append("%(bindingName)s")
args.append("-remove")
args.append("true")

bindingLocation=""
bindingName="PingProviderBindings"

AdminTask.setBinding([item % locals() for item in args])
```

Now you need to perform the steps to bind the necessary resources for the WSSecurity policy type. For the purposes of this example, these steps are as follows:

- Add the service's keystore file as a "trust store." This allows you to trust requesters whose public keys are in your keystore.
- Configure the consumer of incoming signed requests to use the newly added trust store.
- Configure the generator used to generate your signed responses to use your keystore and key.
- Configure the consumer of incoming encrypted requests to use your keystore and key.
- Configure the generator used to generate your encrypted responses to use your keystore and the client's key.

The **AdminTask**.setBinding() command is used for all of these steps. The primary parameter of interest is one called attributes. You can see partial code for how this is used to add the keystore as a trust store in Listing 15.21.

---

[20] See details in the reference section of this chapter.

Listing 15.21   Partial Code for Configuring a Policy Set Binding

```
# Prepare the argument list
args=[]
args.append("-policyType")
args.append("%(policyType)s")
args.append("-attachmentType")
args.append("%(attachmentType)s")
...
# Prepare the nested list of lists for attributes
# attributes is the overall list
# attr is each [key, value] list that will be added
# pre is a prefix part of the property names we are setting.
# factored out for readability of the listing.
pre="application.securityinboundbindingconfig.trustanchor_999."
attributes=[]
attr=[]
attr.append(pre+"keystore.path")
attr.append("%(keystorePath)s")
attributes.append(attr)

attr=[]
attr.append(pre+"name")
attr.append("%(trustAnchorName)s")
attributes.append(attr)

attr=[]
attr.append(pre+"keystore.type")
attr.append("JKS")
attributes.append(attr)

attr=[]
attr.append(pre+"storepass")
attr.append("%(storepass)s")
attributes.append(attr)

...

keystorePath="/tmp/pingServiceKeys.jks"
trustAnchorName="PingServiceTrustStore"
storepass="storew0rd"
```

```
# replace any placeholders in the argument list
al=[items % locals() for items in args]
# add the -attributes argument
al.append("-attributes")
# replace any placeholders in the attributes list ...
# ... and append that [[k0, v0]...[kN,vN]] structure
al.append([[item[0],item[1] % locals()] for item in attributes])


# call setBindings with the constructed argument list
AdminTask.setBinding(al)
```

There are many more parameters that need to be set in a working example. Please visit the companion website, http://www.wasscripting.com, for complete examples.

Actually, one interesting thing is that because of the way **AdminTask**.setBinding() works, you can combine many logical steps into one call, as they are all just properties of the overall policy set binding.

After you have completed a policy set binding, you can export it, as is seen in Listing 15.22. You might wish to import it into Rational Application Developer 7.5 or edit the bindings by hand in a text editor.

Listing 15.22 Export Binding

```
# Prepare Argument List
args=[]
args.append("-bindingName")
args.append("%(bindingName)s")
args.append("-pathName")
args.append("%(pathName)s")


# Export Default Bindings
bindingName="Client sample"
pathName="/tmp/ClientSampleBinding.zip"
AdminTask.exportBinding([item % locals() for item in args])

bindingName="Provider sample"
pathName="/tmp/ProviderSampleBinding.zip"
AdminTask.exportBinding([item % locals() for item in args])
```

Policy Set Attachment

Having created the Policy Set, you now need to attach it to a Web service requester and/or provider to put it into effect. Listing 15.23 illustrates the configuration options on the server side, also called the provider side, of a Web service.

Listing 15.23   Server-Side Policy Attachments

```
# Prepare argument list
args=[]
args.append("-applicationName")
args.append("%(appName)s")
args.append("-attachmentType")
args.append("%(attachmentType)s")
args.append("-policySet")
args.append("%(policySet)s")
args.append("-resources")
args.append("[%(resource)s]")


policySet="PingServicePolicySet"


# Prepare to apply Web service provider attachment

appName="PingServiceApplication"
attachmentType="provider"


# Application Level Attachment
resource="WebService:/"
# Web Service Level Attachment
resource+="PingService.war:"
resource+="{http://services.wasscripting.com/}"
resource+="PingServiceService"
# Endpoint Level Attachment
resource+="/PingServicePort"
# Operation Level Attachment
resource+="/ping"


AdminTask.createPolicySetAttachment([item % locals() for item in args])
```

Listing 15.24 shows the configuration for the client side, also known as the requester side, of a Web service.

Listing 15.24 Client-Side Policy Attachments

```
# Prepare to apply Client-side Web service provider attachment
appName="PingServiceClientApplication"
attachmentType="client"
# Client Side Application Level Attachment
resource="WebService:/"
# Client Side Web Service Level Attachment
resource+="PingServiceClient.war:"
resource+="{http://services.wasscripting.com/}"
resource+="PingServiceService"
# Client Side Endpoint Level Attachment
resource+="/PingServicePort"
# Client Side Operation Level Attachment
resource+="/ping"


AdminTask.createPolicySetAttachment([item % locals() for item in args])
```

You would never attach the policy sets for both the Web service requester and the Web service provider to the same server. We're just trying to illustrate all of the different constructs for the -resources parameter to specify the level to which you want the policy set attached and how those levels relate to one another. You would only build the resource reference out to the desired level.

Notice, too, that other than the name of the WAR file, the resource specification was identical for both the Web service requester and provider.

IMPORTANT **AdminTask**.createPolicySetAttachment()[21] returns a value, specifically an *attachment id*. You will need that when attaching a binding for the policy. You have two choices: You can either assign it to a value now, or attempt to locate it later using **AdminTask**.getPolicySetAttachments().

In Listing 15.25, the id returned, **AdminTask**.createPolicySetAttachment(), is the same as the attachmentId attribute received by calling **AdminTask**.getPolicy SetAttachments().

Given that id, you can now complete the job of associating the Policy Set Attachment and the necessary Policy Set Binding. Use the same mechanism for creating the argument list as before, except that this time instead of setting attributes, set the bindingLocation.

---

[21] See details in the reference section of this chapter.

Listing 15.25   Setting Policy Set Attachments

```
id = AdminTask.createPolicySetAttachment([i % locals() for i in args])
print id
lArgs=args[:4]
lArgs.append("-expandResources")
lArgs.append("*")
print AdminTask.getPolicySetAttachments([i % locals() for i in lArgs])

result:
3263
[resource PingServiceClientApplication]
[resource WebService:/PingServiceClient.war: ... PingServiceService]
[resource WebService:/PingServiceClient.war: ...
PingServiceService/PingServicePort]
[
  [resource WebService:/PingServiceClient.war: ...
PingServiceService/PingServicePort/ping]
  [policySet PingServicePolicySet]
  [policyApplied client]
  [providerPolicySet false]
  [attachmentId 3263]
  [directAttachment true]
]
```

Listing 15.26 associates a policy set binding with an application and policy set attachment.

Listing 15.26   Associate Policy Set Binding with Application and Policy Set Attachment

```
args=[]
args.append("-bindingScope")
args.append("%(bindingScope)s")
args.append("-bindingName")
args.append("%(bindingName)s")
args.append("-attachmentType")
args.append("%(attachmentType)s")

attributes=[]
attr=[]
attr.append("application")
attr.append("%(application)s")
attributes.append(attr)
```

```
attr=[]
attr.append("attachmentId")
attr.append("%(attachmentId)s")
attributes.append(attr)

application="PingServiceApplication"
attachmentId="7"

argList=[items % locals() for items in args]
argList.append("-bindingLocation")
argList.append([[item[0],item[1] % locals()] for item in attributes])

AdminTask.setBinding(argList)
```

Policy Topics Summary

This concludes our look the Policy Sets, Policy Set Attachments, and Policy Set bindings used to configure WS-Security for a Web service provider. Hopefully you have a feel for the kinds of Web services-related topics that you can script in WebSphere. We've discussed what Web services are, how to list them (only works for new Web services using JAX-WS), how to export the WSDL so that you can give it to developers, and the use of Policies for configuring such things as WS-Security. However, there is much more that you can do with Web services and scripting than we can cover in this chapter.

Additional Topics

This last section offers a brief overview of additional Web services functions not covered in detail within this book.

Enable/Disable Endpoints

You can selectively enable and disable the JAX-WS Web services without having to stop the rest of the application. This is performed using **AdminControl** and is discussed in the WebSphere V7 Information Center topic, *Administration of service and endpoint listeners*.

WS-Notification

Web services are often point-to-point, but the WS-Notification specification permits them to participate in a topic-oriented, publish-subscribe, communication model. WebSphere supports WS-Notification, and you could configure those resources using scripting. There are a number of sections in the WebSphere Information Center that provide additional information:

- *Learning about WS-Notification*
- *Using WS-Notification for publish and subscribe messaging for Web services*

Web Services and the Service Integration Bus

Instead of having the Web service requester attach directly to the Web service provider, you can configure Web service endpoints on the Service Integration Bus. There are a number of benefits to this approach. A number of sections in the WebSphere Information Center provide additional information:

- *Learning about bus-enabled Web services*
- *Enabling Web services through the service integration bus*

Mediations

Once you are using the Service Integration Bus, you can perform mediation on the incoming and outgoing messages using SIB Mediations. *Mediation* refers to the ability to modify the routing and content of messages. WebSphere comes with a powerful mediation feature built in, although it is not as easy to use and deploy as the even more powerful capabilities provided by WebSphere Enterprise Service Bus. For addition information, see the following:

- The WebSphere V7 Information Center topic: *Administering Mediations*
- IBM developerWorks: *Mediations made simple* (http://www.ibm.com/developerworks/ webservices/library/ws-mediation/)

Web Services Gateway

The Web services gateway component of WebSphere works with the Service Integration Bus and allows for a single point of control for entire sets of Web services, which may be both internally hosted and externally hosted. The Web services gateway is discussed in the WebSphere V7 Information Center topic, Learning about the Web services gateway.

Online References

The WebSphere Information Center is always a good source of information that you should review. There are specific sections for learning about managing Web services, both in general and specifically via scripting. In addition, we have selected a few of our favorite IBM developer-Works articles that relate to the topics discussed in this chapter.

For additional reading on configuring WS-Security with WebSphere, we recommend the IBM developerWorks tutorial, *Message-level security with JAX-WS on WebSphere Application Server v7* (https://www.ibm.com/developerworks/websphere/tutorials/0905_griffith/). It uses the Integrated Solutions Console and Rational Application Developer, whereas we use scripting, but it goes into more detail on the underlying WS-Security concepts.

For additional reading on WS-Notification support, we recommend the IBM developer-Works articles *WS-Notification in WebSphere Application Server V7: Part 1: Writing JAX-WS Applications for WS-Notification* (http://www.ibm.com/developerworks/websphere/techjournal/0811_partridge/0811_partridge.html) and *WS-Notification in WebSphere Application Server V7:Part 2: Configuring JAX-WS Applications with WS-Security for WS-Notification* (http://www.ibm.com/developerworks/websphere/techjournal/0904_jiang/0904_jiang.html).

For additional reading on JAX-WS using SOAP/JMS, we recommend the IBM developer-Works article *Develop a SOAP/JMS JAX-WS Web services application with WebSphere Application Server V7 and Rational Application Developer V7.5* (http://www.ibm.com/developerworks/websphere/library/tutorials/0903_adams/).

AdminTask Web Services Reference

An application that produces or consumes Web services is installed just like any other application. After it is deployed, there are a lot of possible administrative activities. The groups of **AdminTask** methods you might need to perform those activities depend on which Web service functionality you use. The list of **AdminTask** groups that relate to Web services include the following:

- WSGateway group
- WSNotificationCommands group
- WSNotifierCommands group
- SIBWebServices group
- KeyManagerCommands group
- KeyStoreCommands group
- KeySetGroupCommands group
- PolicySetManagement group
- WebServicesAdmin group

In addition, you might well need the AdminApp.publishWSDL() method[22] to make a WSDL file available to client applications.

The two sections on Web service notifications are outside the scope of this book, as is the WSGateway group. All of the methods in this section are described as they are implemented in version 7.0 of WebSphere Application Server. Some of the **AdminTask** groups did not exist in earlier versions of the product. Some of the methods in existing **AdminTask** groups did not exist in earlier versions of the product.

We present a sampling of the methods in each command group in the order we think you might use them in your scripts. The general pattern for calling **AdminTask** methods is as follows:

---

[22] See "Exporting the WSDL for a Web Service" section in this chapter for details.

```
AdminTask.methodName( target,                                  \
        '[ -argument value -nextArgument value2  ' \
    + '-stepName [ -arg01 val01 -arg02 val02 ] ' \
    + '-nextStepName [ -arg03 val03]  -yetAnotherStep ]' )
```

There might or might not be a target. If there is, it might be a configuration ID or a name. There might or might not be arguments as well. Most often, arguments are name/value pairs. There might or might not be steps, and there might be more than one step. Think of steps as arguments that take either a list of name/value pairs as their value or no argument at all. Bundle all the arguments and all the steps into one big list and pass it to the method.

SIBWebServices Group

The methods in this group allow you to create Web services and wrap them around existing executables as long as those executables can integrate with a messaging service. The Web services that this group manipulates are the JAX-WS Web services.

createSIBWSInboundService

Creates an inbound service. This task cannot be performed when **wsadmin** is started in local mode.

Target (mandatory):

The configuration ID, not the name, of the service integration bus where the inbound service will be created.

Required arguments:

- name—The administrative name of the outbound service.
- wsdlLocation—The Web service WSDL location.

Frequently used optional arguments:

- wsdlServiceNamespace—The Web service namespace.
- wsdlServiceName—The Web service name.
- uddiReference—The UDDI reference.
- destination—The name to use for the associated service destination.

Optional arguments that matter if you enable security:

- userId—The user ID to be used if WSDL is obtained through an authorizing proxy.
- password—The password to be used if WSDL is obtained through an authorizing proxy.

createSIBWSOutboundService

Creates an outbound service. This task cannot be performed when **wsadmin** is started in local mode.

Target (mandatory):

The configuration ID, not the name, of the service integration bus where the outbound service will be created.

Required arguments:

- `name`—The administrative name of the outbound service.

- `wsdlLocation`—The Web service WSDL location.

Frequently used optional arguments:

- `wsdlServiceNamespace`—The Web service namespace.

- `wsdlServiceName`—The Web service name.

- `uddiReference`—The UDDI reference.

- `destination`—The name to use for the associated service destination.

Optional arguments that matter if you enable security:

- `userId`—The user ID to be used if WSDL is obtained through an authorizing proxy.

- `password`—The password to be used if WSDL is obtained through an authorizing proxy.

createSIBWSEndpointListener

Create an endpoint listener on a service integration bus. An endpoint listener is the glue that ties a Web service to a messaging bus.

Target (mandatory):
The configuration ID of the server where the endpoint listener will be created.

Required arguments:

- `name`—Name of the endpoint listener.
- `urlRoot`—Root of the endpoint address URL for Web services accessed using this endpoint listener.
- `wsdlUrlRoot`—Root of the HTTP URL where WSDL associated with this endpoint listener is located.

Occasionally used optional argument:

- `earFile`—Location of the endpoint listener application EAR file.

connectSIBWSEndpointListener

Connect an endpoint listener to a service integration bus. An endpoint listener is the glue that ties a Web service to a messaging bus. This task cannot be performed when **wsadmin** is started in local mode.

Target (mandatory):

The endpoint listener to be connected.

Required argument:

- `bus`—The name of the service integration bus to which the endpoint listener will be connected.

Occasionally used optional argument:

- `replyDestination`—Name to use for the connection's reply destination.

addSIBWSInboundPort

Add an inbound port to an inbound Web service. This task cannot be performed when **wsadmin** is started in local mode.

Target (mandatory):

The configuration ID of the inbound service to which the port will be added.

Required arguments:

- `name`—The name for the inbound port.
- `endpointListener`—The name of the associated endpoint listener.

Frequently used optional arguments: At least one, and possibly two, of these arguments is actually required. If the endpoint listener lives in a cluster, you must supply the name of the cluster. If the endpoint listener lives on an individual server, you must supply the server name and the node name.

- `cluster`—The name of the cluster where the associated endpoint listener lives.
- `node`—The name of the node that contains the server that contains the endpoint listener with which this port will be associated
- `server`—The name of the server where the associated endpoint listener lives.
- `templatePort`—The name of the port in the template WSDL to use as a basis for this port's binding.

addSIBWSOutboundPort

Add an outbound port to an inbound Web service. This task cannot be performed when **wsadmin** is started in local mode.

Target (mandatory):

The configuration ID of the outbound service to which the port will be added.

Required arguments:

- `name`—The name for the outbound port.
- `endpointListener`—The name of the associated endpoint listener.

Frequently used optional arguments:

At least one, and possibly two, of these arguments is actually required. If the endpoint listener lives in a cluster, you must supply the name of the cluster. If the endpoint listener lives on an individual server, you must supply the server name and the node name.

- `cluster`—The name of the cluster where the associated endpoint listener lives.
- `node`—The name of the node that contains the server that contains the endpoint listener with which this port will be associated
- `server`—The name of the server where the associated endpoint listener lives.
- `templatePort`—The name of the port in the template WSDL to use as a basis for this port's binding.

publishSIBWSInboundService

Publish an inbound service to a UDDI registry. This task cannot be performed when **wsadmin** is started in local mode.

Target (mandatory):

The configuration ID of the inbound service to be published.

Required argument:

- `uddiPublication`—The name of a UDDI publication for the inbound service.

Optional arguments that matter if you enable security:

- `userId`—User ID to be used if publishing is done through an authenticating proxy.
- `password`—Password to be used if publishing is done through an authenticating proxy.

KeyManagerCommands

A key manager determines which alias to use during the Secure Sockets Layer (SSL) handshake. There is a default key manager. You can also create a custom key manager.

listKeyManagers

Reports the key managers installed in the product. The arguments serve to limit the scope of the report.

Frequently used optional arguments:

- `scopeName`—Specifies the management scope.

- `all`—Specifies true to list all key managers. True overrides the `scopeName` parameter.

- `displayObjectName`—Specifies `true` to display the list output as ObjectNames and `false` to return SSL configuration alias names. If you do not pass this argument, you get SSL configuration alias names.

createKeyManager

Creates a key manager.

Required argument:

- `name`—Specifies a name to uniquely identify a key manager.

Frequently used optional arguments:

- `algorithm`—Specifies the algorithm name of the `TrustManager` or `KeyManager`.

- `scopeName`—Specifies the management scope.

- `provider`—Specifies the provider.

Occasionally used optional argument:

- `keyManagerClass`—Specifies the custom class that implements the `KeyManager` interface. You may not specify this argument if you specify either the provider or the algorithm argument.

KeyStoreCommands

Keys are managed in keystores so the keystore type can be supported by WebSphere Application Server, provided that the keystores can store the referenced key type. You can configure keys and scope keystores so that they are visible only to particular processes, nodes, clusters, and so on.

listKeyStoreTypes

List the supported keystore types. This method takes no arguments.

listKeyStores

List keystore objects. For the most part, the arguments serve to limit the scope of the query.

Frequently used optional arguments:

- `all`—Specifies `true` to list all keystores. True overrides the `scopeName` parameter. If you do not specify this argument, the default value is `false`.

- `scopeName`—Limits the query to the specified management scope. This argument only matters if you omit all or set all `false`.

- `keyStoreUsage`—Limits the query to keystores for a particular usage. If you omit this argument, you get all keystore usages subject to any scope limitation you might have specified.

createKeyStore

Creates a new keystore.

Required arguments:

- `keyStoreName`—Specifies the unique name to identify the keystore.

- `keyStoreLocation`—Specifies the name of the keystore file. This may either be a fully qualified file name or a relative file name. We recommend passing a fully qualified file name.

- `keyStoreType`—Specifies one of the predefined keystore types. The value you pass must be one of the values returned by **AdminTask**.`listKeyStoreTypes()`.

Frequently used optional arguments:

- `scopeName`—Specifies the management scope.

- `keyStorePassword`—Specifies the password to open the keystore. This argument is specified as optional, but if you try to create a keystore without a password, recent versions of WebSphere Application Server throw an exception.

- `keyStoreDescription`—Statement that describes the keystore.

- `keyStoreProvider`—Specifies the provider for the keystore.

- `keyStoreIsFileBased`—Keystore is file-based.

- `keyStoreUsage`—What the keystore can be used for. Permitted values are `SSLKeys`, `KeySetKeys`, `RootKeys`, `DeletedKeys`, `DefaultSigners`, or `RSATokenKeys`.

- `enableCryptoOperations`—Specifies true to enable cryptographic operations on hardware devices.

Occasionally used optional arguments:

- `controlRegionUser`—Specifies this field if creating a writable keystore object for the control region's keyring. This argument only matters in z/OS environments.

- `servantRegionUser`—Specifies this field if creating a writable keystore object for the servant region's keyring. This argument only matters in z/OS environments.

- `keyStoreHostList`—Specifies a comma-separated the list of hosts where the keystore is remotely managed.

- `keyStorePasswordVerify`—Specifies the confirmation of the password to open the keystore. Most scripts will not pass this value. If your script processes manually generated responses, this argument exists to save your script the trouble of comparing two password entries for equivalence.

- `keyStoreReadOnly`—Specifies whether the keystore can be written to or not.
- `keyStoreInitAtStartup`—Specifies whether the keystore needs to be initialized at server startup or not.
- `keyStoreStashFile`—Specifies whether to stash the keystore password to a file or not. This only applies to the CMS keystore type.

exchangeSigners

Exchange Signer Certificates between two keystores.

Required arguments:

- `keyStoreName1`—Keystore name that will exchange signers with another keystore.
- `keyStoreName2`—Keystore name that will exchange signers with another keystore.
- `keyStoreScope1`—Specifies the management scope.
- `keyStoreScope2`—Specifies the management scope.

Frequently used optional arguments:

- `certificateAliasList1`—Specifies colon-separated list of certificates whose signer will be added to another keystore.
- `certificateAliasList2`—Specifies colon-separated list of certificates whose signer will be added to another keystore.

getKeyStoreInfo

Returns information about a particular keystore.

Required argument:

- `keyStoreName`—Specifies the unique name to identify the keystore.

Frequently used optional argument:

- `scopeName`—Specifies the management scope.

listKeyFileAliases

List personal certificate aliases in a keystore file.

Required arguments:

- `keyFilePath`—Specifies the fully qualified name of the keystore file.

- `keyFilePassword`—Specifies the password to the keystore file.
- `keyFileType`—Specifies the type of the keystore file.

KeySetCommands

The key management infrastructure is based on two basic configuration object types: key sets and key set groups. WebSphere Application Server uses a key set to manage instances of keys of the same type. You can configure a key set to generate a single key or a key pair, depending on the key or key pair generator class. A key set group manages one or more key sets and enables you to configure and generate different key types at the same time. For example, if your application needs both a secret key and key pair for cryptographic operations, you can configure two key sets, one for the key pair and one for the secret key that the key set group manages. The key set group controls the auto-generation characteristics of the keys, including the schedule. The framework can automatically generate keys on a scheduled basis, such as on a particular day of the week and time of day, so that key generation is done during off-peak hours.

createKeySet

Creates a key set.

Required arguments:

- `name`—Specifies the name that uniquely identifies a key set.
- `password`—Specifies the password for the key.
- `keyStoreName`—Specifies the unique name to identify the keystore.
- `aliasPrefix`—Specifies the key alias prefix name.
- `maxKeyReferences`—Specifies the maximum number of keys stored.

Frequently used optional arguments:

- `isKeyPair`—Specifies `true` if the key set is a key pair, `false` otherwise.
- `deleteOldKeys`—Specifies `true` to delete old keys during key generation, `false` to retain old keys.
- `scopeName`—Specifies the management scope.
- `keyStoreScopeName`—Specifies the management scope of the keystore.
- `keyGenerationClass`—Specifies the class used to generate keys.

generateKeyForKeySet

Generate all the keys in a key set.

Required argument:

- `keySetName`—Specifies the name that uniquely identifies a key set.

Frequently used optional arguments:

- `keySetScope`—Specifies the management scope.
- `keySetSaveConfig`—Specifies `true` to automatically save the configuration[23] without calling **`AdminConfig`**`.save()` after adding the key reference, `false` to save to the configuration with a separate command.

modifyKeySet

Modify the attributes of a key set.

Required argument:

- `name`—Specifies the name that uniquely identifies a key set.

Frequently used optional arguments:

- `password`—Specifies the password for the key.
- `keyStoreName`—Specifies the unique name to identify the keystore.
- `aliasPrefix`—Specifies the key alias prefix name.
- `maxKeyReferences`—Specifies the maximum number of keys stored.
- `sKeyPair`—Specifies `true` if the key set is a key pair, `false` otherwise.
- `deleteOldKeys`—Specifies `true` to delete old keys during key generation, `false` to retain old keys.
- `scopeName`—Specifies the management scope.
- `keyStoreScopeName`—Specifies the management scope of the keystore.
- `keyGenerationClass`—Specifies the class used to generate keys.

PolicySetManagement Group

Policies are a very important component of WebSphere Application Server V7 architecture. See Web Service Policy Sets section earlier in the chapter Web Service Policy Sets for details.

addPolicyType

The `addPolicyType` command creates a policy type with default values for the specified policy set. You may indicate whether to enable or disable the added policy type.

---

[23] This is the only method on any of the administrative scripting objects that has such a feature.

Required arguments:

- `policyType`—Specifies the name of the policy to add to the policy set.
- `policySet`—Specifies the policy set name.

Frequently used optional argument:

- `enabled`—If this parameter is set to `true`, the new policy type is enabled in the policy set. If this parameter is set to `false`, the configuration is contained within the policy set, but the configuration does not have an effect on the system.

createPolicySet

The `createPolicySet` command creates a new policy set. Policy types are not created with the policy set. The default indicator is set to `false`.

Required argument:

- `policySet`—Specifies the name of this policySet.

Frequently used optional arguments:

- `description`—Adds a description for the policy set.
- `policySetType`—Specifies the type of policy set. The type must already exist.

createPolicySetAttachment

Creates a new policy set attachment. This method returns a value; specifically it returns an attachment ID. You will need that when attaching a binding for the policy. You have two choices: You can either assign it to a value at invocation time, or you can attempt to locate it later, using **AdminTask**.getPolicySetAttachments().[24]

Required arguments:

- `policySet`—Specifies the policy set name. The `policySet` must already exist.
- `resources`—Specifies the names of the application or trust service resources.

Frequently used optional arguments:

- `applicationName`—Specifies the name of the application. This parameter applies to application and client attachments. It is not applicable to trust service attachments.
- `attachmentType`—Specifies the type of policy set attachments. The value for this parameter must be `application`, `client`, or `system/trust`. The default value is `application`.

---

[24] See **AdminTask**.getPolicySetAttachments() for details.

- `dynamicClient`—Indicates that the client resources should not be validated. The default value for this parameter is `false`.
- `attachmentProperties`—The attachment-specific properties.

listPolicyTypes

Returns a list of the names of the policies configured in the system, in a policy set, or in a binding. The arguments are optional. They serve to limit the scope of the policy types that are returned.

Frequently used optional arguments:

- `policySet`—Specifies the policy set name. For a list of all policy set names, use the `listPolicySets` command.
- `attachmentType`—Specifies the type of policy set attachments. The value for this parameter must be `application`, `client`, or `system/trust`. The default value is `application`.
- `bindingName`—Specifies the name for the binding. The binding name is optional when you are creating a new binding. A name is generated if it is not specified. The binding name is required when you are changing an attachment to use a different existing binding.
- `fromDefaultRepository`—Indicates if the command should use the default repository.
- `enabled`—If this parameter is set to `true`, only the policy types that are enabled in the policy set are listed. If this parameter is set to `false`, all of the policy types in the policy set are listed.

listPolicySets

Returns a list of all existing policy sets. The arguments are optional. They serve to limit the scope of the policy sets that are returned.

Frequently used optional argument:

- `policySetType`—Specifies the type of policy set. Specify `application` to list application policy sets. Specify `system/trust` to list the trust service policy sets. The default value for this parameter is `application`.
- `fromDefaultRepository`—Indicates if the command should use the default repository.

listAttachmentsForPolicySet

Lists the applications to which a specific policy set is attached.

Required argument:

- `policySet`—Specifies the policy set name. The `policySet` must already exist.

Frequently used optional argument:

- `attachmentType`—Specifies the type of policy set attachments. The value for this parameter must be `application`, `client`, or `system/trust`. The default value is `application`.

listAssetsAttachedToPolicySet

Lists the assets to which a specific policy set is attached.

Required argument:

- `policySet`—Specifies the policy set name. The `policySet` must already exist.

Frequently used optional argument:

- `attachmentType`—Specifies the type of policy set attachments. The value for this parameter must be `application`, `client`, or `system/trust`. The default value is `application`.

getPolicySet

Returns general attributes, such as description and default indicator, for the specified policy set.

Required argument:

- `policySet`—Specifies the policy set name. For a list of all policy set names, use the **AdminTask**.`listPolicySets()`.

Frequently used optional argument:

- `fromDefaultRepository`—Indicates if the command should use the default repository. Set this argument to `true` to use the default repository. Set it to `false` or omit it entirely if you do not wish to use the default repository.

getPolicyType

Returns the attributes for a specified policy.

Required arguments:

- `policySet`—Specifies the policy set name.
- `policyType`—Specifies the name of the policy to add to the policy set. The name you pass must be one of the types returned by calling some form of the **AdminTask**.`listPolicySets()` command.[25]

Frequently used optional arguments:

- `attributes`—Specifies the attributes to display. If this parameter is used, the command returns all attributes for the specified policy type as an array of strings.

---

[25] See **AdminTask**.`listPolicySets()` for details.

- `fromDefaultRepository`—Indicates if the command should use the default repository. Set this argument to `true` to use the default repository. Set it to `false` or omit it entirely if you do not wish to use the default repository.

getPolicySetAttachments

Lists the properties for all attachments configured for a specified application, client, or for the trust service. All arguments here are optional; however, it is not possible to call this method without arguments. See arguments for details.

Frequently used optional arguments:

- `applicationName`—Specifies the name of the application. This parameter applies to application and client attachments. It is not applicable to system/trust service attachments. You may not specify this argument for system/trust service attachments.
- `attachmentType`—Specifies the type of policy set attachments. The value for this parameter must be application, client, or system/trust. The default value is application.
- `expandResources`—Provides expanded information that details the attachment properties for each resource. An asterisk (*) character returns all Web services.
- `attachmentProperties`—The attachment-specific properties. This must be some value that can be converted into a `java.util.Properties` object.

getBinding

Returns the binding configuration for a specified policy type and scope.

Frequently used optional arguments:

- `bindingName`—Specifies the name for the binding. The binding name is optional when you are creating a new binding. A name is generated if it is not specified. The binding name is required when you are changing an attachment to use a different existing binding.
- `policyType`—Specifies the name of the policy to add to the policy set. The name you pass must be one of the types returned by calling some form of the **AdminTask**.listPolicySets() command.[26]
- `attributes`—Specifies the attribute values to update. If the `attributes` parameter is not specified, the command only updates the binding location used by the specified attachment. Any value you pass here must be convertible into a `java.util.Properties` object.
- `attachmentType`—Specifies the type of policy set attachments. The value for this parameter must be `application`, `client`, or `system/trust`. The default value is `application`.

---

[26] See `listPolicySets` for details.

getDefaultBindings

Returns the default binding names for a specified domain or server.

Frequently used optional argument:

- `domainName`—Specifies the name of the domain. The domain name is only required when the domain is not the global security domain.

getRequiredBindingVersion

Returns the binding version that is required for a specified asset.

Required argument:

- `assetProps`—Specifies the asset, such as the application name.

importPolicySet

Imports a policy set from a compressed archive onto a server environment. A side-effect of the existence of this method is that you can create policies in one of several ways. You can manipulate the various parts of a policy with methods in this group, or you can edit XML files in a text editor and import the complete set of XML files that make up a given policy.

Frequently used optional arguments:

- `importFile`—Specifies the path name of the archive file to import.
- `defaultPolicySet`—The name of the default policy set to import.
- `policySet`—Specifies the policy set name. For a list of all policy set names, use the `listPolicySets` command.
- `verifyPolicySetType`—Verifies the policy set is of this type.

exportPolicySet

Exports a policy set as an archive that can be copied onto a client environment or imported onto a server environment. A side-effect of the existence of this method is that you can create policies in one of several ways. You can manipulate the various parts of a policy with methods in this group, or you can edit XML files in a text editor and import the complete set of XML files that make up a given policy.

Required arguments:

- `policySet`—Specifies the policy set name. The `policySet` must already exist.
- `pathName`—Specifies the path name of the archive file. It is recommended that you pass a fully qualified file name. Regardless of the operating system that you use, you should use a forward slash as a directory delimiter.

copyPolicySet

Creates a copy of an existing policy set. The default indicator is set to false for the new policy set. You can indicate whether to transfer attachments from the existing policy set to the new policy set.

Required arguments:

- `sourcePolicySet`—Specifies the name of the existing policy set.
- `newPolicySet`—Specifies the name of the new policy set.

Frequently used optional arguments:

- `newDescription`—Adds a description for the policy set or binding.
- `transferAttachments`—If this parameter is set to `true`, all attachments transfer from the source policy set to the new policy set. The default value is `false`.

validatePolicySet

Validates the policies in the policy set.

Required argument:

- `policySet`—Specifies the policy set name. For a list of all policy set names, use the `listPolicySets` command.

importBinding

Imports a binding from a compressed archive onto a server environment. A side-effect of the existence of this method is that you can create bindings in one of several ways. You can manipulate the various parts of a binding with methods in this group, or you can edit XML files in a text editor and import the complete set of XML files that make up a given binding.

Required argument:

- `importFile`—Specifies the path name of the archive file to import. It is recommended that you pass a fully qualified file name. Regardless of the operating system that you use, you should use a forward slash as a directory delimiter.

Frequently used optional arguments:

- `bindingName`—Specifies the name for the binding. The binding name is optional when you are creating a new binding. A name is generated if it is not specified. The binding name is required when you are changing an attachment to use a different existing binding.

- `verifyBindingType`—Verifies the binding is of this type. It is recommended that you set this optional argument to true.

- `domainName`—Specifies the name of the domain. The domain name is only required when the domain[27] is not the global security domain.

exportBinding

Exports a binding as an archive that can be copied onto a client environment or imported onto a server environment. A side-effect of the existence of this method is that you can create bindings in one of several ways. You can manipulate the various parts of a binding with methods in this group, or you can edit XML files in a text editor and import the complete set of XML files that make up a given binding.

Required arguments:

- `bindingName`—Specifies the name for the binding. The binding name is optional when you are creating a new binding. A name is generated if it is not specified. The binding name is required when you are changing an attachment to use a different existing binding.

- `pathName`—Specifies the path name of the archive file. It is recommended that you pass a fully qualified file name. Regardless of the operating system that you use, you should use a forward slash as a directory delimiter.

copyBinding

Creates a copy of an existing binding.

Required arguments:

- `sourceBinding`—Specifies the name of the existing binding.

- `newBinding`—Specifies the name of the binding to which the bindings are copied.

Frequently used optional arguments:

- `domainName`—Specifies the name of the domain. The domain name is required when `newBinding` is part of a security domain. This argument is not required when `newBinding` is part of the global security domain.

- `newDescription`—Adds a description for `newBinding`.

---

[27] See Chapter 12, "Scripting and Security," for additional information about security domains.

setBinding

Updates the binding configuration for a specified policy type and scope. Use this command to add a server-specific binding, update an attachment to use a custom binding, edit binding attributes, or remove a binding. Although strictly speaking, none of the arguments here are required, as a practical matter, you will find yourself passing bindingName very often.

Frequently used optional arguments:

- bindingName—Specifies the name for the binding. The binding name is optional when you are creating a new binding. A name is generated if it is not specified. The binding name is required when you are changing an attachment to use a different existing binding.

- bindingScope—Specifies the scope of the binding. The binding scope is only required when you are changing an attachment to use an existing named binding or when you are removing a named binding from an attachment.

- attachmentType—Specifies the type of policy set attachments. The value for this parameter must be application, client, or system/trust. The default value is application.

- replace—If you set this value to true, the new attributes provided from the command replace the existing attributes. The default value is false.

- attributes[28]—Specifies the attribute values to update. If the attributes parameter is not specified, the command only updates the binding location used by the specified attachment.

- policyType—Specifies the name of the policy to add to the policy set. This name must be one of the names returned by **AdminTask**.listPolicyTypes().[29]

WebServicesAdmin Group

The methods in this group provide information about JAX-WS Web services provided by applications. The entire group is read-only. If you wish to change a JAX-WS Web service, you must edit the WSDL file using the AdminApp.edit() method. If you wish to view any details of a JAX-RPC Web service, you must examine the WSDL file.[30] If you wish to change a JAX-RPC Web service, you must edit the deployment.[31]

---

[28] The system will attempt to create a Java Properties object from whatever value you pass here. That means you must pass some Jython type that can be converted into a java.util.Properties object.

[29] See AdminTask.listPolicyTypes() in this chapter.

[30] See the AdminApp.publishWSDL() method description.

[31] See AdminApp.edit() method and AdminApp.update() method as described in Chapter 10, "The AdminApp Object."

listWebServices

This method lists the deployed Web services in enterprise applications. As of this writing, if there is no application name supplied, then all the Web services in the enterprise applications will are be listed.

Frequently used optional arguments:

- `application`—The deployed enterprise application name that contains Web services.
- `client`—Set `true` if you want client information about the service. Either set to `false` or omit it entirely to get server information about the service.

Steps:

1. `J2EEWSStep`—Lists the Web services.

listWebServiceEndpoints

Lists the Web service endpoints that are port names defined in a Web service in an enterprise application.

Required arguments:

- `application`—The enterprise application name that contains the Web service(s).
- `module`—The module name within the aforementioned application that contains the Web service(s).
- `service`—The Web service name within the aforementioned module whose attributes you want.

Frequently used optional argument:

- `client`—Set to `true` if you want client information about the service. Either set to `false` or omit it entirely to get server information about the service.

Steps:

1. `J2EEWSStep`—Lists the logical endpoints that are port names in a Web service.

listWebServiceOperations

Lists the Web service endpoints that are port names defined in a Web service in an enterprise application.

Required arguments:

- `application`—The enterprise application name that contains the Web service(s).
- `module`—The module name within the aforementioned application that contains the Web service(s).

- `service`—The Web service name within the aforementioned module whose attributes you want.
- `logicalEndpoint`—The name of the logical endpoint within the Web service within the aforementioned module whose attributes you want.

Frequently used optional argument:

- `client`—Set `true` if you want client information about the service. Either set `false` or omit it entirely to get server information about the service.

Steps:

1. `J2EEWSStep`—Lists the operations in a Web service endpoint.

getWebService

Gets the attributes for a given Web service in a given enterprise application.

Required arguments:

- `application`—The enterprise application name that contains the Web service(s).
- `module`—The module name within the aforementioned application that contains the Web service(s).
- `service`—The Web service name within the aforementioned module whose attributes you want.

Frequently used optional argument:

- `client`—Set to `true` if you want client information about the service. Either set it to `false` or omit it entirely to get server information about the service.

Steps

1. `J2EEWSStep`—Lists the attributes for a Web service.

listServices

Lists the services based on generic query properties. It provides more generic query functions than `listWebServices`, `listWebServiceEndpoints`, `listWebServiceOperations`, and `getWebService` commands.

Frequently used optional arguments:

- `queryProps`—The query properties for services.
- `expandResource`—Expand endpoint or operation resource in the service.

## CHAPTER 16

Version 7.0 Scripting Libraries

"Every library is an arsenal."

—*Robert Green Ingersoll*

One of the differences between Version 6.x and Version 7.0 of the product is the addition of some script libraries to version 7.0 that provide routines to assist with common administration functions. This chapter is primarily a reference to these modules, with some comments about their structure and use. We would have preferred to include lots of examples with this chapter, but due to space limitations, we chose to have a section in the companion website (http://www.wasscripting.com) for these examples.

Library Organization

In the installation directory structure, you will find a new directory under the <WAS_HOME> directory named scriptLibraries. Within this directory, there are the following sub-directories:

- application
- resources
- security
- servers
- system
- utilities

Each of these sub-directories contain (either directly or indirectly)[1] a directory named V70, which in turn contains one or more Jython script files with a filename extension of .py. Using a

---

[1] The **resources** subdirectory contains four directories (J2C, JDBC, JMS, and Provider), each of which contains a V70 directory.

recursive directory listing of files with this extension, you can find the complete list of script library files shown in Listing 16.1.[2]

Listing 16.1 `scriptLibrary` Files[3]

```
...\scriptLibraries>dir /b /s *.py
...\scriptLibraries\application\V70\AdminApplication.py
...\scriptLibraries\application\V70\AdminBLA.py
...\scriptLibraries\resources\J2C\V70\AdminJ2C.py
...\scriptLibraries\resources\JDBC\V70\AdminJDBC.py
...\scriptLibraries\resources\JMS\V70\AdminJMS.py
...\scriptLibraries\resources\Provider\V70\AdminResources.py
...\scriptLibraries\security\V70\AdminAuthorizations.py
...\scriptLibraries\servers\V70\AdminClusterManagement.py
...\scriptLibraries\servers\V70\AdminServerManagement.py
...\scriptLibraries\system\V70\AdminNodeGroupManagement.py
...\scriptLibraries\system\V70\AdminNodeManagement.py
...\scriptLibraries\utilities\V70\AdminLibHelp.py
...\scriptLibraries\utilities\V70\AdminUtilities.py
```

How are these files made available to your scripts? Well, when the **wsadmin** command is started, these directories are automatically added to the `sys.path` variable. The fact that these directory names are added to the `sys.path` variable can be shown using a trivial loop construct, as seen in Listing 16.2.[4]

Listing 16.2 Displaying `sys.path` Contents

```
wsadmin>for path in sys.path : print path
wsadmin>
.
C:\IBM\WebSphere\AppServer70\optionalLibraries\jython\Lib
C:/IBM/WebSphere/AppServer70/scriptLibraries/application/V70
C:/IBM/WebSphere/AppServer70/scriptLibraries/resources/J2C/V70
C:/IBM/WebSphere/AppServer70/scriptLibraries/resources/JDBC/V70
C:/IBM/WebSphere/AppServer70/scriptLibraries/resources/JMS/V70
```

---

[2] One way to do this on `*ix` type systems would be to execute (`find . -name "*.py"`) from the `scriptLibraries` directory.

[3] The directory prefix was removed to allow the filenames to better display within this book.

[4] The `<WAS_HOME>\optionalLibraries\jython\Lib` directory contains the standard Jython class files, and the last entry (i.e., `<WAS_HOME>\scripts`) was added by the `WAuJ.py` profile.

```
C:/IBM/WebSphere/AppServer70/scriptLibraries/resources/Provider/V70
C:/IBM/WebSphere/AppServer70/scriptLibraries/security/V70
C:/IBM/WebSphere/AppServer70/scriptLibraries/servers/V70
C:/IBM/WebSphere/AppServer70/scriptLibraries/system/V70
C:/IBM/WebSphere/AppServer70/scriptLibraries/utilities/V70
C:\IBM\WebSphere\AppServer70\scripts
```
wsadmin>

Is there anything else? Oh, yeah. All of the Jython files in these directories are automatically imported during the **wsadmin** environment initialization. You can see this using the `dir()` command when **wsadmin** is first started, as shown in Listing 16.3.[5]

Listing 16.3 Autoloading of `scriptLibraries`

```
wsadmin>dir()
['AdminApp', 'AdminApplication', 'AdminAuthorizations', 'AdminBLA',
'AdminClusterManagement', 'AdminConfig', 'AdminControl', 'AdminJ2C',
'AdminJDBC', 'AdminJMS', 'AdminLibHelp', 'AdminNodeGroupManagement',
'AdminNodeManagement', 'AdminResources', 'AdminServerManagement',
'AdminTask', 'AdminUtilities', 'Help', 'TypedProxy', '__builtin__',
'__doc__', '__name__', 'bsf', 'imp', 'main', 'nested_scopes', 'sys',
'wasroot']
```
wsadmin>

Some of the items returned by the `dir()` command prove quite useful. For example, if you `print <moduleName>.__file__`, where `<moduleName>` is the name of the scripting library file, the result is the fully qualified path and filename to the file from which the code was imported. With having just looked at the scripting libraries directory structure, it should be no surprise to see from where these files were imported.

The steps outlined here illustrate the fact that all of the `*.py` files within these directories are automatically imported and are shown in Listing 16.4.

1. Create a trivial Jython file containing a function and save it in one of these directories, or you can even create a new subdirectory under `scriptLibraries` directory (lines 1–7).

2. Start an interactive **wsadmin** scripting environment (lines 8–11). Note how the `print` statements from the script file are displayed during the initialization phase of **wsadmin** (lines 10–11).

3. Use the `dir()` command to verify that the new module exists and contains the defined function (lines 14–17).

---

[5] Remember that both `nested_scopes` and `wasroot` were added by the `WAuJ.py` profile.

Listing 16.4   Example: Adding Your Own Library

```
 1|...\bin>type ..\scriptLibraries\Bob\bob.py
 2|print r'scriptLibraries\Bob\bob.py'
 3|
 4|  print '__name__ = "%s"' % __name__
 5|
 6|if __name__ == '__main__' or __name__ == 'main' :
 7|  print 'main(%s)' % __name__
 8|...\bin>wsadmin -conntype none -WAuJ
 9|WASX7357I: ...
10|scriptLibraries\Bob\bob.py
11|__name__ = "bob"
12|WASX7411W: Ignoring the following provided option: [-WAuJ]
13|WASX7031I: For help, enter: "print Help.help()"
14|wsadmin>'bob' in dir()
15|1
16|wsadmin>print bob.__file__
17|C:\IBM\WebSphere\AppServer70\scriptLibraries\Bob\bob.py
```

OK, this shows that you can "add your own" library modules and have them automatically loaded by **wsadmin** when it starts. In fact, you can also decide whether you want to include all, or even any, of the existing script libraries. If not, you only need to move, remove, or rename the files (so they no longer have an extension of .py).[6]

> **WARNING**   If you choose to do this, it will make your environment different from the one created as part of the product installation process. As such, it could potentially interfere with a future product update (such as installation of a Fix Pack or cumulative fix). Be sure to document any and all changes to the scriptLibraries directory and provide a process for reliably duplicating the expected and required environmental changes. It would also be reasonable to include a mechanism for verifying that the expected files and changes are in place and possibly restoring the original directory structure and contents prior to a product update.

This raises an interesting question, specifically, "What's the best way to make libraries available for a scripting environment?" Let's review the options:

1. You could specify a file as a command-line option when **wsadmin** is started, using, for example, something like **wsadmin** -profileName myLibrary.py ....

---

[6] Remember, though, that the *.py files are compiled to filename$py.class in the same directory, so these too need to be moved, removed, or renamed.

2. You could modify the appropriate **wsadmin**`.properties` file and include the fully qualified path and filename on the `com.ibm.ws.scripting.profiles` directive, as was suggested in Chapter 7, "Introduction to Admin Objects," where the `WAuJ.py` profile script was discussed.

3. You could create a new library file in an existing (or in a new) directory under `scriptLibraries`.

4. You could create a `scripts` directory under `<WAS_HOME>` and place the library files in it. This directory, if it exists, is added to the `sys.path` variable by the `WAuJ.py` profile script.[7]

   What's the difference between placing a module in this scripts directory and placing it in a subdirectory under `scriptLibraries`? The main difference is that during the initialization of **wsadmin**, only the files with an extension of `.py` under the `scriptLibraries` directory are automatically loaded (imported). Consequently, all of these modules and their objects become immediately available for use by your scripts. For modules in the scripts directory to be made available, just as with the library routines provided with Jython, one of the various `import` statements would need to be used.

Is this a big deal? To some, it can be. Some people and organizations prefer the simplified approach of not automatically loading library files. This means that before a library routine can be used, the presence of an `import` statement documents which library routines or objects will be used by a script. If you tend to execute many, small scripts and do not require the collection of script library files, then the overhead associated with the automatic loading might not be to your liking.

On the other hand, you or your organization might prefer to standardize a set of library routines and objects that must be available for your scripting environment. In this case, you might prefer to use, expand, or extend modules in the `scriptLibraries` directory structure.

Scripting Library Help

In Chapter 7, we used some scripts to display the help text for the **wsadmin** scripting objects. You can do the same sort of thing for the script library modules. Each module includes a `help()` method that can be used to:

- Display the help text and methods for the module (should the optional method/procedure name be unspecified) or
- Display the help text for a specific module method/procedure name (should a valid method/procedure name be provided).

We were hoping that it would be as useful as those seen earlier in Chapter 7. Unfortunately, the help text for the script library modules does not have as much detail about the parameters as expected. The parameters are not identified as required or optional, nor is any description about

---

[7] `WAuJ.py` was covered in the first section of Chapter 7.

the parameters provided. That's the bad news. The good news is that we have the source code to each of the library modules to examine should we need to understand the following:

- A specific parameter and whether it is required or optional
- How the parameters are used within the method
- The **wsadmin** scripting objects that are used to implement the method
- How the library method parameters are related to the scripting object method parameters

The script that was used to display all of the script library help text is available on the download page and is named `ScriptLibrariesHelp.py`. The sample output file that was generated when the script was run is also available from the download page and is named `ScriptLibrariesHelp.out`. Listing 16.5 shows one way to execute this script and some abbreviated output.[8]

One of the things that you can note about this script is how it refers to each of the script library modules as an object. This is true even though the library modules are written in Jython, instead of Java, which is pretty neat.

Because each of the library modules includes a help method, and each help method acts in the same way, the help methods for the library modules are not discussed here.

Listing 16.5   Example Output of `ScriptLibrariesHelp.py` Script

```
 1|...\bin>wsadmin -conntype none -WAuJ -f ScriptLibrariesHelp.py
 2|WASX7357I: ...
 3|#-------------------------------------------------------
 4|# AdminApplication.help()
 5|#-------------------------------------------------------
 6|WASL0001I: The AdminApplication script library provides script
 7|        procedures that configure, administer, and deploy ...
 8|
 9|        The AdminApplication script library provides the ...
10|
11|
12|Group 1: Install and uninstall applications
13|
```

Default Failure Action

Almost all of the script library methods have an optional last parameter called `failonerror` that has a default value of `'false'`, which is interpreted by each routine as an indication that errors

---

[8] If you choose to execute this script yourself, you are encouraged to redirect the output to a file because the output generates more than 4,000 lines of text.

should cause an exception to be thrown. If, instead, you prefer to have the library method terminate with a failure message, specify `'true'` for this value. Listing 16.6 shows an example use of the default `failonerror` parameter (lines 3–11), as well as what happens if a value of `'true'` is provided (lines 12–22). Note how the interactive **wsadmin** session is terminated by the uncaught exception.

Listing 16.6   Example Use of `failonerror`

```
 1|C:\IBM\WebSphere\AppServer70\bin>wsadmin -conntype none -WAuJ
 2|WASX7357I: ...
 3|wsadmin>print AdminApplication.checkIfAppExists('missing' )
 4|- - - - - - - - - - - - - - - - - - - - - - - - - - - - - - - -
 5| AdminApplication:      Check if application exists
 6| Application Name:      missing
 7| Usage: AdminApplication.checkIfAppExists("missing")
 8|- - - - - - - - - - - - - - - - - - - - - - - - - - - - - -
 9|
10|
11|false
12|wsadmin>AdminApplication.checkIfAppExists(None, 'true' )
13|- - - - - - - - - - - - - - - - - - - - - - - - - - - - - - - -
14| AdminApplication:      Check if application exists
15|DEBUG: getExceptionText(): typ=<class exceptions.TypeError ...
16|WARNING: getExceptionText(): value='<exceptions.TypeError  ...
17|DEBUG: getExceptionText(): stackdump='\'Traceback (innermos...
18|WARNING: getExceptionText(): Function= checkIfAppExists  Li...
19|
20|FAILURE: 'checkIfAppExists(None, \'true\'): <exceptions.Typ...
21|
22|Exiting.
```

Because this option parameter is on each and every one of the methods to be discussed, we won't describe it each and every time.

AdminApplication Script Library Module

Let's start by looking at the one of the library modules in more detail. The first in the list is `application\V70\AdminApplication.py`, the help for which identifies its role as "providing script procedures that configure, administer, and deploy applications."

One of the big differences between the script library files and the "other" **wsadmin** scripting objects is that you have access to the source code to see exactly how things are implemented.[9] One of the similarities is that like the **AdminTask** object, many of the script library methods are associated together into groups. For example, in the AdminApplication object, in both the source code comment block at the beginning of the file and in the help text, the 53 methods are associated into the following six command groups:

> Group 1: Install and uninstall applications (13 methods)
>
> Group 2: Queries application configurations (8 methods)
>
> Group 3: Update applications (14 methods)
>
> Group 4: Export applications (3 methods)
>
> Group 5: Configure application deployment (9 methods)
>
> Group 6: Administer applications (6 methods)

AdminApplication Group 1—Install and Uninstall Applications

Looking at either the comment block at the beginning of the source file or at the associated help text, you find the following methods in this group:

```
installAppModulesToDiffServersWithMapModulesToServersOption()
installAppModulesToDiffServersWithPatternMatching()
installAppModulesToMultiServersWithPatternMatching()
installAppModulesToSameServerWithMapModulesToServersOption()
installAppModulesToSameServerWithPatternMatching()
installAppWithClusterOption()
installAppWithDefaultBindingOption()
installAppWithDeployEjbOptions()
installAppWithNodeAndServerOptions()
installAppWithTargetOption()
installAppWithVariousTasksAndNonTasksOptions()
installWarFile()
uninstallApplication()
```

What do you notice about these method names? Some of them are extremely long! It would be very unlikely that anyone could type those long names without making at least one mistake. Thank goodness for copy and paste. The good news about the long names, though, is the fact that the purpose of the method is more likely to be understood just by looking at the method name.

Another thing that might catch your attention when you first look at these methods is the fact all of them have something to do with installing or removing an application. What do these

---

[9] **Warning**: Unfortunately, these script library files have some lines indented using spaces and others using tab characters. This is **not** a best practice, and a product defect has been opened to get this fixed. This warning is provided in case you use an editor that uses other than the "default" operating system tab stops.

methods do that the **AdminApp**.install() method does not? Nothing. In fact each of these methods uses the specified parameters to perform a specialized form of the **AdminApp**.install() method. That is what these scripting libraries are all about—showing you how you might want to build your own collection of specialized routines to perform actions for your environment in a way that conforms to your policies and procedures.

What other differences exist between these methods and those found in the other scripting objects? Unlike the other scripting objects, the scripting library methods:[10]

1. Display a message block with the method name and all specified parameter values.

2. Automatically save the configuration if the method changes the configuration.

3. Use positional parameters in the method signature, which forces all parameters to be specified in the statements where the methods are called.

4. Display a message, upon exit, indicating the success or failure of the requested action.

What does this message block look like? Listing 16.7 shows an example interactive session where one of the AdminApplication install methods gets invoked. Please note that this example does something that I do not expect you to do, which is assign a reference to the function to be called to a variable (fun, for example). The only reason for using this technique in this example was to shorten the statement where the function was called to fit on a single line in this book without having the line wrapped.

Listing 16.7   Sample AdminApplication.install

```
wsadmin>print AdminConfig.list('Server' )
server1(cells/ragibsonNode02Cell/nodes/ragibsonNode03/servers/...
wsadmin>from WAuJ_utilities import ConfigIdAsDict
wsadmin>sDict = ConfigIdAsDict(AdminConfig.list('Server' ) )
wsadmin>svrName, nodeName = sDict[ 'Name' ], sDict[ 'nodes' ]
wsadmin>appName  = 'myApp'
wsadmin>earFile  = r'C:\referenceWEBEAR.ear'
wsadmin>fun = AdminApplication.installAppWithNodeAndServerOptions
wsadmin>fun(appName, earFile, nodeName, svrName )
- - - - - - - - - - - - - - - - - - - - - - - - - - - - - - - - - - - - - - - - -
  AdminApplication:        Install application with -node and ...
  Application name:        myApp
  Ear file to deploy:      C:\referenceWEBEAR.ear
  Node name:               ragibsonNode03
  Server name:             server1
  Usage: AdminApplication.installAppWithNodeAndServerOptions(...
```

---

[10] Other than the help() method, which returns the appropriate help text.

```
. . .
ADMA5013I: Application myApp installed successfully.
OK: installAppWithNodeAndServerOptions('myApp', 'C:\\referen...
```

The good thing about the installation methods in the `AdminApplication` module is that they show how easy it can be to develop modules and methods that suit your particular needs. If your workplace has guidelines for applications, they can be implemented and enforced by library methods such as these. For example, you might be asked to use a specific set of installation options or even use a particular naming convention for items. With scripting libraries like these, you can enforce any kind of protocol or convention that is appropriate for your team, organization, or business.

Yet another thing to consider is the value of grouping related methods together in a module. In the case of this group of methods in the `AdminApplication` module, almost all of them can be used to install an application. The only method that is not is the one that can be used to remove an application (`AdminApplication.uninstallApplication()`, for example). Because the application already exists, the only parameter that needs to be provided is the name of the application to be removed.

Looking at the code used to implement the `uninstallApplication()` method, you can see exactly how it does its job:

1. It verifies that the `appName` parameter value is not an empty string.
2. It verifies that the specified application is a deployed object (using the **AdminConfig**.`getid()` method).
3. A message banner is displayed that identifies the task being performed and the values being used to do the job.
4. It uses the **AdminApp**.`uninstall()` method to remove the application.
5. It uses the **AdminConfig**.`save()` method to save the configuration changes.
6. A status message is displayed indicating the success or failure of the task.

Almost all of the methods in the script library modules follow this same format. Those methods with more parameters require more instructions to verify that every required parameter is valid, but the concept is the same. One of the really nice things about the fact that these library modules is that should you decide that you do not like something (for example, the ubiquitous banner messages that get displayed by each library method), you have a number of options:

1. You could edit the script library files (for example, to remove or disable the messages).[11]
2. You could create your own library files containing the same methods but in a different library files that have your own versions of the code (such as without the messages).

---

[11] This is not recommended because the script library files could be replaced during some product update.

This option has definite possibilities because these would be "new" library files and
would be unlikely to be replaced by a product update.

3. You could delete the `scriptLibraries` directory and all of its contents. This option
    appeals to some because of the reduced number of module imports to be performed dur-
    ing the **wsadmin** initialization phase.

4. You could leave the `scriptLibraries` in place but not make use of any of the library
    files or the methods contained therein. This option appeals to those interested in devel-
    oping their own script libraries, using their own standards and practices.

AdminApplication Group 2—Query Application Configurations

The variety of tasks performed by this group of methods is a bit more diverse than the previous
group. However, the method names again are quite straightforward:

```
checkIfAppExists()
getAppDeployedNodes()
getAppDeploymentTarget()
getTaskInfoForAnApp()
help()
listApplications()
listApplicationsWithTarget()
listModulesInAnApp()
```

The `checkIfAppExists()` method is also easily understood. Given an application name, it
uses the **AdminConfig**.`getid()` method to see if an application of this name exists in the configuration as having been deployed. If so, the method returns `true`; otherwise, `false`.[12]

Sometimes, though, a scripting library method can be surprising. For example, if the
`AdminApplication.getAppDeployedNodes()` method is called with the name of a
deployed application, the result is a list of the nodes on which the application is deployed.[13] So
far, so good. We were very surprised, however, when we called the same method and specified the
name of a non-existent application. We expected an empty list to be returned. Unfortunately, an
exception was thrown. So here is an example of multiple ways to handle the same situation. If
you choose to use the script libraries, you are going to have to write your programs to deal with
the way that these methods handle "error" conditions. If you write your own library methods, you
might decide that for your organization, a different implementation might be more appropriate.

---

[12] In addition to `true` and `false`, there is a possibility of -1 being returned should an error be encountered. In addition, an exception may also be raised. So you might want to consider calling these methods within a `try/except`
statement.

[13] Unfortunately, there is a mistake in the code. In `AdminApplication` on line 4336, the value to be appended
should be `nodeName`, instead of `node`. So, if the `getAppDeployedNodes()` method is called to display the nodes
on which an application is deployed, and the application is deployed on a cluster, a `NameError` exception will be
generated.

Similarly, the `AdminApplication.getAppDeploymentTarget()` method can be used to determine the deployment target attribute for an application. What does that mean? Well, under the covers, this method uses the **`AdminConfig`**`.getid()` method to verify that the specified application has been deployed and at the same time get the `configID` of the deployment configuration object for this application. Then, the **`AdminConfig`**`.showAttribute()` method is used to obtain the deployment targets attribute for this given `configID`. And finally, the returned value is converted to a list.

The `list*()` methods in this group (*i.e.,* `listApplications()`, `listApplications WithTarget()`, and `listModulesInAnApp()`) are very similar to each other. The first, `list Applications()` needs no parameters and simply uses **`AdminApp`**`.list()` to generate the list of deployed applications. The main difference between these two methods is that **`AdminApp`**`.list()` returns a string, and `AdminApplication.listApplications()` returns a list of strings (as well as printing out information about the specific method that was called).

The next method, `listApplicationsWithTarget()`, can be used to list the deployed applications on a specific node. You need only to specify the node name and server name parameters. The last, `listModulesInAnApp()`, can be used to list the modules in a given application. If you want to find the module information for a specific application that is not deployed upon a specific server, specify the second parameter (such as `serverName`) as an empty string (`' '`).

AdminApplication Group 3—Update Applications

It should be relatively easy to guess what kind of methods would be put into this group given the two-word abstract:

```
updateApplicationUsingDefaultMerge()
updateApplicationWithUpdateIgnoreNewOption()
updateApplicationWithUpdateIgnoreOldOption()
addSingleFileToAnAppWithUpdateCommand()
updateSingleFileToAnAppWithUpdateCommand()
deleteSingleFileToAnAppWithUpdateCommand()
addSingleModuleFileToAnAppWithUpdateCommand()
updateSingleModuleFileToAnAppWithUpdateCommand()
addUpdateSingleModuleFileToAnAppWithUpdateCommand
deleteSingleModuleFileToAnAppWithUpdateCommand()
addPartialAppToAnAppWithUpdateCommand()
updatePartialAppToAnAppWithUpdateCommand()
deletePartialAppToAnAppWithUpdateCommand()
updateEntireAppToAnAppWithUpdateCommand()
```

The `updateApplicationUsingDefaultMerge()` method performs a simple call to the **`AdminApp`**`.install()` method, specifying the `'-update'` and `'-appName'` options. So the only parameters needed by this method are the name of the EAR file and the name of the existing application.

The updateApplicationWithUpdateIgnoreNewOption() method makes sense if you are familiar with the update.ignore.new **AdminApp** installation option. This option is applicable for the **AdminApp**.install() method, as long as the 'update' option is specified, and the item being updated is a module file or an application. It requests that bindings from the new version of the item being updated are ignored, thus leaving existing (configured) bindings intact.

The updateApplicationWithUpdateIgnoreOldOption() method is very similar and only differs from the preceding method in that the 'update.ignore.old' option is used so that existing (configured) bindings are overridden by those in the new version of the item being updated.

The addSingleFileToAnAppWithUpdateCommand() method shows how to call the **AdminApp**.update() method and add a file with associated contentURI, a specified application. The updateSingleFileToAnAppWithUpdateCommand() method acts in a very similar fashion and is used to update (replace) an existing file within a specific application. And the deleteSingleFileToAnAppWithUpdateCommand() method[14] does what you probably suspect and removes the specified file from the indicated application.

The next few methods deal with a single module file within an application:

```
addSingleModuleFileToAnAppWithUpdateCommand()
updateSingleModuleFileToAnAppWithUpdateCommand()
addUpdateSingleModuleFileToAnAppWithUpdateCommand()
deleteSingleModuleFileToAnAppWithUpdateCommand()
```

The first of these, the addSingleModuleFileToAnAppWithUpdateCommand() method, as the name implies, adds a single module file to an existing application using the **AdminApp**.update() method (command). The parameters of this method are as follows:

- The application name
- The fully qualified path and file name to be added
- The URI of the content

Looking at the implemen.ation of the method, however, it is surprising to see that the BindJndiForEJBNonMessageBinding option is being used. The next method, updateSingleModuleFileToAnAppWithUpdateCommand(), is used in a similar fashion to update a single module file within an application using the **AdminApp**.update() method. Again, looking at the implementation, it is surprising to see the use of the DataSourceFor20EJBModules option by this routine.

The next method, addUpdateSingleModuleFileToAnAppWithUpdateCommand(), makes use of the addupdate operation to either add a module file, if it does not exist within the application, or to update a module file if present within the application. Interestingly enough, this method does not include any unexpected **AdminApp**.update() options in the routine.

You can use the last of these four methods, deleteSingleModuleFileToAnApp With-UpdateCommand(), to remove a single module file from an application. To do so, you

---

[14] I'm surprised that these grammatically incorrect names are used. I would have thought that they would be named something like updateSingleFileInAnAppWithUpdateCommand() and deleteSingleFileFromAnAppWithUpdate Command().

must provide the application name, the fully qualified path and filename, and the content URI for the specific file within the application.

The next few methods deal with manipulating (that is, adding, updating, or deleting) partial applications to a deployed application. To do this, an input archive file (normally with a `zip` extension) must be prepared. Then, one of the following methods should be executed:

- `addPartialAppToAnAppWithUpdateCommand()`
- `updatePartialAppToAnAppWithUpdateCommand()`
- `deletePartialAppToAnAppWithUpdateCommand()`

The `addPartialAppToAnAppWithUpdateCommand()` method uses the contents of the specified archive file to add things to a specific application. To do this, only the name of the application to be updated and the (fully qualified) name of the input archive file need to be specified.

Likewise, the `updatePartialAppToAnAppWithUpdateCommand()` method will also use the **AdminApp**.`update()` method to modify existing portions of a particular application. It does so using the contents of the specified archive file, and the `deletePartialAppToAnApp WithUpdateCommand()` method uses the specified archive file to remove parts of an existing application.

The last method in this group, that is, `updateEntireAppToAnAppWithUpdate Command()`, also uses the **AdminApp**.`update()` method and an input archive file to modify an existing application. However, it's not certain why it was decided that the following options be included on this call:

```
usedefaultbindings
nodeployejb
MapWebModToVH
```

AdminApplication Group 4—Export Applications

This is the smallest group within the `AdminApplication` library and contains only three methods:

- `exportAnAppToFile()`
- `exportAllApplicationsToDir()`
- `exportAnAppDDLToDir()`

The first of these, `exportAnAppToFile()`, can be used to export the contents of an application to an archive file. To use this method, you need only specify the name of a deployed application and the fully qualified path to the archive file to be created.

The next method, `exportAllApplicationsToDir()`, is even simpler to use. It only needs to be passed the fully qualified path to a directory into which all of the applications will be exported as archive files, each having an extension of `*.ear`.

The last method in this group, `exportAnAppDDLToDir()`, is a simple wrapper to the **AdminApp**.`exportDDL()` method, which lets you export the data definition language (DDL) from a specified application to a specific directory of your choice.

AdminApplication Group 5—Configure Application Deployment

The penultimate `AdminApplication` group deals specifically with the configuration of different parts of deployed applications. Some of these methods show how an individual attribute of a configured item can be modified. For example, the `configureStartingWeightForAn Application()` method can be used to change the starting weight attribute for a specific application. As you might expect, the only values needed by the method are the application name and the starting weight. Unfortunately, the method does not check, or properly handle, the situation where a numeric `startingWeight` is specified by the user. So instead of "doing the reasonable thing," the following, cryptic, error message is displayed:[15]

```
Exception:  exceptions.TypeError  __add__  nor  __radd__  defined for
these operands
```

So in order to use these scripting library routines, be sure that you are going to provide (pass in) values of the appropriate datatype. If you are going to be writing your own methods, it would be wise to include tests for "reasonable datatypes" and to handle them appropriately.

Likewise, the following methods may be used to assign new values for specific application attributes. Unfortunately, each of these methods does minimal parameter checking,[16] so use them with caution:

1. `configureClassLoaderPolicyForAnApplication()`—Can be used to modify the `'warClassLoaderPolicy'` attribute for a deployed application. The only valid settings are `"SINGLE"` and `"MULTIPLE"`.

2. `configureClassLoaderLoadingModeForAnApplication()`—Can be used to modify the `classloader` loading `'mode'` attribute for a deployed application. The only valid settings are `"PARENT_FIRST"` and `"PARENT_LAST"`.

3. `configureApplicationLoading()`—Can be used to modify the `'enable'` value for the `'targetMappings'` attribute of a deployed application. Only `true` or `false` should be specified.

4. `configureLibraryReferenceForAnApplication()`—Create a shared library reference (such as `'LibraryRef'`) for a deployed application.

The next set of methods in this group has a few parameters in addition to the name of a specific application for which the configuration changes are intended.

1. `configureEJBModulesOfAnApplication()`—This method can be used to specify the `startingWeight`, and indicate whether or not the EBJ Modules should be enabled for the specified application.

---

[15] The reason this exception gets generated is because the method includes code to display the parameter values and to do so has each parameter name displayed and tries to use the string concatenation operator (`'+'`) to concatenate the parameter name with the parameter value. Unfortunately, this operator does not allow a number to be concatenated to a string; only two strings may be concatenated.

[16] A test is made to see if the parameter is an empty string or not. A non-empty string is "presumed valid."

2. `configureWebModulesOfAnApplication()`—This method can be used to specify the `startingWeight`, and the `classloader` mode (for example, `'PARENT_FIRST'` or `'PARENT_LAST'`) for a specific web module of a specific application.

3. `configureConnectorModulesOfAnApplication()`—This method can be used to configure the following connector module attributes for a specific application:

   - `j2cconnFactory`
   - `jndiName`
   - `authDataAlias`
   - `connTimeout`

The last method in this group has been saved for last because it is significantly different from the other methods in the group due to the number of parameters it requires. The `configure SessionManagementForAnApplication()` method creates a `sessionManagement` object, with all of its attributes, for a specified application. That's why the method has so many parameters, one for each `sessionManagement` attribute. Unfortunately, like the other methods in this group, this method does minimal checking on the parameter values. Each parameter value is checked to verify that it is not an empty string.[17] If you need this kind of capability, you might need to write some functions that allow you to create and modify individual `sessionManagement` attributes for an application.

AdminApplication Group 6—Start/Stop Applications

The last group of methods can be used to start or stop applications. The first of these methods, `startApplicationOnSingleServer()`, can be used to start an application on a single application server. The good news is that it includes checks for things such as the following:

- Is the application already running?
- Is the application manager active? (If it is not, then applications can't be stopped or started.)

Unfortunately, along with the good news, there appears to be some bad news: The user is required to specify the `nodeName` for the specified application server. This makes sense if the script is connected to a Deployment Manager, but not if the connection is to an unmanaged node.

These methods can be used to start or stop an application on various application servers. Fortunately, the names are explicit enough for you to discern which method to use based upon your specific need.

---

[17] This is really unfortunate because the online documentation (http://publib.boulder.ibm.com/infocenter/wasinfo/v7r0/index.jsp?topic=/com.ibm.websphere.base.doc/info/aes/ae/rxml_7libapp4.html) indicates that the **enableSSLTracking** attribute has been deprecated and suggests that an empty string be specified.

```
startApplicationOnSingleServer()
startApplicationOnAllDeployedTargets()
stopApplicationOnSingleServer()
stopApplicationOnAllDeployedTargets()
startApplicationOnCluster()
stopApplicationOnCluster()
```

For both the `startApplicationOnSingleServer()` and the `stopApplicationOnSingle`
`Server()` methods, you need to provide the application name, the node name, and the server
name. For the `startApplicationOnAllDeployedTargets()` and the `stopApplication`
`OnAllDeployedTargets()` methods, you only need to specify the application name and the
server name. Similarly, for the `startApplicationOnCluster()` and the `stopApplication`
`OnCluster()` methods, you only need specify the application name and the cluster name.

Business-Level Applications (AdminBLA)

The next script library module deals with business-level applications, which are a new concept in
version 7.0 of the product. A business-level application is a configuration entity, similar to an
enterprise application, that can be used to hold the definition of an application from a business
perspective. One of the scripting library files, `AdminBLA.py`,[18] contains a group of methods that
can be used to create, manipulate, and delete business-level application related items.

The `help()` method was described in general terms in the "Scripting Library Help" section, so we do not need to discuss it again. The remainder of the methods in the AdminBLA
library module deal with one of the following types of BLA-related items:

> **Business-Level Applications (BLA) Asset**—An asset represents one or more (binary)
> application files that are stored in an asset repository.

> **CompUnit**—A composition unit represents an asset in the BLA. A CompUnit enables
> the asset contents to interact with other assets in the BLA. It also enables the BLA run-
> time to load and execute asset contents.

The BLA-related methods in this library module are as follows:

- `listBLAs(blaName='', includeDescription='')`—This easily understood method
  can be used to either list all of the business-level applications (if no parameters are specified)
  or a single BLA (if the BLA name is specified). A second optional (boolean) parameter can be
  used to include the BLA description in the result (should one exist).

  The result is a list of string values. Each BLA name will start with `'WebSphere:`
  `blaname='`. If the request specifies that descriptions should also be included, then
  descriptions that exist will follow the BLA name in the list. So if you are going to

---

[18] Remember that the file can be found under the `scriptLibraries` directory under the WebSphere Application
Server installation directory, e.g., `<WAS_HOME>\scriptLibraries\application\V70\AdminBLA.py`.

process the list of all BLA names, be prepared to handle the BLA entries for which no description exists.

- `createEmptyBLA(blaName, description='')`—This method can be used to create a new BLA and specify an optional description for it. The first parameter is required and specifies the name of the BLA to be created. This method will either return a string containing the BLA configuration ID, or an exception will be raised if the specified BLA can't be created (for example, if the specified BLA name already exists or an invalid name was specified).

- `deleteBLA(blaName)`—This method has only one required parameter, which is the name of the BLA to be removed. The result of calling this method will either be a string containing the configuration ID of the BLA that was deleted, or an exception will be raised to indicate an error occurred.

- `startBLA(blaName)`—This method has only one required parameter, which is the name of the BLA to be started. The result of calling this method will either be a string containing a message indicating that the BLA that was started successfully (even if the BLA was previously started), or an exception will be raised to indicate an error occurred.

- `stopBLA(blaName)`—This method has only one required parameter, which is the name of the BLA to be stopped. The result of calling this method will either be a string containing a message indicating that the BLA that was stopped successfully (even if the BLA was previously stopped), or an exception will be raised to indicate an error occurred.

The Asset-related methods in this library module are as follows:

- `importAsset(sourcePath, storageType='')`—This method has only one required parameter; that is, the (complete, or fully qualified) `sourcePath` (path and filename) to the asset file to be imported into the domain configuration. The optional parameter is used to identify what information from the specified file should be saved in the asset repository. The allowed values are as follows:

  - `'FULL'`—Stores the complete binaries from the source file (this is the default value).
  - `'METADATA'`—Stores only the metadata portion of the binary files.
  - `'NONE'`—Stores no binaries in the asset repository.

- `exportAsset(assetID, fileName)`—This method has two required parameters—the name of the asset to be exported and the name of the destination file into which the asset information should be written.

- `editAsset(assetID, description, destinationURL, typeAspect, relationship, filePermission, validate)`—This method is used to modify options specified when the asset was imported. It has seven required parameters, which makes it one of the most complex methods in the scripting libraries. Unfortunately, the banner message displayed by this method says that only the `assetID` is required, but this is not the case. If less than seven parameters are specified, an error message is displayed indicating that seven parameters are required.[19] The parameters to this routine are as follows:

- `assetID`—Specifies the name of the asset to be modified.
- `description`—Specifies new descriptive text to be associated with the asset.
- `destinationURL`—Specifies a new destination URL to be associated with the asset.
- `typeAspect`—Specifies a new type aspect to be associated with the asset.
- `relationship`—Specifies a new asset relationship.
- `filePermission`—Specifies a new asset `filePermission` configuration.
- `validate`—Specifies whether the asset should be validated (`true`), or not (`false`, the default).

- `listAssets(assetID='', includeDescription='', includeDeployUnit='')`— This method has no required parameters. If specified, the `assetID` is the name of the asset to be listed. If this parameter is empty, all registered assets are listed. The other two optional parameters are boolean values, and each defaults to `false`. If the `includeDescription` parameter is specified as `true`, the asset description is returned (should one exist). If the `includeDeployUnit` parameter is specified as `true`, information about the deployable units within the asset are returned.[20]

- `deleteAsset(assetID)`—This method is used to remove the specified asset from the asset repository. The parameter is required and must exist. The fully qualified `assetID` is returned to indicate that the removal operation was a success.

- `viewAsset(assetID)`—This method is used to display the asset settings stored in the repository. Only the asset name, or ID, is allowed, and it must be specified.

The methods in the `AdminBLA` library module related to composition units are as follows:

- `addCompUnit(blaName, cuSourceID, deployUnits, cuName, cuDescription, startingWeight, server, activationPlan)`—This method is used to add a composition unit to a specific BLA. It has eight required parameters, even though the banner message displayed by this method says that only the `blaName` and `cuSourceID` are required. The parameters to this routine are as follows:

  - `blaName`—The name of the BLA to which the composition unit is to be added.
  - `cuSourceID`—The configuration ID of the composition unit to be added.
  - `deployUnits`—The name of the deployable unit for the asset.

---

[19] If the author of the method had actually wanted there to be optional parameters, then a default value should have been specified for each (e.g., `description=" "`). A product defect has been opened to get this issue corrected.

[20] Remember that Jython has a really nice feature where you can use keywords to assign a single optional parameter by name, rather than by position. For example, you could execute a command such as `AdminBLA.listAssets (includeDescription='true')`.

- `cuName`—The name of the composition unit to be added.
- `cuDescription`—The descriptive text for the composition unit to be added.
- `startingWeight`—The starting weight of the composition unit to be added.
- `server`—The name of the server to which the composition unit is to be mapped.
- `activationPlan`—Specifies the activation plan runtime components.

- `listCompUnits(blaName, includeDescription='')`—This method can be used to list the composition units associated with a specific business-level application. The second, optional (boolean) parameter can be used to indicate that the description should be included.

- `editCompUnit(blaName, compUnitID, cuDescription, startingWeight, server, activationPlan)`—This method is used to modify the options specified when the composition unit was created. All six parameters are required. The parameters to this routine are as follows:

  - `blaName`—The name of the BLA with which the composition unit is associated.
  - `compUnitID`—The configuration ID of the composition unit.
  - `cuDescription`—The descriptive text for the composition unit.
  - `startingWeight`—The starting weight of the composition unit.
  - `server`—The name of the server to which the composition unit is to be mapped.
  - `activationPlan`—The activation plan runtime components.

- `deleteCompUnit(blaName, compUnitID)`—This method is used to remove the specified composition unit from the indicated BLA.

- `viewCompUnit(blaName, compUnitID)`—This method is used to display information about the specific composition unit associated with the indicated BLA.

Java 2 Connector (AdminJ2C) Library Module

This library module contains methods related to J2C resources. The three types of operations associated with these types of resources are list, install, and create.

You will be better able to understand the differences between these operations when we take a look at the methods. Because we have already discussed the `help` method, the next easiest to understand are the ones used to list or display information about J2C resources. These methods are as follows:

- `listMessageListenerTypes(j2cRAConfigID)`—This method can be used to list the message listener types associated with the required J2C Resource Adapter identified.

- `listConnectionFactoryInterfaces(j2cRAConfigID)`—In the same way, this method can be used to list the connection factory interfaces associated with the required J2C Resource Adapter identified.

- `listAdminObjectInterfaces(j2cRAConfigID)`—Similarly, this method can be used to list the administrative object interfaces associated with the required J2C Resource Adapter identified.

- `listJ2CResourceAdapters(j2cRAName='')`—This method can be used to list all of the configured J2C Resource Adapters (if no parameter is specified) or to list a specific one given a Resource Adapter Name.

- `listJ2CConnectionFactories(j2cRAConfigID, cfInterface)`—This method can be used to list the J2C connection factories associated with a specific (required) J2C Resource Adapter configuration ID and the (also required) connection factory interface name.

- `listJ2CActivationSpecs(j2cRAConfigID, msgListenerType)`—This method can be used to list the J2C activation specifications associated with a specific (required) J2C Resource Adapter configuration ID, and a specific (required) message listener type.

- `listJ2CAdminObjects(j2cRAConfigID, aoInterface)`—This method can be used to list the J2C administration objects associated with a specific (required) J2C Resource Adapter configuration ID and a specific (required) administration object interface.

- `installJ2CResourceAdapter(nodeName, rarPath, J2CRAName, otherAttrs-List=[])`—This method can be used to install a J2C Resource Adapter to the configuration. The `nodeName`, `rarPath`, and `J2CRAName` parameters are required and specify the name of the node with which the resource adapter is to be associated, the fully qualified path of the RAR file to be installed, and the name of the J2C Resource Adapter to be installed.

The last parameter is optional and can be used to provide a collection of name, value pairs to be used during the installation of the resource adapter.

- `createJ2CConnectionFactory(j2cRAConfigID, j2cCFName, cfInterface, jndiName, otherAttrsList=[])`—This method can be used to create a J2C connection factory. The first four parameters are required and specify the following:

  - The J2C Resource Adapter configuration ID
  - The J2C Connection Factory Name
  - The Connection Factory interface
  - The JNDI Name

The last parameter is optional and can be used to provide a collection of name, value pairs to be used during the creation of the connection factory.

- `createJ2CActivationSpec(j2cRAConfigID, j2cASName, msgListenerType, jndiName, otherAttrsList=[])`—This method is used to create a J2C Activation Specification. The first four parameters are required and specify the following:

- The J2C Resource Adapter configuration ID
- The J2C Activation Specification Name
- The Connection Factory interface
- The JNDI Name

The last parameter is optional and can be used to provide a collection of name, value pairs to be used during the creation of the activation specification.

- `createJ2CAdminObject(j2cRAConfigID, j2cAOName, aoInterface, jndiName, otherAttrsList=[])`—This method is used to create a J2C Administrative Object. The first four parameters are required and specify the following:
  - The J2C Resource Adapter configuration ID
  - The J2C Administrative Object Name
  - The Administrative Object interface
  - The JNDI Name

The last parameter is optional and can be used to provide a collection of name, value pairs to be used during the creation of the activation specification.

AdminJDBC Library Module

This library module contains methods for performing `DataSource` and `JDBCProvider`-related tasks. Some of the methods can be used to query information about these kinds of resources, and the remainder can be used to create these kinds of resources. The query methods are as follows:

- `listDataSources(datasourceName="")`—This method can be used to list one or all the configured `DataSource` configuration IDs. If no name is specified, then the result is a list of all of the configured `DataSource` configIDs. If a single `DataSource` name is specified, only it is used to query if the resource exists. The result could be an empty list.

- `listDataSourceTemplates(templateName="")`—This method can be used to list one or all of the configured `DataSource` Template IDs. If no name is specified, then the result is a list of all the configured `DataSource` Template IDs. If a single template name is specified, only it is used to query if the resource exists. The result might be an empty list.

- `listJDBCProviders(JDBCName="")`—This method can be used to list one or all of the configured `JDBCProvider` configIDs. If no name is specified, the result is a list of all the configured provider IDs. If a single provider name is specified, only it is used to query if the resource exists. The result might be an empty list.

- `listJDBCProviderTemplates(templateName="")`—This method can be used to list one or all the configured `JDBCProvider` template object IDs. If no name is specified, the result is a list of all the configured template object IDs. If a single template name is specified, only it is used to query if the resource exists. The result might be an empty list.

The creation-related methods are the following:

- `createDataSource(nodeName, serverName, JDBCName, datasourceName, otherAttrsList=[])`—This method can be used to create a `DataSource` and has the following required parameters:
  - `nodeName`—Defines the name of the node on which this resource is to be created.
  - `serverName`—Defines the name of the server on which this resource is to be created.
  - `JDBCName`—Defines the JDBC provided to be used for the creation.
  - `datasourceName`—Defines the name of the `DataSource` to be created.

In addition, an optional parameter, `otherAttrsList`, is provided that allows other attributes that are used for the creation of the resource to be specified.

- `createDataSourceUsingTemplate(nodeName, serverName, JDBCName, templateID, datasourceName, otherAttrsList=[])`—Similarly, this method can be used to create a DataSource using an existing DataSource Template ID and has the following required parameters:
  - `nodeName`—Defines the name of the node on which this resource is to be created.
  - `serverName`—Defines the name of the server on which this resource is to be created.
  - `JDBCName`—Defines the JDBC provided to be used for the creation.
  - `templateID`—Defines the template ID to be used for the creation.
  - `datasourceName`—Defines the name of the `DataSource` to be created.

In addition, an optional parameter, `otherAttrsList`, is provided that allows other attributes that are used for the creation of the resource to be specified.

- `createJDBCProvider(nodeName, serverName, JDBCName, implClassName, otherAttrsList=[])`—This method can be used to create a `JDBCProvider` and has the following required parameters:
  - `nodeName`—Defines the name of the node on which this resource is to be created.
  - `serverName`—Defines the name of the server on which this resource is to be created.
  - `JDBCName`—Defines the JDBC provided to be created.
  - `implClassName`—Defines the name of the implementation class to be used for the creation.

In addition, an optional parameter, `otherAttrsList`, is provided that allows other attributes that are used for the creation of the resource to be specified.

- `createJDBCProviderUsingTemplate(nodeName, serverName, templateID, JDBCName, implClassName, otherAttrsList=[])`—Similarly, this method can be used to create a `JDBCProvider` using an existing `JDBCProvider` Template ID and has the following required parameters:
  - `nodeName`—Defines the name of the node on which this resource is to be created.

- `serverName`—Defines the name of the server on which this resource is to be created.
- `templateID`—Defines the ID of the template to be used for the creation request.
- `JDBCName`—Defines the JDBC provided to be used for the creation.
- `implClassName`—Defines the name of the implementation class to be used for the creation.

In addition, an optional parameter, `otherAttrsList`, is provided that allows other attributes that are to be used for the creation of the resource to be specified.

AdminJMS Library Module

This library module contains methods that can be used to query or configure Java Messaging Service (JMS)-related items:

- `listJMSProviderTemplates(templateName="")`—This method can be used to list the configured `JMSProvider` templates. If no template name is provided, all of the configured template IDs are returned in a list. If a name is specified, a list is returned with the matching template IDs if any exist.

- `listGenericJMSConnectionFactoryTemplates(templateName="")`—This met hod can be used to list the generic JMS connection factory templates. If no template name is provided, all of the configured template IDs are returned in a list. If a template name is specified, a list is returned with the matching template IDs if any exist.

- `listGenericJMSDestinationTemplates(templateName="")`—This   method can be used to list the generic JMS destination templates. If no template name is provided, all of the configured template IDs are returned in a list. If a template name is specified, a list is returned with the matching template IDs if any exist.

- `listWASQueueTemplates(templateName="")`—This method can be used to list the WebSphere Application Server queue templates. If no template name is provided, all of the configured template IDs are returned in a list. If a template name is specified, a list is returned with the matching template IDs if any exist.

- `listWASQueueConnectionFactoryTemplates(templateName="")`—This method can be used to list the WebSphere Application Server queue connection factory templates. If no template name is provided, all of the configured template IDs is returned in a list. If a template name is specified, a list is returned with the matching template IDs if any exist.

- `listWASTopicTemplates(templateName="")`—This method can be used to list the WebSphere Application Server topic templates. If no template name is provided, all of the configured template IDs are returned in a list. If a template name is specified, a list is returned with the matching template IDs if any exist.

- `listWASTopicConnectionFactoryTemplates(templateName="")`—This method can be used to list the WebSphere Application Server topic connection factory templates. If no template name is provided, all of the configured template IDs are returned in a list. If a template name is specified, a list is returned with the matching template IDs if any exist.

- `listJMSProviders(JMSProviderName="")`—This method can be used to list the configured JMS providers. If no provider name is provided, all of the configured provider IDs are returned in a list. If a provider name is specified, a list is returned with the matching provider IDs if any exist.

- `listGenericJMSConnectionFactories(JMSCFName="")`—This method can be used to list the generic JMS connection factory IDs. If no JMS connection factory name is provided, all of the configured factory IDs are returned in a list. If a connection factory name is specified, a list is returned with the matching factory IDs if any exist.

- `listGenericJMSDestinations(JMSDestName="")`—This method can be used to list the generic JMS destination IDs. If no destination name is provided, all of the configured destination IDs are returned in a list. If a destination name is specified, a list is returned with the matching destination IDs if any exist.

- `listWASQueues(WASQueueName="")`—This method can be used to list the WebSphere Application Server queue IDs. If no queue name is provided, all of the configured queue IDs are returned in a list. If a queue name is specified, a list is returned with the matching queue ID if one exists.

- `listWASQueueConnectionFactories(WASQueueCFName="")`—This method can be used to list the WebSphere Application Server queue connection factory IDs. If no queue connection factory name is provided, all of the configured IDs are returned in a list. If a queue connection factory name is specified, a list is returned with the matching queue connection factory ID, if one exists.

- `listWASTopics(WASTopicName="")`—This method can be used to list the WebSphere Application Server topics. If no topic name is provided, all of the configured topic IDs are returned in a list. If a topic name is specified, a list is returned with the matching topic ID if one exists.

- `listWASTopicConnectionFactories(WASTopicCFName="")`—This method can be used to list the WebSphere Application Server topic connection factory IDs. If no topic connection factory name is provided, all of the configured IDs are returned in a list. If a topic connection factory name is specified, a list is returned with the matching ID, if one exists.

- `listJMSConnectionFactories(jmscfName="")`—This method can be used to list the configured JMS connection factory IDs. If no connection factory name is provided, all of the configured IDs are returned in a list. If a JMS connection factory name is specified, a list is returned with the matching ID, if one exists.

- `listJMSDestinations(jmsdestName="")`—This method can be used to list the configured JMS destination IDs. If no destination name is provided, all of the configured IDs are returned in a list. If a JMS destination name is specified, a list is returned with the matching ID, if one exists.

- createJMSProvider(nodeName, serverName, JMSProviderName, extInit-ContextFactory, extProviderURL, otherAttrsList=[])—This method can be used to create a JMS provider. The five required parameters are as follows:
  - nodeName—Defines the node on which the provider is to be created.
  - serverName—Defines the server on which the provider is to be created.
  - JMSProviderName—Defines the name of the provider to be created.
  - extInitContextFactory—Defines the Java class name of the initial context factory.
  - extProviderURL—Defines the provider URL for external JNDI lookups.

The optional parameter, otherAttrsList, can be used to specify name/value pairs of values to be used during the resource creation.

- createJMSProviderUsingTemplate(nodeName, serverName, templateID, JMSProviderName, extInitContextFactory, extProviderURL, other-AttrsList=[])—This method can be used to create a JMS provider using a pre-existing template ID. The required parameters are as follows:
- nodeName—Defines the node on which the provider is to be created.
  - serverName—Defines the server on which the provider is to be created.
  - templateID—Defines the template ID to be used during the creation.
  - JMSProviderName—Defines the name of the provider to be created.
  - extInitContextFactory—Defines the Java class name of the initial context factory.
  - extProviderURL—Defines the provider URL for external JNDI lookups.

The optional parameter, otherAttrsList, can be used to specify name/value pairs of values to be used during the resource creation.

- createGenericJMSConnectionFactory(nodeName, serverName, JMSProvider-Name, JMSCFName, jndiName, extJndiName, otherAttrsList=[])—This method can be used to create a generic JMS connection factory. The required parameters are as follows:
  - nodeName—Defines the node on which the provider is to be created.
  - serverName—Defines the server on which the provider is to be created.
  - JMSProviderName—Defines the name of the provider with which the connection factory is to be associated.
  - JMSCFName—Defines the name of the connection factory to be created.
  - jndiName—Defines the JNDI name to be used to bind the connection factory to the namespace.
  - extJndiName—Defines the JNDI name to be used to bind the queue into the application server namespace.

The optional parameter, otherAttrsList, can be used to specify name/value pairs of values to be used during the resource creation.

- createGenericJMSConnectionFactoryUsingTemplate(nodeName, serverName, JMSProviderName, templateID, JMSCFName, jndiName, extJndiName, otherAttrsList=[])—This method can be used to create a generic JMS connection factory using an existing template. The required parameters are as follows:
  - nodeName—Defines the node on which the provider is to be created.
  - serverName—Defines the server on which the provider is to be created.
  - JMSProviderName—Defines the name of the provider with which the connection factory is to be associated.
  - templateID—Defines the template to be used for the creation.
  - JMSCFName—Defines the name of the connection factory to be created.
  - jndiName—Defines the JNDI name to be used to bind the connection factory to the namespace.
  - extJndiName—Defines the JNDI name to be used to bind the queue into the application server namespace.

The optional parameter, otherAttrsList, can be used to specify name/value pairs of values to be used during the resource creation.

- createGenericJMSDestination(nodeName, serverName, JMSProviderName, JMSDestName, jndiName, extJndiName, otherAttrsList=[])—This method can be used to create a generic JMS destination. The required parameters are as follows:
  - nodeName—Defines the node on which the provider is to be created.
  - serverName—Defines the server on which the provider is to be created.
  - JMSProviderName—Defines the name of the provider with which the connection factory is to be associated.
  - JMSDestName—Defines the name of the destination to be created.
  - jndiName—Defines the JNDI name to be used to bind the connection factory to the namespace.
  - extJndiName—Defines the JNDI name to be used to bind the queue into the application server namespace.

The optional parameter, otherAttrsList, can be used to specify name/value pairs of values to be used during the resource creation.

- createGenericJMSDestinationUsingTemplate(nodeName, serverName, JMSProviderName, templateID, JMSDestName, jndiName, extJndiName, otherAttrsList=[])—This method can be used to create a generic JMS destination using an existing template. The required parameters are as follows:
  - nodeName—Defines the node on which the provider is to be created.

- `serverName`—Defines the server on which the provider is to be created.
- `JMSProviderName`—Defines the name of the provider with which the connection factory is to be associated.
- `templateID`—Defines the template to be used for the creation.
- `JMSDestName`—Defines the name of the destination to be created.
- `jndiName`—Defines the JNDI name to be used to bind the connection factory to the namespace.
- `extJndiName`—Defines the JNDI name to be used to bind the queue into the application server namespace.

The optional parameter, `otherAttrsList`, can be used to specify name/value pairs of values to be used during the resource creation.

- `createWASQueue(nodeName, serverName, JMSProviderName, WASQueueName, jndiName, otherAttrsList=[])`—This method can be used to create a WebSphere Application Server queue. The required parameters are as follows:
  - `nodeName`—Defines the node on which the provider is to be created.
  - `serverName`—Defines the server on which the provider is to be created.
  - `JMSProviderName`—Defines the name of the provider with which the connection factory is to be associated.
  - `WASQueueName`—Defines the name of the queue to be created.
  - `jndiName`—Defines the JNDI name to be used to bind the connection factory to the namespace.

The optional parameter, `otherAttrsList`, can be used to specify name/value pairs of values to be used during the resource creation.

- `createWASQueueUsingTemplate(nodeName, serverName, JMSProviderName, templateID, WASQueueName, jndiName, otherAttrsList=[])`—This method can be used to create a WebSphere Application Server queue using an existing template. The required parameters are as follows:
  - `nodeName`—Defines the node on which the provider is to be created.
  - `serverName`—Defines the server on which the provider is to be created.
  - `JMSProviderName`—Defines the name of the provider with which the connection factory is to be associated.
  - `templateID`—Defines the template to be used for the creation.
  - `WASQueueName`—Defines the name of the queue to be created.
  - `jndiName`—Defines the JNDI name to be used to bind the connection factory to the namespace.

The optional parameter, `otherAttrsList`, can be used to specify name/value pairs of values to be used during the resource creation.

- `createWASQueueConnectionFactory(nodeName, serverName, JMSProvider-Name, WASQueueCFName, jndiName, otherAttrsList=[])`—This method can be used to create a WebSphere Application Server connection factory. The required parameters are as follows:
    - `nodeName`—Defines the node on which the provider is to be created.
    - `serverName`—Defines the server on which the provider is to be created.
    - `JMSProviderName`—Defines the name of the provider with which the connection factory is to be associated.
    - `WASQueueCFName`—Defines the name of the connection factory to be created.
    - `jndiName`—Defines the JNDI name to be used to bind the connection factory to the namespace.

The optional parameter, `otherAttrsList`, can be used to specify name/value pairs of values to be used during the resource creation.

- `createWASQueueConnectionFactoryUsingTemplate(nodeName, serverName, JMSProviderName, templateID, WASQueueCFName, jndiName, otherAttrs-List=[])`—This method can be used to create a WebSphere Application Server connection factory using an existing template. The required parameters are as follows:
    - `nodeName`—Defines the node on which the provider is to be created.
    - `serverName`—Defines the server on which the provider is to be created.
    - `JMSProviderName`—Defines the name of the provider with which the connection factory is to be associated.
    - `templateID`—Defines the template to be used for the creation.
    - WASQueueCFName—Defines the name of the connection factory to be created.
    - `jndiName`—Defines the JNDI name to be used to bind the connection factory to the namespace.

The optional parameter, `otherAttrsList`, can be used to specify name/value pairs of values to be used during the resource creation.

- `createWASTopic(nodeName, serverName, JMSProviderName, WASTopicName, jndiName, topic, otherAttrsList=[])`—This method can be used to create a WebSphere Application Server topic. The required parameters are as follows:
    - `nodeName`—Defines the node on which the provider is to be created.
    - `serverName`—Defines the server on which the provider is to be created.
    - `JMSProviderName`—Defines the name of the provider with which the connection factory is to be associated.
    - `WASTopicName`—Defines the name of the topic to be created.
    - `jndiName`—Defines the JNDI name to be used to bind the connection factory to the namespace.

- `topic`—Defines the name of the topic (as a qualification in the topic space) to be used.

The optional parameter, `otherAttrsList`, can be used to specify name/value pairs of values to be used during the resource creation.

- `createWASTopicUsingTemplate(nodeName, serverName, JMSProviderName, templateID, WASTopicName, jndiName, topic, otherAttrsList=[])`—This method can be used to create a WebSphere Application Server topic using an existing template. The required parameters are as follows:
  - `nodeName`—Defines the node on which the provider is to be created.
  - `serverName`—Defines the server on which the provider is to be created.
  - `JMSProviderName`—Defines the name of the provider with which the connection factory is to be associated.
  - `templateID`—Defines the template to be used for the creation.
  - `WASTopicName`—Defines the name of the topic to be created.
  - `jndiName`—Defines the JNDI name to be used to bind the connection factory to the namespace.
  - `topic`—Defines the name of the topic (as a qualification in the topic space) to be used.

The optional parameter, `otherAttrsList`, can be used to specify name/value pairs of values to be used during the resource creation.

- `createWASTopicConnectionFactory(nodeName, serverName, JMSProviderName, WASTopicCFName, jndiName, port, otherAttrsList=[])`—This method can be used to create a WebSphere Application Server topic connection factory. The required parameters are as follows:
  - `nodeName`—Defines the node on which the provider is to be created.
  - `serverName`—Defines the server on which the provider is to be created.
  - `JMSProviderName`—Defines the name of the provider with which the connection factory is to be associated.
  - `WASTopicCFName`—Defines the name of the connection factory to be created.
  - `jndiName`—Defines the JNDI name to be used to bind the connection factory to the namespace.
  - `port`—Defines the port number to be associated with this resource.

The optional parameter, `otherAttrsList`, can be used to specify name/value pairs of values to be used during the resource creation.

- `createWASTopicConnectionFactoryUsingTemplate(nodeName, serverName, JMSProviderName, templateID, WASTopicCFName, jndiName, port, otherAttrsList=[])`—This method can be used to create a WebSphere Application

Server topic connection factory using an existing template. The required parameters are as follows:

- `nodeName`—Defines the node on which the provider is to be created.
- `serverName`—Defines the server on which the provider is to be created.
- `JMSProviderName`—Defines the name of the provider with which the connection factory is to be associated.
- `templateID`—Defines the template to be used for the creation.
- `WASTopicCFName`—Defines the name of the connection factory to be created.
- `jndiName`—Defines the JNDI name to be used to bind the connection factory to the namespace.
- `port`—Defines the port number to be associated with this resource.

The optional parameter, `otherAttrsList`, can be used to specify name/value pairs of values to be used during the resource creation.

- `startListenerPort(nodeName, serverName)`—This method can be used to start the listener ports associated with the specified resource. The required parameters are as follows:
  - `nodeName`—Defines the node with which the listener ports are associated.
  - `serverName`—Defines the server with which the listener ports are associated.

AdminResources Library Module

This library module is a little unusual in that it only contains methods for the creation of the Mail, URL, and resource environment-related items. Let's start by taking a look at the Mail-related creation methods:

- `createMailProvider(nodeName, serverName, mailProviderName)`—This method can be used to create a Mail Provider. The required parameters are as follows:
  - `nodeName`—Defines the node on which the mail provider is to be created.
  - `serverName`—Defines the server for which the mail provider is to be created.
  - `mailProviderName`—Defines the name of the mail provider to be created.
- `createMailSession(nodeName, serverName, mailProviderName, mail-SessionName, jndiName)`—This method can be used to create a mail session for a mail provider. A mail session object is used to authenticate users and control access to the associated mail messaging resources. The required parameters are as follows:
  - `nodeName`—Defines the node on which the mail provider is to be created.
  - `serverName`—Defines the server for which the mail provider is to be created.
  - `mailProviderName`—Defines the name of the mail provider to be used.

- `mailSessionName`—Defines the name of the mail session to be created.
- `jndiName`—Defines the JNDI name of the resource.
- `createProtocolProvider(nodeName, serverName, mailProviderName, protocolProviderName, className, type)`—This method can be used to create a Protocol Provider to provide an implementation class for a specific messaging protocol. The required parameters are as follows:
  - `nodeName`—Defines the node with which the protocol provider is to be associated.
  - `serverName`—Defines the server with which the protocol provider is to be associated.
  - `mailProviderName`—Defines the name of the mail provider to be used.
  - `protocolProviderName`—Defines the name of the protocol provider to be created.
  - `className`—Defines the implementation class name of the protocol provider.
  - `type`—Defines the kind of the protocol provider being created (either `'STORE'` or `'TRANSPORT'`).
- `createCompleteMailProvider(nodeName, serverName, mailProviderName, propertyName, propertyValue, protocolProviderName, className, mailSessionName, jndiName, mailStoreServer, mailStoreUser, mailStorePassword)`—This method can be used to create a Mail Provider using all of the configurable settings. The required parameters are as follows:
  - `nodeName`—Defines the node on which the mail provider is to be created.
  - `serverName`—Defines the server for which the mail provider is to be created.
  - `mailProviderName`—Defines the name of the mail provider to be created.
  - `propertyName`—Defines the name of the custom property.
  - `propertyValue`—Defines the custom property value.
  - `protocolProviderName`—Defines the name of the protocol provider.
  - `className`—Defines the implementation class name of the protocol provider.
  - `mailSessionName`—Defines the name of the session object.
  - `jndiName`—Defines the JNDI name of the resource.
  - `mailStoreServer`—Defines the hostname of the server from which stored mail is retrieved.
  - `mailStoreUser`—Defines the userid of the mail account to be used.
  - `mailStorePassword`—Defines the password of the mail account to be used.
- `createResourceEnvEntries(nodeName, serverName, resEnvProviderName, resEnvEntryName, jndiName)`—This method can be used to create a resource environment entry. The required parameters are as follows:
  - `nodeName`—Defines the node on which the entry is to be created.
  - `serverName`—Defines the server for which the entry is to be created.

- `resEnvProviderName`—Defines the resource environment provider for the entry.

- `resEnvEntryName`—Defines the name of the resource environment entry to be created.

- `jndiName`—Defines the JNDI name of the resource.

- `createResourceEnvProvider(nodeName, serverName, resEnvProviderName)`—This method can be used to create a resource environment provider. The required parameters are as follows:

  - `nodeName`—Defines the node on which the entry is to be created.

  - `serverName`—Defines the server for which the entry is to be created.

  - `resEnvProviderName`—Defines the resource environment provider to be created.

- `createResourceEnvProviderRef(nodeName, serverName, resEnvProviderName, resEnvFactoryClass, resEnvClassName)`—This method can be used to create a resource environment provider reference. The required parameters are as follows:

  - `nodeName`—Defines the node on which the entry is to be created.

  - `serverName`—Defines the server for which the entry is to be created.

  - `resEnvProviderName`—Defines the resource environment provider reference to be created.

  - `resEnvFactoryClass`—Defines the factory class to be used.

  - `resEnvClassName`—Defines the name of the class to be used.

- `createCompleteResourceEnvProvider(nodeName, serverName, resEnvProviderName, propertyName, propertyValue, resEnvFactoryClass, resEnvClassName, resEnvEntryName, jndiName)`—This method can be used to create a resource environment provider by specifying all of the necessary configuration information. The required parameters are as follows:

- `nodeName`—Defines the node on which the entry is to be created.

- `serverName`—Defines the server for which the entry is to be created.

- `resEnvProviderName`—Defines the resource environment provider reference to be created.

- `propertyName`—Defines the name of the custom property.

- `propertyValue`—Defines the custom property value.

- `resEnvFactoryClass`—Defines the factory class to be used.

- `resEnvClassName`—Defines the name of the class to be used.

- `resEnvEntryName`—Defines the name of the resource environment entry.

- `jndiName`—Defines the JNDI name of the resource.

- `createURL(nodeName, serverName, urlProviderName, urlName, jndiName, urlSpec)`—This method can be used to create a URL for a URL Provider. The required parameters are as follows:

- nodeName—Defines the node for which the URL is to be created.
- serverName—Defines the server for which the URL is to be created.
- urlProviderName—Defines the name of the provider for which the URL is to be created.
- urlName—Defines the name of the URL to be created.
- jndiName—Defines the JNDI name of the resource.
- urlSpec—Defines the string from which the URL is formed.
- createURLProvider(nodeName,   serverName,   urlProviderName, streamHandlerClass, protocol)—This method can be used to create a URL Provider. The required parameters are as follows:
  - nodeName—Defines the node for which the URL is to be created.
  - serverName—Defines the server for which the URL is to be created.
  - urlProviderName—Defines the name of the provider to be created.
  - streamHandlerClass—Defines the class to be used for a specific protocol.
  - protocol—Defines the protocol supported by this provider.
- createCompleteURLProvider(nodeName, serverName, urlProviderName, streamHandlerClass, protocol, propertyName, propertyValue, urlName, jndiName, urlSpec)—This method can be used to create a URL provider by specifying all of the necessary configuration information. The required parameters are as follows:
  - nodeName—Defines the node on which the entry is to be created.
  - serverName—Defines the server for which the entry is to be created.
  - urlProviderName—Defines the name of the provider to be created.
  - streamHandlerClass—Defines the class to be used for a specific protocol.
  - protocol—Defines the protocol supported by this provider.
  - propertyName—Defines the name of the custom property.
  - propertyValue—Defines the custom property value.
  - urlName—Defines the name of the URL that specifies a resource.
  - jndiName—Defines the JNDI name of the resource.
  - urlSpec—Defines the string from which the URL is to be formed.
- createJAASAuthenticationAlias(authAlias,   uid,   password)—This method can be used to create a JAAS Authentication Alias. The required parameters are as follows:
  - authAlias—Defines the name of the alias to be created.
  - uid—Defines the userid to be associated with the alias.
  - password—Defines the password for the specified userid.

- `createLibraryRef(libName, appName)`—This method can be used to create a Library Reference. The required parameters are as follows:
  - `libName`—Defines the name of the reference to be created.
  - `appName`—Defines the name of the application associated with the reference.
- `createSharedLibrary(nodeName, serverName, libName, classpath)`—This method can be used to create a Shared Library entry. The required parameters are as follows:
  - `nodeName`—Defines the node on which the library is to be created.
  - `serverName`—Defines the server for which the entry is to be created.
  - `libName`—Defines the name of the library to be created.
  - `classpath`—Defines the classpath to be used with library.
- `createScheduler(nodeName, serverName, schedName, schedJNDI, schedCategory, schedDSJNDI, schedTablePrefix, schedPollInterval, wmName)`—This method can be used to create a Scheduler. The required parameters are as follows:
  - `nodeName`—Defines the node on which the scheduler is to be created.
  - `serverName`—Defines the server for which the scheduler is to be created.
  - `schedName`—Defines the name by which the scheduler is to be referenced.
  - `schedJNDI`—Defines the JNDI name to be associated with the scheduler.
  - `schedCategory`—Defines a string to be associated with the scheduler.
  - `schedDSJNDI`—Defines the name of the data source for persistent tasks.
  - `schedTablePrefix`—Defines a prefix name for scheduler database tables.
  - `schedPollInterval`—Defines an interval, in seconds, used by the schedule to check the database.
  - `wmName`—Defines the work manager JNDI name to be associated with the scheduler.
- `createWorkManager(nodeName, serverName, wmName, wmDesc, wmJNDI, wmCategory, wmNumAlarmThreads, wmMinThreads, wmMaxThreads, wmThreadPriority, wmIsGrowable, wmServiceNames)`—This method can be used to create a JNDI-related work manager. The required parameters are as follows:
  - `nodeName`—Defines the node on which the work manager is to be created.
  - `serverName`—Defines the server for which the work manager is to be created.
  - `wmName`—Defines the name by which the work manager is to be referenced.
  - `wmDesc`—Specifies a description string for the work manager.
  - `wmJNDI`—Specifies a JNDI lookup string for the work manager in the namespace.
  - `wmCategory`—Defines a string to be associated with the work manager.

- `wmNumAlarmThreads`—Defines a number of alarm threads for the work manager.
- `wmMinThreads`—Defines the minimum number of thread for work manager.
- `wmMaxThreads`—Defines the maximum number of thread for work manager.
- `wmThreadPriority`—Defines a priority associated with the work manager.
- `wmIsGrowable`—Defines if the number of threads associated with the work manager can increase (`'true'` or `'false'`).
- `wmServiceNames`—Defines a list of services for the work manager.

AdminAuthorizations Library Module

This library module provides methods related to security authorization. First, let's look at the methods used to query this kind of configuration information:

- `listAuthorizationGroups()`—This method can be used to list the configured authorization groups. A list of all configured groups is returned.

- `listAuthorizationGroupsForUserID(userid)`—This method can be used to list the configured authorization groups for a specific userid. Only one parameter exists and is required. It is used to identify the userid to be used for the query. A list of all associated groups is returned if any exist.

- `listAuthorizationGroupsForGroupID(groupid)`—This method can be used to list the configured authorization groups for a specific group ID. Only one parameter exists and is required. It is used to identify the group ID to be used for the query. A list of all associated groups is returned if any exist.

- `listAuthorizationGroupsOfResource(resourceName)`—This method can be used to list the configured authorization groups for a specific resource. Only one parameter exists and is required. It is used to identify the resource to be used for the query. A list of all associated groups is returned if any exist.

- `listUserIDsOfAuthorizationGroup(authGroup)`—This method can be used to list the userids associated with a specific authorization group. Only one parameter exists and is required. It is used to identify the authorization group to be queried. A list of all associated userids is returned if any exist.

- `listGroupIDsOfAuthorizationGroup(authGroup)`—This method can be used to list the group IDs associated with a specific authorization group. Only one parameter exists and is required. It is used to identify the authorization group to be queried. A list of all associated group IDs is returned if any exist.

- `listResourcesOfAuthorizationGroup(authGroup)`—This method can be used to list the resources associated with a specific authorization group. Only one parameter exists and is required. It is used to identify the authorization group to be queried. A list of all resources is returned if any exist.

- `listResourcesForUserID(userid)`—This method can be used to list the resources associated with a specific userid. Only one parameter exists and is required. It is used to identify the userid to be queried. A list of all resources associated with this userid is returned if any exist.

- `listResourcesForGroupID(groupid)`—This method can be used to list the resources associated with a specific group ID. Only one parameter exists and is required. It is used to identify the group ID to be queried. A list of all resources associated with this group ID is returned if any exist.

- `createAuthorizationGroup(authGroup)`—This method can be used to create a new authorization group. Only one parameter exists and is required. It is used to identify the name of the group to be created.

- `addResourceToAuthorizationGroup(authGroup, resourceName)`—This method can be used to add a new resource to an existing authorization group. Two required parameters exist—the name of the authorization group and the name of the resource to be added.

- `mapUsersToAdminRole(authGroup, roleName, userids)`—This method can be used to map one or more userids to an administrative role in the specified authorization group. The three parameters are required and are as follows:
  - `authGroup`—Identifies the authorization group.
  - `roleName`—Identifies the name of the authorization role for the mapping.
  - `userids`—Identifies the list of affected userids. Even if only one userid is specified, it must be provided in a list.

- `mapGroupsToAdminRole(authGroup, roleName, groupids)`—This method can be used to map one or more group IDs to an administrative role in the specified authorization group. The three parameters are required and are as follows:
  - `authGroup`—Identifies the authorization group.
  - `roleName`—Identifies the name of the authorization role for the mapping.
  - `userids`—Identifies the list of affected group IDs. Even if only one group ID is specified, it must be provided in a list.

- `deleteAuthorizationGroup(authGroup)`—This method can be used to delete an authorization group. Only one parameter exists and is required. It is used to identify the name of the group to be deleted.

- `removeUsersFromAdminRole(authGroup, roleName, userids)`—This method can be used to remove one or more userids from an administrative role in the specified authorization group. The three parameters are required and are as follows:
  - `authGroup`—Identifies the authorization group.
  - `roleName`—Identifies the name of the authorization role for the mapping.
  - `userids`—Identifies the list of affected userids. Even if only one userid is specified, it must be provided in a list.

- `removeGroupsFromAdminRole(authGroup, roleName, groupids)`—This method can be used to remove one or more group IDs from an administrative role in the specified authorization group. The three parameters are required and are as follows:
    - `authGroup`—Identifies the authorization group.
    - `roleName`—Identifies the name of the authorization role for the mapping.
    - `userids`—Identifies the list of affected group IDs. Even if only one group ID is specified, it must be provided in a list.
- `removeResourceFromAuthorizationGroup(authGroup, resourceName)`—This method can be used to remove a resource from an existing authorization group. Two required parameters exist—the name of the authorization group and the name of the resource to be removed.
- `removeUserFromAllAdminRoles(userid)`—This method can be used to remove a user from all administrative roles. Only one (required) parameter exists. It identifies the userid to be removed.
- `removeGroupFromAllAdminRoles (groupid)`—This method can be used to remove a group ID from all administrative roles. Only one (required) parameter exists. It identifies the group ID to be removed.

AdminClusterManagement Library Module

This library module provides methods related to clusters. Let's begin by looking at the methods used to query cluster members:

- `listClusters()`—This method can be used to list the configured clusters. A list of all configured clusters is returned.
- `listClusterMembers(clusterName)`—This method can be used to list the members of a specific clusters. A single, required parameter exists that is used to identify the name of the cluster to be queried. A list of all configured cluster members is returned.
- `checkIfClusterExists (clusterName)`—This method can be used to test if a specified cluster exists. A single, required, parameter exists and is used to specify the cluster name to be tested. A boolean value (`'true'` or `'false'`) is returned.
- `checkIfClusterMemberExists (clusterName, serverMember)`—This method can be used to test if a specified cluster member exists. Two required parameters exists: the name of the cluster to be checked and the name of the server (cluster member) that is expected to be in the specified cluster. A boolean value (`'true'` or `'false'`) is returned.

The next group of methods described deals with the creation of clusters and members:

- `createClusterWithoutMember(clusterName)`—This method can be used to create an empty cluster. A single, required parameter exists and is used to specify the name of the cluster to be created.

- `createClusterWithFirstMember(clusterName, clusterType, nodeName, serverName)`—This method can be used to create a cluster with a single member. All four parameters are required:
  - `clusterName`—Defines the name of the cluster to be created.
  - `clusterType`—Defines the kind of the cluster to be created. It seems kind of silly, though, to require this parameter given that the only valid type is `'APPLICATION_SERVER'`.
  - `nodeName`—Defines the name of the node on which the cluster is to be created.
  - `serverName`—Defines the name of the server to be converted to a cluster member.
- `createClusterMember(clusterName, nodeName, newMember)`—This method can be used to create a cluster member. All three parameters are required:
  - `clusterName`—Defines the name of the cluster on which the member is to be created.
  - `nodeName`—Defines the name of the node on which the member exists.
  - `newMember`—Defines the name of the member to be created.
- `createFirstClusterMemberWithTemplate(clusterName, nodeName, newMember, templateName)`—This method can be used to create a cluster member using a template with this already existing server as the first member. The server will be converted into the first member of the cluster. Any additional members of the cluster that you might create at a later time will have all the applications and all the messaging buses that this model server has. All four parameters are required:
  - `clusterName`—Defines the name of the cluster to be created.
  - `nodeName`—Defines the name of the node on which the member is to be created.
  - `newMember`—Defines the name of the member to be created.
  - `templateName`—Defines the name of the template to be used to create the cluster member.
- `createFirstClusterMemberWithTemplateNodeServer(clusterName, nodeName, newMember, templateNode, templateServer)`—This method can be used to create a new, first cluster member using a template. All five parameters are required:
  - `clusterName`—Defines the name of the cluster for which the member is to be created.
  - `nodeName`—Defines the name of the node on which the member is to be created.
  - `newMember`—Defines the name of the member to be created.
  - `templateNode`—Defines the name of the node on which the template exists.
  - `templateServer`—Defines the name of the server with which the template is associated.

The penultimate group of methods to be described deal with the deletion of clusters and members:

- `deleteCluster(clusterName)`—This method can be used to delete a cluster. A single, required parameter exists and is used to specify the name of the cluster to be deleted.
- `deleteClusterMember(clusterName, nodeName, serverMember)`—This method can be used to delete a cluster member. All three parameters are required:
  - `clusterName`—Defines the name of the cluster containing the member to be deleted.
  - `nodeName`—Defines the name of the node on which the member exists.
  - `serverMember`—Defines the name of the server that is the member to be deleted.

The final group of methods in this library module deal with the stopping and starting of clusters and members:

- `startAllClusters()`—This method can be used to start all configured clusters.
- `startSingleCluster(clusterName)`—This method can be used to start the specified and named cluster.
- `stopAllClusters()`—This method can be used to stop all configured clusters.
- `stopSingleCluster(clusterName)`—This method can be used to stop the specified and named cluster.
- `rippleStartAllClusters()`—This method can be used to stop and then start all members of all clusters.
- `rippleStartSingleCluster(clusterName)`—This method can be used to stop and then start all members of the specified and named cluster.
- `immediateStopAllClusters()`—This method can be used to stop all clusters without allowing time for pending operations of the cluster members to complete gracefully.
- `immediateStopSingleCluster(clusterName)`—This method can be used to stop the specified and named cluster without allowing time for pending operations of the cluster members to complete gracefully.

AdminServerManagement Library Module

This library module, much like the first, `AdminApplication`, contains a large number of methods and is separated into groups. This module, though, is only partitioned into three command groups:

Group 1: `ServerConfiguration` (28 methods)

Group 2: `ServerTracingAndLoggingConfiguration` (8 methods)

Group 3: `OtherServicesConfiguration` (16 methods)

AdminServerManagement: Group 1—Server Configuration

The methods in this group all deal with Server Configuration in one way or another:

- `listServers(serverType="", nodeName="")`—This method can be used to return a list of all of the server configIDs. The two parameters are optional. The first can be used to specify the kind of server being queried (not the name), and the second can be used to specify the name of the node to be queried.

- `listServerTypes(nodeName="")`—This method can be used to return a list of the available server types. The optional parameter can be used to specify the name of the node to be queried.

- `listServerTemplates(version="", serverType="", templateName="")`—This method can be used to return a list of the available server templates. The optional parameters can be used to filter the result based on the template version information, the server type, and/or the template name.

- `createApplicationServer(nodeName, serverName, templateName)`—This method can be used to create a new application server. The three parameters are required and specify the following:
  - `nodeName`—The name of the node on which the server is to be created.
  - `serverName`—The name of the server is to be created.
  - `templateName`—The name of the template to be used for the creation. If a template is not to be used, specify this parameter as an empty string (that is, `''`).

- `createAppServerTemplate(nodeName, serverName, newTemplate)`—This method can be used to create a new application server template. The three parameters are required and specify the following:
  - `nodeName`—The name of the node on which the basis server exists.
  - `serverName`—The name of the basis server.
  - `newTemplate`—The name of the template to be created.

- `createGenericServer(nodeName, serverName, templateName, startCmd, startCmdArgs, workingDir, stopCmd, stopCmdArgs)`—This method can be used to create a new generic server. The parameters are required and specify the following:
  - `nodeName`—The name of the node on which the server is to be created.
  - `serverName`—The name of the server being created.
  - `templateName`—The name of the template to be used during creation.
  - `startCmd`—The fully qualified path and command file name used to start the server.
  - `startCmdArgs`—The arguments to be provided during server startup.
  - `workingDir`—The "current working directory" to be used during server startup.
  - `stopCmd`—The fully qualified path and command file name used to stop the server.

- `stopCmdArgs`—The arguments to be provided during server stop.
- `createWebServer(nodeName, serverName, webPort, webInstallPath, pluginInstallPath, configfile, serviceName, errorLog, accessLog, protocol )`—This method can be used to create a new web server. The parameters are required and specify
  - `nodeName`—The name of the node on which the server is to be created.
  - `serverName`—The name of the server being created.
  - `webPort`—The web server port number or an empty string.
  - `webInstallPath`—The fully qualified path to the IBM HTTP Server installation directory or an empty string.
  - `pluginInstallPath`—The fully qualified path for the web server plugin.
  - `configfile`—The fully qualified path for the web server configuration file.
  - `serviceName`—The name of the Windows service or an empty string.
  - `errorLog`—The fully qualified path to the error log file.
  - `accessLog`—The fully qualified path to the access log file.
  - `protocol`—Defines the type of communication protocol to be used (for example, `'HTTPS'`). If an empty string is specified, `'HTTP'` is used by default.
- `deleteServer(nodeName, serverName)`—This method can be used to delete a server. The parameters are required and specify the name of the node on which the server exists and the name of the server to be deleted.
- `deleteServerTemplate(templateName)`—This method can be used to delete a server template. The parameter is required and specifies the name of the template to be deleted.
- `startAllServers(nodeName)`—This method can be used to start all servers on a specific node. The parameter is required and specifies the name of the node.
- `startSingleServer(nodeName, serverName)`—This method can be used to start a specific server on a particular node. The parameters are required and specify the name of the node on which the server exists and the name of the server to be started.
- `stopAllServers(nodeName )`—This method can be used to stop all servers on a specific node. The parameter is required and specifies the name of the node.
- `stopSingleServer(nodeName, serverName)`—This method can be used to stop a specific server on a particular node. The parameters are required and specify the name of the node on which the server exists and the name of the server to be stopped.
- `listJVMProperties(nodeName, serverName, JVMProperty)`—This method can be used to list one or all of the JVM properties for a specific server on a particular

node. If the list of all properties is to be returned, specify the `JVMProperty` parameter as an empty string.[21]

- `showServerInfo(nodeName, serverName)`—This method can be used to return a list of information about the specified server name that exists on the given node.

- `getJavaHome(nodeName, serverName)`—This method can be used to return a string that identifies the `JAVA_HOME` directory for the specified server.

- `setJVMProperties(nodeName, serverName, classpath, bootClasspath, initHeapsize, maxHeapsize, debugMode, debugArgs)`—This method can be used to set one or more JVM properties for a particular server. The parameters are required but might be specified as an empty string. They are as follows:

  - `nodeName`—The name of the node on which the server exists.

  - `serverName`—The name of the server whose properties are to be modified.

  - `classpath`—Specifies the list of directories to be searched for classes by the JVM.

  - `bootClasspath`—Specifies the list of bootstrap classes and resources for the JVM.

  - `initHeapsize`—Defines the initial Heap size (in megabytes) to be used by the JVM.

  - `maxHeapsize`—Defines the maximum Heap size available for the JVM.

  - `debugMode`—If specified as `'true'`, indicates that the JVM should execute in debug mode.

  - `debugArgs`—If `debugMode` is specified as `'true'`, indicates that debug arguments to be used by the JVM.

- `checkIfServerExists(nodeName, serverName)`—This method can be used to check for the existence of a specific server on a particular node. The result of the call will be either `'true'` or `'false'`.

- `checkIfServerTemplateExists(templateName)`—This method can be used to check for the existence of a specific server template name. The result of the call will be either `'true'` or `'false'`.

- `configureProcessDefinition(nodeName, serverName, otherAttrList=[])`—This method can be used to define a collection of name/value pairs for the process of a specific server on a particular node. The last parameter specifies the list of name/value pairs.

- `configureEndPointsHost(nodeName, serverName, hostName)`—This method can be used to define the hostname to be associated with a specific server on a particular node. The last parameter specifies the "new" hostname.

---

[21] Some might find the returned list awkward to work with and prefer the code shown in Listing 11.10.

- `configureApplicationServerClassloader(nodeName, serverName, policy, mode, libraryName)`—This method can be used to define the classloader properties to be used by a specific server on a particular node. The parameters are required and are as follows:
  - `nodeName`—The name of the node on which the server exists.
  - `serverName`—The name of the server whose classloader properties are to be modified.
  - `policy`—Defines the classloader policy as either `'SINGLE'` or `'MULTIPLE'`.
  - `mode`—Defines the classloader mode as either `'PARENT_FIRST'` or `'APPLICATION_ FIRST'`.
  - `libraryName`—Defines the name of the shared library.
- `queryMBeans(nodeName, serverName, mbeanType)`—This method can be used to query for MBeans of a specific type associated with a specific server on a particular node.
- `viewProductInformation()`—This method can be used to display product version information.[22]
- `getServerPID(nodeName, serverName)`—This method can be used to obtain the process identifier (number) associated with the specified server.
- `getServerProcessType(nodeName, serverName)`—This method can be used to obtain the process type of the specified server (for example, `'UnManagedProcess'`).
- `configureCustomProperty(nodeName, serverName, parentType, propName, propValue, otherAttrList=[])`—This method can be used to define the custom properties for a specific server. All but the last parameter is required and has the following meanings:
  - `nodeName`—The name of the node on which the server exists.
  - `serverName`—The name of the server whose properties are to be set.
  - `parentType`—The kind of component, within the specified server, having the property to be set.
  - `propName`—The name of the property being set.
  - `propValue`—The value of the property being set.
  - `otherAttrList`—An optional name/value pair list of additional attributes to be set.

---

[22] Why this method displays the information via a print statement, rather than returning it to the caller, we do not know.

- configureSessionManagerForServer(nodeName, serverName, session-Persistence Mode, otherAttrList=[])—This method can be used to define the session manager properties for a specific server. All but the last parameter are required. Parameters have the following meanings:
  - nodeName—The name of the node on which the server exists.
  - serverName—The name of the server whose properties are to be set.
  - sessionPersistenceMode—Specifies the session persistence mode (i.e., 'DATABASE', 'DATA_REPLICATION', or 'NONE').
  - otherAttrList—An optional name/value pair list of additional attributes to be set.
  - otherAttrList—An optional name/value pair list of additional attributes to be set.
- configureCookieForServer(nodeName, serverName, cookieName, domain, maxAge, secure, otherAttrList=[])—This method can be used to configure cookies for a specific server. All but the last parameter is required. The parameters have the following meanings:
  - nodeName—The name of the node on which the server exists.
  - serverName—The name of the server whose properties are to be set.
  - cookieName—The name of the cookie being set.
  - domain—The domain to be associated with the session cookie.
  - maxAge—The length of time (in seconds) for which the cookie is to be considered as valid. To have the cookie expire when the browser session ends, use a value of '-1'.
  - secure—Used to indicate that the cookie only applies to secure (i.e., HTTPS) sessions. Default value is 'false'.
  - otherAttrList—An optional name/value pair list of additional attributes to be set.

AdminServerManagement: Group 2—ServerTracingAndLogging Configuration

The methods in this group all deal with logging and tracing for a particular server.

- setTraceSpecification(nodeName, serverName, traceSpec)—This method can be used to dynamically set or change, the trace specification for a specific server. All of the parameters are required and have the following meanings:
  - nodeName—The name of the node on which the server exists.
  - serverName—The name of the server being modified.
  - traceSpec—The trace specification to be used.
- configureTraceService(nodeName, serverName, traceString, outputType, otherAttrList=[])—This method can be used to configure the trace service

for a specific server. Almost all of the parameters are required, and have the following meanings:

- `nodeName`—The name of the node on which the server exists.

- `serverName`—The name of the server being modified.

- `traceString`—The trace string to be stored.

- `outputType`—Defines where the trace is to be written, either `'MEMORY_BUFFER'` or `'SPECIFIED_FILE'`.

- `otherAttrList`—An optional name/value pair list of additional attributes to be set.

- `configureJavaVirtualMachine(jvmConfigID, debugMode, debugArgs, otherAttrList=[])`—This method can be used to configure the JVM for a specific server. Almost all of the parameters are required and have the following meanings:

  - `jvmConfigID`—The configuration ID of the JVM being modified.

  - `debugMode`—Indicates that the JVM should execute in debug mode. If this value is specified as `'true'`, then debug arguments must be specified.

  - `debugArgs`—Specifies the arguments to be used by the JVM in debug mode.

  - `otherAttrList`—An optional name/value pair list of additional attributes to be set.

- `configureServerLogs(nodeName, serverName, logRoot, otherAttrList=[])`—This method can be used to configure the properties related to log files for a specific server. Almost all of the parameters are required and have the following meanings:

  - `nodeName`—The name of the node on which the server exists.

  - `serverName`—The name of the server being modified.

  - `logRoot`—The fully qualified directory in which log files should be written.

  - `otherAttrList`—An optional name/value pair list of additional attributes to be set.

- `configureJavaProcessLogs(jpdConfigID, logRoot, otherAttrList =[])` — This method can be used to configure the properties related to Java Process log files for a specific server. Almost all of the parameters are required and have the following meanings:

  - `jpdConfigID`—The configuration ID of the Java Process being modified.

  - `logRoot`—The fully qualified directory in which log files should be written.

  - `otherAttrList`—An optional name/value pair list of additional attributes to be set.

- `configureRASLoggingService(nodeName, serverName, logRoot, otherAttrList=[])`—This method can be used to configure the properties related to Reliability and Serviceability log service for a specific server. Almost all of the parameters are required and have the following meanings:

  - `nodeName`—The name of the node on which the server exists.

- `serverName`—The name of the server being modified.
- `logRoot`—The fully qualified directory in which log files should be written.
- `otherAttrList`—An optional name/value pair list of additional attributes to be set.

- `configurePerformanceMonitoringService(nodeName, serverName, enable, initialSpecLevel, otherAttrList=[])`—This method can be used to configure the properties related to Performance Monitoring Service for a specific server. Almost all of the parameters are required and have the following meanings:
  - `nodeName`—The name of the node on which the server exists.
  - `serverName`—The name of the server being modified.
  - `enable`—Boolean value (i.e., `'true'` or `'false'`) indicating whether or not the PM Service should be enabled.
  - `initialSpecLevel`—Specifies the PMI statistics to be gathered (one of `'None'`, `'Basic'`, `'Extended'`, `'All'`, or `'Custom'`).
  - `otherAttrList`—An optional name/value pair list of additional attributes to be set.

- `configurePMIRequestMetrics(enable, traceLevel, otherAttrList=[])`—This method can be used to configure the PMI Request Metrics for a specific server. Almost all of the parameters are required and have the following meanings:
  - `enable`—Boolean value (i.e., `'true'` or `'false'`) indicating whether or not the Request Metrics should be gathered.
  - `traceLevel`—Specifies the kind of metrics to be gathered (one of `'None'`, `'HOPS'`, `'PERFORMANCE_DEBUG'`, or `'DEBUG'`).
  - `otherAttrList`—An optional name/value pair list of additional attributes to be set.

AdminServerManagement: Group 3—OtherServicesConfiguration

The methods in this group deal with all of the "other" server configuration topics.

- `configureRuntimeTransactionService(nodeName, serverName, total-TranLifetimeTimeout, clientInactivityTimeout)`—This method can be used to configure the runtime transaction service for a specific server. This service is a component that coordinates updates to resource managers. All of the parameters are required and have the following meanings:
  - `nodeName`—The name of the node on which the server exists.
  - `serverName`—The name of the server with which the runtime service is associated.
  - `totalTranLifetimeTimeout`—Specifies the timeout, in seconds, allowed for a transaction to complete.
  - `clientInactivityTimeout`—Specifies the maximum time, in seconds, between client requests.

- `configureEJBContainer(nodeName, serverName, passivationDir, default-DatasourceJNDIName, otherAttrList=[])`—This method can be used to configure an EJB container for a specific server. Almost all of the parameters are required and have the following meanings:
  - `nodeName`—The name of the node on which the server exists.
  - `serverName`—The name of the server with which the container is to be associated.
  - `passivationDir`—The fully qualified directory into which the container can contain stateful session beans.
  - `defaultDatasourceJNDIName`—Identifies the datasource JNDI name to be used should a name not be specified during application deployment.
- `configureDynamicCache(nodeName,    serverName,    defaultPriority, cacheSize, externalCacheGroupName, externalCacheGroupType, other-AttrList=[])`—This method can be used to configure the dynamic cache for a specific server. Almost all of the parameters are required and have the following meanings:
  - `nodeName`—The name of the node on which the server exists.
  - `serverName`—The name of the server for which the cache is being configured.
  - `defaultPriority`—Defines the default priority for cache entries (numeric value from 1.255).
  - `cacheSize`—Defines the maximum number of entries that the cache may hold.
  - `externalCacheGroupName`—Defines the external name as configured in the `cachespec.xml` file.
  - `externalCacheGroupType`—Defines the external cache group type.
  - `otherAttrList`—An optional name/value pair list of additional attributes to be set.
- `configureMessageListenerService(nodeName, serverName, maxListener-Retry,   listenerRecoveryInterval,   poolingThreshold,   pooling-Timeout, otherAttrList=[])`—This method can be used to configure the message listener service for a specific server. Almost all of the parameters are required and have the following meanings:
- `nodeName`—The name of the node on which the server exists.
  - `serverName`—The name of the server with which the listener service is to be associated.
  - `maxListenerRetry`—The maximum number of retry attempts to be tried when a failure occurs.
  - `listenerRecoveryInterval`—The time (in seconds) between retry attempts.
  - `poolingThreshold`—The maximum number of unused connections in the connection pool.

- poolingTimeout—The time (in milliseconds) that an unused connection is allowed to remain unused before it is destroyed.
- otherAttrList—An optional name/value pair list of additional attributes to be set.
- configureListenerPortForMessageListenerService(nodeName, serverName, lpName, connFactoryJNDIName, destJNDIName, maxMessages, maxRetries, maxSessions, otherAttrList=[])—This method can be used to configure the listener port for a message listener service for a specific server. Almost all of the parameters are required and have the following meanings:
  - nodeName—The name of the node on which the server exists.
  - serverName—The name of the server with which the listener service is associated.
  - lpName—The name by which the port is known.
  - connFactoryJNDIName—The JNDI name for the JMS connection factory.
  - destJNDIName—The JNDI name for the destination.
  - maxMessages—The maximum number of messages that can exist per transaction.
  - maxRetries—The maximum number of attempts to send a message.
  - maxSessions—The maximum number of concurrent sessions that can exist between the listener and the JMS server.
  - otherAttrList—An optional name/value pair list of additional attributes to be set.
- configureThreadPool(nodeName, serverName, parentType, tpName, maxSize, minSize, inactivityTimeout, otherAttrList=[])—This method can be used to configure a thread pool for a specific server. Almost all of the parameters are required and have the following meanings:
  - nodeName—The name of the node on which the server exists.
  - serverName—The name of the server with which the thread pool is to be associated.
  - parentType—The kind of component, within the specified server, used to hold the thread pool.
  - tpName—The name of the thread pool resource.
  - maxSize—The maximum number of threads allowed in the pool.
  - minSize—The minimum number of threads allowed in the pool.
  - inactivityTimeout—The number of milliseconds that a thread is allowed to remain unused before it is reclaimed.
  - otherAttrList—An optional name/value pair list of additional attributes to be set.
- configureStateManageable(nodeName, serverName, parentType, initial-State, otherAttrList=[])—This method can be used to configure the initial state

for a specific server. Almost all of the parameters are required and have the following meanings:

- `nodeName`—The name of the node on which the server exists.

- `serverName`—The name of the server whose state is to be defined.

- `parentType`—The kind of component that contains the specified server.

- `initialState`—The desired initial state of the component (i.e., either `'STOP'` or `'START'`).

- `otherAttrList`—An optional name/value pair list of additional attributes to be set.

- `configureORBService(nodeName, serverName, requestTimeout, request-RetriesCount, requestRetriesDelay, connCacheMax, connCacheMin, locateRequestTimeout, otherAttrList=[])`—This method can be used to configure the ORB Service for a specific server. Almost all of the parameters are required and have the following meanings:

  - `nodeName`—The name of the node on which the server exists.

  - `serverName`—The name of the server whose state is to be defined.

  - `requestTimeout`—The number of seconds to wait before a request expires.

  - `requestRetriesCount`—The number of attempts to be made to send a request.

  - `requestRetriesDelay`—The number of milliseconds to wait between retries.

  - `connCacheMax`—The maximum number of entries allowed in the cache.

  - `connCacheMin`—The minimum number of entries allowed in the cache.

  - `locateRequestTimeout`—The number of seconds that a locate request message is allowed to wait before it expires.

  - `otherAttrList`—An optional name/value pair list of additional attributes to be set.

- `configureTransactionService(nodeName, serverName, totalTran Life-time Timeout, clientInactivityTimeout, maxTransactionTimeout, heuristicRetryLimit, heuristicRetryWait, propogatedOrBMTTran Life-timeTimeout, asyncResponseTimeout, otherAttrList=[])`—This method can be used to configure a Transaction Service for a specific server. Almost all of the parameters are required and have the following meanings:

  - `nodeName`—The name of the node on which the server exists.

  - `serverName`—The name of the server for which the service is being defined.

  - `totalTranLifetimeTimeout`—The maximum time, in seconds, that a transaction is allowed to exist before timeout cleanup is initiated.

  - `clientInactivityTimeout`—The maximum time, in seconds, that a client is allowed to remain inactive.

- `maxTransactionTimeout`—The maximum time, in seconds, that a transaction is allowed to remain active.

- `heuristicRetryLimit`—The maximum number of attempts that the server is allowed to attempt a rollback, or commit.

- `heuristicRetryWait`—The maximum time, in seconds, between rollback or commit requests.

- `propogatedOrBMTTranLifetimeTimeout`—The maximum time, in seconds, that a transaction is allowed to remain inactive before rollback is initiated.

- `asyncResponseTimeout`—The maximum time, in seconds, that the server will wait for a Web Services Atomic Transaction response.

- `otherAttrList`—An optional name/value pair list of additional attributes to be set.

- `configureWebContainer(nodeName, serverName, defaultVirtualHostName, enableServletCaching, otherAttrList=[])`—This method can be used to configure the Web Container for a specific server. Almost all of the parameters are required and have the following meanings:

  - `nodeName`—The name of the node on which the server exists.

  - `serverName`—The name of the server for which the Web Container is being defined.

  - `defaultVirtualHostName`—A name by which the host is to be able to receive request. Valid values include `'default_host'` and `'admin_host'`.

  - `enableServletCaching`—Defines whether or not servlet responses are cachable.

  - `otherAttrList`—An optional name/value pair list of additional attributes to be set.

- `configureHTTPTransportForWebContainer(nodeName, serverName, adjust-Port, external, sslConfig, sslEnabled, otherAttrList=[])`—This method can be used to configure the HTTP Transport for a Web Container in a specific server. Almost all of the parameters are required and have the following meanings:

  - `nodeName`—The name of the node on which the server exists.

  - `serverName`—The name of the server in which the Web Container exists.

  - `adjustPort`—Indicates whether the port number for the Web Container can be automatically adjusted.

  - `external`—Indicates whether the HTTP Transport for the Web Container is external.

  - `sslConfig`—Indicates the SSL type for secure connections between the plugin and the application server (for example, `'DefaultSSLSettings'`).

  - `sslEnabled`—Indicates whether or not secure connections should exist between the plugin and the application server.

- `otherAttrList`—An optional name/value pair list of additional attributes to be set.
- `configureHTTPTransportEndPointForWebContainer(nodeName, serverName, newHostName, newPort, oldHostName="", oldPort="", otherAttrList=[])`—This method can be used to configure the HTTP Transport EndPoint for a Web Container in a specific server. Almost all of the parameters are required and have the following meanings:
  - `nodeName`—The name of the node on which the server exists.
  - `serverName`—The name of the server in which the Web Container exists.
  - `newHostName`—The hostname associated with the EndPoint.
  - `newPort`—The port number associated with the EndPoint.
  - `1dHostName`—This parameter is unused.
  - `oldPort`—This parameter is unused.
  - `otherAttrList`—An optional name/value pair list of additional attributes to be set.
- `configureFileTransferService(nodeName, serverName, retriesCount, retryWaitTime, otherAttrList=[])`—This method can be used to configure the File Transfer Service for a specific server. Almost all of the parameters are required and have the following meanings:
  - `nodeName`—The name of the node on which the server exists.
  - `serverName`—The name of the server being configured.
  - `retriesCount`—The maximum number of retry attempts allowed should an error be encountered.
  - `retryWaitTime`—The number of seconds between retry attempts.
  - `otherAttrList`—An optional name/value pair list of additional attributes to be set.
- `configureAdminService(nodeName, serverName, localAdminProtocolType, remoteAdminProtocolType, otherAttrList=[])`—This method can be used to configure the Administrative Service interface for a specific server. Almost all of the parameters are required and have the following meanings:
  - `nodeName`—The name of the node on which the server exists.
  - `serverName`—The name of the server being configured.
  - `localAdminProtocolType`—Defines the type of connection protocol to be used for a local connection.
  - `remoteAdminProtocolType`—Defines the type of connection protocol to be used for a remote connection.
  - `otherAttrList`—An optional name/value pair list of additional attributes to be set.

- `configureCustomService(nodeName, serverName, className, displayName, classpath, otherAttrList=[])`—This method can be used to configure a Custom Service for a specific server. Almost all of the parameters are required and have the following meanings:
  - `nodeName`—The name of the node on which the server exists.
  - `serverName`—The name of the server being configured.
  - `className`—The name of the custom service class.
  - `displayName`—The name of the service.
  - `classpath`—The classpath used to locate the service Jar files.
  - `otherAttrList`—An optional name/value pair list of additional attributes to be set.

AdminNodeGroupManagement Library Module

This library module contains methods for querying and creating Node Groups.

- `listNodeGroups(nodeName="")`—This method can be used to list one or all of the configured Node Groups. If a `nodeName` is specified, a list is returned containing this name should a Node Group of that name exist. Otherwise, an exception is raised.
- `listNodeGroupMembers(nodeGroupName="")`—This method can be used to list one or all of the configured Node Group members. If a `nodeName` is specified, a list is returned containing the members of the group if that group exists. Otherwise, an exception is raised.
- `listNodeGroupProperties(nodeGroupName)`—This method can be used to list the Node Group properties of the specified group. If a `nodeName` is specified, a list is returned containing the properties of the group if any exist.
- `createNodeGroup(nodeGroupName)`—This method can be used to create a new Node Group of the specified name.
- `createNodeGroupProperty(nodeGroupName, propName, propValue, propDesc, required)`—This method can be used to create a new Node Group Property. All of the parameters are required and have the following values:
  - `nodeGroupName`—The name of the group with which the property is being created.
  - `propName`—The name of the property being created.
  - `propValue`—The property value.
  - `propDesc`—The property description.
  - `required`—Defines whether or not the property is required (`'true'` or `'false'`).
- `addNodeGroupMember(nodeGroupName, nodeName)`—This method can be used to add a node, specified by the `nodeName` parameter to the Node Group specified by the `nodeGroupName` parameter.

- `modifyNodeGroup(nodeGroupName, shortName, description)`—This method can be used to change the `shortName` and/or `description` values for the specified Node Group if either or both have non-empty string values.

- `modifyNodeGroupProperty(nodeGroupName, propName, propValue, propDesc, required)`—This method can be used to change a Node Group Property. All of the parameters are required and have the following values:

  - `nodeGroupName`—The name of the group with which the property is being modified.

  - `propName`—The name of the property being changed.

  - `propValue`—The property value.

  - `propDesc`—The property description.

  - `required`—Defines whether or not the property is required (`'true'` or `'false'`).

- `deleteNodeGroup(nodeGroupName)`—This method can be used to delete the specified Node Group.

- `deleteNodeGroupMember(nodeGroupName, nodeName)`—This method can be used to delete the specified `nodeName` in the specified Node Group.

- `deleteNodeGroupProperty(nodeGroupName, propName)`—This method can be used to delete a specified property, `propName`, from the specified Node Group.

- `checkIfNodeGroupExists (nodeGroupName)`—This method can be used to check that the specified Node Group exists. If the specified group name exists, the result is `'true'`.

- `checkIfNodeExists (nodeGroupName, nodeName)`—This method can be used to check that the specified Node, `nodeName`, exists within the specified Node Group, `nodeGroupName`. If it does, the result is `'true'`.

AdminNodeManagement Library Module

This library module contains methods for manipulating nodes in the cell.

- `listNodes(nodeName="")`—This method can be used to list all or one of the nodes in the cell. The result is a list containing the configIDs of the matching nodes.

- `doesNodeExist(nodeName)`—This method can be used to check for the existence of the given node in the cell. If the node exists, the result is `'true'`.

- `isNodeRunning(nodeName)`—This method can be used to check if the specified node is active. If it is, the result is `'true'`.

- `stopNode(nodeName)`—This method can be used to stop the specified node if it is active.

- `stopNodeAgent(nodeName)`—This method can be used to stop the `nodeagent` for the specified node.
- `restartNodeAgent(nodeName)`—This method can be used to stop and restart the `nodeagent` for the specified node.
- `restartActiveNodes()`—This method can be used to stop and restart the active nodes in the cell.
- `syncNode(nodeName)`—This method can be used to propagate configuration changes to the specified node.
- `syncActiveNodes()`—This method can be used to propagate configuration changes to the active nodes in the cell.
- `configureDiscoveryProtocolOnNode(nodeName, discProtocol)`—This method can be used to configure the discovery protocol, `discProtocol`, for the specified node, `nodeName`.

AdminLibHelp and AdminUtilities Library Modules

The `AdminLibHelp` module contains the scripting library module general `help` method. The `AdminUtilities` module contains "constants" and methods used by the other library modules. It is unlikely that you would be using these methods unless you were writing or rewriting library modules that depended on and required these methods. Therefore, details about these methods are outside the scope of this book.

Summary

This chapter has primarily been a reference for the scripting library modules that are provided with version 7.0 of the IBM WebSphere Application Server. You are encouraged to take a look at the code and determine if the modules, as written, suit your needs. You can then choose to use none, some, or all of these routines in your environment.

Index

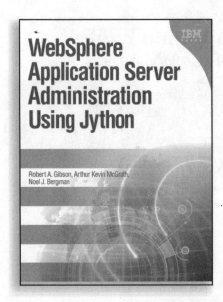